Geographies for Advanced Study
Edited by Emeritus Professor Stanley H. Beaver, MA, FRGS

The British Isles: A Geographic and Economic Survey
Central Europe
Concepts in Climatology
East Africa
Eastern Europe
Geography of Population
Geomorphology
The Glaciations of Wales and Adjoining Regions
An Historical Geography of South Africa
An Historical Geography of Western Europe before 1800
Human Geography
Introduction to Climatic Geomorphology
The Landforms of the Humid Tropics, Forests and Savannas
Malaya, Indonesia, Borneo and the Philippines
North America
Peninsular Malaysia
The Polar World
A Regional Geography of Western Europe
The Scandinavian World
The Semi-Arid World
The Soviet Union
Statistical Methods and the Geographer
Structural Geomorphology
Tropical Agriculture
The Tropical World
Urban Essays: Studies in the Geography of Wales
Urban Geography
West Africa
The Western Mediterranean World

To
Pin, Su-lin and Yu-lin

Peninsular Malaysia

Ooi Jin-Bee

Professor of Geography, University of Singapore

New edition of
Land, People and Economy in Malaya

Longman
London and New York

Longman Group Limited London

Associated companies, branches and representatives
throughout the world

Published in the United States of America
by Longman Inc., New York

© Ooi Jin-Bee 1963
This edition © Longman Group Limited 1976

First published 1963 as *Land, People and Economy in Malaya*
This edition first published 1976

Library of Congress Cataloging in Publication Data

Ooi Jin-Bee
   Peninsular Malaysia.

   (Geographies for advanced study)
   Published in 1963 under title: Land, people, and
   economy in Malaya.
   Bibliography: p.
   Includes index.
   1. Malaya. I. Title.
DS592.05   1976   959.5   75-42166
ISBN 0 582 48185 6

Set in IBM Baskerville 11 on 12pt
and printed in Hong Kong by
Sheck Wah Tong Printing Press

Contents

List of illustrations

Plates

Acknowledgements to the Plates

Plates 1, 2, 4, 5, 6, 7, 8, 9, 10, 13, 15, 16, 17, 18, 20, 21, 23, 26, 27, 28, 29, 30, 32, 33, 34, 35 by the Ministry of Information, Malaysia; Plate 3 by R. Wikkramatileke; Plate 12 by C. A. Keel; Plates 14, 19, by Chee Keng Soon; Plate 22 by Teh Tiong Sa; Plate 31 by the Shell Company, Singapore; Plates 11, 24, 25, 37, 38, are by the author.

Figures

List of illustrations

Tables

Preface to the first edition

I have attempted in these pages to provide a modern systematic study of Malaya which is sufficiently comprehensive to serve as a basic text for students, and as a source of detailed information for other readers, in Malaya and elsewhere, who would like to know more about this rapidly developing country. The first part of the book deals with the natural setting of the Malay Peninsula, the second with the evolution, distribution and composition of the population, and the third with the economic patterns.

I have, in writing this book, drawn on my native knowledge of the country, and have in addition consulted a great number of sources, the most important of which are listed in the bibliography. I have also discussed various aspects of this work with experts and officials in the Federation of Malaya and in Singapore, and I would like to place on record my thanks to them for their advice and suggestions. I am, of course, solely responsible for all statements and opinions expressed in the book. I must also acknowledge my debt to:

Professor S. H. Beaver, for his editorial advice and suggestions. Mr W. L. Dale, for his comments and advice on the chapter on Climate. I am also grateful to Mr Dale as Editor, *The Journal of Tropical Geography*, for kind permission to use parts of my monographs on 'The Mining Landscapes of Kinta' and on 'Rural Development in Tropical Areas, with Special Reference to Malaya' published as Volumes 4 and 12 respectively of the *Journal*; to reprint my article on 'The Rubber Industry of the Federation of Malaya' (Vol. 15, 1961); and to reproduce Section B of Charts 1–12 in W. L. Dale, 'Wind and Drift Currents in the South China Sea' (Vol. 8, 1956), Figures 2, 5 (inset), 6, 7 and 8 in W. L. Dale, 'The Rainfall of Malaya, Part I' (Vol. 13, 1959), Figure 1 in W. L. Dale, 'The Rainfall of Malaya, Part II' (Vol. 14, 1960), and Figure 2 in Kernial Singh Sandhu, 'The Population of Malaya' (Vol. 15, 1961).

Dr J. J. Nossin, for his helpful criticism and suggestions on the chapter on Geological Evolution, Relief and Drainage.

Professor K. M. Buchanan, Editor, *Pacific Viewpoint*, for kind permission to republish my article on 'The Nature and Distribution of the Natural Vegetation of Malaya' (September, 1960).

Members of several Government departments in the Federation of Malaya, in particular Mr N. Subramaniam and Mrs G. H. Leong of the Department of Statistics, for data on aspects of the Malayan economy. The Warden and Fellows of St Antony's College, Oxford, for making it possible for me to complete the final stages of my book at the college.

Professors W. A. R. Wikkramatileke and H. B. Gilliland, Messrs Chee Keng Soon, Charles Keel and Richard D. Smith, the Shell Company of Singapore Ltd and the Straits Times Press for kind permission to reproduce their photographs.

Professor Wikkramatileke, for his support and encouragement at all times.

My wife, for her patience and tolerance.

St Antony's College,   Ooi Jin-Bee
Oxford

December 1962

Preface to the second edition

The original version of this book, which appeared in 1963, was implicitly designed to provide the reader with a synthesis of the major aspects of the land, people and economy of Malaya. In that year a political marriage of territories formerly under British rule took place with the formation of the Federation of Malaysia, consisting of Malaya (now Peninsular Malaysia), Singapore, Sarawak and Sabah (formerly North Borneo). In 1965 Singapore left the Federation and became an independent republic. The Federation today is consequently a reduced unit, made up of Peninsular Malaysia on the mainland, and separated from it by a few hundred miles of the South China Sea, Sarawak and Sabah on the island of Borneo.

Although the title has been changed, the general structure of this edition remains basically the same as that of the first edition. The focus of attention continues to be Peninsular Malaysia, and no attempt has been made to tackle the much larger task of writing a book on the Federation of Malaysia. Reference is made to the Federation of Malaysia from time to time where such reference appears necessary.

The years between these two editions have seen a rapid growth of information, published and unpublished, on Peninsular Malaysia. Relevant material from these sources as well as first-hand data obtained from numerous visits to Peninsular Malaysia have been incorporated here in an attempt to make the revision as thorough and as comprehensive as possible.

The major aim of this book remains the same—to provide a modern systematic study of Peninsular Malaysia which can serve both as a basic text for students as well as a work of reference to other readers. The approach is a simple and orthodox one. That many readers have found the original edition useful is, one hopes, sufficient justification for this revised and expanded version.

I would like to record my thanks to the large number of people in Peninsular Malaysia, officials and others, who have assisted me in various ways and on various occasions. In particular I would like to thank the Chan family in Kuala Lumpur (Mrs Chan Kok Tien and the late Mr Chan

Kok Tien, Mr and Mrs Chan Hua Eng) and Mr and Mrs Tan Jin Eong of Ipoh, for their unfailing kindness and hospitality; Tunku Shamsul Bahrin and his colleagues in the Department of Geography, University of Malaya; Mr S. K. Chung, former Director, Geological Survey of Malaysia; Mrs Esah Yip of the Rubber Research Institute; Mr Poon Puay Kee for drawing the maps and diagrams; Mrs Lim Kim Leng and Mrs Irene Chee for their secretarial help; and Miss Goh Phaik Sim of the Department of Information, Kuala Lumpur, for assistance in obtaining some of the photographs reproduced in the book. I am, of course, solely responsible for the views and opinions expressed in this book.

Ooi Jin-Bee

Singapore, 1975

General note about statistical data

Values given in dollars refer to Malaysian dollars. Malaysian $2.27 = US$1.

The statistical data used in this book are drawn mainly from official sources—statistical bulletins, census reports, government departmental reports, etc. In some cases, e.g. statistics on rubber smallholdings, the figures quoted are estimates, and must be treated with some caution.

The maps and diagrams have been drawn by Mr Poon Puay Kee under the direction of the author.

Glossary of Malay terms

amang: various minerals found as impurities in tin-ore
atap: roofing thatch made from the leaves of the *nipah* palm
belat: a large screen fish-trap
belukar: secondary forest, sometimes also referred to as *utan muda*
bumiputra: lit. 'sons of the soil'
changkol: a hoe
dulang: a wooden platter for washing tin-ore
dusun: orchard, fruit holding
gantang: Imperial gallon (1 gantang of padi weighs approximately 5.5 lb (2.5 kg))
gelam: a swamp tree *Melaleuca leucadendron*
gombang: marine purse-net
kampong: used in two senses: (1) a Malay village or settlement; and (2) a mixed garden composed of a heterogeneous collection of tree and bush crops
karang: tin-bearing ground (lit. coral reef)
kelong: a large marine fish-trap
kuala: estuary, or junction of two streams
kuku kambing: a dibble for planting padi seedlings
ladang: shifting cultivation; a clearing planted to dryland crops
lalang: a coarse grass *Imperata cylindrica*
menuai: to reap padi with a *tuai*
mukim: subdivision of an administrative district
nipah: brackish-water palm *Nipa fruticans*
padi: the growing plant and unhusked grains of *Oryza sativa*
palong: a sluice-box for separating tin-ore from waste material
parang: a long-handled cleaver
penarekan: place where boats are hauled (over watersheds)
permatang: beach ridges
petai: an edible pod, *Parkia speciosa*
picul or *pikul*: $133\frac{1}{3}$ lb (60 kg)
pisau: knife
pompang: a Chinese purse-net

xiv

sabit: sickle
sampan: a small rowboat
sawah: flooded padi field (south Peninsular Malaysia)
seladang: the Malaysian wild buffalo (*Bos gaurus*)
sumatras: local line-squalls, common in the Straits of Malacca
sungei: river, sometimes abbreviated to *S*
tajak: a padi-planter's weedcutter
tuai: a tiny padi-reaping knife
tuba: roots of plants belonging to the genus *Derris*, used for poison-fishing, and commercially valuable as an insecticide

Note on Malay spelling

Malaysia and Indonesia have recently agreed to standardize the spelling of Malay/Indonesian words. Many of the place names in Malaysia have consequently been changed to follow the new spelling. The old spelling has largely been retained in this book, but for the guidance of readers a list of the most common place names with the old and new spellings is given below.

Old Spelling	New Spelling
Alor Star	Alor Setar
Bandar Bharu	Bandar Baru
Johore	Johor
Johore Bharu	Johor Baru
Klang	Kelang
Kluang	Keluang
Kota Bharu	Kota Baru
Kota Star	Kota Setar
Krian	Kerian
Malacca	Melaka
Negri Sembilan	Negeri Sembilan
Penang	Pinang
Tanjong	Tanjung
Trengganu	Terengganu

Acronyms

CGC: Credit Guarantee Corporation
CIC: Capital Investment Council
FAMA: Federal Agricultural Marketing Authority
FELCRA: Federal Land Consolidation and Rehabilitation Authority
FELDA: Federal Land Development Authority (formerly FLDA)
FIDA: Federal Industrial Development Authority
FOA: Farmers' Organization Authority
LPN: Lembaga Padi Nasional (National Padi and Rice Authority)
MAJUIKAN: Fisheries Development Authority, set up to promote the growth of the fishing industry
MAJUTERNAK: Livestock Development Corporation, established to promote the development of the livestock industry
MARA: Majlis Amanah Ra'ayat (an institution established to assist the participation of Malays and other indigenous people in commerce and industry)
MARDI: Malaysian Agricultural Research and Development Institute
MIDF: Malaysian Industrial Development Finance Ltd
MRDC: Malayan Rubber Development Corporation
NEP: New Economic Policy
PERNAS: The National Corporation, established in 1970 to spearhead the Government's efforts in the creation of a Malay commercial and industrial community
RISDA: Rubber Industry Smallholders Development Authority
RRI: Rubber Research Institute
SEDC: State Economic Development Corporation
UDA: Urban Development Authority

PART ONE

The land

Frontispiece   Political Divisions, 1974 (see note on Malay spelling, p. xv).

1
Geological evolution, relief and drainage

The geological evolution of the Malay Peninsula

In early Palaeozoic times an extensive landmass lay between present-day Asia and Australia. This ancient landmass was composed of crystalline rocks such as schists, gneisses and plutonites. Van Bemmelen (1949) calls it the Indonesian Primeval Continent. During the course of the Palaeozoic era parts of this Continent, including the part now occupied by the Malay Peninsula, began to subside, creating geosynclinal conditions. A long period of quiet subsidence and sedimentation was followed in the course of time by a very long and involved cycle of mountain building. The geological history of the Malay Peninsula forms part of the story of this orogenesis, which is still continuing in some areas of present-day Indonesia.

The geosynclinal areas were covered by seas, but their limits are uncertain. It is probable that most of the Indo-Chinese Peninsula, the Malay Peninsula, parts of western Borneo, south-eastern Sumatra and most of Java were covered by such geosynclinal seas, though not all at the same time.

In the part now occupied by the Malay Peninsula, evidence of sedimentation in Upper Cambrian times has been found in the north-west. The sediments included cement-bedded sands, muds, silts and pebbles laid down in shallow waters, on the northwest coast of the Langkawi Islands as well as on a Thai island north of the Langkawis (Procter, 1966). Subsidence continued to Silurian times and geosynclinal conditions appeared to have been created as far south as present-day Selangor. Thick layers of limestone and shales were laid down in the geosyncline—the limestones of this age have been estimated to be 7 500 ft (2 286 m) thick in the Langkawi Islands (Jones, 1961) and 6 000 ft (1 829 m) thick in the Kuala Lumpur area (Gobbett, 1964). Similar fossil-bearing Ordovician—Silurian sedimentary rocks comprising limestone, shale and chert have been discovered in west Perlis, south Kedah, the Kanthan, Grik and Kroh areas of Perak, and the south Bentong area of Pahang (Fig. 1).

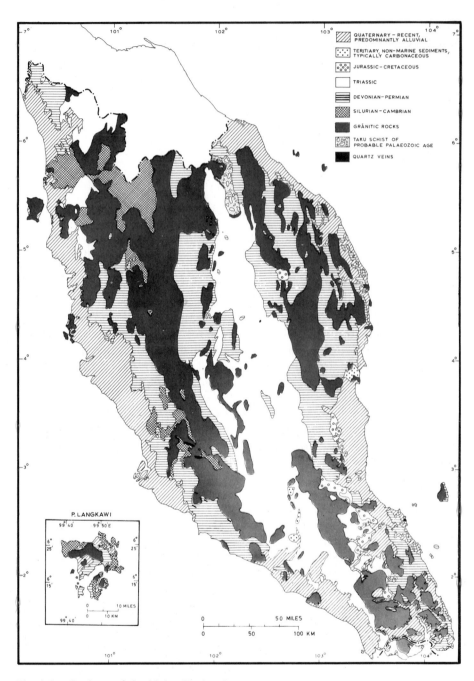

Fig. 1.1   Geology of the Malay Peninsula.

The first of the many phases of orogenesis (mountain-building) affecting the Malay Peninsula occurred in Upper Silurian—Lower Devonian times. This was probably preceded by volcanic activity. Although the orogeny was a minor one, it had the important effect of creating two long narrow geosynclinal basins due to the rise of a geanticlinal ridge occupying the site where the Main Range now stands. The geosynclinal basin west of this ridge was a miogeosyncline in which volcanic activities were absent. In contrast, evidence of subsequent volcanic activity has been found in the eastern geosyncline, which consequently has been termed an eugeosyncline (Chung, 1970).

Sedimentation in the miogeosyncline took place without a break in the shallow seas which covered the area during the Upper Palaeozoic era. The sediments deposited during the Devonian and Carboniferous periods consisted of a succession of limestones at the southern part of the miogeosyncline and of fine-grained non-calcareous materials at the northern end. Limestone rocks of Devonian age have been proved to occur in the Kanthan limestone hill and in southwest Kampar, Perak, where they are about 4 000 ft (1 219 m) thick. Carboniferous fossils and rocks have been found in Perlis, Kedah and Perak.

The sedimentation record in the eugeosyncline appeared to have been different in detail from that in the west. Sediments of Devonian age in west-central Pahang consisted of conglomerates, quartzites, graptolitic shales and cherts, which have been intruded by basic rocks. These rocks were previously known as the Foothills Formation and the 'Older Arenaceous Series'. Carboniferous rocks are widespread along the east coast where they were probably laid down in a shallow water marine environment. In the Kuantan area they consisted of carbonaceous shales, phyllites, quartzites and limestone bands. In central Pahang they were made up of thick successions of limestone. In southern Kelantan the Carboniferous sediments discovered were calcareous mudstones intercalated with pyroclastics (Chung, 1970).

In Upper Carboniferous—Lower Permian times another period of orogenesis was accompanied by the emplacement of granite in many parts of Peninsular Malaysia. Radiometric datings have established these granites, the oldest known to date, to be 280 to 300 million years old (Snelling *et al.*, 1968).

According to van Bemmelen (1949) a period of orogenesis in Carbo—Permian times affected the area where the present Anambas Island is located (east of the present east coast of Peninsular Malaysia). A geanticline was pushed up in this zone, with compensatory subsidence of the adjacent regions. The border deep north of the geanticline was situated in the area where Natuna Island now stands. The wide and shallow southern border deep extended from the eastern half of present-day Peninsular Malaysia (with the Kelantan—Trengganu Border Range and the Tahan Range as central axis) to the island of Karimata and the

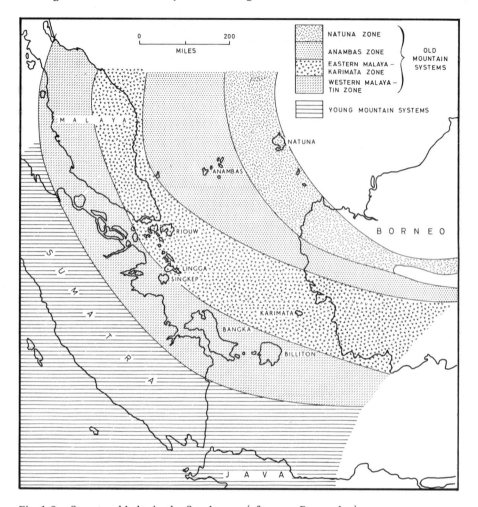

Fig. 1.2   Structural belts in the Sunda area (after van Bemmelen).

southern part of West Borneo (Fig. 1.2). Both deeps were centres of volcanic activity. The products of vulcanism in the southern deep were the clastic ejectamenta formerly classified as the Pahang Volcanic Series (a term no longer in use; the rocks are now known to be more widespread in distribution and cover a wider range of time—Carboniferous to Triassic—than was once thought).

The next phase in the evolution of the Malay Peninsula occurred at the end of the Palaeozoic era when the geosynclinal strip along eastern Peninsular Malaysia, Karimata and the southern part of West Borneo was uplifted by orogenic forces. The geanticlinal ridges so formed were intruded by granitic magma. The uplift of a geanticline along eastern Peninsular Malaysia brought about compensatory subsidence along western Peninsular Malaysia. During Triassic times subaerial denudation and subsidence of the geanticlinal ridges resulted in a general lowering of the relief so that by late Triassic times the sea again covered most of the Malay Peninsula. At the same time a phase of active vulcanism set in along eastern Peninsular Malaysia. The volcanic products were conformably interbedded with the sedimentary rocks of the so-called Younger Arenaceous Series, laid down in the shallow sea. The material eroded off the mountains of eastern Peninsular Malaysia during Triassic time helped to fill in the western Malaysian geosyncline (referred to as the Tin Zone by van Bemmelen).

Van Bemmelen states that in early Jurassic times the eastern Peninsular Malaysia—Karimata zone was uplifted by orogenic forces for the second time, to form imposing mountain ranges which were probably also volcanic. The mountains were again intruded by granitic magma, in composition more homogeneous and richer in silica than the granitic intrusions of the earlier period of orogenesis. During the process of orogenesis the thick sedimentary cover deposited in the earlier periods of sedimentation slipped from the shoulders of the rising basement and piled up in the adjacent subsiding troughs. Parts of the crystalline basement with their cloaks of Carbo—Permian and Triassic sediments also began to slide towards the western Malaysian geosyncline (Tin Zone), thus helping to fill it up. Sedimentation of the western Malaysian geosyncline continued during Middle Jurassic times, and appeared to have been almost completed by late Jurassic times, when the stage was set for the final and most important phase in the evolution of the Malay Peninsula—the upraising of the mountain chain along western Peninsular Malaysia.

In late Jurassic and early Cretaceous times the centre of diastrophism had shifted from the eastern Peninsular Malaysia—Karimata zone to the western Peninsular Malaysia—Tin Zone (Fig. 1.2). A mountain chain was pushed up from the western Peninsular Malaysian geosyncline. During this period all the major intrusive masses of western Peninsular Malaysia were emplaced by tin-bearing granitic batholiths. Similar intrusions occurred in the islands of Singkep, Bangka and Biliton.

This phase of mountain building gave rise to a double orogen in the Malay Peninsula, consisting of two parallel mountain arcs. The younger and more imposing outer arc, which was non-volcanic, was dominated by the mountain range now known as the Main Range, some 300 miles (483 km) long and from 30 to 40 miles (48—64 km) wide, and in places over 7 000 ft (2 134 m) above present-day sea-level. The Benom Range of western Pahang, occupying about 560 square miles (1 683 sq km) and rising to a maximum height of 6 916 ft (2 124 m), as well as the complementary synclinorium of the Main Range foothills, were the other major structures formed during this orogenic phase. The inner or eastern arc, comprising the Kelantan—Trengganu Boundary Range (or the East Coast

7

Range) and the Tahan Range, was made up of remnants of the older volcanic chain of the eastern Peninsular Malaysia—Karimata zone.

The Main Range, with its heavy load of compressed sediments, formed an unstable geanticlinal structure which later collapsed under its own weight. Some of the collapsed parts slumped towards the new geosyncline located over eastern Sumatra, which was later (in Middle Cretaceous times) pushed up into a new mountain chain as the centre of diastrophism shifted westwards. By this time orogenic forces in the Malaysian area had waned.

The intrusion of the granitic batholiths in the central Sunda area during the Permo—Triassic—Jurassic phases of mountain building and their subsequent crystallization consolidated the whole region into a rigid continental block, now known as the Sunda Shelf or the Sunda Platform. The Malay Peninsula today forms the western part of this Shelf.

This account of the geological evolution of the Peninsular Malaysian landmass by van Bemmelen appears to need modification in the light of subsequent findings, particularly with regards to the period when the main orogenesis took place. Although the biggest interruption in sedimentation in Peninsular Malaysia occurred in Jurassic times, radiometric datings of the granites so far have not established the existence of Jurassic granites. Geologists of the Malaysian Geological Survey Department believe that the main orogeny in the Peninsular Malaysian geosyncline ended in the Triassic, and that the sequence of geologic events after the Upper Carboniferous—Lower Permian orogeny was as outlined below (Chung, 1970).

Sedimentation in the geosynclines continued in the Permian, the sediments being typically calcareous. In the miogeosyncline limestone development in the Lower Permian is estimated to be 3 500 ft (1 067 m) thick in the Langkawis and about 2 000 ft (610 m) thick in Perlis. The limestones thin out eastwards and southwards in Kedah and are only 500 ft (152 m) thick in Kampar. In the eugeosyncline the Permian succession is also mainly calcareous, but with associated shales, siltstones, quartzites and volcanics. The sedimentation record shows that the sea had reached southwards to Johore by the Middle Permian.

The end of the Permian witnessed the onset of another period of orogenesis which was associated with the rise of volcanic island arcs and large-scale granitic intrusions. This orogeny reached its climax in the Lower Triassic, and appeared to have affected most parts of the country. Radiometric datings indicate a major period of granite emplacement in the Lower Triassic (about 230 million years ago).

The end of this period of orogenesis was followed by a change in the pattern of deposition in Middle Triassic times, characterized by flysch-type sedimentation under neritic conditions. Deposition continued from the Middle Triassic to the Upper Triassic. Widespread volcanic activity occurred in the eugeosyncline, the volcanics being andesite, intermediate to acid pyroclastic rocks and some lavas. Volcanic rocks of Triassic age occupy an area of about 180 square miles (466 sq km) in Peninsular Malaysia today (Pimm, 1967). In south-central Pahang the volcanics are predominantly acid tuffs. In southeast Johore the initial period of vulcanism was relatively quiescent, then mildly explosive with lava flows, and finally strongly explosive (Grubb, 1968).

The Upper Triassic heralded the onset of the main orogeny. Accompanied by granite intrusions, it brought sedimentation in the existing geosynclines to a close by uplift and folding. Radiometric datings have confirmed that a major period of granite emplacement occurred in the Malay Peninsula 175 to 200 million years ago, in the Upper Triassic. The orogeny converted the existing geosynclines into a landmass and established the present structural trend of the country. This orogeny was accompanied by granite emplacement. It is probable that much of the mineralization of the Peninsular Malaysian landmass occurred during this period of granite emplacement in Early Jurassic times. Many of the mineral deposits such as tin (cassiterite), wolframite, scheelite, haematite and gold are genetically related to the granites and are either hydrothermal veins or pyrometasomatic replacements at or near the contact between the granite and the invaded sediments.

During the Jurassic trough-like sedimentary basins developed on the eastern part of the peninsula from Gunong Gagau in the north to Gunong Panti in the south. West of these basins was an upland area of granites and Palaeozoic sediments. The sediments that were laid down after the emergence of this primitive Peninsular Malaysian landmass were mainly continental in character, in contrast to the marine sediments laid down in pre-Jurassic times. Deposition in the basins took place under fluvial, lacustrine and deltaic conditions, the sediments being mainly sandstones, conglomerates and shales with small coal seams and volcanics. In the states of Kelantan, Pahang and Johore these postorogenic sediments are from 1 000 to 1 800 ft (305–549 m) thick. In the Gunong Gagau area they occur at elevations of over 4 000 ft (1 219 m) above sea-level, but in Johore they are only about 200 ft (61 m) above sea-level.

Radiometric (potassium/argon) datings have established four major periods of granite emplacements in Peninsular Malaysia—in pre-Lower Triassic, Upper Triassic, Jurassic–Cretaceous, and post-Upper Cretaceous to Lower Tertiary times (Chung, 1970). The emplacement of granites and the earth movements that preceded it and continued during and after their emplacement brought about folding as well as contact, thermal and regional metamosphism of the sedimentary rocks. There appears to be a close correlation between the geological age of the rocks and the degree of folding: the old Palaeozoic sediments are more intensely folded and more deformed than the younger sediments.

9

Argillaceous, arenaceous and calcareous rocks have been altered by regional metamorphism in various parts of the country. The Taku Schists of north Kelantan, for example, are the products of deep-seated regional metamorphism. They occupy a sharply-defined surface area of 300 square miles (777 sq km) and are named after the Sungei Taku. They are composed of metamorphosed argillaceous and arenaceous rocks interbedded with or intruded by basic igneous rocks. The metamorphism which produced the Taku Schists has been shown by radiometric dating to have taken place in Middle to Lower Triassic times (MacDonald, 1967).

Thermal metamorphism is usually associated with the intrusion of the major granite masses and is generally confined to narrow aureoles around the granite masses. The degree of metamorphism can vary considerably, not only from one granite body to another, but also around the peripheries of the same granite body. The metamorphic rocks produced by thermal metamorphism would naturally depend on the nature of the original rocks. Arenaceous and rudaceous rocks have been converted into hard, coarse-grained quartz hornfels, quartz schists and quartz mica-schists. Calcareous rocks have usually been altered to form a crystalline marble with considerable variations in grain size depending on distance from the granite. Argillaceous rocks which have suffered metamorphism due to the intrusion of granite have been converted to indurated shale, phyllite, mica-schist and hornfels. Volcanic rocks have suffered degrees of alteration which vary with the severity of metamorphism. Andesites close to and against the granite contact may be altered by the replacement of pyroxene by amphibole.

The granitic magma, on cooling, solidified as granite and other plutonic rocks such as hornblende-granite, syenite diorite and gabbro. These were initially buried under a thick overburden of sedimentary rocks. As stated earlier, most of the mineral wealth of Peninsular Malaysia is derived from the granite. The rich alluvial tin fields of Larut, the Kinta Valley, the Klang Valley and Negri Sembilan are located on the western flanks of the Main Range, while the other tin fields are associated with smaller granite intrusions.

The Upper Triassic orogeny probably established the present structural framework of the Malay Peninsula. This framework has remained substantially the same, though the relief has everywhere been greatly reduced by denudation, and the shape of the Peninsula has varied over the years as a result of sedimentation along the coastal peripheries as well as fluctuations in the relative levels of land and sea.

As soon as the primitive Peninsular Malaysian landmass appeared from the geosynclinal sea it was subjected to weathering, probably of tropical intensity, which in time stripped off tens of thousands of feet of sedimentary and metamorphic rocks, in places laying bare the underlying granite and other igneous rocks. For example, the thick cover of sedi-

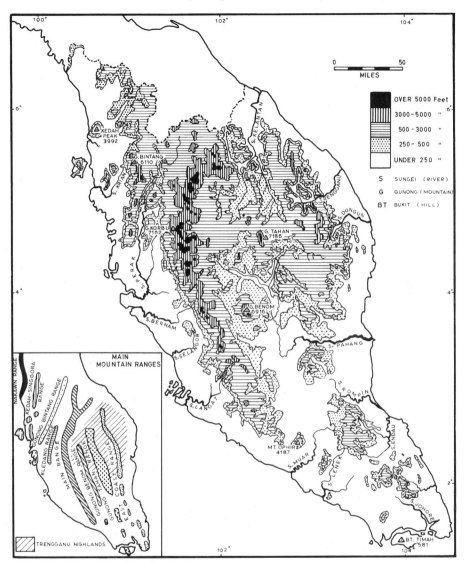

Fig. 1.3   Relief and main mountain ranges.

mentary rocks of the present-day Bintang Range, the Kledang Range, the Main Range, the Benom Range and the East Coast Range (Fig. 1.3) have been almost entirely removed by subaerial denudation over millions of years, so that today their granite cores lie exposed. The weathering processes are accelerated under the conditions of constantly high temperatures and heavy rainfall which prevail in the Peninsula, and weathering extends to great depths. Quartzites and sandstones break down into loose sands, while shale reverts to clay. The weathered zone may exceed 100 ft (30 m) in depth. Schists and phyllites readily weather

11

to clay. Limestones being more soluble in water have, of all the geological formations, suffered the greatest downgrading. The weathering of limestone does not lead to the formation of the weathered products normal to other rocks, but to the solution of the limestone itself. Only a thin covering of dark red earth remains after its solution. Prolonged weathering has resulted in the removal of most of the thick mantle of limestone which once covered a large part of the Peninsula, and today the limestone in valleys such as that of Kinta is buried under a layer of alluvium. Granite disintegrates under tropical weathering to a red, orange or yellow soft mass which may be anything from 6 to 200 ft (2—61 m) in depth. Core-boulders which have resisted weathering are commonly found within the weathered mass.

The twin processes of weathering and erosion have reduced the Peninsular Malaysian landmass to an advanced stage of maturity. The great thicknesses of sedimentary rocks which were stripped off the crests of the mountain ranges were, for the most part, carried out to sea. Part of this transported material was deposited in the large alluvial plains. In some cases the upraised, metamorphosed sediments have proved unusually resistant to erosion, the best example being the Tahan Range (Fig. 1.3) which is composed of quartzites and sandstones.

The geological record of the Malay Peninsula shows that during Tertiary times, long after the formation of the Peninsular Malaysian landmass, coal-bearing strata were laid down, probably in isolated freshwater swamps and lakes, in many widely separated places. They are known to occur in five localities: in the north at Bukit Arang on the Perlis—Thailand border; at Enggor near Kuala Kangsar in Perak; at Batu Arang in Selangor where the deposits consist of beds of shale, sandstone, coal and conglomerate resting unconformably on quartzites and phyllite of Triassic age; near Kluang and Nyor in Johore; at Kepong in Johore (Fig. 1.1). Some coal was mined from the Enggor coalfield before it closed down in 1928. The Batu Arang coalfield in Selangor produced more than 15 million tons of coal between 1915 and 1960, when it was finally forced to close down as a result of competition from imported fuel oil. None of the other deposits contain coal of any economic importance. The total area of the five Tertiary coal-bearing outcrops is less than 100 square miles (259 sq km).

From the end of the Tertiary to the present day, that is, during the Quaternary, alluvium brought down by the rivers has caused widespread sedimentation along the coasts of Peninsular Malaysia. Wide alluvial plains have been built up from the bases of the inland mountain ranges to the coast. These coastal plains average about 20 miles (32 km) in width along western Peninsular Malaysia, broadening out to a maximum of 40 miles (64 km) in west-central Peninsular Malaysia, in the lower courses of the Perak and Bernam rivers. They are narrower along eastern Peninsular Malaysia, the maximum width being about 20 miles

(32 km) along the lower course of the Pahang River. These recent and unconsolidated sediments have been deposited under both marine and fluvial conditions. They vary in thickness from about 30 ft (9 m) around Kampar, to 80 to 100 ft (24—30 m) around Ipoh, to 150 to 250 ft (46—76 m) in Telok Anson District, to 365 ft (111 m) at Sitiawan, and to about 450 ft (137 m) around Kuala Perak and Kuala Bernam.

The inland valleys are covered with a thin mantle of recent river muds, sands and gravels, while the upland areas usually have a cover of eluvial material of varying thickness. Included with these deposits of Pleistocene and Recent age are the deposits of rhyolite ash which have been found in Perak and Pahang. They are believed to have originated from the prehistoric volcanic eruption at Toba (now Lake Toba) in Sumatra.

The development and present position of the coastal alluvial plains of Peninsular Malaysia are related to the changes in the relative levels of land and sea which have occurred in the Quaternary. There is no general agreement as yet on the number and magnitude of eustatic changes that have occurred in the Malay Peninsula and the Sunda area. There appeared to have been several (probably three) phases of high sea-level in Sundaland before the final transgression at the end of the Quaternary. During such periods (which might be correlated with the melting of the great ice sheets in the higher latitudes), the sea covered much of Sundaland, reducing it to a number of archipelagoes. In the Peninsula the physical evidence of a maximum high sea-level includes that of an eroded marine terrace on the Dindings coast about 250 ft (76 m) above present mean sea-level and marine platforms of about 230 ft (70 m) in the Kinta Valley. During this and the three other probable periods of transgression, the coastlines receded and the lower portions of the drainage systems were drowned, creating extensive neritic conditions for alluvial deposits. The streams filled in their drowned estuaries and, as sedimentation continued, extended the alluvial formations seawards.

Conversely, the eustatic lowerings of sea-level in the Peninsula and Sundaland during the Quaternary periods of glaciation exposed much of the area as dry land as the sea receded and the coastlines were extended. According to Scrivenor, the Middle Pleistocene was probably the period of maximum lowering in the Peninsula, when sea-level stood about 328 ft (100 m) lower than present mean sea-level. The Malay Peninsula, Sumatra, Java and Borneo were then probably connected to the Asian mainland by dry land. During this and other periods of exposure the rivers of the Peninsular Malaysian landmass might have been rejuvenated, renewing downcutting of their valleys. The present drowned tin alluvials of Bangka and Singkep were probably produced during one or more of these phases of lowered sea-level.

The final melting of the great ice sheets at the close of the Pleistocene brought about a rise in sea-level of 262 to 328 ft (80—100 m) in Sundaland, submerging the lower parts under a shallow sea, and producing the present Sunda Shelf or Sunda Platform. Sea-level in the Malay Peninsula at that time was thought to have been about 50 ft (15 m) higher than present mean sea-level. Fitch, on the basis of evidence in the form of beach ridges, caves at different levels in limestone hills, river terraces, and rapids at Sungei Karang, believes that the land in East Pahang has risen twice in recent times, the first being an uplift of 20 ft (6 m) and the second 10 ft (3 m). There might have been an earlier rise of about 20 ft (6 m). Nossin, working on the beach ridges of north-eastern Johore, has recorded evidence of a recent fall in sea-level of about 20 ft (6 m).

Relief

The Peninsula of Peninsular Malaysia extends from latitude 1° 20′ N to latitude 6° 40′ N, and from longitude 99° 35′ E to longitude 104° 20′ E. The total length of this long and narrow peninsula is about 500 miles (804 km). The peninsula is linked, at its northern end, to the mainland of Asia by the Kra Isthmus, which at its narrowest is only about 40 miles (64 km) wide. The island of Singapore lies at the southern extremity of the peninsula and is separated from it by a shallow strait—the Strait of Johore. The island of Singapore is physically linked to Peninsular Malaysia by a causeway across the Strait, but is politically separate from it.

Peninsular Malaysia covers a total area of 50 886 square miles (131 794 sq km); in contrast, the Republic of Singapore, together with its adjacent tiny islands, occupy only 224.5 square miles (583 sq km). About one-half of the total area of Peninsular Malaysia is covered by granite and other non-volcanic igneous rocks, about one-third by stratified rocks older than the granite, and the remainder by alluvium. Highlands cover a large part of the country, and over half of the total area is more than 500 ft (152 m) above sea-level (Fig. 1.3). Singapore is an island of subdued relief, with its highest hill—Bukit Timah—rising to only 581 ft (177 m) above sea-level.

The Malay Peninsula forms part of the old continental block known as the Sunda Platform. Most of the Platform is at present inundated by uniformly shallow seas following the rise in sea-level at the close of the Pleistocene when the great polar ice caps melted. The portions of the Platform which are not submerged are the Malay Peninsula, southern Thailand, southern Indo-China, eastern Sumatra, northern Java and the island of Borneo. That part of the Platform between the Malay Peninsula and western Borneo is an old stable region which has been peneplaned. The partial submergence of this peneplane has left groups of rocky islands—Natuna, Anambas, Rhio-Lingga, Bangka, Billiton, Karimata and Karimundjawa (Fig. 1.2)—between present-day Peninsular Malaysia and western Borneo.

Orographically, Peninsular Malaysia is dominated by its mountainous core, which in detail consists of a series of roughly parallel mountain ranges aligned longitudinally (Fig. 1.3, inset). The Benom Range, the Main Range and the subsidiary ranges west of the Main Range are the remains of an ancient mountain system described earlier. The Tahan Range and the East Coast Range of eastern Peninsular Malaysia are the remnants of a still older mountain system formed at the end of the Palaeozoic. Tropical weathering and erosion over these millions of years have, except in the case of Tahan Range, removed the cloaks of sedimentary rocks with which these mountain ranges were once clad, subdued their relief and exposed their crystalline cores.

Scrivenor has described the structure of Peninsular Malaysia as consisting of eight mountain or hill ranges. These are, from west to east (Fig. 1.3):

1. *The Nakawn Range*, a low ridge in the extreme northwest of Peninsular Malaysia. The southern half of this ridge is of limestone, and forms the boundary between Perlis and Thailand.

2. *The Kedah–Singgora Range*, and its southerly continuations. It is composed of quartzite with granite outcrops, and runs from Singgora in Thailand to west-central Kedah. Outliers of this Range include the granite mountain Gunong Perak, the quartzite mountain Kedah Peak, the low granite hills forming the boundary of south Kedah and Province Wellesley, and the island granite mass of Penang.

3. *The Bintang Range*, dominated by the peak of Bintang, 6 103 ft (1 868 m). This granite range runs from southern Thailand through Intan in upper Perak to Bruas. The granite southern hills of the Dindings are outliers of the Range.

4. *The Kledang Range*, an offshoot of the Main Range. Where it separates itself from the Main Range (in the vicinity of Enggor), the Kledang Range has an average elevation of over 3 000 ft (914 m), but south of Gunong Hijau the Range drops from about 2 000 ft (610 m) to below 250 ft (76 m). The range is formed of granite.

5. *The Main Range*, composed mostly of granite with some patches of altered stratified rocks. The top of Gunong Korbu (7 162 ft (2 188 m)) is of phyllite. The Main Range is the most prominent and continuous of the mountain ranges of Peninsular Malaysia. It runs all the way from the Thai border with elevations rarely less than 3 000 ft (914 m) and peaks of over 7 000 ft (2 134 m) to as far south as Negri Sembilan where its altitude gradually diminishes until it abuts on the coastal plain in Malacca. It has an average width of 30 to 40 miles (48–64 km) and is continuous for about 300 miles (483 km). On the east the Range is flanked by foothills of sedimentary rocks, wide tracts of which have been converted by dynamic metamorphism into schistose conglomerate, schistose quartzite, quartz schist, phyllite and mica schist.

6. *The Benom Range*, which takes its name from Gunong Benom, 6 916 ft (2 114 m) high. The Range is of granite and is believed to have

been formed at the same time as the Main Range. South of the Benom Range are some small isolated hills composed of the same hornblende-granite as the Benom. The best known of these outliers is Mount Ophir (4 187 ft (1 295 m)), located near the meeting point of the boundaries of Negri Sembilan, Malacca and Johore. The granite of this outcrop has been deeply weathered, although many of the slopes are steep and bare. The Benom Range is flanked on the west by a range of foothills composed of ultra-basic rocks of post-Triassic age, with individual hills rising to 2 000 ft (610 m).

7. *The Tahan Range*, named after Gunong Tahan, which rises 7 186 ft (2 207 m) above sea-level and is the highest mountain in Peninsular Malaysia. This range is composed of sedimentary rocks—conglomerate quartzite, sandstone and shale—which have been over-folded. Along many parts of the Range the greater resistance of the quartzite to weathering has resulted in a markedly rugged outline with frequent cliffs and an occasional canyon. The jagged outline of the Tahan Range contrasts sharply with the smooth, gently curving outlines of the Benom and other granite ranges. Another unusual feature of the Tahan Range is that it has only a sparse cover of vegetation because of the poverty of the soils derived from quartzite and shale. The continuity of the Range is interrupted by the Rompin River. The Range extends southwards as low ridges along east-central Johore, and as the Mount Faber ridge in Singapore.

8. *The East Coast Range*, extending from the Kelantan coast in the north, through interior Trengganu, to the Pahang River. The Range is

Plate 1   Bukit Jugra, a low outcrop of porphyritic granite, located in the Klang—Kuala Langat coastal plain. The granite contains occasional oval patches of mica and tourmaline. Aplites and pegmatites are also abundantly developed. The hill is now a forest reserve, but past cultivation has denuded some of its sides (see p. 21).

discontinuous south of the Pahang River, and is marked by low granite hills standing above swamp level and by granite ridges in eastern and south-eastern Johore.

The Trengganu Highlands (Fig. 1.3, inset) occupy the area bounded by the lower Pahang River, the eastern flanks of the Main Range, south Kelantan, and the whole of Trengganu inland from the coast and consist of the northern parts of the Benom, Tahan and East Coast Ranges and their foothills, the whole forming a highly dissected mountainous mass with deep narrow valleys. The average height of the Highlands is about 2 500 ft (762 m).

The limestones of Peninsular Malaysia are often buried under a layer of alluvium. But in parts of central and north Peninsular Malaysia limestone hills with precipitous sides are distinctive features of the landscape: on either side of the Pahang—Kelantan border in the headwaters of the

Plate 2 The Batu Caves, an historic landmark near Kuala Lumpur. The precipitous sides of this limestone outcrop are bare, an unusual phenomenon in a country where the slopes of most mountains and hills are smooth and rounded and characteristically covered with a thick mantle of forest. The local solution of limestone has enlarged the joints and cracks of the outcrop, resulting in the formation of many small cavities and several large caves. The vegetation in such limestone areas differs from that of lowland rain forest, being made up of species which are adapted to semi-drought conditions caused by the rapid run-off and percolation of rain water and to the thin, alkaline soils (see p. 18).

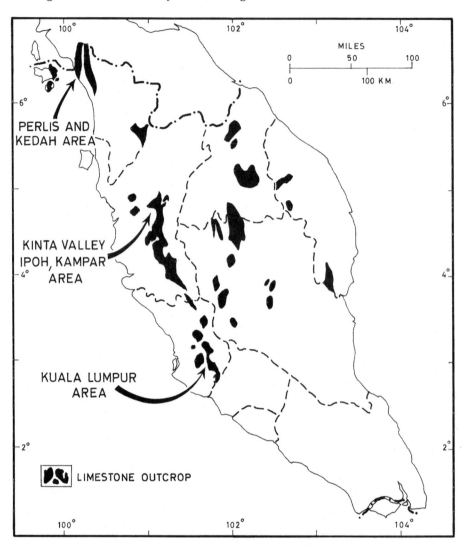

Fig. 1.4   Limestone outcrops (after Hutchison, 1968).

Galas, the Kuantan District, the upper Sungei Lipis Valley east of Raub, and some other areas in Pahang, at Kanching and Batu near Kuala Lumpur, in the Kinta Valley and the Sungei Siput and Batang Padang areas of Perak, along the Perak—Kedah border southeast of Baling, in the headwaters of the Sungei Muda and the alluvial plain of north Kedah, along the western part of the Perlis—Thai border, and in the Langkawi Islands (Fig. 1.4). These limestone hills are from a few hundred feet to over 2 000 ft (610 m) high. They are conspicuous landmarks not because of their height but because of their characteristic steep sides which are often bare of vegetation and of the fact that they are often isolated hills rising abruptly from flat land. The appearance of these hills contrasts sharply with the rounded slopes and open valleys associated with the other geological formations of Peninsular Malaysia. Erosion of the lime-stone formations has produced a karst topography consisting of intricate patterns of caves, caverns, swallow-hollows, underground river courses, dry valleys, potholes and chasms. Many of the caves are of great size, as for example Gua Badak on the south side of Bukit Chuping in Perlis. A large Chinese temple has been built in one of the caves of Gunong Rapat, a limestone hill near Ipoh. Other caves attain exceptional length: those at Perlis Tin Mines at Wang Tangga are over 6 000 ft (1 829 m) in length. Stalactites and stalagmites are commonly found in the caves. Along the limestone ridge which separates Perlis from Thailand are great basins and hollows known locally as *wangs*. Each consists of a low-lying flat piece of land surrounded on all sides by vertical limestone cliffs. Some of the *wangs* are large enough to support Malay settlements. This limestone ridge is also honey-combed with solution caves and passages cut by subterranean streams. Some of the caves contain rich deposits of tin-ore and of guano (Jones, 1965).

A number of theories have been advanced to account for the origin of these hills. They include block faulting, folding, plastic flow, aeolian erosion, marine erosion and subaerial erosion. Of these subaerial erosion (modified by marine erosion) is the most plausible in that it is the only theory which can account for the formation of all the limestone hills in Peninsular Malaysia (Paton, 1964). The high solubility and the different rates of erosion in limestone with active erosion taking place at the lowest levels, in which highly acid water may be constantly available from swamps and streams in low-lying areas or from the sea, would tend to produce a topography of vertical cliffs rising from relatively flat platforms. The great mechanical strength of limestone allows for the support of overhanging cliffs. The collapse of such overhangs in the latter stages of the cycle of erosion would produce steep-sided and isolated hills (Fig. 1.5).

The type of limestone topography found in Peninsular Malaysia is in fact a function of the lithology of the rock rather than the nature of the erosive processes. The landforms produced on impure limestone are similar to those associated with non-calcareous rocks (see Fig. 1.5). In Perlis the impure limestone of Ordovician—Silurian age forms fairly well-rounded hills with poorly developed cliffs (Paton, 1964). But most of the limestones of Peninsular Malaysia are of exceptional purity (Hutchison, 1968), and the landforms associated with them are high and isolated hills with vertical sides.

The large extensive plains which are characteristic features of the land-scapes of Burma, Thailand and Indo-China are not found in Peninsular Malaysia. The only flat pieces of land of any size are the coastal plains

19

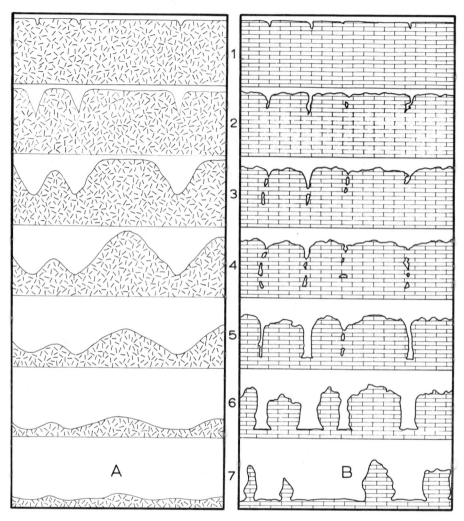

Fig. 1.5   Stages in the cycle of erosion on (A) silicate rocks and (B) limestone (after Paton, 1964).

which lie between the mountainous core and the coast on either side of the Peninsula. There is a sharp demarcation between the flat coastal plains and the steep mountain ranges, which is seen in the sharp angle in the profile of the rivers at the foot of the mountains. Scrivenor attributes the contrast between the lowlands and the mountains to marine denudation, which carved out wide valleys in the bedrock during the Pleistocene period of low sea-level. These valleys were subsequently filled with alluvium. The depth of the original valleys is indicated by the great thickness (up to 450 ft (137 m) in places) of alluvium which now covers the modern riverbeds and the bedrock.

These flat coastal plains have a gentle gradient. For example, the average gradient of the Pahang riverbed between Kuala Lipis and Kuala Pahang on the coast is only about 0.9 ft per mile, that is, less than 1 in 5 280. The gradient of the lower course of the Perak River is about 1 in 7 000. The coastal plains are most extensive along western Peninsular Malaysia. They average about 20 miles (48 km) in width, and reach their maximum width in the lower courses of the Perak and Bernam rivers where the alluvium extends inland for some 40 miles (64 km). The continuity of the western plains is broken in the region between Port Dickson in Negri Sembilan and Tanjong Kling in Malacca where the older sedimentary rocks extend to the coast, and there are only local patches of alluvium. The western plains continue, south of Tanjong Kling, as a narrow band of alluvium which broadens out all along the Johore coast. The central Malacca—Johore stretch of the western plains is interrupted in three places by granite outliers—at Serkam in south Malacca, near Parit Jawa south of Bandar Maharani (Muar) and at Bandar Penggaram (Batu Pahat).

The alluvial deposits of the western plains are predominantly clayey in composition, the actual succession in depth varying from place to place. Those of north Selangor, for example, consist of a dark-blue clay which is comparatively free from sand but with a high proportion of decaying vegetation. A bore sunk on a site on the Bernam River in north Selangor showed the following succession: a top layer of clay with beds of sand 69 ft (21 m) thick, followed by a 7 ft (2 m) layer of sandstone, beneath which was another thick (57 ft (17 m)) layer of clay with sand, followed again by a 15 ft (4.6 m) layer of sandstone, then a 24 ft (7.3 m) layer of clay with vegetable matter, and a 73 ft (22 m) bed of sand with gas and water, and finally a 135 ft (41 m) layer of clay with sandy beds. The bore was sunk to a depth of 380 ft (116 m) without reaching the bottom of the alluvium. The alluvium in the swampy stretch north of Batang Berjuntai in the Selangor River valley averages 87 ft (26.5 m) in depth. Here the surface is covered by peat with an average thickness of 20 ft (6 m). Beneath the peat is a layer of soft, grey clay about 30 ft (9 m) thick, followed by sandy clay, sand and gravel at the lower levels. The discovery of sea-shells and brackish water at various depths in a bore sunk in the south Perak alluvium at Bangan Datoh indicates that the coastal plains are made up of marine as well as fluvial deposits.

The process of land aggradation is going on rapidly along the west coast, resulting in a gradual widening of the coastal plains. Rapid sedimentation and the comparatively calm seas of the Straits of Malacca have caused the building up of large tracts of alluvial flats along the coast. Some of these flats extend far seawards, raising the sea floor to such an extent that the sea in such places has become very shallow. For example, the 3 fathom (5.5 m) limit opposite Jeram in Kuala Selangor was 26 miles (67 km) out to sea in 1919, and is probably further out today. The

21

alluvial flats which are inundated by high tides are usually colonized by mangroves. Mangrove swamps occupy a belt which stretches practically uninterruptedly from Perlis to Johore. Along this part of Peninsular Malaysia the coastline is very slowly being pushed out into the Straits of Malacca as the mangrove swamps extend by degrees outwards into the sea. As the process of encroachment continues the innermost or landward edges of the mangroves pass beyond the limits of the tides. The mangroves then give way to other species of the rain forest which can tolerate the different conditions of soil and water. In time to come this piece of land is entirely won from the sea and becomes a part of the total land area of the Peninsula, provided that in the meantime sea-level does not change. The indiscriminate felling of the mangroves can slow down the process of land aggradation appreciably since the mud and drifting vegetation which are normally trapped within the stilt roots of the mangroves are thereby exposed and may be carried away by waves or tidal currents.

The coastal plains on the eastern side of the Peninsula are much narrower and less continuous than those of the west. The major expanses of flat land are the Kelantan and the Pahang—Rompin—Endau deltas, separated from each other by the Trengganu Highlands which come close to the Trengganu coast. The greatest width of the eastern plains is in the Pahang delta where the alluvium extends inland for about 20 miles (32 km). Elsewhere the plains are much less developed and limited to narrow localized areas such as that along the Sedili coast of Johore. In the Kuantan riverine area the coastal alluvium goes down to a depth of 169 ft (51 m). It consists of sandy deposits near the coast, and of alternating beds of peaty clay, silt and sand in the inland areas. Along the Trengganu coast between Kuala Trengganu and Kemaman and along most of the Johore coast south of Mersing there are only narrow bands of coarse beach sands between the foothills and the sea.

The coastal landscape of eastern Peninsular Malaysia is distinctly different from that of the west. The mud flats and mangrove swamps so characteristic of the west coast are here limited in their distribution to some parts of the tidal reaches of sheltered river mouths, such as those of the Mersing, Endau, Pahang, Pahang Tua, Trengganu and Kelantan rivers. Instead, long sandy beaches dominate the coast. The entire length of the coast faces the great expanse of the South China Sea. There is no protective land barrier between the coast and the South China Sea, unlike the position in western Peninsular Malaysia where the landmass of Sumatra stands between the Indian Ocean and the coast. During the northeast monsoon the winds and waves that beat along the eastern shores of the Peninsula are therefore fiercer and rougher than those normally encountered along the western shores at all times of the year. These, together with the strong currents which flow off the east coast, combine to prevent the formation of mud flats. The beaches are sandy. Sand banks

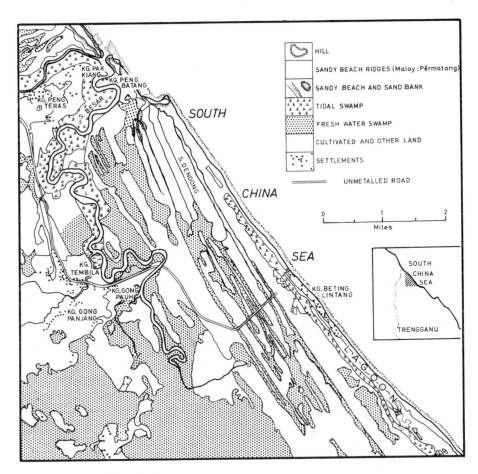

Fig. 1.6   Beach ridges in Trengganu.

and sand bars have been built up across the mouths of most rivers. These sand banks and bars constantly shift and alter their positions, especially after a flood or a storm, and they are a major obstacle to navigation in these areas.

A characteristic and prominent feature of the coastal landscape of eastern Johore, Pahang, Trengganu and Kelantan is the series of long, low ridges which are aligned more or less parallel to the shoreline, sometimes extending several miles inland (Fig. 1.6). These beach ridges are known locally as *permatang*. They are composed mainly of sand, and support only a very poor growth of coastal vegetation—sea-side grasses, low bushes of Cape rhododendron, and a few scattered trees. The swales or depressions between the *permatang*[1] are often seasonally or permanently

[1] For this and other Malay terms, italicized, see the Glossary on p. xiv.

23

flooded, and are covered with swamp vegetation except where they have been cleared for cultivation.

A number of theories involving tectonic uplift of the land and eustatic changes in sea-level have been put forward to explain the formation of these *permatang*. Fitch recognizes two main series of *permatang* between Kuantan and Kemaman, the older series located 1 to 4 miles (1.6–6.4 km) inland and standing up to 36 ft (11 m) above present sea-level, and the younger series located between 2½ miles (4 km) inland and the present coast, with a maximum height of 15 ft (4.6 m). He states that they were formed as a result of the post-Pleistocene uplift of the land. The older series were formed when the land emerged 20 ft (6 m) relative to the sea, and the younger series when the land emerged a further 10 ft (3 m) relative to the sea.

Nossin found no evidence of recent tectonic uplift of the land in north-eastern Johore. The *permatang* in the Mersing–Endau area extend more than 4½ miles (7 km) inland from the coast. Their elevation increases with distance from the coast, and reaches a maximum of 25 ft (7.6 m) above sea-level at the furthest point inland. Nossin postulates that the present inland *permatang* were formed at a period when the sea-level was about 20 ft (6 m) higher than it is now. The subsequent fall in sea-level (in recent or subrecent times) resulted in the formation of a succession of beach ridges as the sea withdrew to its present position.

Permatang also occur along parts of the west coast. Along the coast of north Perak and Province Wellesley, for example, these beach ridges rise to heights of between 17 to 30 ft (5–9 m) above mean sea-level.

Drainage

The constant and heavy rainfall of the Malay Peninsula gives rise to a dense network of rivers and streams, though there is no one single large river dominating the drainage pattern as, for example, the Menam Chao Praya dominates the drainage pattern of Thailand. The largest river in Peninsular Malaysia—the Sungei Pahang—has a length of only slightly over 270 miles (434 km) and a catchment area of about 11 250 square miles (29 137 sq km). The catchment areas of the other three large rivers are: Sungei Perak 5 850 square miles (15 151 sq km); Sungei Kelantan 4 900 square miles (12 691 sq km) and Sungei Muda 1 650 square miles (4 273 sq km). All the other rivers have catchment areas of less than 1 000 square miles (2 590 sq km).

The year-round precipitation ensures perennial stream flow, but although no river course is ever completely dry at any time of the year, the torrential and localized nature of the rainfall causes rapid fluctuations in the volume of water transported by the rivers. Very heavy falls may occur within the space of a few minutes or a few hours at any period of the year. The most intense rainstorm recorded in Peninsular Malaysia was

2 in (51 mm) in 15 minutes at Kuala Lumpur. Falls of high intensities are more likely to occur over a longer period along the east coast during the northeast monsoon. The maximum recorded was 24 in (610 mm) in 24 hours near Kuantan. More than 10 in (254 mm) of rain in 24 hours may be expected along the east coast once in every ten years (Wycherley, 1969a). When such exceptionally heavy rainfall occurs in a catchment area, the volume of water that enters the river channels will be beyond their capacity to transport, so that the excess water runs over the banks and floods the surrounding plain. While most Peninsular Malaysian rivers and streams are subject to occasional flooding, those in eastern Peninsular Malaysia flood more or less regularly during the northeast monsoon when very heavy rainfall occurs over a period of about four months (November to February). In the Pahang delta, for example, floods now occur annually, though the older farmers living there still remember the time when floods were only of occasional incidence and the bed of the Sungei Pahang was very much deeper than it is now. Sometimes, as in 1926, 1948, 1954, 1965, 1969 and 1970 there are peninsula-wide floods which may paralyse normal work for days or even for weeks at a time. The most destructive flood in Peninsular Malaysia within living memory occurred in December 1970 when river levels rose in places from 80 to 105 ft (24—32 m) above normal.

The natural regime of any river whose catchment is under natural vegetation is normally in a state of dynamic equilibrium. Changes tend to occur very gradually. But the uncontrolled forest clearing and mining activities of earlier years have disrupted the natural regimes of Peninsular Malaysian rivers, especially those west of the Main Range. The large quantities of eroded material deposited in the rivers have silted up their channels and turned these rivers into wide shallow meandering streams. The tendancy for such rivers to flood has thus been seriously aggravated. Such floods affect not only agricultural areas but also population centres, most of which had their origins as riverine settlements (*see* Leigh and Low, 1973). The silting up of the Kinta River, due to mining activities in the Kinta Valley, has led to frequent flooding in the areas around Ipoh and Telok Anson, just as the accumulation of silt in the Klang River has increased the occurrence of floods in Kuala Lumpur.

Stream flow in the upper reaches of Peninsular Malaysian rivers and streams is usually swift and strong, but slow and sluggish in the middle and lower courses. The main mountain ranges which run more or less parallel to the west coast form a continuous watershed from the northern borders of Peninsular Malaysia to Malacca. The rivers west of this watershed have relatively short courses. Their gradients in the upper courses are very steep: some rivers drop about 4 000 ft (1 219 m) in less than 15 miles (24 km) before they emerge onto the coastal plains. The very rapid decrease in the flow rates of the rivers at the foot of the mountains reduces the carrying capacity of the rivers, and causes them to drop their load of the coarser-grained material on the landward margins of the western alluvial plains. The finer-grained material are carried by the slow meandering rivers and deposited at the river mouths and along the coastal stretches. There is therefore a roughly parallel zoning of marine and riverine sediments on the west coast.

The rivers east of the main watershed are much faster flowing in the lower reaches and, with their greater carrying capacity, transport large quantities of coarse-grained material to the river mouths. This material is subjected to strong wave and current action during the northeast monsoon, and is eventually deposited along the coast and shoreline to form the extensive beach ridges known as *permatang*.

Waterfalls and rapids are common features in streams which have their headwaters in hilly country. Falls are often caused by streams encountering some highly resistant rocks (e.g. igneous dykes) while deepening their valleys. They also develop where the streams cut their valleys through rocks of very unequal hardness, as at the contacts between granite and sedimentary rocks. The waterfalls vary considerably in height, form and volume of water. Most of them are small, but exceptionally large falls occur in places as, for example, those on the Sungei Pelepak Kanan, a tributary of the Sungei Johore, and those on the Sungei Pandan, a tributary of the Sungei Kuantan. Rapids are caused in many cases by the recession of the waterfalls. Others occur where streams are eroding rocks of unequal hardness.

While the headwaters of most rivers exhibit such indications of youthfulness as steep gradients, waterfalls and rapids, the lower courses, in contrast, characteristically show signs of maturity such as braided channels, meanders, ox-bows and levees. The river profiles thus present a typically flattened appearance, and have been influenced by Quaternary changes in sea-level and progressive sedimentation by the over-loaded rivers. During periods of rising sea-level in the Quaternary the base-levels of rivers and streams in the Peninsula were raised. The effect of this has been to reduce the downcutting power of the rivers and streams, encourage the formation of meanders, extend the area of impeded drainage far inland and induce progressive sedimentation along the coasts on both sides of the Peninsula.

The rivers and streams all flow into the surrounding seas; there are no areas of internal drainage in Peninsular Malaysia. There is only one large natural lake—Lake Chini, located some 50 miles (80 km) from the mouth of the Sungei Pahang (Fig. 1.7). Chenderoh Lake has been created as a result of the damming of the upper course of the Sungei Perak for the generation of hydroelectric power. Tasek Bera, which takes its name from the Sungei Bera, a tributary of the Sungei Pahang, is an elongated swamp whose boundaries are considerably extended during the rainy northeast monsoon. The junctions of many tributaries of rivers flowing in granite country are often blocked by landslide debris, damming the

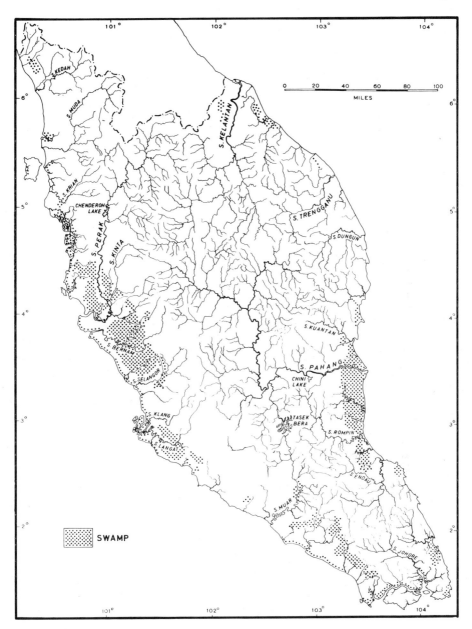

Fig. 1.7   The drainage pattern.

flow of water and creating long, shallow lakes, which, however, are only
temporary features on the landscape, disappearing as soon as the natural
dams have been breached. These temporary lakes are more commonly
found in eastern Peninsular Malaysia because of the greater frequency

27

with which landslides occur in this part of the Peninsula, especially after the heavy rains of the northeast monsoon. Small, shallow lagoons are also common along the east coast where drainage has been impeded by the sea banking up sand.

The very gentle gradients of the rivers flowing along the western alluvial plains have resulted in the formation of large expanses of both tidal and freshwater swamps. Roe attributes the swamps of western Peninsular Malaysia to subsidence of the west coast. Although extensive areas of swamp in western Peninsular Malaysia have been drained for agriculture, especially in Perlis, Kedah, Province Wellesley, Krian, the Sungei Manik area of Perak and along the Selangor and Johore coasts, swamps still cover large parts of the alluvial plains (Fig. 1.7). Freshwater swamps in eastern Peninsular Malaysia have developed where drainage has been impeded by beach ridges. Most of these swamps are being filled in with heavy clay carried down by rivers. Such in-filling has resulted in many instances in fully impeding drainage and has led to the formation of permanently flooded swamps. Many of the smaller rivers of eastern Peninsular Malaysia, particularly those of the Pahang—Rompin—Endau deltaic regions, disappear into the freshwater swamps, emerging only where they debouch into the sea. Much of the drainage of the coastal plains and freshwater swamps on both sides of the Peninsula is under control for padi cultivation.

The main factor which sets the drainage pattern of north and central Peninsular Malaysia (Fig. 1.7) is the series of mountain ranges aligned in a roughly north—south direction and running with the grain of the Peninsula from the north to end in a number of outliers in Malacca and Johore (Fig. 1.3, inset). In general the tributaries flow east and west at right angles to the mountain ranges, whereas the main rivers follow a longitudinal course along the strike of the rocks before making a right-angled turn, usually at the break of slope between the mountains and the plains, and meandering out to sea on either side of the Peninsula. The two major rivers—the Perak and the Pahang—both exhibit such a pattern of flow, the one debouching into the Straits of Malacca and the other into the South China Sea. The Sungei Kelantan, however, rising in the Trengganu Highlands and the eastern flanks of the Main Range, flows in a northerly direction straight out into the South China Sea. The overall result is a more or less rectangular pattern of drainage, with longitudinal, often subsequent lines predominating in the middle courses of the rivers, and latitudinal lines in the upper and lower courses.

Advanced erosion and the absence of any pronounced relief features in the south are responsible for the dendritic drainage pattern in this section of the Peninsula. There is irregular branching in all directions, and the tributaries join the main streams at all angles. Marshes and swamps extend far inland from the coasts, and the rivers are generally slow-moving, with ill-defined channels.

2
Climate

The Malay Peninsula has an equatorial climate, though insularity and exposure to monsoonal effects result in its climate being slightly different in detail from that of, say, the equatorial areas of the Congo and Amazon Basins. The differences are not so much in temperature as in rainfall, and again not so much in its total volume as in its annual distribution. The other characteristic features of the climate of the Peninsula are the constantly high temperatures and the absence of a cold season. Seasonality in the Peninsula, as in other parts of the tropics, is a function of rainfall rather than of temperature.

The narrowness of the Peninsula and the central location of the mountain ranges with flanking flat coastal plains facilitate the inland penetration of maritime influences. Although Peninsular Malaysia is a mountainous country, none of the mountains attains any great altitude, and only two of them—Gunong Tahan and Gunong Korbu—rise to just over 7 000 ft (2 134 m) above sea-level. They are therefore well below the snowline, which in the equatorial zone is about 16 000 ft (4 877 m) and snow and frost are never encountered in the Peninsula. The lowest absolute minimum temperature recorded at Cameron Highlands, 4 750 ft (1 448 m) above sea-level, was 36° F or 2.2° C (January 1937).

Climate is the chief control of vegetation type, and the rain forest of the Malay Peninsula is the climax vegetation of the equatorial climate. The rain forest in its turn has a modifying influence on the climate. Nearly three-quarters of the total land area of Peninsular Malaysia is still forested, and the transpiration from the dense vegetative cover increases the humidity of the air and the potentiality for rain to fall. The forest cover also affects the climate near the ground, moderating temperatures by absorbing heat in the process of evaporation from the foliage and by casting shade.

Pressure

During the northern winter the air overlying the Asian continent increases in density as temperatures fall. High pressure areas are built up over Siberia (the 'Siberian High') and the Indian subcontinent. At this period the Southern Hemisphere is experiencing its summer. The air overlying the Australian continent becomes lighter as temperatures rise. A low pressure area develops over the continent. There is therefore, in these months, a continuous pressure gradient across the equatorial regions from the high pressure over Asia to the low pressure over Australia. North of the Equator this gradient is associated with north-easterly winds of the northeast monsoon. During the northern summer a reversal of circulation takes place as pressures fall over Asia and a high pressure area develops over Australia.

Over equatorial Southeast Asia seasonal pressure changes are very small, the maximum range being less than 2 millibars. Over the Malay Peninsula these seasonal variations are masked by the daily variations in pressure which are more pronounced and range between 3 and 4.3 millibars. At Temerloh, for instance, the atmospheric pressure may vary from 1 011 millibars at 0900 hours to 1 006.7 millibars at 1500 hours. Such a great daily variation of pressure is typical of these equatorial latitudes and stands in marked contrast to the 1 millibar diurnal variation common in the middle latitudes.

Winds

The Malay Peninsula and the other parts of Southeast Asia come under the influence of eight or nine major air-streams which have their sources in northeast and central Siberia, north India, Tibet, the North Pacific, Australia, the South Indian Ocean and the South Pacific. They converge over Southeast Asia from three main directions during the course of a year, to form a pattern of air-stream boundaries as illustrated in Fig. 2.1. The boundary AB is the Northern Equatorial Air-stream Boundary; BC is the Southern Equatorial Air-stream Boundary, while BD is the Combined Air-stream Boundary. Figure 2.1 shows a pattern which obtains only in October, April and May. At other times of the year, only two main boundaries—the Northern and Southern Equatorial Air-stream Boundaries (AB and BC)—prevail over Southeast Asia.

The boundaries are constantly shifting with changes in the speed and direction of the air-streams. The winds that blow over Peninsular Malaysia and the other parts of Southeast Asia are related to the air-streams. It is the wind with its accompanying rains which, more than any other climatic element, gives the climate of Peninsular Malaysia a seasonal rhythm. The advance and retreat of the air-streams that cross the Peninsula follow a recognizable pattern, and are responsible for the division of the year into four seasons: (1) the northeast monsoon, (2) the southwest monsoon, and (3) and (4) the transitional periods between the monsoons. The northeast monsoon arrives in November or early December, and lasts until March. During this period air-streams from the

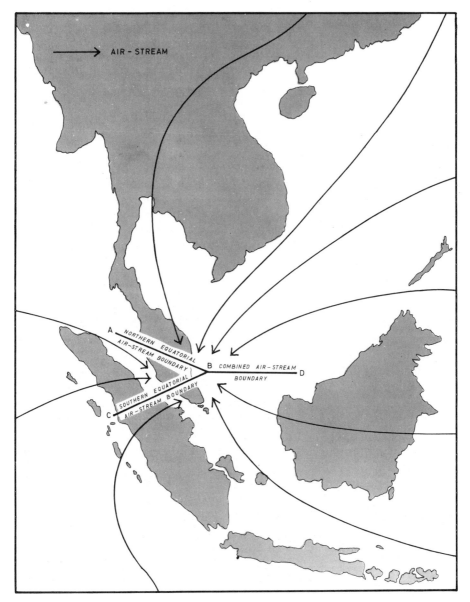

Fig. 2.1 Principal air-streams affecting Peninsular Malaysia and air-stream boundaries.

northeast sweep over the Peninsula. The northeast monsoon gives way to a transitional period of five to seven weeks' duration, when winds are weak and variable. The northeast monsoon retreats from southern Peninsular Malaysia earlier in the year, so that the transitional period in this part of the Peninsula usually coincides with the month of April, while the north part experiences it in May. The southwest monsoon then follows, lasting from June to September or early October. This monsoon only prevails over northern Peninsular Malaysia. South of latitude 5° N the country experiences light southerly winds. Neither the south-westerlies nor the southerlies are as strong as the north-easterlies, and they may be masked by land and sea breezes in coastal areas. The monsoon is then followed by another transitional period during October and early November. This general pattern of the wind seasons is mirrored in the rainfall regime of the Peninsula.

Figures 2.2 to 2.7 show the surface winds which blow over Southeast Asia, the position of the air-stream boundaries and the percentage frequencies of the surface winds in four stations in Peninsular Malaysia for each month of the year. October is selected as the starting point of the month-by-month analysis of surface wind conditions as it marks the retreat of the southwest monsoon and the advance of the northeast monsoon over the region.

October (Fig. 2.2).   This is the transitional month between the southwest and the northeast monsoons. The pattern of the air-stream boundaries is similar to that depicted in Fig. 2.1. The Northern Equatorial Air-stream Boundary (AB) separates the retreating south-westerlies from the advancing north-easterlies, while the Southern Equatorial Air-stream Boundary (BC) divides the same south-westerlies from the southerlies. At about latitude 10° N, and east of longitude 110° E the two boundaries merge to form the Combined Boundary (BD). Surface winds in the Malay Peninsula are weak and variable, with speeds seldom exceeding 12 m.p.h. (19 k.p.h.). In north Peninsular Malaysia a high percentage—39 per cent at Penang and 23 per cent at Kota Bharu—of the days of this month experience calms. At Kota Bharu 50 per cent of the days of the month experience winds from the west, southwest and south. In south Peninsular Malaysia a very small percentage of the wind observations show a calm—only 3 per cent at Kuala Pahang and 1 per cent at Malacca. For 33 per cent of the time, winds at Kuala Pahang are from the west, while westerly winds also attain a high frequency at Malacca (20 per cent).

November (Fig. 2.2).   During this month the air-streams originating from northeast and central Siberia and the North Pacific advance southwards, pushing the Northern Equatorial Air-stream Boundary (AB) across the South China Sea to a position parallel with the east coast of Peninsular Malaysia, while the Southern Equatorial Air-stream Boundary (BC), separating the westerlies from the southerlies, is located at latitude 5° S. Surface winds over northern Peninsular Malaysia are light and variable. Penang experiences a calm on 36 per cent of the days of this month, with winds reaching speeds of less than 8 m.p.h. (13 k.p.h.) from the

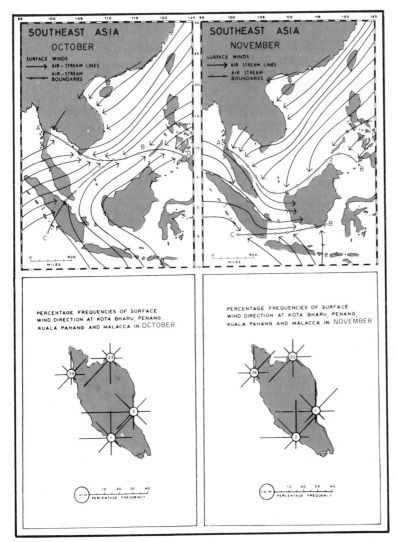

Fig. 2.2 Surface winds and air-stream boundaries over Southeast Asia (*top*), and percentage frequencies of surface winds over the Malay Peninsula (*bottom*), October and November.

north and northeast for 23 per cent of the time. Kota Bharu has calm weather on 20 per cent of the days of the month, and light winds from the southwest quadrant for 43 per cent of the time. Southern Peninsular Malaysia, again, has very few days of calm. Malacca has light winds from four directions: west (22 per cent frequency), northwest (15 per cent), north (21 per cent) and northeast (20 per cent). Kuala Pahang also receives most of its winds from these four directions, with occasional

33

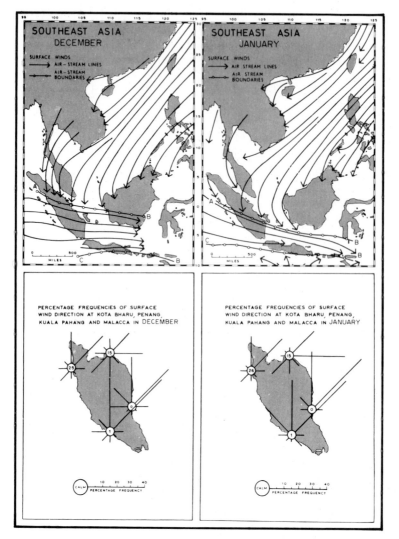

Fig. 2.3 Surface winds and air-stream boundaries over Southeast Asia (*top*), and percentage frequencies of surface winds over the Malay Peninsula (*bottom*), December and January.

gusts from the north and northeast reaching speeds of 13 to 24 m.p.h. (21—39 k.p.h.).

December (Fig. 2.3).   The Northern Equatorial Air-stream Boundary (AB) now advances to a position parallel to the Equator. The northeast monsoon is now established over the Malay Peninsula, as is apparent from the decrease in the percentage of calms throughout the country and the high proportion of the winds blowing from the north and northeast.

Penang has the lowest percentage of calms (25 per cent) for the year during this month. Thirty-two per cent of the days of the month have winds from the north and northeast. Kota Bharu has a 15 per cent frequency of calms, and a 35 per cent frequency of winds from the northeast and east. The pattern of winds in southern Peninsular Malaysia reflects to a more pronounced extent the advance of the northeast monsoon. At Kuala Pahang 63 per cent of the days have winds from the north and northeast, 40 per cent reaching speeds of 13 to 24 m.p.h. At Malacca 71 per cent of the days have winds from these two directions, though only 13 per cent reach speeds of 13 to 24 m.p.h.

January (Fig. 2.3). The Northern Equatorial Air-stream Boundary (AB) advances to its most southerly position, astride the Java Sea. The pattern of winds in north Peninsular Malaysia is similar to that in December, with Kota Bharu recording a higher frequency (54 per cent) of winds from the northeast and east. Both the frequencies and the average speeds of the northerlies and the north-easterlies in south Peninsular Malaysia increase considerably. At Kuala Pahang the frequency of the winds from these two directions increases to 90 per cent, with 64 per cent attaining speeds of 13 to 24 m.p.h. At Malacca their frequency increases to 83 per cent, and 27 per cent blow with speeds of 13 to 24 m.p.h.

February (Fig. 2.4). With the retreat of the northeast monsoon the Northern Equatorial Air-stream Boundary (AB) moves northwards, its mean position for the month being similar to that of December. The wind pattern in Peninsular Malaysia is also basically similar to that in December, with the exception that Penang records a higher frequency (34 per cent) of calms.

March (Fig. 2.4). The retreat of the monsoon is marked by a further slight northward shift of the Northern Equatorial Air-stream Boundary (AB). A higher frequency of calms is observed in the north—40 per cent at Penang and 22 per cent at Kota Bharu. The prevailing surface winds along the east coast of Peninsular Malaysia are still from the north-eastern quadrant—40 per cent of the days at Kota Bharu and 70 per cent at Kuala Pahang. But the wind patterns along the west coast do not indicate the presence of the northeast monsoon. At Malacca the prevailing surface winds are from the north and northwest (59 per cent frequency), while at Penang winds from the western quadrant are more frequent (28 per cent) than from the north-eastern quadrant (24 per cent).

April (Fig. 2.5). The pattern of the air-stream boundaries in this month is similar to that of October, but the position of the boundaries is south of Singapore. April is the transitional period between monsoons in

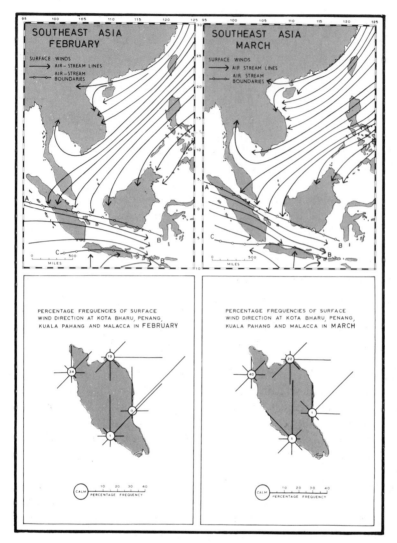

Fig. 2.4 Surface winds and air-stream boundaries over Southeast Asia (*top*), and percentage frequencies of surface winds over the Malay Peninsula (*bottom*), February and March.

southern Peninsular Malaysia. Wind patterns are indeterminate in this part of the Peninsula. At Kuala Pahang 38 per cent of the days of the month experience winds from the northeast and east. At Malacca winds blow with a 43 per cent frequency from the north and northeast, and a 36 per cent frequency from the western quadrant. Wind conditions in north Peninsular Malaysia are much the same as those recorded for March, except that at Kota Bharu the frequency of winds from the northeast and east drops to 27 per cent.

36

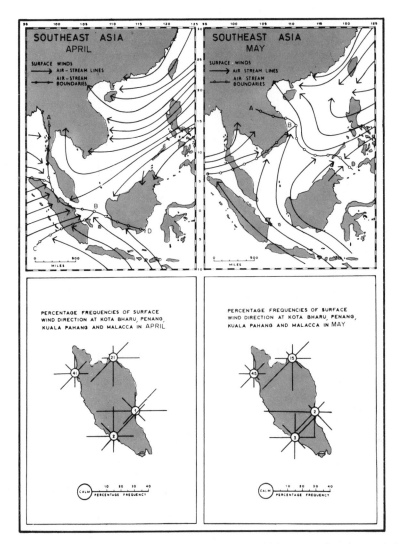

Fig. 2.5 Surface winds and air-stream boundaries over Southeast Asia (*top*), and percentage frequencies of surface winds over the Malay Peninsula (*bottom*), April and May.

May (Fig. 2.5).   The pattern of the air-stream boundaries is similar to that for April, but the position of the boundaries is now north of the Malay Peninsula. The withdrawal of the north-easterlies is reflected in the wind patterns in Peninsular Malaysia. North Peninsular Malaysia continues to have a high incidence of calms—48 per cent at Penang and 15 per cent at Kota Bharu. Sixty-five per cent of the days at Kota Bharu have winds from the southwest quadrant. At Kuala Pahang winds also blow with the greatest frequency (64 per cent) from the southwest quadrant.

37

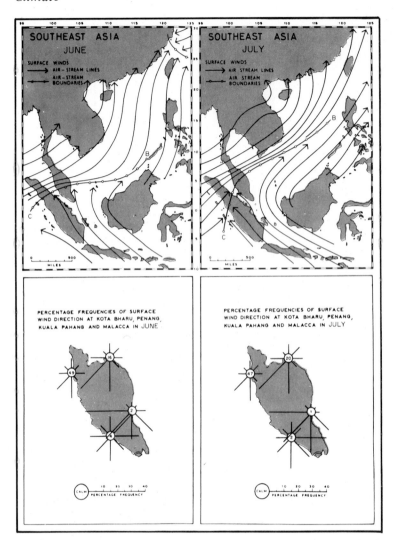

Fig. 2.6 Surface winds and air-stream boundaries over Southeast Asia (*top*), and percentage frequencies of surface winds over the Malay Peninsula (*bottom*), June and July.

June (Fig. 2.6). With the onset of the southwest monsoon air-streams from the southwest prevail over northern Peninsular Malaysia, while southerlies prevail over south Peninsular Malaysia. The Southern Equatorial Air-stream Boundary (BC) marks the meeting zone of these air-streams. Wind conditions throughout the Peninsula differ very little from those in May.

July (Fig. 2.6). The Southern Equatorial Air-stream Boundary (BC)

38

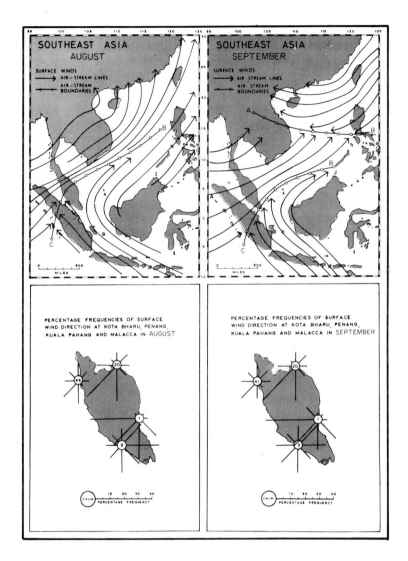

Fig. 2.7   Surface winds and air-stream boundaries over Southeast Asia (*top*), and percentage frequencies of surface winds over the Malay Peninsula (*bottom*), August and September.

now advances slightly northwards. Wind patterns in north Peninsular Malaysia remain remarkably similar to those in May and June. At Kuala Pahang most of the winds are light (less than 13 m.p.h. (21 k.p.h.)) and blow from the southwest quadrant. At Malacca, however, 55 per cent of the days have winds from the southeast quadrant.

August (Fig. 2.7).   There is little change in the mean position of the

39

Southern Equatorial Air-stream Boundary (BC), and wind conditions throughout Peninsular Malaysia are much similar to those for July.

September (Fig. 2.7). The southwest monsoon begins to retreat. The Northern Equatorial Air-stream Boundary (AB) advances to a position between the centre of the Indo-Chinese peninsula and the Philippines, while the Southern Equatorial Air-stream Boundary (BC) now lies between Singapore and Palawan Island. Surface winds in north Peninsular Malaysia are light and are often reduced to a calm. Penang has 41 per cent of the days with calm weather, while Kota Bharu has 20 per cent. Winds at the latter station are predominantly from the southwest quadrant. Kuala Pahang has 75 per cent of the days with winds from the same quadrant, but Malacca has winds as frequently from the northeast (41 per cent) as from the southwest (40 per cent). Wind speeds throughout the Peninsula remain less than 13 m.p.h.

Land and sea breezes

These diurnal winds are caused by differential heating and cooling over land and sea. The sea breeze generally sets in about 10 a.m., steadily gathering strength until it blows with greatest force in the early afternoon, and finally dies away at sunset. There is a short interim period before the land breeze begins to blow in the late evening and night. The land breeze is seldom as strong as the sea breeze. The breezes are only felt for a distance of about 10 miles (16 km) from the shore, and inland areas do not have these diurnal winds.

The regularity of the breezes varies with the season of the year, and the location of the area in relation to the monsoons. In general the breezes are best developed during the intermonsoon periods and when the monsoons are weak. At Kuala Trengganu, during these periods, the sea breeze reaches maximum speed at about 2 p.m. or 3 p.m. The breeze at its maximum averages 7 to 8 m.p.h. (11–13 k.p.h.). The land breeze reaches maximum force at about 6 a.m. At its maximum it averages 4 to 5 m.p.h. (6–8 k.p.h.).

In the Straits of Malacca, during these periods, the sea breeze usually sets in between 10 a.m. and 11 a.m., and attains maximum force at about 4 p.m. The average speed of the breeze at its maximum is 11.5 m.p.h. (18 k.p.h.). The land breeze sets in between 8 p.m. and 9 p.m. and blows until about 9 a.m. At its maximum, the land breeze seldom exceeds 8 m.p.h. (13 k.p.h.).

The position is different during the monsoons. During the northeast monsoon the prevailing north-easterlies attain sufficient force to mask and even entirely prevent the development of the land breeze along the east coast and the sea breeze along the west coast of the Peninsula. Conversely, the north-easterlies during this period reinforce the sea breeze along the east coast, and the land breeze along the west coast. A reversal of this pattern occurs during the southwest monsoon.

Squalls

Surface winds over the Peninsula are generally light, their speeds seldom exceeding 18 m.p.h. (29 k.p.h.) with gusts of less than 30 m.p.h. (48 k.p.h.). Occasionally, however, gusts may exceed 30 m.p.h. A squall is defined by Watts (1954) as a storm with gusts of over 30 m.p.h. accompanied by marked changes in wind direction and sudden increases of wind-speed. Such storms can sometimes be quite violent and cause considerable damage to shipping, buildings and other structures which lie in their paths. The torrential rain which accompanies them may cause local floods, destroy crops[1] and impede normal traffic flow. Winds may reach speeds of 40 m.p.h. (64 k.p.h.) or more within a few minutes. Local squalls may occur as a result of some local configuration of the land disturbing the smooth passage of an air-stream. Other local squalls may occur in association with isolated cumulonimbus.

Line-squalls are usually, though not necessarily, accompanied by continuous lines of cumulonimbus clouds with equally strong winds at every point along them. Line-squalls may accompany a moving air-stream boundary. Sometimes the seaward flow of an air-stream at an upper level may retard the development of a sea breeze, so that when the breeze does set in, the air over the land has had time to warm up to such an extent that its temperature is several degrees higher than the sea breeze. The colder sea breeze thereby undercuts the warm air over the land, resulting in the formation of convective cloud and a line-squall parallel to the coast. Similarly, the land breeze may on occasion begin as a line-squall because of an air flow from sea to land delaying the development of the land breeze sufficiently to cause the air over the land to cool considerably. When the land breeze eventually moves out to sea, it undercuts the warmer air over the sea, and a line-squall may then develop.

The incidence of squalls in the Malay Peninsula varies from place to place and according to the period of the year. Table 2.1 shows that squalls occur with the greatest frequency along the coastal parts of southern Peninsular Malaysia: Mersing had a total of 218 squalls and 72 line-squalls over a two-year period, while Kuala Pahang, at the mouth of the Pahang River, recorded a total of 155 squalls and 52 line-squalls. A similar pattern obtains along the coasts of western Peninsular Malaysia: Malacca recorded a total of 182 squalls and 90 line-squalls while Bukit Jeram, on the Selangor coast, had a total of 146 squalls and 90 line-squalls.

---

[1] It has been found, for example, that high yielding rubber trees derived from Clone 501 are distinctively susceptible to wind damage and are liable to be blown down during a squall.

Table 2.1   Number of squalls and line-squalls in Peninsular Malaysia over a two-year period (1936 and 1937)

	Period of the year								Total over the two-year period	
	Nov.–Feb.		March–April		May–Aug.		Sept.–Oct.			
	Squalls	Line-squalls	Squalls	Line-squalls	Squalls	Line-squalls	Squalls	Line-squalls	Squalls	Line-squalls
Western Peninsular Malaysia										
Penang (Bayan Lepas)	6	4	10	6	54	36	24	18	94	64
Sitiawan	6	6	Nil	Nil	16	16	2	Nil	24	22
Kuala Lumpur	26	6	14	2	42	18	30	14	112	40
Bukit Jeram	28	8	18	12	74	52	26	18	146	90
Malacca	46	20	14	6	78	46	44	18	182	90
Eastern Peninsular Malaysia										
Kota Bharu	8	Nil	4	Nil	68	22	26	14	106	36
Kuala Pahang	42	8	11	2	66	30	36	12	155	52
Kuala Lipis	8	2	20	6	36	28	28	8	92	44
Mersing	54	8	24	10	90	34	50	20	218	72

The incidence of squalls and line-squalls is higher over all parts of the Peninsula during May to August, as Table 2.1 reveals clearly. The line-squalls which occur along the coast between Port Swettenham and Singapore during this period are known locally as 'sumatras'. These 'sumatras' have the following characteristic features: (*a*) they are not associated with a moving air-stream boundary but lie entirely within a single air-stream, (*b*) they almost always occur at night or in the early morning, and (*c*) they are accompanied by strong cold squalls with gusts of over 50 m.p.h. (80.5 k.p.h.) where the 'sumatras' are well-developed. In most cases these 'sumatras' are accompanied by a continuous line (which may be up to 200 miles (322 km long)) of huge cumulus or cumulonimbus. Their cause is not yet fully understood.

The incidence of squalls in Peninsular Malaysia is low during November to February, in marked contrast to the high incidence during May to August. Most of the squalls during November to February occur in the early afternoon as local convective storms. Except at Malacca, line-squalls are rare in Peninsular Malaysia at this period. Table 2.1 also shows that the frequency of occurrence of squalls and line-squalls during the months of September—October is higher than that during the months of March—April, and even higher than that during November to February.

Temperature

The Malay Peninsula, with its southernmost extremity just north of latitude 1° N and its northern boundaries at about latitude 7° N, lies within a zone where the sun's angular elevation above the horizon is high for all the year. But insularity, heavy rainfall, high relative humidities and a constant heavy cloud-cover considerably moderate temperature, so that the excessive summer temperatures which occur at the higher tropical latitudes are never recorded here. Temperatures remain uniformly high throughout the Peninsula and throughout the year. Figure 2.8 shows that the mean annual temperature is strikingly similar for all places in lowland Malaya. Kluang in central Johore has the lowest (78° F; 25.6° C) mean annual temperature of the nine lowland stations, whilst Grik, some 50 miles (80.5 km) inland from the Province Wellesley coast, has the highest—80.5° F (26.9° C). The other seven lowland stations have mean annual temperatures between 78° and 80° F. Cameron Highlands, 4 750 ft (1 448 m) above mean sea-level, has a mean of 64° F (17.8° C), but altitudinal lowering of the temperature is of little human significance in a country where the population is concentrated in the lowlands.

Figure 2.8 also illustrates the monotonous uniformity of the mean monthly temperatures throughout the Peninsula. Temperatures for most of the months of the year for most places in lowland Malaysia are

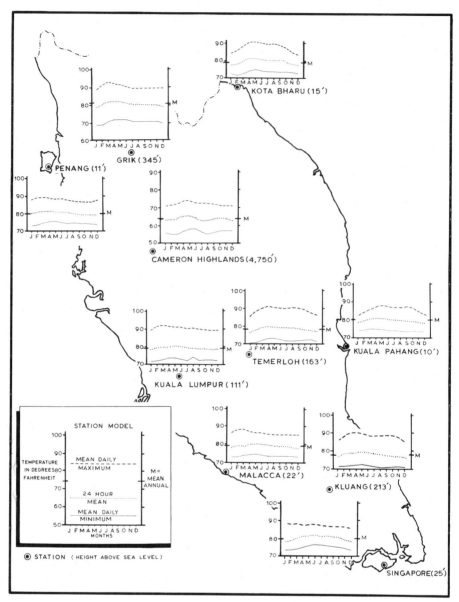

Fig. 2.8   Mean temperatures at selected stations.

between 78° and 82° F (25.6–27.8° C). However, there is a small but noticeable drop in mean monthly temperatures in eastern Peninsular Malaysia during the northeast monsoon. Kota Bharu, for example, has mean monthly temperatures of 77 to 78° F (25–25.6° C) for the monsoon months of November to February, while Temerloh, about 70 miles (113 km) upstream from the mouth of the Pahang River, experiences a similar drop in temperature during this period. This fall in the average values in eastern Peninsular Malaysia is probably due to the low day temperatures brought about by the overcast skies and heavy rainfall of the monsoons. It is also possible that the fall in average temperature values may be due to the fact that eastern Peninsular Malaysia is under the influence of air-streams from higher, and cooler, latitudes at this time of the year. Cameron Highlands experiences temperatures of between 63° and 65° F (17.2–18.3° C) for all the months of the year.

The mean annual range is consequently very small everywhere in the Peninsula, along the coasts as well as in the interior, in the lowlands and the uplands (Table 2.2). Penang (Bayan Lepas aerodrome), Kuala Pahang at the mouth of the Pahang River, Kuala Lumpur in the Klang Valley, Malacca on the south-western coast and Kluang in central Johore, all record a mean annual range of only 2° F (1.1° C), while Cameron Highlands has a range of 2.5° F. Kota Bharu and Singapore both have a slightly higher range of 4° F.

As is typical of the equatorial latitudes, the mean diurnal range (that is, the difference between the mean of the daily maxima and the mean of the daily minima observed over a long period) is greater than the mean annual range, although the diurnal range is still very small when compared with that of the dry tropics. For this reason, the 'winter' of equatorial and tropical areas may be said to fall at night when the lowest temperatures are experienced. Mean daily minima for places throughout the lowlands fall between 69° and 76° F (20.6–24.4° C) (Fig. 2.8). Most areas record minima of 71 to 74° F (21.7–23.3° C). Mean daily maxima, however, show greater variation. Places in eastern Peninsular Malaysia experience a drop in maximum temperatures during the northeast monsoon. Thus the mean daily maxima at Kota Bharu are 83 to 86° F (28.3–30° C) for the months of November to February, and 87 to 90° F (30.6–32.2° C) for the rest of the year. A similar pattern obtains for Kuala Pahang. At Temerloh the fall in daily maximum temperatures is confined only to the months of December and January when mean daily maxima are 85 to 86° F (29.4–30° C). For the remainder of the year the maxima are between 88° and 91° F (31.1–32.8° C) (Fig. 2.8).

The mean daily maxima are generally higher in the interior of the Peninsula (e.g. 89–93° F at Grik) than along the coast (e.g. 86–89° F at Penang). The mean daily minima are also lower in the interior (e.g. 69–72° F at Grik) than along the coast (e.g. 73–75° F at Penang). The result is that interior locations have a more pronounced diurnal range of temperatures than places along the coast. Thus Kuala Lumpur, Temerloh, Grik and Kluang all have a diurnal range of 16 to 19° F (5.3–7° C), while the coastal stations of Kota Bharu, Kuala Pahang, Malacca and Penang have a range of 11 to 14° F (2.5–4.2° C) (Table 2.2). At Cameron Highlands the range is 16° F (5.3° C) (mean maxima of 72° F and mean minima of 56° F).

Table 2.2 Temperature ranges and extremes of temperature at selected stations

Lowland stations	Mean annual range		Mean diurnal range		Absolute maximum		Absolute minimum		Extreme range	
	°F	°C	°F	°C	°F	°C	°F	°C	°F	°C
Kota Bharu	4	−2.2	14	−7.8	96	+35.6	62	+16.7	34	+18.9
Penang (Bayan Lepas)	2	−1.1	13	−7.2	94	+34.4	65	+18.3	29	−16.1
Kuala Pahang	2	−1.1	11.5	−6.4	93	+33.9	65	+18.3	28	−15.6
Temerloh	3	−1.7	17	−9.4	97	+36.1	64	+17.8	33	+18.3
Kuala Lumpur	2	−1.1	18	−10.0	98	+36.7	64	+17.8	34	+18.9
Malacca	2	−1.1	13	−7.2	95	+35.0	66	+18.9	29	−16.1
Kluang	2	−1.1	16	−8.9	96	+35.6	64	+17.8	32	17.8
Grik	3	−1.7	19	−10.6	99	+37.2	60	+15.6	39	+21.5
Singapore	4	−2.2	12	−6.7	95	+35.0	67	+19.4	28	−15.6
Cameron Highlands										
(4 750 ft)	2.5	−1.4	16	−8.9	80	+26.7	36	+2.2	44	+24.4

In Peninsular Malaysia extreme temperatures show the same constancy and the same small range as mean temperatures. The thermometer seldom rises above 100° F (37.8° C) or falls below 60° F (15.6° C) (Table 2.2). The highest temperature recorded in the Peninsula was 103° F (39.4° C) at Pulau Langkawi on a day in March 1931. The lowest temperature recorded in the lowlands was 60° F, at Grik on several occasions, at Lenggong on a day in 1937 and again in 1939, and at Kulim on a day in 1937. The extreme range in the lowlands seldom exceeds 40° F (18.7° C) (Table 2.2). At Cameron Highlands the extreme range is greater as an absolute maximum of 80° F (26.7° C) and an absolute minimum of 36° F (2.2° C) have been recorded. Such a range, however, has not been observed for the other highland stations in the Peninsula.

Relative humidity

Relative humidity is persistently high in all parts of the Malay Peninsula. The average values recorded for a large number of stations in different locations show remarkable uniformity. Most of the stations have a mean relative humidity of 82 to 86 per cent, rising to nearly 90 per cent in the highland areas. The constantly high temperature and high relative humidity which are characteristic features of the Peninsular Malaysian climate are far from the optimum for comfort, health and sustained physical work.

Over the Peninsula relative humidities vary to some extent with changes in the monsoons, but these variations are not great, and the mean values in the months of highest and lowest relative humidity do not exceed 13 per cent in any part of the country. Figure 2.9 shows the average monthly variation of relative humidity for each of the main rainfall regions of Peninsular Malaysia: the northwest (Alor Star), the east (Kota Bharu), the west (Kuala Lumpur), the southwest (Kluang), and the Port Dickson—Muar coast (Malacca), as well as the highlands (Cameron Highlands). In all cases the monthly variations are the result of variations in the mean daily minima as the mean daily maxima lie between 95 and 100 per cent for all stations. The greatest variation (nearly 13 per cent) of the average monthly values of relative humidity is recorded at Alor Star. Mean monthly relative humidity reaches a peak of about 88 per cent in October, and decreases during the northeast monsoon to a low of 76 per cent in February. It then increases to a secondary peak of 85 per cent in May, and remains around that level during the southwest monsoon. Mean monthly relative humidity at Kota Bharu is between 82 and 84 per cent for most of the year except in October, November and December when the onset of the northeast monsoon causes it to rise to 86, 88 and 87 per cent respectively. Kuala Lumpur has a wave pattern of relative humidity, with crests of 85 to 86 per cent occurring in April and May and again in November, and troughs of 81 to 82 per cent in

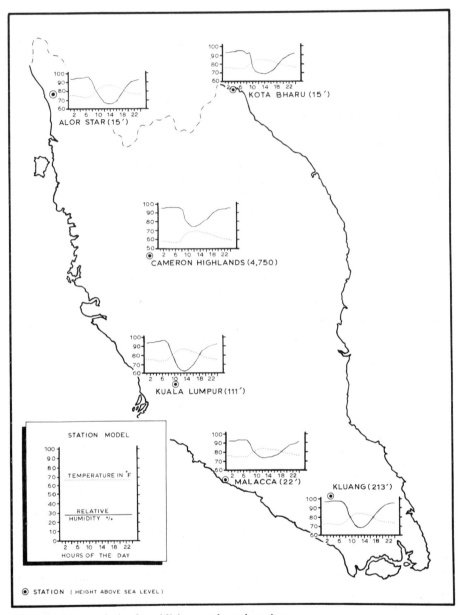

Fig. 2.9   Mean relative humidities at selected stations.

February and July—August. The same pattern is recorded at Malacca, Kluang and Cameron Highlands.

Figure 2.10 shows the hourly values of relative humidity in relation to temperature for the same selected stations from the main rainfall regions. The diurnal cycle is the same for all stations throughout Peninsular Malaysia: during the night and the early hours of the morning tempera-

48

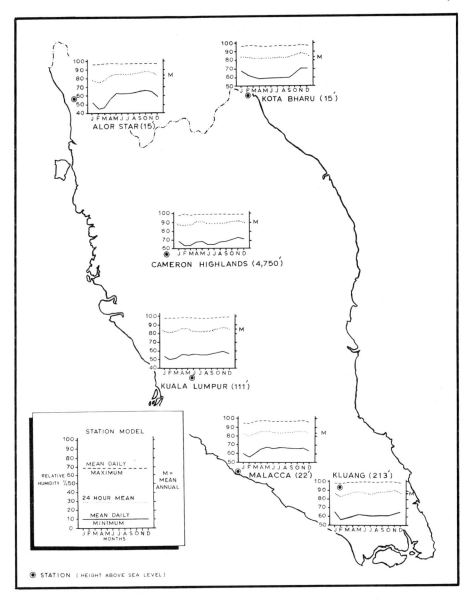

Fig. 2.10 Hourly values of temperature and relative humidity at selected stations.

tures fall gradually until they reach a minimum of 72 to 75° F (22.2–23.9° C) at about 6 and 7 a.m. in the lowlands, and 58° F (14.4° C) in the highlands. As temperatures fall, relative humidity increases progressively until it reaches a maximum of 93 to 98 per cent during the hours of lowest temperatures. A state of near saturation now

49

exists. Temperatures are still in the seventies in the lowlands at 8 a.m., but climb abruptly to 82 to 83° F (about 28° C) between 9 a.m. and 10 a.m. and 66 to 68° F (19–20° C) in the highlands. As a result there is a sudden decrease in relative humidity during this period, values falling by 7 per cent in the case of Malacca (from 89 per cent at 8 a.m. to 82 per cent at 9 a.m.) to as much as 17 per cent at Kota Bharu (from 93 per cent at 9 a.m. to 76 per cent at 10 a.m.). Thereafter temperatures rise steadily to a maximum of 84 to 87° F (28.9–30.6° C) at 1 p.m. in the lowlands and 70° F (21.1° C) in the highlands, and relative humidities drop to their lowest levels for the 24-hour period: to 62 to 74 per cent in the lowlands and 75 per cent in the highlands. There is a slow but steady fall in temperatures and a rise in relative humidities as the afternoon advances, gives away to evening and then to night. However, the relative humidity of a place may increase suddenly when a shower or thunderstorm occurs.

The diurnal range of relative humidity is much greater than the annual range, and is greater for inland areas than for coastal or highland. Thus the coastal stations of Kota Bharu and Malacca have a range of 26 and 19 per cent respectively, while the inland stations of Kuala Lumpur and Kluang have a range of 34 and 29 per cent. Cameron Highlands has a diurnal range of 21 per cent.

Rainfall

In the tropics the seasons are marked by changes in rainfall rather than changes in temperature. Wet and dry seasons take the place of winter and summer. While there is no real 'dry' season in the Malay Peninsula, the rainfall does vary sufficiently at different periods in the year to justify a classification of the rainfall regime into seasons of lesser or greater rainfall. Then again, because of the size of the Peninsula, its position in relation to the main air-streams and the mountain ranges which lie athwart these air-streams, there is a great difference in the amount of rain which falls in any one region in the Peninsula at any one season. Much of the rainfall is convective in origin and therefore localized in distribution, with heavy falls in some areas and none in adjacent areas.

Rainfall types

The rainfall regime of a place is affected, to a varying extent (depending upon local conditions of position and relief), by the type of rainfall that is experienced in that place. Precipitation in the Peninsula at any one time may derive from one or a combination of these four types of rainfall:

1. Orographic rainfall. Orographic ascent causes some of the moisture that the air-streams have picked up from the surrounding tropical seas to be precipitated in the form of heavy falls of rain. The degree of uplift need not be very much to induce precipitation. Such rainfall is particularly important during the monsoons when the prevailing winds are stronger and more regular, and consequently capable of greater uplift when they encounter land barriers such as mountain ranges, plateau escarpments and even moderately high hills. Cooling, condensation and precipitation then occur, usually on the windward slopes. The Main Range and the other subsidiary ranges which are aligned transversely to the path of both the monsoons receive considerable rain on the western flanks during the southwest monsoon and the eastern flanks during the northeast monsoon.

2. Convectional or instability rainfall. Differential heating and cooling of the earth's surface may result in the formation of huge cumulonimbus clouds which attain a vertical depth of several miles. In Peninsular Malaysia the rain which falls from such clouds is usually of great intensity, but of limited duration and affecting only a small area. Such showers last for periods of one to six hours, but the rate of precipitation may be as much as 2 to 3 in (51—76 mm) per hour. A single cumulonimbus cloud may bring rain to an area of less than 1 square mile (2.59 sq km) or as much as 24 square miles (62 sq km). Much of the rain which falls in the Peninsula, especially in April, is of this type.

3. Boundary rainfall. As has been described in the section on winds, eight or nine major air-streams blow across the Peninsula in the course of a year. Where two or more of them converge to form an air-stream boundary up-currents are initiated, followed by cloud formation and heavy precipitation. Such boundary rain commonly marks the onset of the monsoons, and may persist for several days in areas because of the slow rate of movement of the air-stream boundary.

4. Squall rainfall. Squalls, including line-squalls and 'sumatras', are important sources of rain in the Malay Peninsula. Very intense falls of rain lasting for only a few minutes but occasionally up to two hours may be experienced during a squall.

Annual rainfall

The areal distribution of annual rainfall reflects the interplay of the seasonal winds and orography on precipitation. The main differences in the regional distribution of rainfall arise from changes in the major air-streams and from the positional factor relative to the rain-inducing barrier of the main mountain ranges of the Peninsula.

Figure 2.11 shows the distribution of annual rainfall in the Peninsula. There are two exceptionally wet belts where rainfall totals more than 110 in (2 794 mm) a year. The first and major belt covers the entire

51

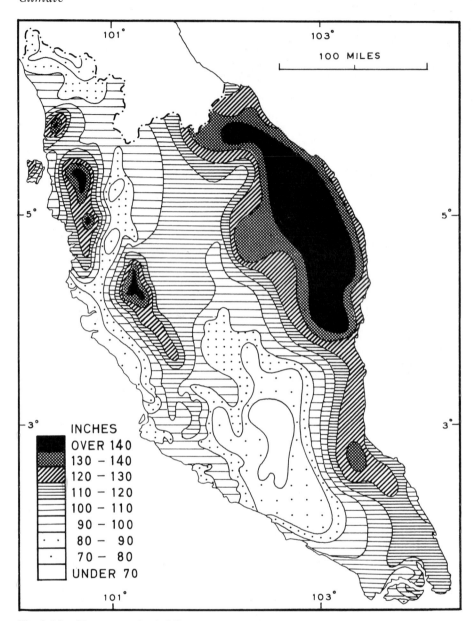

Fig. 2.11   Mean annual rainfall.

length of eastern Peninsular Malaysia, and is broad in the mountainous
north and narrow in the southern half. Within this eastern wet belt is a
smaller belt running from the Kelantan delta to the vicinity of Kuantan
and including most of Trengganu State where rainfall totals are still
higher, being between 130 and 170 in (3 302–4 318 mm) a year.
Between one-third and one-half of the annual total rainfall of eastern

Peninsular Malaysia falls during the northeast monsoon. The heaviest falls are experienced along the foothills of Trengganu where an average of 160 in (4 064 mm) is received a year.

The other wet belt lies along the north-western Peninsular Malaysia and runs from the coastal parts of central Kedah in a southeasterly direction to the vicinity of Tanjong Malim, the continuity of the belt being interrupted by the Perak River valley which receives less than 90 in (2 286 mm) a year. In contrast to the eastern wet belt, the western belt is narrow and confined to the northern half of western Peninsular Malaysia. Heavy falls of rain are not experienced along the southern half of western Peninsular Malaysia probably because of the sheltering effect of the Sumatran Mountains.

There are three 'dry' belts where rainfall totals are less than 90 in (2 286 mm) a year. All are in western Peninsular Malaysia. The first small belt includes Perlis and north-western Kedah. The second covers the coastal districts of Perak and Selangor and extends inland along the Perak River valley. The third and largest belt runs from the Muar–Malacca coast northwards to the vicinity of Temerloh, and includes north-western Johore, most of Malacca State, the inland districts of Negri Sembilan and the south-western parts of Pahang.

All the other parts of the Peninsula receive between 90 and 110 in (2 286–2 794 mm) of rain a year.

These are the broad trends. The distribution over local areas, however, shows wide variations, even over comparatively short distances. As would be expected, the heaviest falls and the highest totals occur on the windward slopes of the main mountain ranges. Maxwell's Hill (3 400 ft (1 036 m)) has an annual rainfall of 201 in (5 105 mm), while Taiping, at the foot of the Hill, has 166 in (4 216 mm). Hill stations higher than Maxwell's Hill but exposed to winds robbed of much of their rain-load when passing over the Sumatran Mountains receive considerably less rain; Cameron Highlands (4 750 ft (1 448 m)) has a total of 107 in (2 718 mm), and Fraser's Hill (4 289 ft (1 308 m)) has 109 in (2 769 mm). The relatively low total received by Cameron Highlands is also due to its being in a sheltered highland valley.

At the other end of the scale, the lowest annual total occurs in Jelebu District, which receives 65 in (1 651 mm). This is again due to its protected location, being ringed in on all sides by mountains.

Monthly rainfall

Figures 2.12, 2.13 and 2.14 show the monthly rainfall distribution as worked out by Dale (1959). They should be consulted in conjunction with Figs 2.2 and 2.7 which show the surface winds and the position of the air-stream boundaries from month to month. October is again selected as the starting point of the month-to-month analysis of monthly

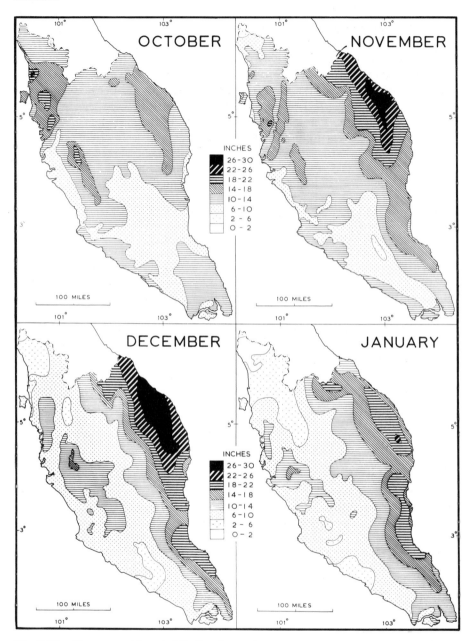

Fig. 2.12   Mean monthly rainfall, October to January.

rainfall, being the transitional month between the retreating southwest monsoon and the advancing northeast monsoon.

October (Fig. 2.12) is the transitional month between the monsoons. The highest rainfall (18 to 22 in (457–559 mm)) is experienced in

54

north-western Peninsular Malaysia. This is also the wettest month of the year for this part of the Peninsula. Western Peninsular Malaysia in general receives heavier rain than eastern Peninsular Malaysia.

November (Fig. 2.12) marks the onset of the northeast monsoon. The heaviest rainfall occurs in a belt running from the Kelantan delta to southern Trengganu, with totals of 18 to 30 in (457–762 mm). The rest of Peninsular Malaysia, except the extreme northwest and a large part of the western half of south Peninsular Malaysia, receive fairly heavy falls of between 10 and 18 in (254–457 mm).

December (Fig. 2.12) brings very heavy boundary and orographic rain to the entire length of eastern Peninsular Malaysia as the Northern Equatorial Air-stream Boundary (Fig. 2.3) passes slowly across the Peninsula from the northeast to the southwest. It is the rainiest month of the year in Peninsular Malaysia, but with most of the rain distinctly localized to the east coast. A broad belt along this part of the Peninsula receives 14 to 30 in (356–762 mm).

January (Fig. 2.12) has a rainfall pattern similar to that of December, but totals are lower and eastern Peninsular Malaysia receives between 10 and 22 in (254–559 mm). The rest of the country, apart from a small area in west-central Peninsular Malaysia, receives less than 10 in of rain. This is the wettest month of the year for southern Johore.

February (Fig. 2.13) is a month of low rainfall for all of Peninsular Malaysia with totals amounting to less than half those for December. Although the northeast monsoon is still blowing with undiminished strength, it brings little rain to the east coast. Kota Bharu, for example, has only 5 in (127 mm), Dungun 6 in (152 mm), Temerloh 4 in (102 mm) and Mersing 9 in (229 mm) of rain during the month. Most of the Peninsula north of latitude 5° N receives less rain in this month than for any other month of the year.

March (Fig. 2.13) is a month of slightly heavier rainfall, with most parts of the Peninsula receiving between 6 and 10 in. There are two narrow wetter belts, one running along the foothills and plains of west-central Peninsular Malaysia, and the other a coastal zone running from southern Trengganu to the southern extremity of Johore. Both belts have totals of between 10 and 14 in.

April (Fig. 2.13) is the transitional period between the retreating northeast monsoon and the advancing southwest monsoon. Calm conditions prevail for much of the time, and convectional rainfall is important. The western wetter belt of March has extended to include a considerably larger area of country, with some parts receiving 18 to 22 in of rain. However, this is a month of low rainfall for eastern Peninsular Malaysia, with totals of 6 to 10 in, except for a slightly wetter zone astride the southern Trengganu–Pahang border. North-eastern Peninsular Malaysia is the driest part of the Peninsula, with totals of less than 6 in.

May (Fig. 2.13) marks the onset of the southwest monsoon over

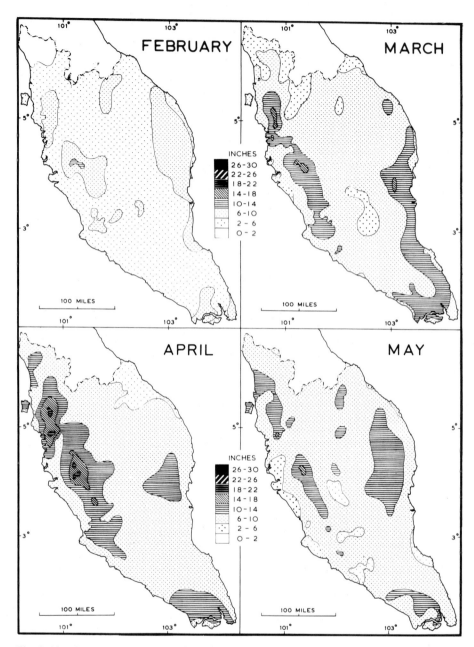

Fig. 2.13   Mean monthly rainfall, February to May.

northern Peninsular Malaysia, but there is no significant increase in rainfall in western Peninsular Malaysia during this month. Most of the country receives between 6 and 10 in of rain, with belts and zones of slightly higher and slightly lower rainfall.

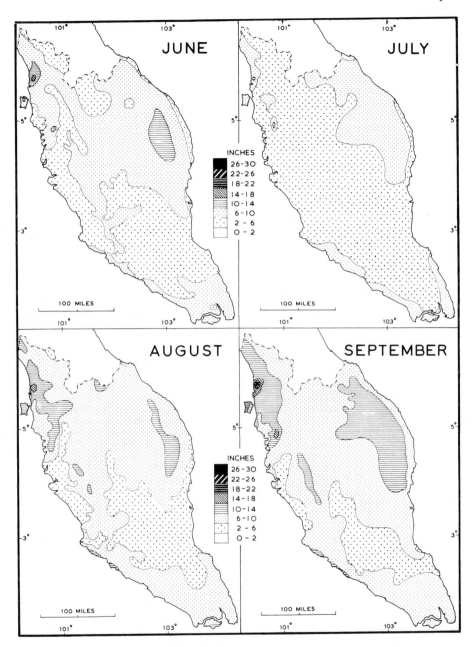

Fig. 2.14   Mean monthly rainfall, June to September.

June (Fig. 2.14) is a month of still lower rainfall for most of Peninsular Malaysia, with totals of between 6 and 10 in for the northern half of the Peninsula, and between 2 and 6 in for most of the southern half, except southern Johore.

57

July (Fig. 2.14) is the driest month of the year for most of Peninsular Malaysia, with totals of less than 6 in everywhere except in the Kelantan delta and most of Trengganu where totals are between 6 and 10 in.

August (Fig. 2.14) is a period of slightly heavier rain for most places except in the Pahang–Rompin–Endau deltas and along the Perak–Selangor coast where totals remain less than 6 in.

September (Fig. 2.14) sees a further increase in rainfall throughout the country, particularly in north-western Peninsular Malaysia and Trengganu. Although the period from May to September sees the southwest monsoon established over northern Peninsular Malaysia, the monsoon does not bring heavy rain to the Peninsula. In fact, one of the months of the monsoon—July—is the driest for most of Peninsular Malaysia. The monsoon does, however, bring more rain to northern than to southern Peninsular Malaysia.

The daily rain cycle

The daily rain cycle varies with the time of the year and the location of the station (whether coastal, inland, eastern or western). For example, half of the total amount of rain which falls during the northeast monsoon at Kuala Lumpur, located some 25 miles (40 km) inland from the Selangor coast, falls between the hours of 2 p.m. and 6 p.m., whilst Bukit Jeram, on the Selangor coast, receives its rain spread more evenly over the hours of the day during this period. During the southwest monsoon, however, Bukit Jeram receives one-quarter of its rain during the hours of 2 a.m. and 6 a.m., whilst Kuala Lumpur has a more even distribution pattern, though there is still a pronounced afternoon maximum.

The diurnal and seasonal distribution of rainfall over a five-year period for seventeen lowland and two highland stations in Peninsular Malaysia is shown in Fig. 2.15 (Wycherley, 1967). For the seventeen lowland stations the mean annual rainfall is 95.6 in (2 428 mm). The records show that, over the five-year period, 21 per cent of the rain fell between midnight and 6 a.m., 16 per cent between 6 a.m. and noon, 35 per cent between noon and 6 p.m., and 28 per cent between 6 p.m. and midnight. There is therefore a greater tendency for rain to fall in the afternoon and at night than at any other time. This tendency is even more pronounced in inland areas in Peninsular Malaysia. Figure 2.16 shows the daily cycle of rain according to the time of day at Kuala Lumpur. The very low incidence of rain during the morning hours (only 3½ per cent between 8 a.m. and noon), and the very high incidence during the afternoon and early evening (71 per cent between noon and 8 p.m.) are strikingly illustrated in the graph. Such a pattern is common in many other inland areas.

However, coastal locations experience a different diurnal rainfall

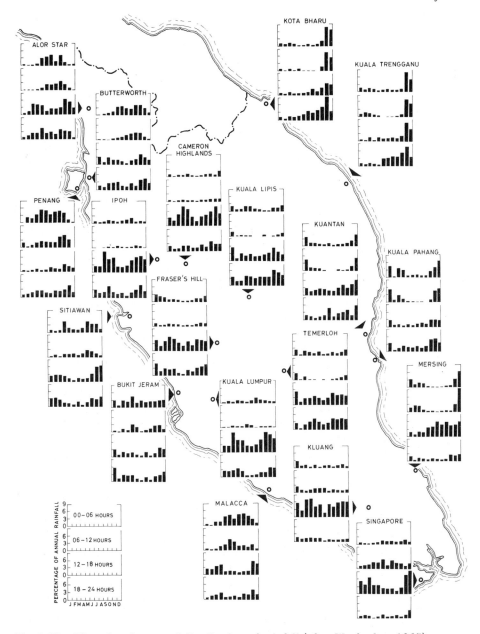

Fig. 2.15 Diurnal and seasonal distribution of rainfall (after Wycherley, 1967).

regime. Stations along the west coast have an afternoon peak during the northeast monsoon and a night or early morning peak during the southwest monsoon. Areas along the east coast have a fairly even distribution of rainfall during the northeast monsoon, with a small but noticeable

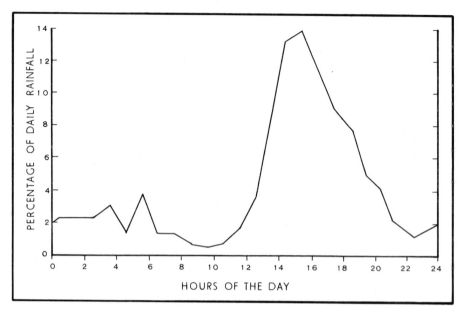

Fig. 2.16   The daily rain cycle at Kuala Lumpur.

peak at night and in the early morning. For the rest of the year the maximum occurs in the afternoon or evening (Nieuwolt, 1968).

The island of Singapore, located at a latitude of only 1° 20′ N, has its own distinctive diurnal regime. Rain is most frequent from 3 p.m. to 4 p.m. from December to March, with a small secondary maximum at about 6 a.m. in December and January. After April, rain in the afternoon begins to decline in frequency and importance, while early morning rain becomes increasingly frequent. A high percentage of the rain in September and October falls between 6 a.m. and 8 a.m. (Watts, 1954).

Rain-days

Figure 2.17 shows the average number of rain-days[1] per year in Peninsular Malaysia as worked out by Dale (1960). Wycherley (1967) has found that there is a strong positive correlation between the number of rainy days and the total rainfall received in nineteen stations in Peninsular Malaysia for sixty consecutive months. However, an area may have a great number of rain-days and yet receive a lesser amount of rain in a year than another area with a smaller number of rain-days but which receives its rain in long, sustained spells. The outstanding example is eastern Johore which has the greatest number of rain-days in the eastern

[1] A rain-day is defined as a 24-hour period beginning at 0730 hours local time, in which 0.01 in or more of rain is recorded.

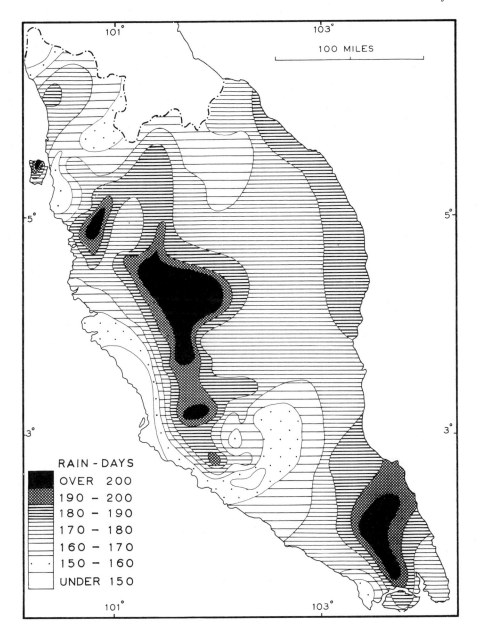

Fig. 2.17   Average number of rain-days per year.

wet belt but yet receives the lowest rainfall in the belt. The number of rain-days in any station may vary considerably from year to year. Georgetown, for example, had 119 rain-days in 1894 and 229 in 1949.

In general there is a close and direct relationship between relief and the number of days in which rain falls. Thus the Main Range between Fraser's Hill and Cameron Highlands receives more than 200 rain-days in a year. But the mountains of eastern Peninsular Malaysia have fewer rain-days than those in western Peninsular Malaysia because they lie in the rain-shadow of the Main Range during the southwest monsoon and also because much of the rainfall in this region is concentrated within the relatively brief period of the northeast monsoon. The eastern lowlands, however, have more rain-days than the western lowlands. The range in the eastern lowlands is from 174 rain-days per year at Pekan to 198 at Mersing, while that in the western lowlands is from 134 at Kuala Selangor to 223 at Taiping.

Rainfall regions

Dale (1959) has divided Peninsular Malaysia into five rainfall regions, each with its distinctive pattern of rainfall distribution (Fig. 2.18).

1. Northwest. This region includes that part of Peninsular Malaysia lying north of about 5° N latitude and west of 101° E longitude. Its rainfall regime is typically equatorial, with two maxima occurring during the transitional periods between the monsoons, and two minima during the monsoons. The distinguishing feature of the rainfall pattern in this region is the low amount received during the months of December, January and February, when the other parts of the Peninsula, especially eastern Peninsular Malaysia, have heavy rainfall.

2. West. This region covers that part of the western lowlands between 2° 40' and 5° N latitude, and that part of interior Peninsular Malaysia west of a line drawn from the Thai border running between the Main Range and the Trengganu Highlands and running southwards in a wide curve to end at the west coast north of Port Dickson. The pattern of distribution is similar to that of the northwest region, with two maxima occurring in April and October—November, and two minima in February and July. Places along the coast may receive as much as half of the total annual rainfall during the northeast monsoon, but, in general, the rainfall is more evenly distributed throughout the year than in the northwest region, and dry spells do not last for more than a week or two, and only very occasionally for as long as a month. Within this region is the southerly extension of the western wet belt where rainfall totals are between 110 and 140 in (2 794—3 556 mm) a year.

3. Port Dickson—Muar coast. This region covers that part of the coast roughly between Port Dickson and Muar, and extending up to 15 miles (24 km) inland. The pattern of distribution is different from that of the

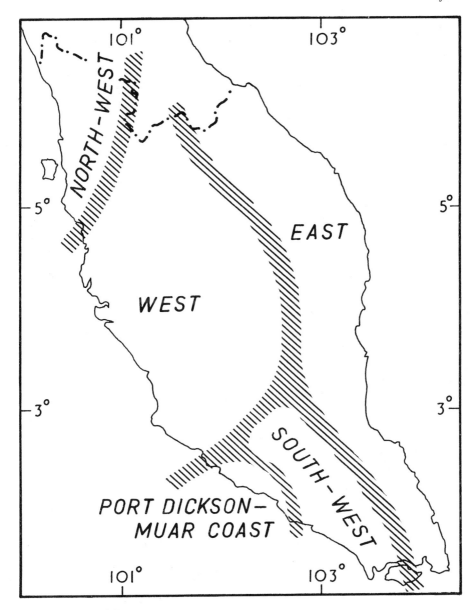

Fig. 2.18   Rainfall regions.

rest of Peninsular Malaysia in that there is only one maximum and one minimum a year. In contrast to the west region, 45 per cent of the annual rainfall is received during the southwest monsoon, and only 36 per cent during the northeast monsoon. Much of the rainfall during the southwest monsoon is from the heavy falls associated with 'sumatras' and to boundary rain during the 'summer' months.

63

4. Southwest. This region extends from the south-western coast of Johore to cover the inland areas of Negri Sembilan and southwest Pahang. Rainfall in this region ranges from less than 70 to 110 in (1 778–2 794 mm) a year, and is distributed evenly throughout the year. The northeast monsoon brings only slightly heavier rain than the southwest monsoon.

5. East. This region covers the whole of eastern Peninsular Malaysia, from Kelantan to eastern Johore. It receives only one primary maximum and one primary minimum during the year, the maximum occurring in November and December in the north and later in the south. The minimum varies from place to place and from year to year, and may fall in April, June or July. The rainfall pattern in this region is more markedly seasonal than in the rest of Peninsular Malaysia, as much as 60 per cent of the annual total falling during the northeast monsoon, 26 per cent during the southwest monsoon and only 14 per cent during the transitional months of April and October.

Rainfall intensity and soil erosion

Much of the precipitation in the Malay Peninsula occurs as thunderstorms, when high intensities of rainfall are recorded. The intensity with which the rain falls has an important bearing on soil erosion and soil conservation in tropical agriculture. In exposed localities such as cultivation clearings, heavy falls of rain concentrated within a short spell may wash away valuable top-soil. The direct impact of falling raindrops has considerable eroding effect on exposed soil, as can be seen in any railway cutting or embankment or the exposed face of a fresh landslip in Peninsular Malaysia. Here one often finds little earth pillars, each with a small pebble, leaf or twig on the top acting as a resistant or protective shield while the rest of the surface soil around it is cut away by the falling drops of rain.

Every particular type of soil absorbs rain by percolation up to a certain limit; rain which falls in excess of this limit accumulates, runs over the surface and erodes the soil. The maximum amount of moisture which a soil can absorb depends on its mechanical composition (whether clay, sand, silt, etc.) and on the amount of moisture already present in it. In Peninsular Malaysia it has been calculated that for an average open soil the maximum absorptive rate is about 3 in (76 mm) of water per hour; in very sandy soils the rate may be twice this figure but most Peninsular Malaysian soils have a rate of less than 3 in.

Local downpours in the Peninsula may occasionally reach intensities of 6 in or more per hour; at Kuala Lumpur a maximal intensity of 8 in (203 mm) an hour has been recorded during a 15-minute instability thunderstorm (Wycherley, 1967). Steady continuous rain falling for long periods has much the same erosive effect as short intense falls because the soil has little chance to dry out in between falls. At Johore Bahru, for example, heavy rain fell almost without ceasing for nearly a week in February 1925. This is an exceptional occurrence, and the normal pattern is one of heavy falls within short periods. On the east coast, however, rainfall of relatively low intensities (about 1/10 in/hr; 2.5 mm/hr) may occur over a sustained period of four or five days.

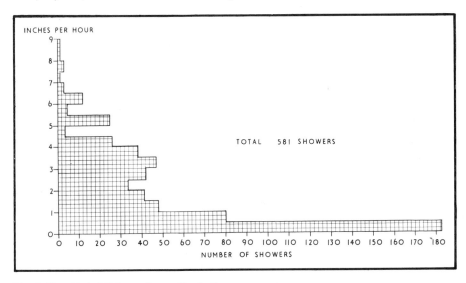

Fig. 2.19   Rainfall intensity at Kuala Lumpur.

Records have been kept at Kuala Lumpur of the maximum intensity reached during each shower of rain for 581 consecutive showers. The results are shown in Fig. 2.19. It will be seen that 26½ per cent (154 showers) of the 581 showers fell with a maximum intensity of more than 3 in per hour. In effect this meant that an average of one in four showers fell with an intensity greater than the absorptive rate for an average open soil in Peninsular Malaysia, with consequent erosive effect on the soil.

The need, therefore, for keeping the soil covered is clear—in heavy forest the thick vegetation and the forest canopy absorb the heaviest impact of the raindrops, but wherever the forest is felled for cultivation, especially on hill slopes, its protective function is lost. The amount of top-soil which will be removed by subsequent water erosion depends on three factors: (*a*) the interval between the time of exposure of the soil and the establishment of a new protective cover of planted crops; (*b*) the type of crop planted—in general perennial tree crops with thick foliage such as rubber are better for soil conservation than short-term crops such as tapioca, hill padi, or maize; and (*c*) the slope of the land: for example, it has been found that a rubber plantation on a 30° slope and without the additional protection of ground cover-crops lost an average of 17 tons of top-soil per acre (42 000 kg/ha) per annum. The significance of this loss is apparent when it is realized that Peninsular Malaysian soils have, with few exceptions, a low content of organic matter and humus, and that this organic matter is concentrated on the top few inches of the soil. The erosive effect of tropical downpours is further illustrated by findings on soil losses from run-off in Cameron Highlands: in virgin climax rain forest soil losses amounted to 300 lb per acre (336 kg/ha) per annum; in tea plantations practising selective weeding losses were 6 000 lb per acre (6 725 kg/ha); and in vegetable gardens which were clean-weeded losses were 9 000 lb per acre (10 088 kg/ha) (Shallow, 1956).

Clouds and sunshine

All the ten international cloud types occur over the Peninsula at various times: the high clouds (cirrus, cirrostratus and cirrocumulus), the middle clouds (altocumulus and altostratus), the low clouds (nimbostratus, stratus and stratocumulus), and the heap clouds or clouds with vertical development (cumulus and cumulonimbus). But the most characteristic and common clouds in the Peninsula are cumulus and cumulonimbus. These convection clouds may be formed not only as a result of direct solar heating of the ground, but by any process which causes uplift to occur. The equatorial atmosphere is nearly always conditionally unstable, and strong upward currents arising from a variety of causes favour cumuliform development.

The life-cycle of a tropical convective cloud is made up of three stages (Frost, 1954):

1. The cumulus or building stage, when a general updraught prevails, and the cloud tops build up to a height of less than 30 000 ft (9 144 m). This stage lasts for 30 to 60 minutes.
2. The active cumulonimbus stage. In the low latitudes of the Malay Peninsula the transition from cumulus to cumulonimbus cloud occurs at a height of between 30 000 and 33 000 ft (10 058 m). During this stage, which also lasts for 30 to 60 minutes, the cloud continues to build up vertically, and may on occasion reach the level of the tropopause, about 55 000 ft (16 764 m). The edges of the cloud have a characteristic fibrous appearance when it is at this active stage.
3. The dissipating cumulonimbus stage, which lasts for less than 30 minutes, and recognizable by the formation of the anvil.

Cloudiness is one of the characteristic features of an equatorial maritime climate such as is experienced in the Peninsula. It is partly responsible for keeping temperatures in these latitudes uniform, by

Table 2.3   The mean daily amount of cloud at selected stations

| | *Amount of cloud* (in tenths) | | | | | | | | | | | | |
	J	F	M	A	M	J	J	A	S	O	N	D	Year
Alor Star	6	6	6	7	7	7	8	8	8	8	8	7	7
Kota Bharu	7	5	5	5	7	7	7	7	7	7	7	7	6.5
Temerloh	8	7	7	8	7	8	8	8	8	9	9	8	8
Kuala Lumpur	7	7	7	8	7	8	7	8	8	8	8	8	8
Bukit Jeram	7	6	7	7	7	7	7	7	7	8	8	7	7
Mersing	7	6	6	6	6	7	7	7	7	8	8	8	7
Malacca	7	7	7	7	7	7	7	7	7	8	8	8	7
Kluang	7	6	7	7	7	7	7	8	8	8	8	8	7
Singapore	7	7	7	7	7	7	6	7	7	7	7	7	7
Cameron Highlands (4 750 ft)	7	7	7	8	8	8	8	8	8	9	8	8	8

checking solar radiation by day and terrestrial radiation by night. Table 2.3 shows the mean daily amount of cloud (in tenths of the sky covered) at representative stations in the Malay Peninsula. High cloud amounts are recorded for all places, the mean annual cloudiness ranging from six-and-a-half-tenths at Kota Bharu to eight-tenths at Kuala Lumpur, Temerloh and Cameron Highlands. The monthly distribution of cloud cover shows only slight variations from place to place.

Singapore has a uniform pattern, with seven-tenths of the sky covered for all the months of the year except June, when the amount of cloud is one-tenth less. All the other stations show a slight increase in cloudiness in the last quarter of the year, coinciding with the end of the southwest monsoon, the transitional period, and the onset of the northeast monsoon.

The general high cloudiness is also seen in the high average number of overcast days in the Malay Peninsula (Table 2.4). In lowland Peninsular Malaysia the annual average varies from 116 days at Bukit Jeram, on the Selangor coast, to 180 and 181 at Kuala Lumpur and Temerloh, while at Cameron Highlands the average is 214 days per year. There is a general increase in the number of overcast days per month during the last quarter of the year. But these average conditions do not reveal the great fluctuations in the number of overcast days in individual years at each station. For example, Bukit Jeram had only 27 overcast days in 1930 and 207 in 1937, while Singapore had a low of 83 days in 1933 and a high of 225 days in 1952 and Mersing a low of 53 days in 1930 and a high of 209 days in 1947. Cameron Highlands recorded a low of 135 overcast days in 1931, and a record total of 338 overcast days in 1951.

Table 2.4   The average number of overcast* days at selected stations

	J	F	M	A	M	J	J	A	S	O	N	D	Year
Alor Star	8	7	8	10	16	14	17	16	18	20	18	18	170
Kota Bharu	12	8	7	6	11	11	13	12	13	15	16	16	140
Temerloh	17	11	12	14	14	15	13	14	14	18	20	19	181
Kuala Lumpur	13	10	12	14	13	14	14	14	16	21	21	18	180
Bukit Jeram	10	5	9	7	8	5	10	9	12	15	14	12	116
Mersing	16	10	8	8	10	11	11	11	10	16	17	18	146
Malacca	13	11	13	13	13	12	13	12	15	19	18	18	170
Kluang	14	9	11	13	12	10	12	11	13	19	20	16	160
Singapore	16	12	11	11	12	12	12	13	13	17	18	19	166
Cameron Highlands	16	10	13	16	18	15	18	20	22	23	22	21	214

* On an overcast day the mean amount of clouds at hours of observation covers more than six-tenths of the sky. It should be noted that the British Meteorological Office defines 'overcast' as a sky completely obscured by clouds. When seven-eighths of the sky is obscured the official term is 'overcast with openings'.

Clear cloudless days are rare in the southern part of the Peninsula. Singapore, for example, had only thirty-three days of blue sky (when the mean amount of cloud covers less than two-tenths of the sky) over a sixteen-year period, the maximum number recorded in a year being eight (in 1933). The number of clear days increases slightly with increase in latitude, and the northern-most parts of the Peninsula—Alor Star and Kota Bharu—receive on an average ten days of blue sky in a year. Cloudiness in highland areas is very marked, and Cameron Highlands has only twenty-seven days of blue sky over a sixteen-year period, of which ten occurred in the year 1931.

Daylight in the Malay Peninsula lasts for about 12 hours, the length of day varying only slightly throughout the year because of the low latitude of the Peninsula and its small latitudinal extent. The difference between the longest and shortest days at Singapore is only 9 minutes, at Kuala Lumpur 20 minutes, and at Alor Star, in the north, 37 minutes. The duration of bright sunshine (Table 2.5) is therefore only affected to a small extent by differences in day lengths due to latitudinal differences. It is, however, greatly affected by the amount of cloud cover. At Singapore, where the cloud cover is high throughout the year (Table 2.3), the average duration of bright sunshine is only 5.8 hours a day, with little variation from month to month. The average duration is still less at Kluang and Kuala Lumpur, with 5.5 and 5.4 hours per day respectively. At both these places the cloud cover increases towards the end of the year, and the average duration of bright sunshine falls correspondingly. A similar pattern obtains for the other lowland areas. At Cameron Highlands cloudiness is higher than in the lowlands, and the average

Table 2.5   The average duration of bright sunshine at selected stations

	Hours of bright sunshine												
	J	F	M	A	M	J	J	A	S	O	N	D	Year
Alor Star	8.0	8.5	8.3	7.9	7.0	6.5	6.3	6.5	5.7	5.5	5.5	6.7	6.8
Kota Bharu	6.1	8.0	8.3	8.4	6.8	6.9	6.8	7.3	6.3	5.8	4.9	4.9	6.7
Temerloh	5.2	6.6	6.6	6.5	6.4	6.3	6.4	6.5	5.8	5.3	4.8	4.7	5.9
Kuala Lumpur	5.4	6.8	5.8	5.7	5.6	5.9	5.6	5.6	5.0	4.6	4.2	4.7	5.4
Bukit Jeram	6.7	8.5	7.3	7.0	7.1	7.5	6.9	6.9	6.3	5.7	5.8	6.1	6.8
Mersing	5.2	7.3	7.3	7.1	6.9	6.7	6.6	6.7	6.1	5.3	4.9	4.7	6.2
Malacca	6.0	7.5	7.2	6.8	6.7	6.8	6.6	6.4	5.9	5.8	5.6	5.8	6.4
Kluang	5.3	7.2	6.0	5.8	5.9	5.6	6.1	5.6	4.9	4.6	4.5	4.5	5.5
Singapore	5.0	6.6	6.2	5.9	6.1	6.4	6.6	6.2	5.8	5.2	4.8	4.7	5.8
Cameron Highlands	4.3	5.5	5.1	4.8	4.7	5.4	5.1	4.8	4.1	3.7	3.4	3.7	4.5

duration of bright sunshine is only 4.5 hours a day. In the lowlands of Peninsular Malaysia the average number of hours of bright sunshine varies from 2 000 to 2 600 per year. In general the average tends to increase from south to north and from east to west (Dale, 1964).

3
Soils

Soil may be defined as the superficial layer of fairly loose earth which results from the weathering, decomposition and transformation of the underlying parent-rock through the action of physico-chemical and biological agents. It is a medium in which live a very large number of plants, animals and micro-organisms.

The type of soil that develops in any area depends on the interplay of five major factors:

1. The nature of the parent material.
2. The climate of the area.
3. The plant life as well as the organisms in the soil.
4. Topography and drainage.
5. The length of time the soil processes have been at work.

In Peninsular Malaysia the parent material and the various rock types from which it is derived have a controlling influence on soil types, and up to recent years Malaysian soils had been classified according to their parent material. The different rock types break down to form soils with distinctive profiles. The granites and associated rock formations which occur extensively throughout the Peninsula, particularly in the mountain ranges and upland areas, weather down into deep coarse sandy clay loams containing about 30 per cent clay and 20 per cent coarse sand. Such soils provide a good physical medium for plant growth, and are especially suitable for tree crops. Their potentiality for development however is less than might be expected because of the fact that they occur largely in areas which are too steep for cultivation. The sedimentary rocks break down into soils of varying textures and fertility status, while the basic rocks such as basalt and andesite produce deep reddish-brown soils which are not only physically excellent for tree crops but are also the most fertile in the country.

While on the macro-scale the soil patterns of Peninsular Malaysia are closely associated with the nature of the parent material, at a lower scale differences in climatic conditions (which affect the extent of leaching that occurs), vegetation, topography and drainage as well as time (as a soil-forming factor) operate to produce a great complexity of soils, each with its own characteristic profile.

Soil classes

Up to 1957 soil surveys were conducted on an *ad hoc* basis only, but in the decade 1957—67 a systematic reconnaissance soil survey of the entire country was carried out, the basic classification unit being the soil series, defined as 'a grouping of soil with similar profiles, similar temperature

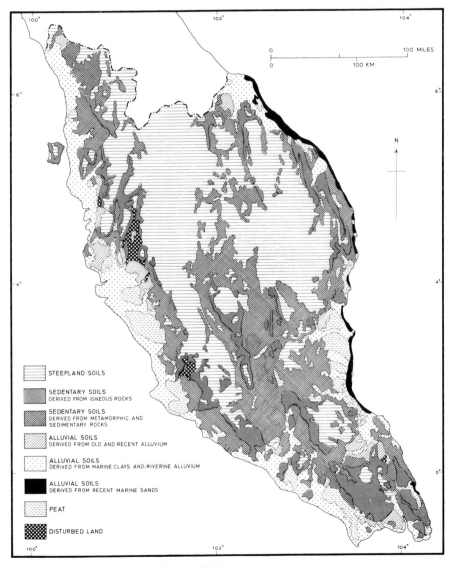

Fig. 3.1   Reconnaissance soil map, 1968.

71

Table 3.1 Main soil classes, Peninsular Malaysia

State	Area (hectares)						Total	Per cent
	Class 1*	Class 2†	Class 3‡	Class 4§	Class 5¶	Padi soils‖		
Johore	646 020	298 260	373 780	351 600	236 750	—	1 906 410	14.5
Kedah	126 630	50 020	208 580	5 340	411 500	145 970	948 040	7.3
Kelantan	79 200	258 890	34 560	35 810	967 680	120 960	1 497 100	11.4
Malacca	67 100	24 320	47 590	20 640	6 070	—	165 720	1.3
Negri Sembilan	124 360	100 120	214 490	9 510	219 550	—	668 030	5.1
Pahang	739 670	287 260	465 040	351 280	1 762 140	—	3 605 390	27.3
Penang and Prov. Wellesley	16 470	14 040	19 020	13 230	19 590	21 290	103 640	0.8
Perak	379 160	150 510	196 280	181 470	1 160 270	12 100	2 079 790	15.7
Perlis	5 500	—	28 810	—	8 980	36 790	80 080	0.7
Selangor	258 400	95 020	19 510	237 760	205 220	—	815 910	6.1
Trengganu	203 240	45 490	277 740	107 240	637 770	23 550	1 295 030	9.8
Peninsular Malaysia (Total)	2 645 750	1 323 930	1 885 400	1 313 880	5 635 520	360 660	13 165 140	100.0
Per cent	20.1	10.1	14.3	10.0	42.8	2.7	100.0	

Source: *Based on Law and Selvadurai, 1968, p. 239.*

and moisture regimes, and the same or very similar parent material' (Leamy and Panton, 1966, p. 64). The soil map which was produced as a result of this survey (Fig. 3.1) was drawn up using the soil association as the main mapping unit (the soil association is defined as two or more soil series which are geographically and topographically associated in a defined proportional pattern; Law and Selvadurai, 1968, p. 229). The other mapping units employed were urban and mined lands, steepland, and padi soils.

Table 3.1 shows the distribution of the main soil classes in Peninsular Malaysia. Soil classification is based on the suitability of the soils for agricultural development. The parameters used in classifying the soils include nutrient status, drainage conditions, gradient, texture, structure, acid sulphate conditions, salinity, rockiness, organic horizon and the degree of human interference. Each or all of these factors may pose a limitation to crop growth on a sustained yield basis. The soil is thus classified according to the growth-limiting factors which occur in it, and will fall into one of the following five suitability classes used in the Malaysian classification (Wong, 1970a):

Class 1. These soils are deep, well-drained, friable and have good water- and nutrient-retention qualities. They occur on slopes of less than 12°, and can be utilized for a wide range of crops, including padi. They occur on 20 per cent of the total landmass of Peninsular Malaysia, the largest areas being in Pahang, Johore, Perak, Selangor and Trengganu (Table 3.1). Eight soil associations belong to this class.

Footnotes to Table 3.1

* Comprising the following soil associations: Kuantan; Segamat–Katong–Jempol; Rengam–Jerangau–Kg. Kolam–Tampin; Prang; Munchong–Bungor–Serdang; Serdang–Munchong–Jeram; Selangor–Briah–Kangkong; Briah–Akob.

† Comprising the following soil associations: Kala–Rengam; Serdang–Munchong–Seremban; Munchong–Malacca–Serdang; Bungor–Serdang–Malacca; Bungor–Durian–Tavy; Serdang–Kedah; Durian–Munchong–Serdang; Batang Merbau–Munchong; Batang Merbau–Durian; Chenian; Pohoi–Batang Merbau–Serdang; Harimau–Tampoi–Ulu Tiram; Telemong–Akob–Local Alluvium; Selangor–Organic Clays and Mucks; Selangor–Telok.

‡ Comprising the following soil associations: Batu Anam–Bungor–Malacca; Batu Anam–Durian; Batu Anam–Durian–Malacca; Durian–Malacca–Tavy; Kulai–Yong Peng; Batu Anam–Malacca–Tavy; Kuala Brang–Serdang–Munchong; Marang–Batu Anam–Bungor; Durian–Kuala Brang; Pohoi–Durian–Tavy; Kawang–Klau; Holyrood–Lunas–Rasau; Sogomana–Sitiawan; Organic Clay and Mucks; Batu Anam–Marang–Apek; Kuala Brang–Serdang–Marang–Apek; Gajah Mati–Malacca; Kemuning–Munchong; Malacca–Munchong–Tavy; Pokok Sena–Padang Besar; Manik–Sogomana.

§ Comprising the following soil associations: Marang–Apek; Malacca–Tavy; Rudua–Rusila–Jambu; Krangi–Linau–Telok; Peat.

¶ Comprising urban and mined land and steepland.

‖ Comprising soils developed from recent marine sediments, riverine alluvium, subrecent alluvium and mixed marine–fluvial deposits (*see* Ng, 1968b).

Class 2. These soils also occur on flat to rolling terrain, but because they have one or more growth-limiting factors they are suitable for a narrower range of crops than Class 1 soils. Ten per cent of Peninsular Malaysia is covered by such soils, with Pahang, Johore, Kelantan, Perak and Negri Sembilan possessing the largest areas (Table 3.1). Fifteen soil associations are in this category.

Class 3. These soils occur on a wider range of slopes. Their capacity to support crops on a sustained yield basis is poor, but with a high standard of management some of these soils can support rubber and oil-palm. Fourteen per cent of Peninsular Malaysia is covered by such soils, the largest areas being found in Pahang, Johore, Trengganu, Negri Sembilan, Kedah and Perak (Table 3.1). Twenty soil associations are in this category.

Class 4. The agricultural potential of these soils is very poor because of their having more than one serious growth-limiting factor. Only a very narrow range of crops can be grown on such soils (e.g. pineapples on peat). Ten per cent of Peninsular Malaysia is covered by these soils, mainly in Johore, Pahang, Selangor, Perak and Trengganu (Table 3.1). Five soil associations are in this category.

Class 5. These soils include those on land disturbed by urban development or by mining activities. Mined-over land usually consists of sterile tin tailings. Soils which have developed on slopes of more than 20° also belong to this class. They occur on the mountain ranges and uplands of Peninsular Malaysia and cover nearly 43 per cent of the total land area (Table 3.1). The soils in this class are not considered suitable for agricultural development, but are likely to be retained for forest.

Main soil groups

The soils described in this section fall into three main categories: (*a*) sedentary; (*b*) alluvial; including organic soils and peat; and (*c*) steepland soils. Further subdivision is based on the influence of the parent rocks or material on the formation of the soils.

Sedentary soils

Sedentary soils derived from igneous rocks. The igneous rocks of Peninsular Malaysia include both extrusive and intrusive rocks of basic, intermediate and acid composition. Granite is the most important of these rocks. Most of the mountain ranges are of granite. However, only 10 per cent of the sedentary soils of Peninsular Malaysia below the 250 ft (76 m) contour line are derived from granite. Weathering of granite takes place to great depths, the average being 30 ft (9 m). The product of weathering is a soft mass of material which may be red, orange or yellow in colour, within which may be large numbers of 'core boulders' which have resisted decomposition. The soils derived from granite are clayey owing to the presence of kaolinite. In general the soils which have developed from granite and other acid igneous rocks are of good quality. Class 1 soils include the Jerangau Series (derived from granodiorite) and the Rengam Series (granite); the other soils are of Class 3 quality—the Yong Peng, Kala and Tampin Series (granite) and the Kulai Series (rhyolite). Granite-derived soils provide a very good physical medium for plant growth, and are especially suitable for tree crops.

The best sedentary soils of Peninsular Malaysia are derived from the basic and intermediate igneous rocks such as basalt, anderite, rhyolite and volcanic agglomerates. They are distributed on the eastern part of the country, from Trengganu to Pahang to Johore. Basalt-derived soils such as the Kuantan Series are only of local importance, and are found mainly in the Bukit Goh Forest Reserve near Kuantan. They are chocolate-coloured soils with well-developed structures, and are considered suitable for most crops. Andesite-derived soils include the Segamat and Katong Series, found on rolling to hilly terrain from north Johore (near Segamat) to central Pahang (the Jengka Triangle) to south Trengganu. They are very friable, deep, well-structured, yellowish-red to red clays and are both Class 1 soils. Small pockets of soils formed from volcanic tuffs and volcanic agglomerates also occur in Johore and central Pahang (Jempol Series).

Sedentary soils derived from metamorphic rocks. These include soils derived from the argillaceous, arenaceous and calcareous rocks that have been altered by metamorphism. Such rocks have been converted into quartz schists, quartz hornfels, indurated shale, mica schist, and in the case of limestone, into marble. The area covered by these soils is small, and consequently they are only of limited agricultural importance. Schist-derived soils cover undulating to hilly terrain in Selangor, Johore, Pahang and Kelantan. They are friable, have clayey textures and well-developed structures. The iron content tends to be high and in some cases iron concretions may be present, as in the Prang Series. The three schist-derived soils identified have been classified as Class 1 (Prang Series), Class 2 (Batang Merbau Series) and Class 3 (Seremban Series).

Limestone soils are too limited in extent to be of significance to agriculture other than locally. They occur in a narrow zone around the slopes and bases of limestone outcrops in Perlis, Perak and Pahang. They are reddish in colour, clay loam in texture and are well structured with a deep uniform profile. They have no concretionary layer and differ from the run of Peninsular Malaysian soils in being slightly alkaline. The soils identified include the Langkawi Series, developed on limestone slopes, the Kaki Bukit Series, developed at the base of limestone cliffs and slopes, the Kodiang Series, and the Weng Series, derived from calcareous shales.

Sedentary soils derived from sedimentary rocks. These soils occupy the largest area in Peninsular Malaysia. Those derived from shale and quartzite alone cover about 90 per cent of all the sedentary soils found below the 250 ft (76 m) contour line. The most important of these rocks are quartzites, shales and coarse conglomerate. The other sedimentaries are chert and associated shales. The quartzites have generally been weathered back into sandstone at the surface. The shales are grey to greenish in colour in their unweathered form, but on weathering become reddish or orange, or may be bleached white. Some of the shales have a high carbon content (up to 54 per cent). The coarse conglomerates contains pebbles of granite, rhyolite or quartz prophyry, and carbonaceous shale and chert, and weather down into loose sands and pebbly gravels. Chert is characteristically flinty in appearance, and breaks down into angular fragments.

The soils derived from sedimentary rocks are distributed over the major portion of the foothill and undulating lowland regions of the Peninsula where the greatest commercial agricultural development has taken place. The soils being derived from such a heterogeneous series of rocks are, as would be expected, extremely variable in composition and nutrient status. On the whole, however, most of them are of low inherent fertility and their agricultural value lies not so much in the amount of nutrients in them as in their physical properties and the type of terrain on which they occur.

The nature of the parent material determines the depth to which weathering can take place. Where the parent material is hard sandstone or schists, the resultant soil is shallow and gravelly, but where the bedrock is shaly, weathering may be up to 30 ft (9 m) deep. Soils derived from schists, shales and phyllites contain varying amounts of ferruginous concretions usually deposited in a pan which hardens into a slag-like mass on exposure. Where the pan is near the surface, rubber trees do not grow well because the hardpan resists root penetration and prevents normal root development. As a rule the soil structure deteriorates on exposure, and such soils are unsuitable for crops which do not provide adequate cover to the soil surface. They are, however, capable of supporting good growths of tree crops such as rubber, and many of the rubber areas of the Peninsula have been established on these soils.

The soils derived from argillaceous sedimentary rocks such as shales are of varied quality, the decisive factor often being the iron content in the rocks. Shale-derived soils with average iron content are well structured, friable at the top and free from laterite. The most common soil is the Munchong Series which occurs on gently rolling terrain in western

Peninsular Malaysia and also in Pahang. It is a deep, friable reddish-brown silty clay soil of first class quality.

Iron-rich shales develop into soils with a lateritized zone close to the surface. This laterite layer acts as a physical barrier to root development and such soils are therefore not considered suitable for tree crops, although rubber is grown where the laterite layer occurs at deeper levels. The Malacca, Changloon, Gajah Mati and Padang Besar Series belong to this class of soils. The Malacca Series is the most widespread and occurs in Malacca, Johore, Pahang and Negri Sembilan.

Iron-poor shales, on the other hand, develop into soils that are weakly structured. The subsoil is very firm and tends to restrict root development. They are represented by the Apak Series, found on undulating land in Johore and Trengganu, and the Batu Anam Series which occurs extensively from west and central Johore to Negri Sembilan to central Pahang.

The soils derived from arenaceous sedimentary rocks such as quartzites, sandstones and conglomerates usually have deep, well-structured profiles, and occur on gently rolling to fairly steep terrain. They are considered suitable for tree crops, except where slopes are too steep or the soil too shallow (Kedah Series). The most common soil is the sandstone-derived Serdang Series which occurs throughout the country. It is a Class 1 soil, supporting good stands of oil-palm and rubber. A soil of more limited distribution and Class 3 quality is the Pokok Sena Series formed on quartzite/sandstone on flat to rolling terrain in Kedah and Johore.

Alluvial soils

Alluvium blankets about 8 500 square miles (22 000 sq km) of Peninsular Malaysia, the cover of alluvium varying from a few to 500 ft (152 m) in thickness. This alluvium is the result of fluvial and marine sedimentation and the soils derived from it are thus quite different from the sedentary soils described in the previous section. The agricultural value of the alluvial soils depends to a great extent on their age, the origin of the alluvium, as well as on the level of the permanent water table—the waterlogged soils being excessively acid and usually poor.

The alluvial soils are distributed along the west in a nearly continuous belt from Perlis to Selangor. The continuity of this belt is interrupted at Port Dickson/Malacca where outliers of the main mountain ranges come close to the coast. From south Malacca to the south-western end of Johore is another large belt of alluvial soils. The width of the western alluvial belt varies from 5 to 50 miles (8–80 km). These soils are more limited in distribution along the east coast. A large expanse occurs in the Kelantan delta, with a narrow south-easterly extension to Kuala Trengganu. The largest area lies between Kuantan and Mersing, and includes the deltas and estuarine plains of the Kuantan, Pahang, Rompin and Endau rivers. Occupying narrow strips of land along the coastlines of the east are the recent marine sands known locally as 'bris'. The total area under 'bris' is about 400 000 acres (161 900 ha).

Alluvial soils derived from marine alluvium.   In general there are four main types of soils derived from marine alluvium. The saline soils of the Kranji Series (Class 4) which have developed in the mangrove swamps of the west coast belong to the first type. They are structureless soils derived from very recent marine or estuarine deposits. Such soils are subject to regular sea water inundation and are therefore salt-saturated. Bunding and drainage are necessary before cultivation (of coconut and padi) can take place.

The second type consists of better drained coastal marine clays represented by the Selangor and Kangkong Series. They are among the most fertile soils in Peninsular Malaysia, being little leached and having high reserves of organic plant nutrients as well as phosphorus, potassium and magnesium. Such soils are widely distributed along the west coast from Perlis to Johore, and are often separated from the sea by the Kranji Series. They are heavy textured soils, well to moderately structured and dark brown to grey in colour. The agricultural potentialities of these soils depend on the drainage conditions: when well drained they are of Class 1 quality and will support good crops of rubber, oil-palm, coconut, banana, fruit and other perennial as well as annual crops including wet padi.

The third type includes the Class 4 soils known as acid sulphate soils, 'cat-clays', or 'gelam' soils formed in a brackish water environment under conditions of impeded drainage. They are highly acid (pH 3 or less) and contain large quantities of sulphur compounds. The parent material is a dark, structureless clay which blackens on exposure. The soils emit a strong sulphurous smell and are characterized by an organic top-soil and abundant decayed plant residues in the subsoil. They are represented by the Telok, Guar and Linau Series, covering an estimated area of 200 000 acres (80 900 ha) of coastal land in Kedah, Perlis, Malacca and southwest Johore, of which about 60 000 acres (24 280 ha) are under padi, mainly in Kedah, and the rest under coconut, oil-palm, rubber, or is uncleared (Chow and Ng, 1969). They are thus of considerable agricultural importance, but require heavy investments in drainage and liming prior to cultivation. They also offer good potential for pisciculture, and very good yields of fish have been obtained experimentally from fish ponds in acid sulphurous areas (Kanapathy, 1966).

The fourth type is made up of the Class 4 soils which have developed on the sandy beach ridges of the east coast, and in places in Perak and Selangor. They are represented by the Rudua, Rusila and Jambu Series, and are the most coarse-textured and among the least fertile soils in the country. The Rudua Series is found on the old beach ridges which run parallel to the coast from Kelantan to Johore. The soils are very loose and can only support very poor stands of coconut and cashew nut. The Jambu Series is similar to the Rudua, except that it has developed on raised beach ridges in Perak, Pahang, Selangor and Johore. The Rusila Series, on the other hand, occurs on the flat narrow swampy areas between the beach ridges. Drainage is very poor because of the high water table. Peat occurs in the waterlogged portions. Padi is the only crop planted on this soil, but yields are low. The best use to which such soils could be put to would be for pasture, livestock, and coconut.

Alluvial soils derived from recent riverine alluvium. These soils occur on the levees and flood plains of the larger rivers as well as the alluvial flats of the smaller rivers and streams. Where the rivers and streams are still actively depositing alluvium during floods or monsoons the soils are very youthful and show little horizon differentiation. They are represented by the Briah, Akob, Telemong and the Merbau Patah Series, and are of Class 2 to 3 quality. Their agricultural value lies in their youth and hence their high nutrient content, but they are subject to constant water table fluctuations and tend to become waterlogged during wet periods. Along the western coastal plains the riverine alluvium is deposited over the marine clay and yields a dark brown, well-structured silty clay soil which, with good drainage, is suitable for a wide range of tree crops as well as padi. On the east coast the better-drained levees of the rivers such as the Pahang and Trengganu rivers have a yellowish-brown clay loam or silt loam (Telemong Series) on which rubber, fruit and annual crops such as tobacco, maize, groundnut, tapioca and sweet potato are grown. The shallow depressions behind the levees usually have soils of the Akob Series. These are imperfectly drained and are usually suitable only for padi.

Alluvial soils derived from sub-recent alluvium. These are soils which have developed on the older sediments found on raised terraces and platforms standing 20 to 50 ft (6—15 m) above sea-level. Some of the terraces in east Pahang with such soils are at elevations of 50 to 150 ft (15—46 m). The soils are of variable texture, colour and drainage status. At the lower elevations they are represented by the Holyrood Series, a brownish-yellow sandy loam, very friable, weakly structured to almost structureless, with a very low nutrient status and deficient in trace elements. They are Class 3 soils found on sandy terrace alluvium near the coasts of Perlis, Perak and Pahang and the old beach ridges of Johore and Kelantan. Trial plantings of a nutrient-demanding crop such as oil-palm have proved unsuccessful on this soil, but it will support crops such as maize, tapioca and sugar-cane. Heavier-textured soils have developed on the subrecent alluvium of Perak, represented by the silty clay loams and silty clays of the Sogomana and the Sitiawan Series. They are of Class 2 and Class 3 quality respectively, and can support rubber as well as oil-palm (Sitiawan Series).

At higher elevations the subrecent alluvial soils are represented by the Rasau Series, found mainly in east Pahang. This soil has a texture of sandy clay loam, and a firmer consistence than the Holyrood Series. But it is highly leached and very poor in plant nutrients, so that while physically and topographically it is suitable for tree crops, a heavy fertilization programme is necessary for successful establishment.

Alluvial soils derived from older alluvium. These soils have developed on the alluvium deposited during the Pleistocene under littoral—estuarine—fluviatile conditions when sea-level was about 250 ft (76 m) higher than today. Most of the older alluvium occurs in south Johore (and eastern Singapore), but small areas have also been identified in Perak, Selangor and Pahang (Burton, 1964). The soils derived from it include the Harimau, Ulu Tram, Tampoi, Kawang, Klau and Tai Tak Series. They closely resemble granite-derived soils in colour and texture, but are poorer in nutrient status, and are known to suffer from manganese deficiency. The most widespread soils are the Harimau and Ulu Tiram Series. The former is a brownish-yellow sandy clay loam with a blocky structure. It occurs on gently to strongly sloping terrain below the 300 ft (91 m) contour line, in Johore, Pahang and Perak. Although of Class 2 quality because of manganese deficiency, it will support excellent stands of oil-palm if properly fertilized. Several thousand acres of oil-palm have been planted on both these soils.

Organic soils and peat

These include the organic clays, muck soils and peat which are common not only in the Peninsula but everywhere in the poorly drained parts of Southeast Asia where rainfall is heavy and well distributed. The total area under these soils, collectively known as the Inland Swamp Association, is over 2 million acres (809 000 ha) or over 6 per cent of the total land area of Peninsular Malaysia. They are distributed in the poorly drained coastal areas of Perak, Selangor, Johore, Pahang, Trengganu and Kelantan (Fig. 3.2). These organic soils have been classified as (1) Organic Clays and Mucks and (2) Peat. Organic clays and mucks usually form the transitional soils between peat and the other (mineral) soils of Peninsular Malaysia. The clays are differentiated from the mucks in having a loss on ignition of up to 25 per cent, while the mucks have a loss on ignition of 25 to 65 per cent. Peat proper has a loss on ignition of 65 per cent or more, that is, there will be less than 35 per cent mineral matter in the ash that remains after the peat has been ignited to 1 382° F (750° C) for 1 hour.

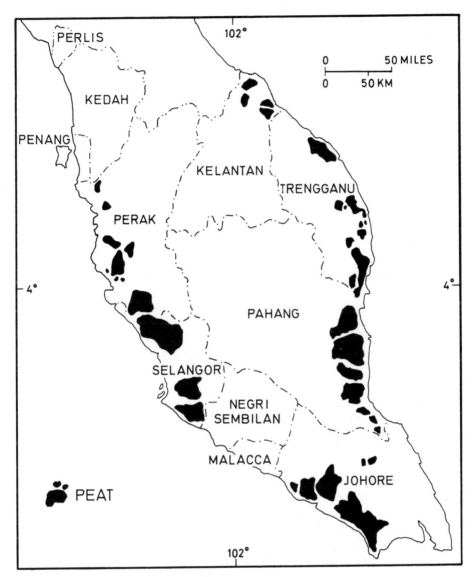

Fig. 3.2   Peat soils (after Tay, 1969).

The organic clays and mucks consist of an organic layer less than 5 ft (1.5 m) thick, overlying clay along the west coast and sand along the east coast. The organic clays usually have a strongly developed crumb structure and are black to dark brown in colour; the mucks have a weakly developed crumb structure and are black to reddish-brown in colour, while their subsoil horizon usually occurs at a deeper level.

Peat covers an area of about 1.9 million acres (769 000 ha), but despite its abundance it has not been developed to any great extent for

81

agriculture mainly because of the special problems it poses to farming. Peat is made up of plant residues which have accumulated under conditions of restricted drainage over a long period of time. The standing water in such areas inhibits the activities of those micro-organisms which live on free oxygen from the air whilst encouraging decomposition by anaerobic micro-organisms. The type of peat which is formed under these conditions depends on the type of vegetation in the area. Most of the Peninsular Malaysian peats are between 2 ft (0.6 m) and 40 ft (12 m) thick, and consist of a compact amorphous mass of woody material (roots, tree stumps, twigs and leaves) at various stages of decomposition. Peat soils are poor in nutrient status, highly acid (pH 3 to 4.5), and are commonly also deficient in micro-nutrients such as boron, zinc, molybdenum and copper.

The agricultural value of peat soils is moderate at best. Cultivation is difficult because of three major problems: the high water table in peat areas; the depth of the peat; and the inability of peat soils to support heavy machinery. Peat soils are usually waterlogged, and some form of drainage has to be carried out before cultivation is possible. Furthermore drainage has to be carefully controlled because too rapid drainage reduces the peat to a brown dry powder which is impossible to recondition. Good drainage is especially necessary for tree crops such as rubber, coconut and oil-palm. Even then the progressive shrinkage of the peat with time may lead to root exposure, and the lack of anchorage in the soft peat may cause the taller and heavier trees to fall over.

The depth of the peat layer is an important factor determining the suitability of peat soils for agriculture. Shallow peat 2 to 3 ft (0.6—0.9 m) deep overlying clay offers the best prospects for crops such as vegetables and other annuals. Tapioca and papaya grow well in shallow peat. Coffee has been successfully established on peat in the Klang area. Padi, however, does not do well in such soils. Peat soils exceeding 5 ft (1.5 m) in depth are not usually recommended for agricultural development because very few crops can grow in such soils. Pineapple is an exception. The successful cultivation of pineapple on deep peat has made possible the opening up of large expanses of deep peat land which otherwise would have been of poor agricultural potential. In fact, pineapple cultivation is confined exclusively to peat soils, and almost all the crop area under pineapple in Peninsular Malaysia is on peat. In addition some 88 000 acres (35 600 ha) of forested peat land in southwest Johore have been earmarked as potential pineapple land (Tay, 1969).

Peat contains large quantities of undecayed timber. This factor, coupled with the poor load-bearing capacity of peat soils, render the use of agricultural machinery an impracticable proposition, so that the large-scale cultivation of peat soils poses special management problems. The pineapple industry established on the peat soils of southwest Johore is thus singularly labour-intensive.

Steepland soils

The steepland soils are the shallow and juvenile soils that develop on slopes greater than 20°. Such steepland occurs as low as 150 ft (46 m) above sea-level in quartzite and schist hills, above the 250 ft (76 m) contour in the foothills region near the Main Range, and above the 500 ft (152 m) contour at the Main Range. In general, the 250 ft contour line can be taken as the lower limit of steepland soils. These soils commonly have shallow profiles and are considered immature or juvenile as the rate of soil formation from the parent rocks is offset by the rapid rate of natural erosion. Although they cover some 41 per cent of the total land area of Peninsular Malaysia their shallowness and extreme susceptibility to erosion when exposed limit their potentiality for agricultural development. The upland areas where such soils are found are therefore likely to remain under the protection of their forest cover rather than be opened up for agriculture.

Soil productivity

All Peninsular Malaysian soils that have developed *in situ* from the parent rock formations are pedologically mature, and have been subjected to a very long period of intensive tropical weathering. As a general rule, such soils are infertile in spite of the fact that they may have been derived from different parent rocks. In a humid tropical climate where the annual precipitation exceeds the annual evaporation, water continually percolates downwards through the soil and in the process chemically breaks down all but the very resistant minerals and leaches the organic matter that is present in the upper layers, so that the soil is eventually exhausted of most of its plant food. The soluble bases are removed early and the soil becomes highly acid. In the Malay Peninsula, where there is no distinct dry season, leaching goes on without a break. The rocks of the Peninsula have been exposed to such tropical weathering for a very long period of time. The end-product of intensive and prolonged weathering is a reddish-brown to yellowish material, commonly seen exposed in road-cuttings, construction sites, erosion gullies and other places where the vegetation and top-soil have been removed to reveal the underlying layers. The colour of these red and yellow soils is derived from the iron and aluminium oxides which remain after the other constituents (the bases, magnesia, calcium oxide and silica) have been leached out. These soils, which may attain great depths (30 ft (9 m) or more), are common not only in the Malay Peninsula but also in the other tropical areas of the world where similar climatic conditions prevail.

Continuous leaching has eliminated a large number of the valuable chemical constituents of Malaysian soils and they are usually very poor in inorganic plant nutrients such as phosphorus and nitrogen. Soil analysis data have confirmed that the phosphorus content of Peninsular Malaysian soils is low. The only soils with high phosphorus levels are those derived from basalt (e.g. Kauntan Series). The soils derived from intermediate igneous rocks and the recent marine clays show moderate levels of phosphorus. The nitrogen contents of the sedentary soils are 0.1 to 0.2 per cent in the top-soil and less than 0.1 per cent in the sub-soil. The alluvial soils are just as poor in nitrogen as the sedentary soils.

Due to this deficiency in inorganic plant nutrients the fertility of the soils is largely dependent on the amount of organic matter present, which in turn is dependent on vegetation factors, climatic factors and on the previous history of the soil. The amount of organic matter in Malaysian soils has been found to be very low when compared with that of soils in temperate countries. The Malaysian soils which have developed *in situ* usually have a humus layer less than 6 in (152 mm) thick. In undisturbed forest the organic matter content may be 3 to 4 per cent, but on cleared and cultivated land it is usually only 1 to 2 per cent. The subsoil layers have very low values of organic matter—usually less than 1 per cent. The only soils which have higher values of organic matter are the recent marine clays (e.g. the Selangor Series) with 2 to 6 per cent.

Peninsular Malaysian soils are also poor in other macro-nutrients such as potassium, magnesium, calcium and sulphur. On the whole, the recent marine clays appear to be the best endowed soils while the sedentary soils have an inherently low nutrient status, although they may differ greatly in individual properties. Less is known about the micro-nutrients status of Peninsular Malaysian soils, but available information indicates that rubber and oil-palm planted on subrecent and old alluvial soils suffer from manganese deficiency.

Yet it has often been maintained that the lushness of the vegetation which covers nearly three-quarters of the total land area of Peninsular Malaysia and once covered the entire area is visible proof that the soils are rich rather than poor. The apparent paradox can be explained thus:

The high uniform heat and humidity of the Malay Peninsula favour the rapid destruction of humus and nitrogen in the soil. The destructive process can be slowed down or countered in two ways: (*a*) through the addition of large quantities of organic material to replace those that have been destroyed or used up; and (*b*) through keeping the soil temperatures at or below about 77° F (25° C), the level at which the process of humus formation gives place to humus breakdown. Both of these requirements are fulfilled in the rain forest. The soil temperature at or near the surface in the undisturbed forested plains of the Peninsula is about 77° F (25° C), with only slight daily variations, and at this temperature humus formation and decomposition are at equilibrium. Such relatively low temperatures are due to the heavy shade provided by the dense foliage and the transpiration of the trees. The direct rays of the sun do not fall on the soil surface, and it has been calculated that the intensity of light at ground level in the Malaysian rain forest is only one-hundredth that of direct sunlight. The air is very still at this level and nearly always saturated; there is thus little variation in temperature due to the movement of the air.

The organic matter which is lost through leaching, erosion or through being taken up by plants is replaced in this manner: the decomposition of the parent rock through chemical weathering releases plant nutrients which are absorbed in dilute solution by deep-rooted plants. These plants shed leaves, flowers, fruit and branches which fall on to the forest floor. Occasionally whole tree trunks may also fall down. All these are immediately set upon by termites, ants and other insects. Rain water also partially dissolves the vegetation remains, which are subsequently attacked by soil micro-organisms—fungi, bacteria and protozoa. The activities of the micro-organisms transform the plant remains into various gases and acids, a dark-coloured residue (humus) from which plant nutrients are set free. The nutrients are quickly absorbed again by the plants, especially those shallow rooted ones which are only capable of taking up their food from the surface layers of the soil. The stock of organic matter (the raw material of humus) is replenished by a constant rain of dead vegetable matter falling on to the forest floor.

A closed cycle is thus set up, in which the plant food is circulated from the top-soil, taken up by the plants, and then returned to the soil again in the form of dead matter to start the process anew. The resources of the parent rock underlying the top-soil are tapped to make good the losses due to drainage and erosion. The entire process takes place many times faster than in temperate forests, and a small amount of nutrients circulating rapidly suffices to maintain the dense vegetation of the tropical rain forest. To put it in the words of Ramann: 'The tropical forest works with a small capital of nutrients and a rapid turnover.'

The luxuriance of the rain forest then is not due to inherent soil fertility, but rather to the special conditions of shade and temperature, and the abundance of vegetative raw material from which the small capital of plant nutrients is built up, expended and rebuilt. The cycle continues as long as conditions remain stable, that is, as long as the forest stands.

When the forest is cut down the cycle is broken, the nutrient capital is rapidly exhausted and the soil reduced to a low level of fertility. The initial effect of forest clearing is to expose the soil surface to the direct rays of the sun, thereby raising the soil temperatures to such a degree that the rate of humus decomposition and oxidation is greatly accelerated. At the same time the flow of plant waste from the forest is arrested and the small store of plant nutrients in the top layers of the soil rapidly depleted. What follows after depends on the subsequent course of events. If the forest is allowed to regenerate itself immediately the process of soil impoverishment is arrested before much harm can be done. But if there is a long period of cultivation after the forest is cleared, and especially if the crops do not provide a good permanent foliage cover, the soil structure, humus content and nutrient status of the soil are radically altered and will progressively deteriorate.

Apart from fertility, the productivity of Malaysian soils depends also on their physical structure. The structure of forest soils is usually good, being porous and resistant to erosion, due to the activities of micro-organisms which bind loose particles of soil into friable crumbs. Under stable conditions of forest growth the number of micro-organisms remains in equilibrium, but when the forest is cut down microbial activity is reduced and the soil structure consequently breaks down. It becomes massive, compacted and very hard, and may deteriorate to the state of 'excessive granulation' when the soil provides too few contacts for plants to take in water and nutrients. One of the major problems of agriculture in Malaysia and in other tropical areas is how to preserve a good soil structure on soils which have been cleared of their original vegetation and cultivated continuously over a period of years.

The process of soil degradation of forested soils following forest clearing is shown diagrammatically in Fig. 3.3. Profile A shows a typical soil

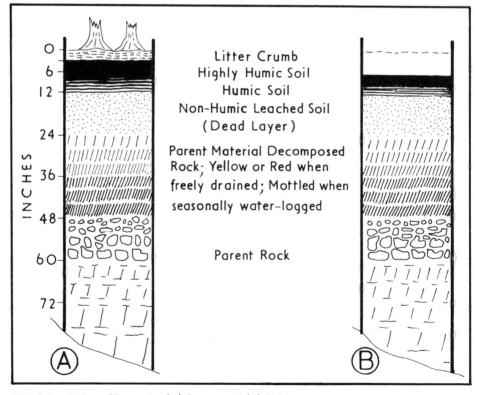

Fig. 3.3   Soil profiles under (A) forest, and (B) field crops.

profile under undisturbed forest. The trees tend to obtain their food more and more from the organic layers of the first 3 in (76 mm) of soil (which are replenished from dead vegetative matter) and on the mineral layer immediately below which is enriched by organic matter washed down. Below the 1 ft (0.3 m) layer is a highly acid, infertile dead layer of soil almost totally leached of nutrients. Below this, the soil grades gradually to undecomposed parent rock. Profile B shows the result after the forest has been cleared, burnt and cultivated. The humus top layer has disappeared, including the litter crumb, and the profile is said to be 'truncated'. The soil fertility now largely depends upon the amount of nutrients left in the original parent rock; this is usually low. The process of degradation and leaching following crop cultivation leads first to a deficiency in nitrogen, and later to phosphorus deficiency, and then to a shortage of bases like magnesium, calcium and potassium, and finally to certain essential trace elements losses. As well as losing its original

Table 3.2   Response of rubber and oil-palm to fertilizers

Soil series	Fertilizers	Increase in yield (per cent)	
		Rubber	Oil-palm
Rengam (ex-jungle)	N	1.5	8
	P	3	5
	K	—	33
	Mg	—	2
	NPK Mg	—	25
Rengam (cultivated)	K	22	—
Serdang (ex-jungle)	NP	17	—
	PK	13	—
	NPK	22	—
Munchong (ex-jungle)	Mg	7	—
	NP	3	—
Malacca (cultivated)	NK	18	—
Selangor (cultivated)	N	5–10	—
Selangor (replant)	N	6	—
	K	8	—
Durian (ex-jungle)	N	—	12
	P	—	22
	K	—	2
Batu Anam (ex-jungle)	N	—	10
	P	—	15
	K	—	22

Source: *Based on data in Ng and Law (1971), p. 137.*

fertility, the soil's physical structure also breaks down and becomes an unfavourable medium for plant growth.

It is apparent that the luxuriance of the rain forest is not a true indication of the fertility status of the soils. In fact, as has been seen, the majority of Peninsular Malaysian soils are poor, strongly leached and require the use of fertilizers on a regular basis in order to minimize inherent fertility as well as productivity deficiencies and to support crops on a sustained yield basis. The response of two major crops—rubber and oil-palm—to fertilizers is in some instances quite dramatic: increases in yields of up to 22 per cent for rubber and of 33 per cent for oil-palm have been recorded (Table 3.2). These findings provide confirmation of the impoverished condition of Peninsular Malaysian soils, and point clearly to the necessity of making adequate provisions for fertilizer use in any programme of agricultural development in the country.

4
Vegetation

In the last survey of Peninsular Malaysia's land resources carried out in 1966 it was established that nearly 70 per cent of the land area was still covered with dense, evergreen forest, the characteristic vegetation of the hot, wet tropics. Part of this forest consisted of logged forest, but most of it was under primary forest cover. Forty-three per cent of the total land area was covered with peat swamps, forest on slopes greater than 20° and forest on flat land within valley re-entrants, all of which are unlikely to be developed for agricultural use. It is therefore likely that this 43 per cent of the land area of the country will remain under permanent forest cover.

This forest, which is usually referred to as tropical rain forest, has developed as a result of the uniformly high temperatures and heavy, evenly distributed rainfall of the Peninsula; it is the climax vegetation of the equatorial climate. Within this general term, the rain forest shows different aspects and floristic composition according to locality. It is modified locally by the nature of the soil, whether lateritic or sandy, dry and well-drained, or swampy and liable to flooding. For example, the forest which is established on the steep limestone hills of Perlis and the Kinta Valley is different in composition from the ordinary lowland forest in that the plant species are those which can adapt themselves to a calcareous soil as well as dry conditions. The mangrove swamp forests and the peat swamp forests are two special edaphic types of forest which occupy large areas in the Peninsula. The tropical rain forest is also modified locally by altitude; with increasing altitude the lowland rain forest gives way to hill and montane forest, a result of temperature changes rather than of rainfall. In the Peninsula the altitude of 1 000 ft (305 m) is roughly the transitional zone between lowland rain forest and hill forest, 2 500 ft (762 m) the transitional zone between hill forest and upper hill forest, and 4 000 ft (1 219 m) that between upper hill forest and montane forest. These altitudes are approximations only, for the transition between one forest type and another is always gradual and nearly imperceptible. At the same time it must be realized that, apart from temperature, other climatic elements such as rainfall, humidity,

89

wind velocity and sunshine also vary with altitude, but not uniformly and consistently as in the case of temperature. Because of this fact, the actual altitudinal limits of the vegetation zones are different on different mountain ranges in the Malay Peninsula, and may vary even on different parts of the same mountain. The zones also tend to be lower on small isolated hills and mountains than on continuous ranges. Thus, for example, the *Dipterocarpaceae*, the dominant family in the lowland tropical rain forests, reach the upper limit of growth at about 4 000 ft (1 219 m) in the main mountain ranges, and this altitude is taken as the approximate dividing line between hill forest and mountain forest. But the upper limit of the *Dipterocarpaceae* on the isolated mountains is much less than 4 000 ft: it is, for example, only 2 750 ft (838 m) on Gunong Belumut in Johore. Similarly upper montane forest species can be found at lower elevations on exposed ridges than in normal circumstances.

Figure 4.1 shows the distribution of the main types of vegetation in the Malay Peninsula. Lowland tropical rain forest covers the largest area; the other vegetation types are limited in their distribution by one or more factors—either altitude, as in the case of mountain forests, or soils and location, as in the case of mangrove, beach and freshwater swamp forests.

Mangrove swamp forest

Mangroves are species of evergreen trees inhabiting tidal land in the tropics. Mangrove forests occupy some 547 square miles (1 417 sq km) in the Malay Peninsula. More than 95 per cent of these forests are distributed along the west coast, where they form a discontinuous belt stretching from Perlis to Johore. The largest areas are in Perak (200 square miles (518 sq km)), Selangor (150 square miles (388 sq km)) and Johore (140 square miles (363 sq km)). The belt varies in width from a few yards to 12 miles (19 km). The continuity of the belt is broken by numerous tidal creeks which cut off islands of different sizes. Exposure to wave action and other adverse environmental conditions limit the extent of mangroves in the east coast; they are here confined to river mouths and occupy areas seldom exceeding 2 to 3 square miles (5—8 sq km). The mangrove forests of the Peninsula are exceptionally luxuriant and consist of at least seventeen 'principal' species and twenty-three 'subsidiary' species. Associated with these are the nipah palm (*Nipa fruticans*), the nibong palm (*Oncosperma tigillarium*) and various weeds and ferns.

Mangrove trees are adapted to maritime conditions and cannot survive in fresh water or on land. The seedlings are unable to withstand strong waves and surf, and for this reason mangrove forests can only develop in sheltered locations, as found along the west coast of the Peninsula. Extensive mud banks are built up in such quiet localities through deposi-

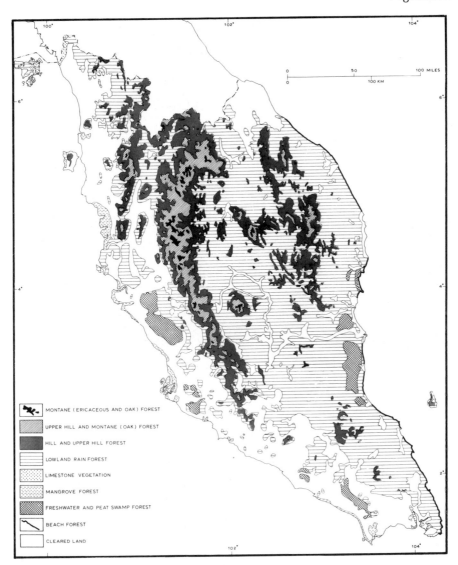

Fig. 4.1   Vegetation types.

tion and silting, and these form favourable sites for mangrove development. Muddy beaches are the rule on the west coast but the exception on the east. The soil requirements vary with the different species of mangrove but the best soil is deep, well-aerated mud, rich in humus but with little or no sand. The larger part of the mangrove swamps of the west coast is covered with such soil.

There is a definite relationship between the distribution of the major species of mangroves and the frequency of tidal inundation of the land

91

Plate 3   Mature mangrove forest, Pulau Klang. Such mangrove forests are valuable sources of poles, firewood and charcoal. The forest areas are worked on a rotation basis (see p. 90).

they colonize. Table 4.1 summarizes this relationship as worked out by Watson (1928) for mangroves growing in the neighbourhood of Port Klang.

Table 4.1   Frequency of tidal inundation and distribution of main mangrove species

Land flooded by	Number of times flooded per month	Main mangrove species
All high tides	56–62	None
Medium high tides	45–59	*Avicennia* and *Sonneratia griffithii*
Normal high tides	20–45	Most species, but *Rhizophora* predominates
Spring high tides	2–20	*Bruguiera*
Abnormal or equinoctial tides	0–2	*Bruguiera gymmorhiza*

The main types of mangrove communities are:

1. *The* Avicennia Sonneratia Griffithii *type.* The first stage in the formation of a mangrove swamp is the colonization of mud banks or sand banks which are exposed at neap tides. The pioneer species are usually *Avicennia alba* and *A. intermedia.* In the river estuaries, however, the new ground is first colonized by *Sonneratia alba.*

2. *The* Rhizophora *type.* The second or middle phase of mangrove swamp formation is usually the replacement of the pioneer species by *Rhizophora* as the level of the mud bank is built up and the pioneer fringe extends seaward. The land is now inundated by normal high tides but with dry periods of from four to eight days twice each month at neap tides. Other conditions which are necessary for the establishment of *Rhizophora* are soils which have been aerated and enriched by the pioneer species, and which contain little or no sand. The main species of *Rhizophora* are *R. conjugata* and *R. mucronata. Rhizophora* forests cover two-thirds or more of the total area of mangrove swamps on the Malay Peninsula, and they provide the bulk of the mangrove products (e.g. firewood, timber, charcoal and tanbark) which are extracted annually. The Malay name for *Rhizophora* is *bakau.* In Perak, where the mangrove forests are best developed, the annual yield per acre is about 3 000 cubic ft (85 cu m), but the yield from the average mangrove forest in the Malay Peninsula is usually much less than this.

3. *The* Bruguiera *type.* There are many species of *Bruguiera. Bruguiera caryophylloides* forms thick pure stands where the soil is a stiff clay and flooded only by the spring tides. It is confined to the sea-face of the mangrove belt and is usually absent in the river estuaries. *Bruguiera gymnorhiza* occupies the driest section of the tidal land—subject to inundation only during the spring and the equinoctial tides. It marks the final stage in the development of the mangrove forests and the beginning of the transition to the inland lowland rain forest. The soil has a noticeable sand content, and on the landward side the ground level may be raised above the level of even the highest tides through the deposition of sediments and dead organic matter and the activities of burrowing prawns. *Bruguiera gymnorhiza* grows to a great size if left undisturbed; individual stands may have trees up to 120 ft (37 m) high and 8 ft (2.4 m) girth. The Malay name for this species is *tumu merah.*

The mangrove swamps on the west coast of the Peninsula are continually extending seawards into the Straits of Malacca, and as this process continues the seaward face is gradually colonized by the pioneer species of mangrove, while the landward side of the swamps is converted into dry land as the ground level is raised and the mangroves give way to inland rain forest. The process is a very slow one, and may be interrupted by uncontrolled felling of the forests, as well as by tidal and sea current changes and riverine erosion.

Along the brackish water zone of estuaries mangroves give way to brackish water palms—nipah (*Nipa fruticans*) and nibong (*Oncosperma*). Nipah is used extensively for thatching, and nibong poles, which can withstand prolonged submersion in sea water, are employed in the construction of fishing stakes.

Beach and 'heath' forests of the east coast

The mud banks and mangrove forests which characteristically line the west coast of the Malay Peninsula are absent along the east coast, except in the sheltered river mouths. Instead, sandy or gravelly beaches dominate the coastal landscape from Johore to Kelantan, their continuity broken only by the mouths of the rivers which debouch into the South China Sea. At intervals along the coast and extending for some distance inland from the shoreline are the old beach ridges known locally as *permatang*. These are usually arranged in a series parallel to the line of the coast, the channels between successive ridges enclosing lagoons in various stages of reclamation by swamp vegetation. In other places the sandy beaches give way inland to sand flats or sandy plains.

Beach forests develop on these sandy or gravelly beaches and, like the mangrove forests, owe their presence and character to special soil and water conditions. These forests are rarely more than 120 ft (37 m) wide, and are established above the level of all except the highest tides.

The typical vegetation of the sandy foreshores comprises low-growing herbaceous plants, which occupy a narrow zone immediately above tide level. Many of the plants have a trailing habit, sending long runners over the surface of the sand. The most common of these are the creeper *Ipomoea pes-caprae* and the creeping grass *Ischaemum muticum*. The majority of the species which colonize this zone are capable of withstanding occasional submergence in sea water and are unharmed by the high salt content of the soil. The screw-pine, *Pandanus fascicularis* (Malay: *mengkuang*), with its pineapple-like fruit, may occur scattered or in groups. But the most striking and distinctive species in this foreshore zone is the casuarina tree *Casuarina equisetfolia* (Malay: *ru* or *aru*). Its area of natural distribution is along the east coast of the Peninsula; elsewhere, the casuarina is planted. It is a quick growing pioneer of the sandy shores, capable of attaining a height of 100 ft (30 m) in twenty-five years. The seedlings are unable to survive in thick forest or dense shade or even in the carpet of fallen needles under the mature casuarina trees. For this reason the casuarinas can only regenerate themselves naturally if the shore is continually building itself seawards and providing the seedlings with a succession of open sandy beaches in which to establish themselves. At Telok Subong on the east coast of Johore and in several places along the Pahang coast the stands of casuarina attain a width of several hundred yards, but the normal pattern is a very narrow strip or even a single line of such trees along the sea front. Many of the casuarina stands along the east coast have been cut down for firewood or, in places, to make way for coconut holdings.

Inland from the fringe of casuarina and the narrow zone of low growing herbaceous plants, shrubs and trees become increasingly common. The trees may form a dense belt of woodland or may be scattered in groups with open spaces between. The sandy ridges of the *permatang* support forest of a xerophytic type known as 'heath' forest. The soils here are almost pure sand below the top few inches, and some of the profiles may contain a lateritic iron pan close to the surface. In such locations the characteristic trees are various species of *Eugenia*, particularly *E. grandis* (Malay: *jambu laut* or *jambu jembar*) and small trees such as *Garcinia hombroniana* (Malay: *beruas*), *Vaccinium malaccense* (Malay: *setumbar*), and *Glochidion* (Malay: *membatu*). In parts of the south Pahang and the Kuantan coasts the sandy ridges carry almost pure stands of *Hopea mutans* (Malay: *giam*) and *Shorea materialis* (Malay: *balau pasir*).

This 'heath' forest is an edaphic climax forest and differs from lowland rain forest in that it has a simpler composition and structure, with a main storey only about 50 to 70 ft (15–21 m) high, and emergents reaching to about 100 ft (30 m). This forest, which grows on sand, degrades easily into scrub when disturbed, and in fact uncontrolled exploitation over the years has destroyed most of the forest that used to cover large parts of the east coast. Today this forest is very poorly represented in Peninsular Malaysia, and in fact only three small remnants of 'heath' forest remain–in the Jambu Bongkok Forest Reserve north of Dungun, the Menchali Forest Reserve north of Kuala Rompin, and in the Tanjong Hantu Forest Reserve in the Dindings. A very open scrub is established on forest areas which have been cleared for cultivation and subsequently abandoned. Such scrub is often razed by fire, ultimately degrading into either an open grassland of tufted grasses or parkland with scattered trees and shrubs.

The channels and low-lying ground between the *permatang* are usually permanently or seasonally swampy and support trees adapted to growing in waterlogged soils. In swamps that are not more than a few feet deep, the typical tree is *Melaleuca leucadendron* (Malay: *gelam*). Gelam forest is a fire climax forest which occupies scattered areas of low-lying land in Kedah, Malacca, Negri Sembilan, Kelantan and Trengganu. The tree, which grows to about 70 ft (21 m) tall, has a thick laminated bark which is fire-resistant so that under conditions of accidental or man-induced seasonal burning which kills off less resistant species it soon establishes itself as the dominant species, much in the way *Imperata cylindrica*

95

(Malay: *lalang*) does. However unlike lalang, gelam has a useful role to play in the rural setting in that it is a valuable source of firewood, charcoal and caulking material. Parts of the gelam forest in Kelantan are worked for these products on a felling cycle of ten years. The forest is deliberately fired once a year during the dry season to maintain species domination.

Freshwater swamp forest

The 1966 land-use survey of Peninsular Malaysia established that the total area covered by swamp forest of all types, including mangrove forests, freshwater swamp forest, peat swamp forest, nipah and gelam forest, amounted to 9 per cent of the total land area of the country. Freshwater swamp forest and peat swamp forest cover the largest areas, and are particularly important in the wet lowlands of Pahang, Perak, Selangor, Johore and Trengganu (Fig. 4.1).

Freshwater swamp forest occurs in locations which are characterized by a seasonal or semi-permanent abundance of water on or near the surface of the ground. The swamps vary considerably in the level of standing water and consequently also in vegetational character. The water in these swamps is mineral-rich and non-acid, in contrast to the very acid water in peat swamps. The vegetation which develops under such conditions varies from open scrub with a few tall trees, to 60 to 100 ft (18–30 m) tall forest, with single species often dominant. Such forest is different in species composition from the forest which develops on a deep peat swamp. Hardwood timber trees such as *Campnosperma* spp. (Malay: *terentang*), *Shorea* spp. (Malay: *meranti*), *Koompassia malaccensis* (Malay: *kempas*), *Hopea mutans* (Malay: *giam*), especially in the seasonal swamps of east Johore, and *Fagraea crenulata* (Malay: *malabera*), which occurs as a narrow belt in the swampy depressions between the beach ridges of the east coast, are of scattered occurrence but in general they are not found in sufficiently large numbers for the swamp forests to be regarded as of prime commercial value.

Single species dominance is also a marked feature of these forests: notable examples are the sedges, screw pines, rattans and palms which occupy large areas in Rompin and Tasek Bera (Pahang) and in Sungei Tinggi (Selangor).

Peat swamp forest

This is an edaphic climax formation established on peat. The distribution and nature of peat have been discussed in the previous chapter (see also Fig. 3.3). The vegetation that has developed on such soils is a specialized one, and depending on the depth of peat as well as extent of water-logging, may range from pure stands of stemless palms, to pole-type forest, to the typical three-storeyed peat swamp forest. The first storey consists of small trees and saplings reaching 30 to 60 ft (9—18 m) above ground level; the second of 90 to 100 ft (27—30 m) trees; the third of scattered emergents reaching a height of 100 to 120 ft (30—36 m). Peat swamp forest is usually more open in aspect than lowland rain forest, and is also more uniform in species representation.

In contrast to freshwater swamp forest, peat swamp forest is of great commercial importance. Available data from commercial enumerations of peat swamp forest in Perak, Selangor, Pahang and Trengganu indicate that each acre (0.4 ha) of forest may have between ten and twenty trees of 4 ft girth breast height. The common timber trees found in such forests are *Cratoxylon arborescens* (Malay: *geronggang*), *Gonystylus bancanus* (Malay: *ramin*), *Dryobalanops aromatica* (Malay: *kapur*), *Koompassia malaccensis* (Malay: *kempas*), *Tetramerista glabra* (Malay: *punah*), and various species of *Shorea* (Malay: *meranti*). Of these *kempas*, although the commonest large species in some swamps (notably in Selangor), is frequently not exploited because of the tendency for its timber to split on seasoning. Two other species—*punah* and *ramin*—have been found to be unable to regenerate themselves, but the other species in peat swamp forest will yield between 15 to 24 tons per acre with silvicultural treatment. It has therefore been suggested that because of difficulty of growing crops other than pineapples on deep peat, land with such peat soils be laid aside for the production of timber.

Lowland rain forest

The most important characteristic of the lowland rain forest of the Malay Peninsula is the remarkable wealth of species. There are no less than 8 000 species of flowering plants, and at least 2 500 of these are trees. A typical acre of forest has about 200 trees of about 100 different species, besides a great number of shrubs, herbs, lianes and epiphytes. In fact, the floristic composition of the lowland rain forest of the Malay Peninsula is probably the richest in the world. The other outstanding feature of the rain forest is that the large majority of the plants are woody and attain the size and dimensions of trees. Not only do trees predominate in the forest, but the undergrowth consists mainly of woody plants, and most of the climbing plants as well as a few of the epiphytes are also woody. The continuous growing season in the Peninsula favours the growth of woody plants as against herbaceous and other smaller plants, while the very long period over which the flora has been evolving probably explains the extraordinary number of different species of forest trees in this part of the tropics.

Although the lowland rain forest consists of an extremely rich flora, the different species of plants are distributed in the greatest disorder and only occasionally are one or two species dominant within the forest community. The different species vary in the space they occupy, some being restricted to localized sectors of the forest and others distributed over very large expanses. This lack of order in distribution of species and the general heterogeneity of the rain forest stand in contrast to the uniform external appearance of the forest, especially when viewed from the air. The rain forest is evergreen, and its general appearance remains the same throughout the year. A few trees may lose their leaves at different times of the year, but these are too scattered and insignificant in number to have any affect on the green of the forest canopy.

The rain forest trees of the Malay Peninsula as a whole have several physiognomic features in common, a result of the adaptation of different species to similar ecological conditions. The tree trunks are usually tall and straight, and are branchless except near the top; the crowns of these trees interlock with each other to form a continuous canopy. Many of the trees have buttresses at the base to provide additional support as their roots do not penetrate far into the soil. Other trees support themselves by the aid of adventitious roots which originate at the lower part of the trunk; these roots hold up the trees much in the same way as wires hold up a telegraph pole. The bark is usually smooth and thin, commonly light grey in colour but sometimes reddish-brown. The leaves are generally large, leathery and dark green in colour. The flowers are small and inconspicuously coloured; large and colourful flowers are rare.

The undergrowth of the Malaysian rain forest consists of shrubs, small palms, herbaceous plants, gingers of varying sizes, ferns, and large numbers of sapling and seedling trees. Contrary to popular belief, the undergrowth in mature rain forest is not impenetrable. It is only on river banks or in forest clearings where sunlight reaches the ground that the undergrowth becomes dense enough to make progress extremely difficult if not impossible. The ground of the forest is not everywhere covered with a thick carpet of dead vegetation, but is often quite bare beneath a thin layer of fallen leaves and branches. The herbaceous ground plants are sparse and grow best on slopes where the light is slightly stronger.

Apart from trees, shrubs and ground herbs, all of which are strong enough to support themselves, the rain forest includes also two types of plants which are dependent on others for support, namely, the climbers which grow from the soil but support themselves on trees up to the upper level of the forest where there is better light; and secondly the epiphytes which do not grow from the soil but perch themselves on the branches and trunks of the trees. Most of the climbers are woody (lianes) and grow to very great lengths, hanging down from the forest canopy in great loops and festoons. They belong to a great many families, and there is a good proportion of economic plants among the lianes, of which the rattans are perhaps the best known. A rattan cane may grow to a length of 200 ft (61 m) or more. There are more than 100 species of rattans in the Malay Peninsula, the majority of them belonging to genus *Calamus*.

The epiphytes are a very abundant plant community in the rain forest.

They include large numbers of orchids and other flowering plants and many ferns. They are adapted to an arboreal existence where the most pressing problem is water supply. Many epiphytes have fleshy leaves, or leaves which minimize water loss from transpiration. Orchids have pseudo-bulbs which act as reservoirs for water; other epiphytes have long aerial roots which absorb water from the atmosphere.

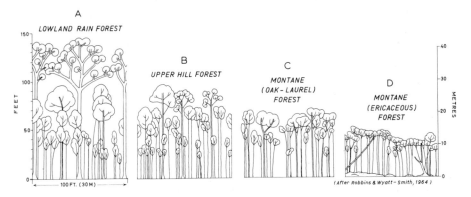

Fig. 4.2   Profiles of altitudinal forest types in Peninsular Malaysia. Profiles A and B include many forest types of different heights and floristic composition but share a common three-storey structure, in contrast to the two-storey structure of Profile C and the single-storey structure of Profile D.

It is apparent that the lowland rain forest is extremely complex in character and is composed of numerous plant types, mostly woody in structure. The forest as a whole is arranged in several storeys or strata— layers of trees whose crowns are more or less of the same average height. In the Malay Peninsula, as in other tropical regions of the world, the primary rain forest communities are arranged in three main tree storeys (Fig. 4.2A). In addition, there are also two layers of undergrowth, so that there are five storeys in all between the forest floor and the crowns of the highest trees. The topmost storey is made up of very large trees most of which are valuable as timber trees; the most important of them are species of *Dipterocarpus* (Malay: *keruing*), *Dryobalanops aromatica* (Malay: *kapur*), *Shorea* (Malay: *meranti*), *Dyera costulata* (Malay: *jelutong*), and occasionally some other species. Most of the species in this storey are light-demanders. Their crowns do not start until 80 or 100 ft (24—30 m) above ground and may rise to 130 to 180 ft (40—55 m). Very occasionally some trees may reach heights of over 200 ft (61 m); the tallest tree recorded in Peninsular Malaysia measured 265 ft (81 m). It is common to discover three or more top-storey trees growing together and separated from the neighbouring groups by fairly pronounced gaps.

The second storey is in fact, the main storey, in that the crowns of the trees here interlock with each other to form a continuous closed canopy,

99

sometimes referred to as the 'roof' of the forest. The tree crowns are usually smaller and more compact than those of the top-storey trees, and they begin from 50 ft (15 m) above ground level, rising to 80 to 100 ft (24—30 m).

The third storey is composed of trees which do not reach over 50 or 60 ft (15—18 m) in height. This storey is composed of a very large number of species, especially members of the families *Annonaceae, Euphorbiaceae* and *Flacourtiaceae*. However, few of the species here are of economic importance.

Beneath these three main tree strata is a layer composed of shrubs, palms and herbaceous plants, and under this is the last and fifth layer comprising the ground flora of ferns, herbs, low-growing palms such as the bertam palm (*Eugeissonia tristis*) and the pinang palm (*Pinanga* spp.), and also seedlings of the species making up the tree strata. It must be remembered that this stratification of the forest vegetation into five storeys is not a rigid one, and the spaces between the storeys may be occupied by species growing gradually from a lower stratum to a higher one.

The lowland rain forest contains more than 350 species of trees which yield timber, excluding the timber trees of the seashores, freshwater swamps and mountains. The most important species from the commercial point of view are those of the family *Dipterocarpaceae*; these collectively provide three-quarters or more of the timber output of Peninsular Malaysia. Most of the species of this family require a hot, wet climate for optimum growth, and few of them are found in the Peninsula north of the 7° N latitude. They are distributed throughout the Peninsula from sea-level to more than 4 000 ft (1 219 m) altitude. They grow in a variety of situations, on poorly drained land as well as steep slopes, but seem to attain their best development in undulating or hilly country. The trees are large and generally belong to the first two storeys of the rain forest. A characteristic feature is the presence of wings on the fruit of most species, a mechanism that aids the dispersal of the seeds. The principal species of the family are the heavy hardwoods, *Balanocarpus heimii* (Malay: *chengal*), *Shorea* (*meranti*), *Hopea* (*giam*), *Eushora* (*balau*), and *Vatica* (*resak*); the medium hardwoods, *Dipterocarpus* (*keruing*) and *Dryobalanops* (*kapur* and *kelandan*); and the light hardwoods, *Shorea* (red, white and yellow *meranti*), most species of *Hopea* (*merawan*) and *Anisoptera* (*mersawa*). Many of the species are gregarious to some extent; *Dryobalanops aromatica* (*kapur*), for instance, is abundant in forests near the east coast. The most abundant of the groups is the *meranti*; they constitute about 17 per cent of the number of trees of commercial size in Peninsular Malaysia. There are usually between three to five trees of commercial size per acre. The next most abundant group is *keruing*, usually making up about 9 per cent of the total number of trees of commercial size, with about two trees of such size per acre of forest. The heavy hardwoods are more restricted in distribution; patches of forest of 20 to 100 acres (8—40 ha) in extent in the east coast may have two or three trees of commercial size in them.

Apart from the species belonging to *Dipterocarpaceae*, four other main species also produce valuable timber—*Intsia palembanica* (*merbau*), *Koompassia malaccensis* (*kempas*), *Dyera costulata* (*jelutong*) and *Tarrietia* (*mengkulang*). In addition, there are many other species which yield timber, some of which are used for special purposes such as boat-building, tool handles and fence posts. Among these are species of the families *Lauraceae, Sapotaceae, Burseraceae* and *Myristicaceae*, as well as species of *Eugenia, Calophyllum, Dillenia* and *Durio*.

Hill (*Dipterocarp*) forest

At about 1 000 ft (305 m) altitude in the inland mountain ranges the floristic composition of the lowland rain forest changes slightly to include many species which do not occur in the lowlands, while the lowland species, although still present, become less common. The characteristic forest tree is *Shorea curtisii* (Malay: *seraya*), which usually occupies the tops of ridges and spurs and which tends to be gregarious, to the extent that it forms a distinct association known locally as seraya-ridge forest.

The valleys on which hill forest is established are narrow and steep-sided. The floors carry a rich herbaceous vegetation, including gingers and ferns and *Saraca* species (Malay: *gapis*). The valuable hardwood *terentang* commonly grows on the valley sides, as well as *Pometia pinnata* (Malay: *kasai*) and *Intsia palembanica* (Malay: *merbau*). On the upper slopes *seraya* becomes dominant, with other dipterocarps such as *Shorea laevis* (Malay: *balau kamus*), *S. multiflora* (Malay: *damar hitam*), *S. faguetiana* (Malay: *damar siput*) and *S. macroptera* (Malay: *melantai*). The undergrowth is dominated by the stemless palm *Eugeissona triste* (Malay: *bertam*) which may form thickets up to 20 ft (6 m) tall.

At about 2 500 ft (762 m) altitude the floristic composition of the hill forest changes gradually, such changes being associated with the altitudinal lowering of temperatures. This altitude marks the approximate lower limit of the *Upper Hill (Dipterocarp) Forest*, but, as in the case of hill forest, the limit may be lower in coastal ranges or isolated mountains. At this level the lowland and hill species of the Dipterocarp family begin to give way to the highland species, of which *Shorea platyclados* (Malay: *meranti bukit*) is the most common. Other dipterocarps which occur, but with less frequency, are *S. ovata* (Malay: *meranti sarang punai bukit*), *S. ciliata* (Malay: *balau gunong*) and *Dipterocarpus retusus* (Malay: *keruing gunong*). One of the few indigenous conifers in the Peninsula, and also one of the largest upper hill forest trees, is *Agathis alba* (Malay: *damar minyak*).

101

The upper hill forest is similar to the forests at lower levels in having a three-storeyed structure, although the separation between the second and upper storey is not as clear-cut as in the lowland forest (Fig. 4.2B). Other differences are: a more even though less tall upper storey; smaller trees (less than 5 ft in girth); lower frequency of occurrence of buttresses; and a greater depth of forest litter due to a slowing down of the rate of decomposition with reduced temperatures. The undergrowth is generally denser than in the lowland rain forest, and contains a large number of bamboos, climbers and epiphytes. Towards the higher levels of the forest the trees decrease markedly in height. At around 4 000 ft (1 219 m) most species of dipterocarps disappear, while oaks and laurels become more common as the hill forest species give way to mountain species.

Montane forest

Two types of montane forest can be recognized in Peninsular Malaysia: montane oak—laurel forest and montane ericaceous forest. The altitudinal range of the former is about 3 500 to 5 000 ft (1 067—1 524 m) above sea-level, but may in instances be wider—from 3 000 to 6 000 ft (914—1 829 m). The characteristic trees of this forest are members of the (oak and laurel) families *Fagaceae* and *Lauraceae*. In drier areas with poorer soils the dominant trees may be conifers such as *Agathis alba*, *Podocarpus neriifolius*, *P. imbricatus*, *Dacrydium beccarii*, *D. elatum* and *D. falciforme*. Apart from floristic composition, the montane oak—laurel forest also differs from lowland rain forest in its structure in having two-storeys instead of three (Fig. 4.2C). The trees are also smaller and seldom exceed 80 ft (24 m) in height. The canopy is smooth, with no giant emergents to break its uniformity. The shrub layer is composed of rattans, stemmed palms and tree ferns. Epiphytes are common. The lower temperatures caused by increased altitude result in thicker litter and humus accumulation. The ground surface is usually covered with liverworts and mosses.

With increasing altitude the oak—laurel forest gives way to montane ericaceous forest, the lower limit of which usually occurs at about 6 000 ft (1 829 m) above sea-level. On ridges and isolated mountains such as Gunong Blumut in Johore it may occur as low as 3 000 ft (914 m). Generally it develops best in the cloud belt, and indeed such forest is sometimes referred to as cloud forest or moss forest in other tropical areas. In this moist environment of mists and clouds there is an abundance of mosses and other epiphytes, including epiphytic orchids. The forest itself is single-storeyed and is composed of stunted trees between 10 and 50 ft (3—15 m) in height (Fig. 4.2D). The common trees and shrubs belong to the Ericaceae (Heath) family, represented by species of *Pieris*, *Rhododendron* and *Vaccinium*. The trees are often twisted and gnarled and sometimes prostrate; their trunks are typically clothed with liverworts, mosses and filmy ferns. Members of many temperate families are also represented in the mixed forest. A characteristic feature of forest floor is the thick accumulation of acid humus soil and peat (as much as 4 ft (1.2 m) thick, as in Gunong Ulu Kali).

Other forest types

Among the other minor forest types in Peninsular Malaysia are those that have developed on sites with extreme drainage and on sites that suffer from severe moisture deficiency due to violent winds or low temperatures such as in limestone areas, quartz dykes and quartzite ridges. The flora of the limestone hills is distinctive, and may even differ from one hill to the next. Henderson (1939) has made a study of the vegetation of the limestone hills and established that out of the 747 recorded species 196 were limestone species and had not been found growing in other habitats in Peninsular Malaysia. The vegetation growing in the calcareous soils at the base of the limestone cliffs and in the large depressions (*wangs*) and gulleys consists of high forest including commercial timber trees such as *Dipterocarpus cornutus, Dryobalanops oblongifolia, Intsia palembanica, Shorea ovalis* and *Chickrassia tabularis*. Most of the species growing in lowland rain forest are represented here.

The hills themselves offer a less hospitable site for plants, and in fact the characteristic plants on the limestone faces, rocky outcrops and ledges are small herbs and rock-loving species of the lowland communities. The dipterocarps are only represented by a few species, notably *Hopea ferrea, Peutacme siamensis* and *Shorea talura*; these grow to only small-tree height, and may even be found as shrubs. Some rare species have disappeared with the destruction of the vegetation through quarrying operations.

Secondary forest or *belukar*

The area covered by primary (or climax) rain forest is continually decreasing in Peninsular Malaysia. Its retreat can be traced a very long way back when the first cultivators reached the Malay Peninsula and started to clear the forest in small patches in order to grow their crops. The process was accelerated as the population of cultivators (including the Malays, who practised permanent or sedentary agriculture based on wet padi, and the aborigines and occasional Malay who practised shifting or *ladang* cultivation) increased with later migrations as well as natural growth. But the greatest encroachment was made during the last 150 years when large areas of forested land were cleared for mining and especially for cash-crop cultivation. At the same time other forested land was cleared in order to grow some of the food crops needed to support the large number of immigrants who poured into the country from China and India. It is inevitable that further encroachments will be made on the remaining areas of forested land for mining, agriculture, urban and transport development and other land-uses as the need arises and the population increases.

But all the land that was cleared of its primary forest is not under agriculture or some other form of productive land-use; a part of it, covering some thousands of square miles, is abandoned land under stands of grasses or other secondary growth, some of which is in the process of reverting to climax rain forest. These secondary plant communities are known as *belukar* or sometimes as *utan muda* (young forest). Unlike the other types of natural vegetation already described, the distribution of *belukar* is not determined by soil, climate or other natural agencies, but by man, who in deciding to choose a particular piece of land clears it of its forest growth, and later abandons it, determines by his actions the location of that area of secondary forest. For this reason, the distribution of *belukar* does not follow a definite natural pattern as in the case of the other types.

The area under secondary growth of one type or another is larger than is generally realized. Perhaps the most important cause of the destruction of primary rain forest which gives rise to *belukar* is the system of shifting cultivation which is practised by the aboriginal tribes (the Sakai or Senoi and the Jakun or Proto-Malay) and also by a few Malays living in the more remote and inaccessible areas of the Peninsula. The system depends on the felling of a patch of forest, the burning of the fallen trees and the cultivation of a few food crops on the patch so cleared. After one or more crops have been harvested, the plot is abandoned and a new one started elsewhere. The old plot meanwhile is colonized by secondary plant communities. The extent of abandoned land once under shifting cultivation (*ladang*) and now under various stages of regeneration to climax rain forest is not known, but the 1966 Land-Use Survey showed that there were 18 300 acres (7 280 ha) of land under shifting cultivation, mainly in Pahang (47 per cent), Perak (27 per cent) and Kelantan (19 per cent). These aboriginal groups seldom recultivate an old holding which has reverted to secondary forest, but prefer to clear a new patch of forest because it is likely to yield better crops and to suffer less from the depredations of pests. Since it takes a very long time for an abandoned clearing to re-establish itself as climax rain forest it is unlikely that the area of fully regenerated forest is keeping pace with the area being cut down or newly abandoned, more so in view of the very long history of *ladang* cultivation in the Peninsula.

Apart from *ladangs*, there are also large areas of land once under some form of agriculture or mining and now abandoned because of loss of soil fertility or of mineral exhaustion. In the western Tin and Rubber Belt, and particularly in the Kinta Valley, the Larut tin fields of Taiping and the Selangor tin fields, the mined-over land covers some thousands of acres. Still larger areas have been devastated as a result of indiscriminate agricultural practices in the past. Thousands of square miles of protected forest reserves were cut down for short-term food crops during the Japanese occupation and subsequently abandoned. In Penang, Malacca and Johore the 'soil-mining' methods of agriculture used by the early pioneers in growing such crops as pepper, gambier, tapioca and pineapples have left their mark on the landscape in the shape of rolling acres of *lalang*—the ubiquitous and obnoxious weed *Imperata cylindrica*. An indication of the extent of such degraded land is given in the 1966 Land-Use Survey, which showed that there were almost 1 500 000 acres (607 000 ha) of scrub forest in Peninsular Malaysia, mainly in Pahang, Johore, Kedah, Perak, Trengganu and Kelantan.

The *belukar* which appears on a site which has been abandoned varies according to the previous history of the site. Where the forest has been completely cleared and the area cultivated for three or more years, abandonment soon leads to an invasion by *lalang* grass. *Lalang* burns easily but because of its underground rhizomes it recovers quickly from a fire which may totally kill off other plants. Repeated firing results in the area being dominated by *lalang*, thus seriously delaying regeneration by forest species. If left undisturbed, however, the *lalang* patch, will, in the course of time and provided that megaspores are available within a reasonable distance, be invaded by pioneer plant species such as *Melastoma malabathricum* and *Eupatorium odoratum*. Later woody species such as *Macaranga, Mallotus, Glochidion* and *Bridelia* take possession of the area; they form a close canopy up to 30 ft (9 m) high. Under their shelter seedlings of forest trees take root and gradually the original type of rain forest is re-established. The transformation from *belukar* to primary rain forest may take up to 250 years or more.

Where the period of cultivation before abandonment is less than two years and the soil is less seriously degraded, a dense secondary forest is quickly established. The dormant seeds and coppice shoots of jungle trees, as well as the pioneer species of plants, rapidly invade the site and compete with each other for living space. The secondary species, which are light-demanding and short-lived in any case, eventually succumb to the shade of the jungle species.

The character of *belukar* varies not only with the degree of felling and the period of cultivation or other forms of land-use but also with the physical nature of the soil. *Belukar* is a portmanteau term which covers all stages of natural succession from light scrub to high forest difficult to distinguish from primary rain forest. 'Typical' *belukar* consists of a large number of herbs, herbaceous creepers and climbers and light-demanding shrubs and tree species which are not characteristic of primary rain forest. They grow in haphazard profusion, but a few species are often gregarious in a patch-like manner. The thick undergrowth is very difficult to penetrate. The general appearance and floristic composition of *belukar* are also different from that of primary rain forest. The trees are smaller in size and the canopy lower, though when viewed from above it has a more level surface than primary forest.

PART TWO
The people

5

The evolution of the population pattern

The population of Peninsular Malaysia[1] has changed considerably in numbers as well as composition over the years since the British first obtained a foothold in the Malay Peninsula with the founding of Penang (or Prince of Wales Island as it was then called) in 1786. Most of these changes occurred as a result of the large-scale migration of Chinese and Indians into the country during the period following the establishment of British rule in the Malay States up to the beginning of the Second World War. But in order to obtain a clearer picture of the evolution of the population pattern it is necessary to go back further in time and trace the pattern as it was in the days immediately prior to the advent of the British.

Pre-British period population pattern

The pattern of population distribution in the period immediately preceding the founding of Penang was fairly simple. On the coastal swamps flanking the central mountainous core and on the jungle-covered slopes of the mountain ranges lived small wandering groups of aborigines whose economies covered the hunting, gathering and shifting cultivation stages. Towards the northern parts of the Peninsula were several distinct tribes of Negritoes, small woolly-headed nomads known locally as Semang in Kedah and Perak and as Pangan in Kelantan. Their traditional habitat was the coastal forests and swamps bordering the mountain ranges of upper Perak, Kelantan and Trengganu, but their wanderings sometimes led them to the jungles of Pahang. With the coming of the lowland Malays and later of other immigrant races, the Negritoes in the course of time were pushed into the interior towards the remote mountain slopes. The Negritoes were hunters and gatherers, practising no

[1] In this chapter all references to Peninsular Malaysia up to 1946 refer to both Peninsular Malaysia and Singapore. After 1946, the term does *not* cover the Republic of Singapore. For further details on the political evolution of Peninsular Malaysia, see time chart (p. 418) showing major political changes in the Malay Peninsula and Borneo.

agriculture but entirely dependent on the jungle and rivers for their food. They built no permanent houses but only crude shelters constructed from sticks and leaves.

The largest of the aboriginal groups collectively known as the Senoi (or more popularly but erroneously as the Sakai) were distributed on the mountains and foothills of the central mountain ranges, seldom venturing on to the plains. The Senoi had a more advanced economy than the Negritoes, and practised some form of *ladang* or shifting cultivation in addition to hunting and food-gathering. Their houses were more substantial than the crude leaf-shelters of the Negritoes. As the feature of shifting cultivation is movement and impermanency, the pattern of population distribution of the Senoi was also constantly changing, although movements of these hill tribes were generally limited to the mountains and slopes of central Peninsular Malaysia.

The third group of aborigines were the Jakuns (or Proto-Malays), primarily of Mongoloid stock. The chief subgroups were the Mantera and the Biduanda of Negri Sembilan and Malacca, and the Orang Ulu, Orang Kanak and Orang Laut of Johore. They were distributed in the southern lowlands of the Peninsula and had a culture akin to that of the lowland Malays, their dialects especially showing recognizable traces of several centuries of contact with the historical Malay tongue. Many of them practised shifting cultivation while some tribes, such as the Orang Laut, settled in fishing villages on the west coast of Johore. Many of them were assimilated into the Malay groups, the rest being distributed in the remoter swamps and jungles of southern Peninsular Malaysia.

The numbers of the aboriginal population of the Malay Peninsula cannot be fixed with any degree of accuracy. Newbold, writing in 1839, estimated that there were some 9 000 aborigines around that period, but it is likely that there may have been more. The population density of all these aboriginal groups varied considerably. Small pockets of settlement in the *ladangs* might have a density of anything from five to twenty persons per square mile, while large tracts of the surrounding jungle were entirely uninhabited.

Apart from the aborigines, the other major population group in the Malay Peninsula was formed by the lowland Malays (sometimes also known as Deutero-Malays or Coastal Malays). Ethnically resembling the Malays of Indonesia, the Malay in the Peninsula is descended from the 'Proto-Malay plus many foreign strains derived from intermarriage with Chinese from the Chou period onwards, with Indians from Bengal and the Deccan, with Thais and Arabs' (Winstedt). The distribution of the Malays followed a definite pattern set by the physical geography of the country. The heavy and uniform rainfall gives rise to a multiplicity of rivers which are narrow and swift in their upper courses and slow and meandering where they flow along the broad flat plains flanking the mountainous core. These rivers in their turn set the original pattern of

Malay settlement on the lowlands and coastal areas. The easiest lines of movement in the landscape of mangrove and freshwater swamp and forest were along the rivers. Wet padi cultivation, the basis of Malay agriculture, also tended to draw the Malays towards flat irrigable land near a convenient source of water. The sea and rivers were the natural sources of fish, and the rivers served as bathing places and provided potable water as well as water for the padi fields. All these considerations served to attract settlement to sites located near to sea and river, the most frequently settled sites being riverine, deltaic and estuarine areas. When the Malays first found their way to the Peninsula, overland and later by sea from Indonesia, the river mouths were always the foci of settlement. From these central locations offshoots of the original settlement expanded either coastwise or up the river or, more usually, in both directions. Malay settlements, in contrast to the amorphous nature of the aboriginal groupings, thus assumed a definite form and shape derived from ribbon development along the coast and along river banks.

The mouth of a river was a strategic location, commanding lines of movement both along the coast and along the rivers. The old Malay political units were sited at these focal points for military as well as economic reasons. The head of each riverine state was the Raja or Sultan, who wielded absolute power. Each sultanate was separated from the next by forested interfluves which acted as a no-man's land, but there were no well-defined boundaries to indicate where one ruler's control ended and the next began. There was a large number of these isolated petty kingdoms during the eighteenth century, and it was by a slow process of absorption of weaker sultanates by stronger ones that the nine Malay States which exist today came into being.

The Malays followed a simple subsistence economy founded on padi cultivation, with fish as the main supplement. There was no pressure on the land. The economy had a flexibility which solved increases in population numbers by bringing more land under cultivation. There are no reliable figures on the total Malay population in the Peninsula at this period. Newbold estimated the population of the States in 1835–36 to be 280 680 (Table 5.1).

The total does not include the population in the islands of Penang and Singapore, or that of Malacca. Purcell estimated the total Malay population in the Malay States in 1830 to be about 200 000 and diminishing.

Population changes 1800–74

The period between the founding of the Straits Settlements of Penang and Province Wellesley, Singapore and Malacca and the extension of British rule to the Malay States saw only minor changes in the basic population pattern of the Peninsula. These changes were mainly the result of the influx of Chinese and Indians into the Straits Settlements as

Table 5.1   Estimated population in Peninsular Malaysia, 1835—36

State	Total population	State	Total population
Perak	35 000	Pahang	40 000
Selangor	12 000	Johore	25 000
Rembau	9 000	Kedah and Ligor	50 000
Sungei Ujong	3 600	Kelantan	50 000
Johol	3 080	Trengganu	30 000
Jempol	2 000	Kemaman	1 000
Jelebu	2 000	Patani	10 000
Sri Menanti	8 000	Total	280 680

they came under British rule, and of some Chinese miners and traders into the Malay States. In addition there were also small numbers of Europeans consisting chiefly of British administrators and military personnel.

Penang was occupied by the British East India Company in 1786. A strip of land on the mainland named Province Wellesley was added to it in 1800. There were no Chinese or Indians in the Settlement at that date, but within a very few years substantial numbers of them began to settle in both the island and Province Wellesley. The Chinese were engaged in a variety of occupations. Many were traders and shopkeepers, others were labourers, while some took to their traditional occupation of farming, not cultivating padi but the more remunerative cash crops like vegetables, cloves, nutmegs and sugar. The Indians migrated to Penang as merchants, petty traders and domestic and agricultural labourers. A number of them were *sepoys* responsible, under their British officers, for maintaining law and order in the Settlement. By 1812 there were 7 000 Indians in a total population of 26 000 in Penang and Province Wellesley, and by 1820 some 8 500 Indians were enumerated in Penang Island alone. In the same year there were 8 300 Chinese in the island. After 1825 the immigrant population of the Straits Settlements was swelled by the arrival of convicts from India. Singapore, Penang and Malacca were then being used as convict stations, the flow averaging over 900 convicts per annum during the years 1832 to 1837.

Singapore, founded in 1819, had only a few Malay fishermen and no immigrant population. Within three years there were some 4 700 people on the island, of whom 1 150 were Chinese. The different immigrant races at first settled wherever they liked, but later the Chinese, Indians, Bugis and Malays were alloted settlement areas on a plan worked out by Raffles. The immigrant population followed much the same occupations as those in Penang, the class of people most encouraged in the early years being merchants and traders. There were also a number of agriculturalists working in the European plantations of cloves, nutmegs and sugar. The Chinese farmers were more interested in growing gambier and pepper and in market-gardening. The Bugis farmers were principally engaged in pineapple cultivation. The population continued to grow rapidly and by 1850 there were about 53 000 people in Singapore, 28 000 of them Chinese.

Malacca had already had a long history of foreign domination by the Portuguese and the Dutch before it finally passed into British hands in 1824. Although Indian influence had been dominant in the Peninsula until the advent of Islam in the fifteenth century, the Indians did not settle in the country, and until the era of modern immigration, which began in the nineteenth century, the number of Indians in Peninsular Malaysia was insignificant. Malacca had a total population of nearly 25 000 in 1826, of which only 2 300 were Indians. Similarly the Chinese, although they had trade and diplomatic relations with the Malay kingdoms from an early period, did not settle permanently in the country until after Malacca was founded. There were some 2 160 Chinese in a total population of 9 630 in Malacca in 1750. The number of Chinese increased to 4 100 in 1826. They were the principal traders in the Settlement, but were also engaged in a great variety of other occupations including farming.

Thus the basic population pattern of aborigines in the interior highlands and lowland Malays around the coasts was altered to some extent in the nineteenth century by the addition of an immigrant group composed largely of Chinese and Indians distributed in the three British possessions—Penang, Singapore and Malacca. By 1871 the immigrant element of the population in the Straits Settlements had become numerically almost as important as the Malays, as shown in Table 5.2.

Table 5.2   The immigrant and Malay population in the Straits Settlements, 1871

Race	*Penang*	*Singapore*	*Malacca*	*Total*
Chinese	36 561	54 572	13 482	104 615
Indians	18 611	11 501	3 278	33 390
Europeans	433	1 946	50	2 429
Eurasians and others	2 409	2 951	2 850	8 210
Total immigrant population	58 014	70 970	19 660	148 644
Total Malay population	75 216	26 141*	58 096	159 453
Grand total	133 230	97 111	77 756	308 097

* The Malays in Singapore included a large number of immigrant Malays from Indonesia.

The population pattern in the Malay States remained much the same until the latter half of the nineteenth century when Chinese miners began to enter in increasingly large numbers. In 1830 there were already about 15 000 to 20 000 Chinese, mainly miners and traders.

In addition there were some Chinese squatters cultivating pepper and gambier in south Johore. However, it was not agriculture but tin-mining which was responsible for the influx of Chinese into the Peninsula. The discovery of rich deposits of tin in the Larut district in 1850 turned it from a little-known and almost uninhabited area to a busy and densely populated mining camp swarming with thousands of Chinese miners (40 000 in 1872). A similar discovery in the Klang Valley saw the influx of miners in Selangor, their numbers growing to 17 000 by 1871. Chinese miners also penetrated into, and set up camp in, the fabulously rich Kinta Valley, as well as the tin fields of Negri Sembilan where there were 15 000 miners in Sungei Ujong in 1874. The influx of Chinese to these new mining fields was so great that the Malay rulers began to find it difficult to maintain order, and the situation soon got out of hand as rival factions of Chinese quarrelled and fought with each other as well as with the Malay overlords over the possession of mining land, and also over the monopoly of opium, liquor and other supplies to the miners.

Plate 4   Port Weld on the Perak coast, with the Main Range in the background. This small town served as the main outlet for tin from the Larut tin fields in the early days of mining in Peninsular Malaysia. Fishing continues to be an important industry in this town.

Plate 5   Taiping, a town located on the foothills of the Main Range. Taiping was originally a mining village in the Larut tin field. Tin mining is still being carried on though on a much reduced scale.

Chinese secret societies played a prominent part in these internecine quarrels.

The turbulent conditions in the Malay States threatened to spread to the Straits Settlements. Normal economic activities in the Settlements were also hampered. Up to this juncture the British Government was reluctant to interfere in the internal affairs of the Malay States. But in 1873, when conditions were becoming chaotic, the British Government reversed its non-interference policy and decided to step in and try to restore law and order in the Peninsula. Both Perak and Selangor were brought under British protection in 1874. Sungei Ujong, one of the Negri Sembilan ('Nine States'), also came under British rule in the same year, and was joined by the other states in subsequent years to form the State of Negri Sembilan. British rule gradually spread to cover the rest of the Peninsula, Pahang accepting protection in 1888, Kelantan, Trengganu, Kedah and Perlis in 1909, and finally Johore in 1914. Peninsular Malaysia was then made up of three major political units—the *Straits Settlements* of Singapore, Malacca, Penang and Province Wellesley; the *Federated Malay States* of Perak, Selangor, Negri Sembilan and Pahang; and the *Unfederated Malay States* of Kedah, Perlis, Kelantan, Trengganu and Johore.

The establishment of the *Pax Britannica* paved the way for economic development in Peninsular Malaysia. Immigration was actively encouraged by the British as a necessary means to development, and the years between 1874 and the beginning of the Second World War saw the influx of Chinese, Indians and immigrant Indonesians in such numbers as to alter the population pattern of the country completely, turning it from a little-known country inhabited by a few hundred thousand Malays and some aborigines to a major producer of rubber and tin with a large (5.5 million in 1941) multiracial population composed of two major groups—the Malays and the Chinese—and an important minority, the Indians and Pakistanis. The next section is devoted to tracing the growth of this immigrant population from 1874 to 1941.

Immigrant population growth

The Chinese

The stabilization of conditions in the western Malay States laid the foundation for the large-scale and systematic exploitation of the tin deposits in these areas. Immigration was completely unrestricted until the Great Depression of the 1930s, and the Chinese continued to flow into the Peninsula in great numbers to trade and to work in the tin mines, and, later, in the rubber holdings and other agricultural enterprises. The continual influx of Chinese into Peninsular Malaysia was due to a number of factors. Most of the immigrant Chinese originated from south-eastern China, from the provinces of Fukien, Kwangtung and Kwangsi and the island of Hainan south of Kwangtung. The natural resources of these regions were limited. There was extreme pressure of population on available cultivable land, which eventually forced many to seek a better livelihood overseas. Peninsular Malaysia, among the countries of the *Nanyang*, offered the best prospects to the migrants, not only because of the opportunities for trade and mining, but also because of the policy of active encouragement followed by the British who, having acquired the Malay States, realized that development would be seriously hampered in this sparsely peopled land without cheap and plentiful labour. Indeed, the demand for labour was so great that a system of recruitment was established for tapping the south Chinese sources of labour.

There was a considerable expansion in the tin-mining industry in the 1880s which followed on the increased demand for tin and the discovery of further deposits along the western foothills. In 1898 there was a phenomenal rise in the price of tin which was reflected in the abnormally high wages being paid for mining labour. This, in turn, stimulated the flow of labour from South China to such an extent that in the two years 1899 and 1900 an estimated 100 000 adult Chinese arrived in the

Federated Malay States. Chinese migration into Selangor and Perak during the period 1881–1900 totalled 1 681 711, while the number which entered the Federated Malay States during the same period came to nearly 2 million. The overall result was that by 1901 there were more Chinese than Malays in the two States of Perak and Selangor and, in fact, the Chinese nearly equalled the Malays in numbers in the Federated Malay States, there being 301 463 Chinese as compared with 313 205 Malays.

Although the development of the tin-mining industry gave the original impetus to Chinese migration, the interests of later migrants expanded to cover a wide range of other economic activities, in particular rubber growing when the crop began to attract the attention of planters in Peninsular Malaysia. The bulk of the labour in the tin mines continued to be Chinese, but the introduction of labour-saving machinery, especially dredges (1912), reduced the need for such labour. The largest number of labourers employed in the mines was 225 000 in 1913. The number gradually declined after that year, and by 1939 only 73 000 were employed, although the output from the mines remained much the same, 51 090 tons in 1939 as compared with 50 126 in 1913.

At the beginning of the twentieth century rubber had come into the agricultural scene, and the end of the first decade saw a phenomenal boom which greatly stimulated the cultivation of the crop. Most of the labour employed in the rubber estates was Indian, but a large number of Chinese were also engaged in this new venture. In 1911, 60 per cent of the estate population in the Federated Malay States was Indian, 25 per cent Chinese and most of the rest Malay. The total Chinese estate population was about 40 000 of which some 10 000 were Hainanese, and the rest Cantonese, Hakka, Hokkien and Teochew. In 1931, 35 per cent of the total population engaged in rubber cultivation in the Federated Malay States was Chinese. The Chinese proportion in the Straits Settlements was 32 per cent, in Johore 49 per cent, in Kedah 16 per cent and in Kelantan 13 per cent. By 1941 the number of Chinese employed in estates of 25 acres (10 ha) and over was 50 000 in the Federated Malay States, 7 500 in the Straits Settlements, 33 000 in Johore and 4 500 in Kedah.

The characteristic feature of Chinese migration to Peninsular Malaysia was that it was motivated entirely by economic reasons. The Chinese came to the country with but one desire—to make their fortunes before returning to their original homes. Few had any intention of settling permanently in the Peninsula. Movements of Chinese to and from South China were therefore extremely fluid, more so as transport was modernized and steamers replaced the old sailing junks. The frequency and directions of these movements were geared to the existing state of the economy, periods of economic boom resulting in a new influx of labour and periods of depression causing a return flow of migrants to China. At most times there was a constant stream of new immigrants from China landing at the Peninsular Malaysian ports and making their way inland to the mines, the estates and the new towns that were springing up along western Peninsular Malaysia. Thus in 1881 some 89 900 Chinese landed at Penang and Singapore, the number increasing to 224 000 in 1901 and to 278 000 in 1913. The First World War put a temporary halt to immigration, but the postwar years were years of prosperity. The number of immigrants reached its record total of 435 708 during the boom year of 1927. During this year only 303 497 Chinese left Peninsular Malaysia for China, so that there was a net surplus of over 102 000. In contrast, the depression year of 1931 saw 304 655 leaving the country as against 191 690 who arrived. In the decade 1921 to 1930 2 317 941 Chinese entered Peninsular Malaysia and 1 937 941 left it, so that the migrational surplus was 480 000.

The export economies of Peninsular Malaysia based on rubber and tin were highly susceptible to price fluctuations in the world markets. In such a situation a flexible labour force was desirable in order to enable quick adjustments to be made to suit the changing market conditions, including a reduction of the labour force to a minimum in a period of low prices. The general world depression of the 1930s greatly affected the economy, and there was a country-wide retrenchment of labour employed in the rubber estates, tin mines and other enterprises. At the beginning of the depression (1930) 167 903 Chinese left the country for China, including some 13 000 destitutes repatriated at government expense. However, the exodus was less than the influx, for during the same year 242 149 Chinese arrived in Peninsular Malaysia, most of whom could not find work and only increased the number of unemployed. It became necessary to prevent more labourers from entering the country, and in August 1930 the Immigration Restriction Ordinance was enforced which stopped direct immigration to the Federated Malay States and imposed a quota upon the number of labourers who could enter the Straits Settlements. More and more Chinese began to leave, and the migrational deficit in 1932 was half a million. The Aliens Ordinance of 1933 further restricted immigration of all adult males of all classes, with the object of regulating 'the admission of aliens in accordance with the political, social and economic needs for the moment of the various administrations'. The quota system applied only to male labour. From 1934 to 1938 female immigration was unrestricted, with the result that there was a migrational surplus of 190 000 Chinese women. It became necessary to restrict the entry of women also, and this restriction was consequently imposed shortly before the start of the Second World War. This imposition marked the end of the major phase of Chinese migration to Peninsular Malaysia.

The net result of Chinese migration from the middle of the nineteenth century to the beginning of the Second World War was to add a major racial component to the population pattern of the country. It has been estimated that at least 5 million Chinese entered Peninsular Malaysia during the nineteenth century, and a further 2 million between 1900 and 1940. The large majority of them returned to China, but a significant number decided, for one reason or another, to settle in the Peninsula. Thus the Chinese population in Peninsular Malaysia grew from 104 615 (Straits Settlements only) in 1871 to 2 418 615 or 44 per cent of the total population in 1941 (Table 5.3).

Table 5.3   Growth of the Chinese population in Peninsular Malaysia, 1871–1941

Year	Total population	Chinese	
		Number	Percentage of total population
1871*	308 097	104 615	34
1891†	910 123	391 418	43
1901	1 227 195	583 396	48
1911	2 644 489	914 143	35
1921	3 338 545	1 170 551	36
1931	4 345 503	1 703 528	39
1941	5 545 173	2 418 615	44

* Straits Settlements only.
† Straits Settlements and Federated Malay States only.

The Indians

While modern Chinese immigration was originally associated with the exploitation of tin, modern Indian immigration was closely linked with the agricultural development of Peninsular Malaysia, in particular with the rise of the rubber industry in the twentieth century. Most of the Indians in Peninsular Malaysia before the establishment of British rule in the Malay States were in the Straits Settlements. The census of 1871 enumerated 33 390 Indians out of a total population of 308 097 in the Straits Settlements. When British rule was extended to cover the Federated Malay States from 1874 onwards, the F.M.S. Government vigorously pursued a policy of encouraging commercial agriculture. Up to the turn of the century the agricultural enterprises based on spices, tapioca, sugar-cane and coffee met with uneven success because of competition from overseas producers, price fluctuations, plant diseases and lack of agricultural knowledge on the part of the pioneers. Most of the capital invested was Chinese. British and European capital was little committed until the development of coffee and later rubber plantations. By the end of the nineteenth century there were some forty sugar plantations covering 50 000 acres and employing 8 000 to 9 000 labourers in Perak, while

119

the Selangor Annual Report for 1896 stated that there were seventy-two European-owned coffee estates covering 47 000 acres and employing 4 000 Indian and Javanese labourers.

In addition to the demand for labour generated by these new agricultural enterprises, there was also a substantial demand for workers to help in the contruction of railways and roads. Most of the labourers were immigrants from India, and by 1891 the Indian population had increased to 74 104 in the Straits Settlements and the Federated Malay States. A decade later the total was 115 532. But the greatest influx of Indians did not occur until rubber became the premier export crop of the country.

Rubber was an experimental crop during the turn of the century, and up to 1905 only 50 000 acres (20 000 ha) had been planted. But the growing demand for rubber forced prices to boom levels in 1906, and again in 1909–12. Profits from rubber were far higher than could be obtained from any other revenue crop, and there was a general rush to clear jungle land, and even land under other crops, for rubber. The acreage under rubber leaped to 290 000 (117 000 ha) in 1909, and continued to expand throughout the next three decades in spite of fluctuating market conditions until, by 1940, the planted acreage was 3 481 000 (1 400 000 ha). Natural conditions of soil and climate in the Malay Peninsula were found to be ideal for the growth of rubber. especially on the well-drained soils as found along the western foothills.

By the first decade of the twentieth century the skeleton of what was to become an excellent railway and road network had already been laid to serve the mining industry, and was conveniently placed to serve the transport needs of the planters as well, being connected to the deepwater ports of Penang and Port Swettenham (now Port Klang) as points of entry for labour and supplies, and of exit for rubber. The major problem which the planters had to face was the labour shortage, as the rapidity with which the rubber acreage expanded created an unprecedented demand for workers. The planters could not look to the indigenous population as the Malays were then few in number, and too much tied to their own self-subsistence economy, with its irregular hours of work and variety of occupations, to have either the inclination or the economic incentive to abandon these for hard, sustained and monotonous work on a rubber estate. The other alternative sources of labour were the immigrant Chinese, Javanese and Indians. Although the Chinese were already present in large numbers in the Peninsula, they were very much preoccupied with their mining, trading and other economic activities, and only a few chose to be wage-earners on a rubber estate. Moreover, the planters were reluctant to employ Chinese labourers as they were 'inclined to be disorderly, cost more in police supervision and gave more trouble'.[1] Javanese labour was difficult to recruit, and was also

[1] Report of the Commissioners of Enquiry into the State of Labour in the Straits Settlements and the Protected Malay States, 1890 (Singapore, 1890), para. 451.

difficult to manage. In the circumstances the South Indian labourer was the logical choice, being well-behaved, hardworking and willing to accept low wages. The demand for South Indian labourers came at a time when there was widespread unemployment and underemployment in India due to the rapidly increasing population. Large numbers of labourers were therefore easily persuaded to emigrate to Peninsular Malaysia.

Unlike the flow of Chinese into Peninsular Malaysia, the migration of Indians was an organized movement from the start. Until the imposition of quotas on all immigration into Peninsular Malaysia in the 1930s, most Indian labour immigration was of the assisted type, that is, the labourer was paid his passage to Peninsular Malaysia by his employer or, later, by the Indian Immigration Committee. The average length of service was three years, so that there was a constant return flow to India as those labourers who did not renew their contracts returned to their original homes. Indian labour migration continued until 1938 when the Indian Government put a ban on the emigration of all unskilled workers to Peninsular Malaysia. In addition to this labour migration was the migration of Indians from the higher economic classes—professional people, merchants, petty contractors, moneylenders, shopkeepers and pedlars—all of whom were attracted by the good prospects in Peninsular Malaysia. Most of these were from North India.

The number of Indian labourers and other Indians who arrived in Peninsular Malaysia and the number who returned to India during the period 1881—1940 are shown in Table 5.4.

Table 5.4   Arrivals and departures of Indians in/from Peninsular Malaysia, 1881—1940

Period	Arrivals	Departures	Migrational balance
1881—89	137 898	n.a.	n.a.
1891—1900	n.a.	n.a.	n.a.
1901—10	421 038	245 298	+175 740
1911—20	908 100	561 913	+346 187
1921—30	887 751	703 809	+183 942
1931—40	764 449	720 374	+44 075

Total +749 944

n.a. = Information not available

Between 1901 and 1940 there was a migration surplus of three-quarters of a million Indians, most of them labourers. The greatest influx of Indians took place between 1910 and the Great Depression. The period 1931—40 recorded a migrational surplus of only 44 000 mainly because of the depression which led to the imposition of immigration control and the Indian Government's action in banning emigration in 1938.

The net result of Indian immigration into Peninsular Malaysia was to increase the Indian component of the Malayan population until by 1941 it constituted 14 per cent of the total population (Table 5.5).

Table 5.5   Growth of the Indian population in Peninsular Malaysia, 1871–1941

Year	Total population	Indians	
		Number	Percentage of total population
1871*	308 097	33 390	11
1891†	910 123	74 081	8
1901	1 227 195	115 536	9
1911	2 644 489	267 159	10
1921	3 338 545	471 536	15
1931	4 345 503	621 774	14
1941	5 545 173	767 693	14

* Straits Settlements only.
† Straits Settlements and Federated Malay States only.

The Indonesians

The large-scale migration of Chinese and Indians to the Malay Peninsula has been well documented and well publicized. Not so well known is the equally important but less spectacular migration of Indonesians to Peninsular Malaysia during the same period. There were two main reasons for this: in the first place there was a general lack of accurate statistics on Indonesian migration. While the Chinese and Indian migrants came in through the main ports, the Indonesians trickled in at various points in the country and, except in the case of Javanese indentured labourers, no record of their number was kept. Secondly the distinction between the local Malays and Indonesians, especially those from Sumatra, is not very obvious, and indeed has sometimes been ignored in the compilation of vital statistics. The 1931 Census of Population, for example, showed all Sumatrans born in Peninsular Malaysia as Malays, thereby increasing the proportion of indigenous Malays to immigrant Indonesians.

The migration of peoples of Malay stock from Indonesia to the Malay Peninsula has been going on for centuries. Most of them were from the neighbouring islands of Java, Sumatra and Sulawesi as well as the lesser islands such as tiny Bawean. Most of the settlers came across in a series of insignificant waves which at times assumed substantial proportions, as, for example, the movement of the Minangkabau from Sumatra to Negri Sembilan in the fourteenth century, and that of the Bugis to Selangor in the eighteenth century. Such immigration has continued to recent times but has been overshadowed by the more spectacular movements of Chinese and Indians to the Peninsula. The immigrants from Sumatra intermarried freely with the Malays already settled in Peninsular Malaysia, while the Boyanese from Bawean, the Bugis from Sulawesi and the Javanese might retain their individuality for some time before they were assimilated into the local Malay population. Assimilation has been greatly facilitated by the fact that these immigrants shared a common anthropological origin, a basically similar language and were Muslims. During the period of British rule and up to the present time, all such people were recognized as 'Malays' (*see* Shamsul Bahrin, 1970).

The Indonesian immigrants came to Peninsular Malaysia with the primary motive of settling on the land as peasant farmers. Unlike the Indians, only a few of the immigrants took to wage-earning in the rubber estates and other large establishments. Most of such labourers were from Java. After the establishment of British rule in the Malay States and towards the end of the nineteenth century when coffee and rubber were introduced as revenue crops, the European planters had to recruit labour from whatever sources were available. In addition to Indian and Chinese labourers, some of the pioneer planters also employed Javanese, although the total number of Javanese labourers never at any time made up a large proportion of the total estate labour force. The Javanese were hard working and, in fact, some planters preferred them to Indians or Chinese as labourers, but recruitment from the former Netherlands East Indies was both difficult and expensive. Javanese immigration was regularized in 1909 with the passing of laws requiring that all Javanese estate labour imported into Peninsular Malaysia be indentured. This regulation remained in force until 1932. The lack of any recruiting machinery in the Netherlands East Indies and the success of the system of free immigration from India both worked against increasing the flow of Javanese labour into Peninsular Malaysia. In consequence the total number of Malaysian estate labourers (Javanese mainly, but also including other Indonesians and indigenous Malays) enumerated in the 1921 census of population was only 37 753, or 10 per cent of the total estate population. By 1931 it had dropped to 28 455 out of a total estate population of 423 851. The total number of Javanese employed as labourers in 1937 was only 15 603. The restriction on Indian emigration imposed by the Indian Government in 1938 created a shortage of labour in estates, public works and other fields of employment. A move was started by the United Planting Association of Malaya urging the Government to use the Indian Immigration Fund to assist Javanese labourers to come into the country, but the Japanese invasion prevented anything concrete emerging from the proposal.

123

In contrast to the limited number of Javanese and other Indonesians who entered the country as labourers and wage-earners, the number of Indonesian immigrants who came to farm and settle in Peninsular Malaysia was quite considerable during the period under discussion. Research by Shamsul Bahrin (1967*a*, *b*) has shown that the occupational patterns of the Indonesian immigrants varied with their place of origin and their place of settlement—the Bugis were traders and merchants in Singapore but cash-crop smallholders in Johore; the Sumatrans came originally as petty miners and tradesmen but later settled as farmers in the hill-and-valley districts of western Peninsular Malaysia; the Boyanese were largely urban, and took on jobs as drivers, gardeners and peons; while the Banjarese and Javanese were mainly agriculturalists. In terms of numbers, however, the majority of the Indonesian migrants were farmers, and their distribution reflected their interest in agriculture and agricultural land. As Fig. 5.1 shows, most of them settled along the coastal fringes of the west, mainly in Krian, in the Kuala Selangor area (between Lower Perak and Kuala Langat), in southwest Johore, and in Johore Bahru/Singapore.

The extent of the flow of Indonesian migrants to the country in the first four decades of the century can be measured roughly by the official statistics of the number of Indonesians by year of first arrival over the period (Table 5.6). Almost all (95%) of the 88 000 Indonesian immigrants who settled in Peninsular Malaysia did so during the first forty years of this century. This was a period in the country's economic history when land was being opened up on a large scale for both plantation and smallholding agriculture. The largest numbers of Indonesian migrants arrived in Peninsular Malaysia between 1911 and 1940, attracted by the opportunities offered in a land undergoing rapid economic development, more specifically by the ease with which land could be acquired for the cultivation of wet padi, rubber and coconut.

The Malay population (that is, the indigenous Malays and other

Table 5.6   Immigrant Indonesians by year of first arrival in Peninsular Malaysia

State/settlement	1910 or earlier	1911–20	1921–30	1931–40	Total
Singapore	1 000	2 000	4 000	6 000	13 000
Johore	4 000	10 000	12 000	7 000	33 000
Selangor	3 000	7 000	6 000	4 000	20 000
Perak	3 000	4 000	3 000	2 000	12 000
Other States	2 000	3 000	3 000	2 000	10 000
Total	13 000	26 000	28 000	21 000	88 000

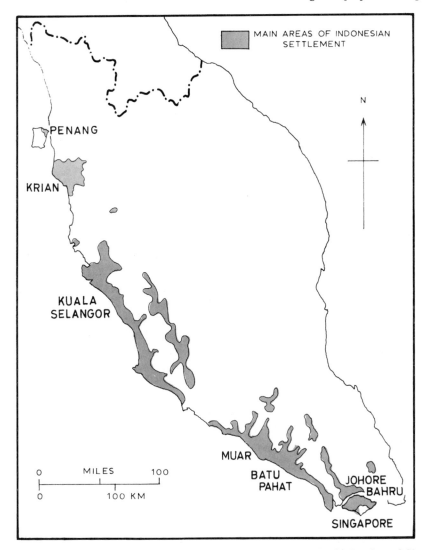

Fig. 5.1 Main areas of Indonesian settlement in Peninsular Malaysia and Singapore, 1947 (based on Fig. 3 in Shamsul Bahrin, 1967*a*).

Malaysians)[1] increased from 1 400 000 in 1911 to 2 248 000 in 1941. What proportions of this increase were due to the excess of births over deaths and what due to immigration cannot be determined accurately because of the lack of migration statistics. However the 1931 and 1947

[1] The official definition of a Malay is a person belonging to the Malay race or any Malaysian race, who habitually speaks the Malay language or any Malaysian language and professes the Muslim religion. The term therefore covers both the indigenous Malays and immigrant Malaysians. For convenience, further references to Malays will also refer to both these groups.

census reports showed that the percentage of Indonesians in the total Malay population declined from 14.5 in 1931 to 12.3 in 1947. It would be fair to assume that at the outbreak of the Second World War the Indonesians made up about 13 per cent of the total Malay population in Peninsular Malaysia and Singapore.

The postwar period has seen a general decline in the percentage of Indonesians to the total Malay population—from 12.3 in 1947 to 8.7 in 1957 and only 4.8 in 1970—providing an indication of the rate of assimilation of the Indonesian groups into the Malay community as well as of the decline in importance of immigration as a factor in swelling the Indonesian population of the country.

Stabilization and postwar growth

By the start of the Pacific War the influx of immigrant Chinese, Indians and Indonesians had completely altered the pattern and character of the population of Peninsular Malaysia. The position is illustrated in Table 5.7. Within the space of less than a century the Chinese had entered and settled in the Peninsula (including Singapore) in such large numbers that they outnumbered the Malays in 1941, while the Indians formed a substantial majority in the now multiracial society of Peninsular Malaysia.[1] The bulk of the immigrant population was spread along a broad coastal belt in western Peninsular Malaysia running from Kedah

Table 5.7　The number and composition of the population in Peninsular Malaysia, 1941

Race	Number	Percentage of total
Chinese	2 418 615	44
Malays	2 248 579	40.5
Indians	767 693	14
Europeans	30 251	0.5
Eurasians and others	80 035	1
Total	5 545 173	100.0

[1] With the separation of Singapore, with its large (730 133 in 1947) Chinese population, and the mainland into two separate political units, first by the establishment of the Malayan Union and then by the formation of the Federation of Malaya and the Colony (now the Republic) of Singapore in 1948, the Malays became numerically superior to the Chinese. Malays formed 49.5 per cent of the total population in the Federation in 1947, and the Chinese 38.4 per cent.

southwards to the tip of the Peninsula. The eastern boundary of this belt coincided with the line taken by the western flanks of the Main Range except in the south where the boundary ran roughly along central Johore. Here were found the tin and rubber industries as well as the main ports. The Chinese were distributed largely in the urban and tin-mining areas, and to a lesser extent in the rubber estates. Most of the Indians were dispersed in the rubber estates with two zones of concentration, the Kuala Lumpur to Malacca and the Kinta to Butterworth rubber areas, and the remainder in urban centres. The Malay population was spread along the traditional padi and fishing areas in the north-eastern and north-western parts of the Peninsula, mainly on coastal locations. A further proportion of the Malays were also located in the coastal parts on both sides of the Peninsula, and in riverine areas in the interior. Broadly speaking there was little overlapping in the distribution of the immigrant peoples and the Malays since the economic interests of the former lay in the urban centres and the tin and rubber areas which were located nearer the foothills than the coast, while those of the Malays were on the coastal and riverine lands associated with their padi and fishing economy.

Up to 1941 the characteristic feature of both Chinese and Indian migration to Peninsular Malaysia was its temporary nature. None of these two groups of people came to the country with a view to permanent settlement, although over the years a substantial number of them did decide to make it their permanent home. The temporary nature of Chinese and Indian migration was reflected in the ill-balanced sex ratio and the low percentage of local-born among both these racial groups. In 1891 there were 654 Chinese men to every 100 Chinese women in the Straits Settlements. The sex ratio among the Indians was even more unbalanced, there being 5 555 Indian men to every 100 Indian women in the Straits Settlements and the Federated Malay States. When the first pan-Malayan census was taken in 1911 the sex ratio of the Chinese was 405 men to every 100 women and of the Indians was 325 men to every 100 women. The sex ratio improved to 100:195 in 1931 in the case of the Chinese and to 100:207 in the case of the Indians. The percentage of local-born Chinese in 1921 was only 22 and of Indians 12. The number of local-born Chinese increased to 31 per cent of the total Chinese population in 1931, while that of the Indians rose to 21 per cent.

The improved sex ratio and the greater number of local-born in 1931 were indicative of a degree of stabilization among the immigrant population. But it was not until after the Great Depression of the 1930s that a succession of events occurred which collectively helped further to stabilize the population.

While the Indian Government had made it mandatory that there should be two females for every three males emigrating to Peninsular Malaysia as early as 1922, the character of Chinese immigration did not change, with males predominating, until the Aliens Ordinance of 1933

127

severely restricted the number of males entering Peninsular Malaysia but allowed the entry of females. The passing of the Ordinance and the subsequent Japanese invasion of China in 1937 caused a flood of Chinese women into the Peninsula which vastly improved the sex ratio of the Chinese population and encouraged the establishment of families in the country of their adoption. It also encouraged the formation of new social links in the country and led to the decay of old ones in China.

When the Indian Government banned emigration of unskilled labour to Peninsular Malaysia in 1938, and the Peninsular Malaysian Government put a ban on the entry of Chinese women shortly before the start of the Pacific War, immigration, which up to then had been the prime factor in altering the population pattern of Peninsular Malaysia and increasing its population, ceased to be of major importance in the further development of the social geography of the Peninsula. By this time many of the Chinese had created extensive economic ties and interests, and the guaranteed protection of these by a paternal government naturally made the Chinese reluctant to leave Peninsular Malaysia and abandon the fruits of many years of labour. Life, even for the common labourer, was very much easier in the rapidly developing Peninsula than in the old, over-crowded villages of China. Finally, the immobilization of traffic between South China and Peninsular Malaysia over the long period from the beginning of the Japanese occupation of the South Chinese ports in 1937, to the end of the Pacific War, and the Communist conquest of China in 1949, forced many Chinese who would normally have returned to their homeland to stay on and, at the same time, fostered and strengthened the economic and social bonds holding them to Peninsular Malaysia. A new generation of local-born Chinese who had never seen the country of their fathers and grandfathers came into being. The overall tendency to permanent settlement is indicated by the improvement in the sex ratio from 100:195 in 1931 to 100:123 in 1947, and the increase in the number of local-born Chinese from 31 per cent of the total Chinese to 62.5 per cent. This tendency to permanent settlement was less pronounced in the case of the Indians, whose sex ratio in 1947 was 100:146. Only 50 per cent of the Indian population was born locally. In contrast, 95 per cent of the Malay population was local-born in 1947.

The total population of the Malay Peninsula increased to 5 848 910 in 1947, made up of 4 908 086 in the Federation of Malaya (Peninsular Malaysia) and 940 824 in Singapore. Most of the increase in the inter-censal years 1931–47 was due to a natural increase of the population and not to the influence of immigration. The increases were confined to the Chinese and Malay segments of the population. The Indians, on the contrary, declined in numbers from 621 774 in 1931 to 599 616 in 1947 in Peninsular Malaysia and Singapore, due to the deaths from malnutri-tion of thousands of unemployed estate labourers during the Japanese occupation, the loss of most of the 50 000 Indians forced to work in the notorious Burma—Siam railway project and the fall in the birth-rate of the Indians as a result of these factors.

The end of the war, the recovery and further development of the economy and the extension of health and medical facilities to most parts of the country have resulted in a great increase in the numbers of all the main racial groups as the birth rates remained high and the death rates declined. Table 5.8 illustrates the position in the census years 1947, 1957, and 1970.

The greater rate of increase of the Malays has improved their position relative to the total population from 49.5 per cent in 1947 to 49.8 per cent in 1957 to 53.2 per cent in 1970. Conversely, there has been a relative decline in the proportion of Chinese to the total population, from 38.4 per cent in 1947, to 37.2 per cent in 1957, to 35.4 per cent in 1970. The position of the Indians has fluctuated in the postwar period, partly because of inclusion of Pakistanis and Ceylonese (Sri Lankans) as part of the Indian community in the 1947 census, their exclusion in the 1957 census, and reinclusion in the 1970 census. Nevertheless the Indians have declined marginally in positional importance since 1947, and in 1970 formed only 10.6 per cent of the total population. The decrease in the percentage of Other Races in the inter-censal period 1957—70 was due to the transfer of the Pakistanis and Ceylonese from this category to the 'Indians' category.

The twenty-three years between the 1947 and 1970 censuses have seen a marked tendency on the part of all the peoples to settle down permanently in the country. This stabilization of the population is indicated by the higher percentage of persons born locally, as well as by the improvement in the sex ratios—from a female : male ratio of 100 : 112 in 1947 to 100 : 106.5 in 1957 to 100 : 102 in 1970. The ratio among the Malays has always been slightly in favour of the females (100 : 99). The ratios among the Chinese/Indians have shown the most dramatic improvement—from 123 in 1947 to 102 in 1970 in the case of the Chinese, and from 146 in 1947 to 113 in 1970 in the case of the Indians.

With the cessation of large-scale immigration and the passage of time the Peninsular Malaysian population has become almost 'normal' in its structure. It is highly unlikely that migration will play any major role in causing population change in the future, although there is the possibility of a small outflow of Peninsular Malaysians to East Malaysia as it is opened up for development.[1] Internally the multiracial pattern of population will persist as cultural and religious differences stand in the way of intermarriage between the Malays, the Chinese and the Indians.

[1] Migration to East Malaysia is channelled through the Malaysian Migration Fund Board, which was established in 1966 mainly to meet the needs of the planting industry of Sabah. The Board was responsible for the flow of about 6 000 workers to Sabah from Peninsular Malaysia (up to mid-1972).

Table 5.8 Population growth in Peninsular Malaysia, 1947–70

	Census year 1947		Census year 1957			Census year 1970		
	Persons	Per cent	Persons	Per cent	Increase over 1947 (per cent)	Persons	Per cent	Increase over 1957 (per cent)
Malays	2 427 834	49.5	3 125 474	49.8	29	4 685 838	53.2	50
Chinese	1 884 534	38.4	2 333 756	37.2	24	3 122 350	35.4	34
Indians	530 638	10.8	735 038	11.7	38	932 629	10.6	27
Others	65 080	1.3	84 490	1.3	30	69 531	0.8	−8
Total	4 908 086	100.0	6 278 758	100.0	28	8 810 348	100.0	40

However, a great deal of progress has been made since independence to foster a sense of national identity among the peoples of the country.

Malaysia: demographic position in 1970

The total population of Malaysia in 1970 was 10 439 530, made up of 46.8 per cent Malays, 34 per cent Chinese, 9 per cent Indians and the remainder Dayaks, Kadazans and other races. The main demographic features of this population are summarized in Table 5.9. As is obvious from the table, most of the population of Malaysia are found in Peninsular Malaysia where densities are eight times as high as in the Borneo territories. All the three states experienced very high rates of population growth in the inter-censal periods, Sabah standing out with a growth rate which must be about the highest in the world! This rapid increase was due not only to a remarkable fall in death rates but also to a substantial in-migration of Malays and Indonesians.

Table 5.9   The main demographic features of the population of Malaysia

Territory	Population (1970)	Density		Annual rate of increases (per cent)	Sex ratios (female:male)	Urban* concentration (per cent)
		per sq mile	per sq km			
Peninsular Malaysia	8 810 348	172	66	3.1 (1957–70)	100 : 101.6	29
Sarawak	975 918	20	8	3.1 (1960–70)	100 : 101.3	15
Sabah	653 264	22	8	4.4 (1960–70)	100 : 107.9	16.5

* 'Urban' is defined as all gazetted administrative areas with a population of 10 000 or more.

The fact that a high percentage of the Malaysian population is young implies that the rate of population increases will continue to remain high as these youths reach the reproductive age. The country will thus have to face the attendant problems of finding employment for the large numbers who enter the labour force each year and of trying to raise levels of living in a situation where economic gains are in danger of being eroded by the pressure of an ever-increasing number of people on the land.

The sex ratio of the Malaysian population as a whole reflects the long-term effects of immigration during the inter-war years, when more males than females entered the country. Thus there still was a preponderance of males to females in 1970, the actual female:male ratio in 1970 being 100:102. In general the sex ratio of a racial group which has been influenced by migration would show this male dominant pattern as in the case of the Chinese (100:103), the Indians (100:113) and the Other Races (100:125), while the ratio of a long-settled indigenous group

131

would show a slight preponderance of females, e.g. the Malays (100:99), the Dayaks (100:99) and the Kadazans (100:99.9). On a state level the importance of immigration as a factor in population growth is reflected in the case of Sabah by its abnormal sex ratio of 100:107.9 (Table 5.9). Within Sabah the ratio of the Malay population was 100:157, and that of the Other Races 100:140.

The other important feature of the population geography of Malaysia is the rural/urban distribution of the people. Seventy-three per cent of the total Malaysian population live in the rural areas; the rest are in the urban centres. This level of urban population is higher than that of every country in Southeast Asia except Singapore and Brunei, and is an indicator of the more diversified and developed state of the Malaysian economy when compared with those in most of the other countries in the region. The contrast among the various ethnic groups in Malaysia is striking—the Chinese show the highest level of urban concentration, with 46 per cent living in urban areas; the Indians are the second most urbanized community (35 per cent) while the Other Races are third (31 per cent). The other groups are still predominantly rural in distribution —85 per cent of the Malays are in the rural areas, and 95 per cent or more of the indigenous peoples of Sarawak and Sabah are located in the more remote and isolated parts of the country.

6

The pattern of population distribution

Peninsular Malaysia, with its 8.8 million people (1970 census) spread over an area of nearly 51 000 square miles (132 000 sq km) has a density of population of 172 persons per square mile (66 persons per sq km). The average population density has increased by almost 40 per cent since the 1957 census, and the country now is as densely populated as Indonesia and Thailand, though it is not as crowded as the Philippines and the two Vietnams.

The overall density of population, however, does not convey a true picture of the situation, since it assumes that all the people are distributed evenly over the entire surface area of the political territory of Peninsular Malaysia. In actual fact, the population is distributed in an extremely uneven manner. Extensive areas of land are almost devoid of population or only very thinly populated, while in contrast many parts of western and north-eastern Peninsular Malaysia have rural densities approaching those of the Menam or Irrawaddy deltas. Figures 6.1 and 6.3 show the distribution and density of population based on 1970 census data. The pattern of population distribution is fairly simple, being made up of the following elements: two zones of high population densities, one extending all the way along western Peninsular Malaysia from Perlis in the north to Pontian (Johore) in the south, and including the crowded island of Penang, and the other located in north-eastern Peninsular Malaysia and centred round the Kelantan and Trengganu deltas. The rest of the Peninsula, consisting of the forested uplands of the interior and other parts of eastern Peninsular Malaysia, is sparsely populated.

High population densities

The western belt

Figure 6.3 shows that there are forty-two districts in western Peninsular Malaysia with more than 100 persons per square mile (40 persons per sq km). These districts are all located in a continuous belt 25 to 75 miles

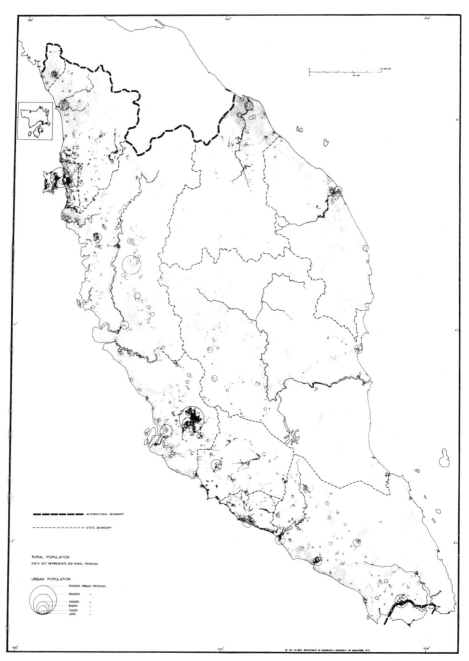

Fig. 6.1   Distribution of population, 1970.

(40–120 km) wide running the entire length of the Peninsula. A comparison of the situation in 1957 (Fig. 6.2) will show that the western belt
of high densities has been enlarged in the inter-censal period to include

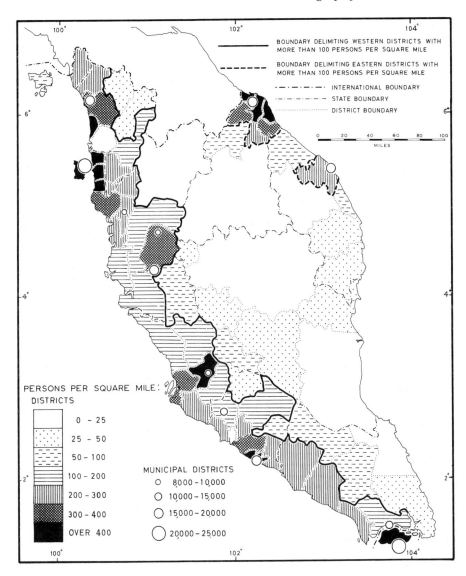

Fig. 6.2   Density of population, 1957.

the districts of Langkawi in Kedah, Batang Padang in Perak, Tampin in Negri Sembilan and Segamat and Kluang in Johore.

The total area and number of people in 1970 within this belt of high densities is shown in Table 6.1. It will be seen that 78 per cent of the total population of Peninsular Malaysia was distributed in this belt, over an area which constitutes 37 per cent of the total area of the country. Another 9 per cent of the total population was distributed in the

Table 6.1   Area and number of people within the western belt, 1970

State	Area		Population (to nearest '000)	Density	
	sq. mile	sq. km		per sq. mile	per sq. km
Perlis	310	803	121 000	390	150
Kedah (districts of P. Langkawi, Kubang Paus, Kota Star, Yen, Kuala Muda, Baling, Kulim and Bandar Bahru only)	2 499	6 472	885 000	354	136
Penang and Province Wellesley	398	1 031	775 000	1 947	752
Perak (all districts except Upper Perak)	5 356	14 011	1 507 000	281	107
Selangor	3 166	8 340	1 631 000	515	195
Negri Sembilan (all districts except Jelebu)	2 022	5 284	449 000	222	84
Malacca	640	1 658	404 000	631	243
Johore (districts of Batu Pahat, Muar, Pontian, Segamat, Kluang and Johore Bahru only)	4 691	12 173	1 181 000	251	97
Total	19 082	49 772	6 953 000	364	139

Kelantan and Trengganu deltas (Fig. 6.3) which occupy 4 per cent of the Peninsular Malaysian land area. In contrast, the remaining three-fifths of the country had a population of only 1 037 000 or 13 per cent of the total population of Peninsular Malaysia.

The average density along the western belt was 364 persons per square mile (139 persons per sq km), more than twice the average for Peninsular Malaysia as a whole. The boundaries of the belt also delimit the area of maximum economic development in the country. Both the high degree of economic development and high population densities are the result of a combination of circumstances that has made western Peninsular Malaysia specially favourable to settlement. Part of the explanation lies

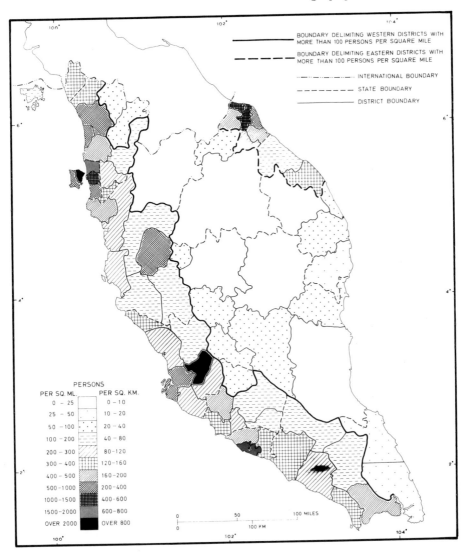

Fig. 6.3   Density of population, 1970.

in the better environmental conditions along this belt. Western Peninsular Malaysia, protected from the direct force of the southwest
monsoon by the great landmass of Sumatra and from the northeast
monsoon by the central mountain ranges of the Peninsula, has always
held greater attractions for the settler than the exposed backwater of the
South China Sea that borders the eastern coast. The sheltered waters of
the Straits of Malacca and the presence of deep-water harbours along the
western coast have served to attract ocean-going vessels to this part of

137

the Peninsula, both in the days of sailing ships and today. Consequently sea-borne traders and sea-borne immigrants have landed and settled along the west coast in far greater numbers than on the east.

Malaysian soils are generally old and poor, being highly leached and suited only to a limited range of crops. The best of these are the alluvial soils deposited by the rivers and constantly enriched by fresh alluvium over the older layers. Here, again, the sheltered west coast provides the better conditions for fluvial deposition. Since the early days of history the first Malay colonists to come to the Peninsula have chosen to settle on the estuarine plains and deltaic plains of the west. With the exception of the Kelantan and Trengganu deltas of the northeast, Malay settlements in eastern Peninsular Malaysia were of little importance.

But perhaps the greatest single factor that has influenced the pattern of population distribution was the existence of large and easily accessible deposits of tin along the western flanks and valleys of the Main Range. As seen in the previous chapter, these rich deposits were the original magnet that drew thousands of Chinese miners to the western foothills. The exploitation of tin resources was responsible directly or indirectly for the establishment of British rule over the Malay States, the influx of Chinese to mine, trade and later to settle in the country, and the establishment of modern land transport in this part of the Peninsula. When rubber was introduced as a major export crop, the first plantations were started in the western belt, not so much because of environmental conditions as because of transport availability and proximity to good ports as points of entry for Indian labour, materials and food, and of exit for rubber. The success of both the tin and rubber industries provided the revenue for the extension of the rail and road networks along western Peninsular Malaysia, which in turn served to concentrate subsequent rubber and other agricultural development in this area. Further, thousands of immigrants from South China, South India and neighbouring Indonesia flocked in to share in and contribute to the wealth of the country, and eventually a substantial number decided to settle here permanently. There is thus a juxtaposition of agricultural smallholdings, mining areas, and large plantations, and an admixture of Malays (including immigrant Indonesians), Chinese and Indians settled in a continuous belt of high density along the entire length of western Peninsular Malaysia.

A large proportion of the Chinese and Indians live in towns distributed along this western belt. In 1970, thirty-five of the forty-nine urban centres with a population of over 10 000 each were located here. The population in these thirty-five urban centres totalled 2 220 000 or 87 per cent of the total urban population of Peninsular Malaysia. Only four—Kota Bahru, Kuala Trengganu, Kuantan and Bentong—of the twenty-six towns in Peninsular Malaysia with more than 20 000 inhabitants were located outside the western belt.

138

Within the belt of dense settlement are found five main areas of exceptionally high population densities, ranging from 300 to over 2 000 persons per square mile (800 persons per sq km) (Fig. 6.3). The first of these includes the districts of Kota Star, Yen, Kuala Muda and Bandar Bahru in Kedah, the entire state of Penang and Province Wellesley and the district of Krian in Perak. Together they make up a continuous belt of thickly peopled country along the northwest coast of the Peninsula. This is a zone of intensive fishing and agricultural activities based on the cultivation of padi, rubber and coconuts, and also of trade centred round the port of Penang. The area has experienced a long history of settlement and development. Here, too, is located the second largest town in Peninsular Malaysia, Georgetown, which had a population of 269 000 in 1970. The second area of exceptionally high population densities is the Kinta Valley, lying between two granite ranges—the Kledang Range on the west and part of the Main Range on the east—and since the 1880s associated with the most intensive mining activities. It is still the premier tin-mining region of Peninsular Malaysia, but over the years most of the richest deposits have been worked out. Cash-crop cultivation has also become important in the Valley, and there are nearly 100 000 acres (40 500 ha) of rubber occupying non-stanniferous land. The early development of Kinta was characterized by a mushroom growth of mining camps, some of which disappeared but others of which persisted and later grew into permanent towns. One—Ipoh—has grown to become the third largest town in Peninsular Malaysia with a population of 248 000 in 1970, as well as an important industrial centre.

The third area is the Klang Valley, made up of the districts of Kuala Lumpur and Klang (Fig. 6.3). The population of this area of 746 square miles (1 932 sq km) was 1 110 000 in 1970, giving an average density of 1 488 persons per square mile (574 persons per sq km). The Valley is a region of important agricultural uses of land, mining activities, trade, industrial and urban functions. The modern development of the Valley was first associated with the discovery of rich tin deposits at about the same time as the discovery of similar deposits in the Kinta Valley. Klang, and later Port Swettenham (now Port Klang), served as ports and points of entry to the region. Kuala Lumpur grew in a similar way as Ipoh from a small mining village to a major town. When rubber was first introduced to Peninsular Malaysia some of the pioneer plantations were established on the old coffee estates in this Valley. From these varied beginnings the economic base has broadened rapidly with the development of the tin and rubber industries, the expansion of the port functions of Port Klang as one of the two major ports of Peninsular Malaysia, and the development of manufacturing industries in the industrial estates of Petaling Jaya and Batu Tiga. Kuala Lumpur occupies a strategic location in the western belt, being the focal point of land and air routes, and connected to Port Klang by an excellent highway. As the Federal capital, it is the administrative centre of Malaysia and also the largest city in the country, with a population (excluding Petaling Jaya) of 452 000 in 1970. Also within the Valley is the fifth largest town in Peninsular Malaysia—Klang, which had a population of 114 000 in 1970.

The fourth region of dense settlement comprises the districts of Seremban and Port Dickson in Negri Sembilan, the whole of Malacca state and the district of Muar in Johore. Within this region are the two major towns of Seremban (population: 81 000 in 1970) and Malacca (population: 87 000 in 1970). This is an old settled region with a long history of trade, mining and agricultural development. The tin-mining activities associated with the early history of Seremban have declined considerably in significance and today Seremban's economic structure is based mainly on agriculture (rubber and oil-palm) and the modern manufacturing industries which have been set up in the 400 acre (162 ha) Senawang industrial estate. Port Dickson district is an area of intensive plantation-crop agriculture in the interior, and oil refineries at Port Dickson itself. The attractive sandy beaches south of Port Dickson support a steady tourist industry. The trading activities of the port of Malacca, especially the barter trade with Indonesia, have dwindled to insignificance. The establishment of the proposed new port in the deep waters of Tanjong Kling may result in a trade revival. Traditionally Malacca state has been an area of cash-cropping based on the cultivation of fruits and coconuts in smallholdings and rubber in smallholdings as well as in plantations. Padi is a long-established subsistence crop. The economic foundations of the state are being broadened with the setting up of free trade zones and small industrial estates (at Ayer Kroh, Tanjong Kling and near Jasin town) which have attracted a number of labour-intensive enterprises, notably electronics companies. Malacca town, of historic fame, had a population of 87 000 in 1970, making it the eighth largest town in Peninsular Malaysia.

The fifth area of dense population concentration in the western belt is at the southern extremity of the Peninsula, comprising the districts of Johore Bahru and Pontian. This is a region of varied economic activities, focused on the smallholder and plantation cultivation of rubber, oil-palm, coconut, pineapples and pepper in the rural areas, and on industrial, administrative, trade (including the substantial tourist trade from Singapore) and transport functions in the urban centres, mainly in Johore Bahru. Apart from the textile mills, car assembly plants and other enterprises which have been established for a number of years in the industrial estates of Scudai, Tampoi and Jalan Larkin, other industries will be channelled to the new industrial estate at Pasir Gudang, 12 miles (19 km) east of Johore Bahru. Pasir Gudang is planned to cover an area of 2 800 acres (1 133 ha), with a free trade zone of 150 acres (61 ha), and a new port. A new airport has also been built at Senai, 18 miles (29 km) from Johore Bahru. Johore Bahru itself has grown considerably in size in the inter-censal period 1957—70 and is now the fourth largest town in Peninsular Malaysia, with a population of 136 000 in 1970.

The north-eastern belt

This belt of high densities is composed of two major nuclei of population centred around the Kelantan and Trengganu deltas linked together by the less densely populated district of Besut (Fig. 6.3). Nine per cent of the total population of Peninsular Malaysia were distributed in this belt (Table 6.2).

Table 6.2   Area and number of people within the north-eastern belt, 1970

State	*Area*		*Population (to nearest '000)*	*Density*	
	sq. mile	sq. km		per sq. mile	per sq. km
Kelantan (districts of Tumpat, Pasir Mas, Kota Kharu, Bachok, Pasir Puteh, and Machang only)	918	2 378	567 000	617	238
Trengganu (districts of Kuala Trengganu and Besut only)	1 203	3 116	253 000	210	81
Total	2 121	5 494	820 000	386	149

This is traditionally a fishing and agricultural region with an overwhelming Malay population, with a history of settlement going back several centuries. Isolated from the rest of the country by the forbidding barrier of the Main Range and the Trengganu Highlands, the northeast has remained very much an area of smallholdings and fishing villages. Except for the urban centres of Kota Bahru and Kuala Trengganu, the landscape bears little evidence of the impact of the modern economy. Padi and kampong cultivation and fishing still remain the customary occupations inextricably bound up with the Malays' way of life. Rubber, that symbol of the modern economy, is subsidiary to padi as the main crop. There was no sudden rush to plant rubber as happened in many parts of western Peninsular Malaysia, but rather an unobtrusive introduction of the tree into the traditional kampong setting without upsetting the normal pattern of life. In recent years tobacco has become an important offseason crop in the Kelantan delta. Progress has also been made in padi cultivation with the establishment of the Kemubu and Besut padi

141

irrigation schemes which will enable farmers to double-crop their padi land. The isolation from which this region suffers will be diminished considerably when the east—west highway linking Kota Bharu to Butterworth is completed.

Within the north-eastern belt is an area of exceptionally high population densities. This is the lower part of the Kelantan delta where rural densities are among the highest in the country: 980 persons per square mile (392 persons per sq km) in Kota Bharu (excluding the town), and 1 125 persons per square mile (450 persons per sq km) in Tumpat (Fig. 6.3). The high densities in this low-lying coastal area are mainly the result of natural increase over an extended period of settlement and owe little to migrational surplus. Kota Bharu town itself had 55 000 people in 1970 as compared with 38 000 in 1957, while the population of Kuala Trengganu town was 53 000 in 1970.

Low population density areas

The central uplands and eastern areas

The western belt of high densities is bordered on the eastern interior side by a number of discontiguous districts with densities of between 50 and 100 persons per square mile (20—40 persons per sq km) (Fig. 6.3). These are, in point of fact, part of the western belt in that they have all the characteristic features of the belt, but because development has been less intensive and population densities relatively lower they remain outside the boundaries of the belt.

Elsewhere densities vary from nothing over large parts of the mountainous core to 50 to 100 persons per square mile (20—40 persons per sq km) in the coastal districts of Trengganu, Pahang and east Johore, and the districts of central Pahang. The uplands of the Peninsula are negative areas except in the hill resorts of Cameron Highlands, Fraser's Hill, Maxwell's Hill, and Genting Highlands. Agricultural development in Peninsular Malaysia has remained below the 1 000 ft (305 m) contour line, while tin-mining has also been focused on the recovery of the alluvial and detrital deposits of the valleys and foothills. The exploitation of timber resources has again been confined to forested land below 1 000 ft. The only people who inhabit the uplands in any number are the aboriginal groups of hunters and gatherers and shifting cultivators. Thus there is a close correlation between the districts of less than 25 persons per square mile (10 persons per sq km) and the forested uplands of the Peninsula (compare Fig. 1.3 with Fig. 6.3).

Another area of exceptionally low densities is that made up of the coastal plains of the lower Pahang, Rompin and Endau rivers. Much of this area is covered with freshwater peat swamps which so far have not been put to productive use. The swamplands of the Pahang delta are also infested with the mosquito vectors of filariasis, a crippling disease whose characteristic manifestation in the later stages is a grotesque swelling of the lower limbs. Settlements in this area are few and far between, and are confined to Malay fishing villages along the coast, a few riverine kampongs and some logging camps. Most of this region is administratively in the district of Pekan, which in 1970 had only 70 000 persons spread over an area of 3 683 square miles (19 persons per square mile (7 persons per sq km), and only one small town, Pekan, with a population of 4 700. However, parts of this region have been earmarked for extensive development under the Pahang Tenggara scheme, which covers an area amounting to almost 30 per cent of the total area of Pahang state.

Three districts in eastern Peninsular Malaysia have densities of between 25 to 50 persons per square mile (10–20 persons per sq km): Kemaman in Trengganu and Mersing and Kota Tinggi in Johore. All are coastal districts. Settlement in Kemaman is concentrated along the coastal zone, and is based on the traditional east coast economic activities of fishing, padi cultivation and kampong cultivation of food crops, rubber and coconut. The two Johore districts have a more varied economic base, including plantation agriculture of rubber and oil-palm, mining of tin at Pelapah Kanan and Jemaluang and of bauxite at Telok Ramumia, and logging. Settlement however is thin and scattered, occurring mainly in pockets and along the main trunk roads. The entire southeastern part of Johore stretching from Kota Tinggi town to the coast and the Penggerang peninsula is to be developed as part of the Johore Tenggara scheme, resulting ultimately in denser concentrations of population in this region.

The urban population and urbanization

Urbanization may be defined as a process of population concentration in towns and cities, that is, in urban areas. The term 'urban' may be defined on the basis of one or more criteria—size, function, demographic density as well as legal, administrative, economic and social criteria. The most widely used is that of size, and in the majority of countries, including Peninsular Malaysia, a population cluster with well-defined boundaries and containing more than a certain number of people is classified as an urban centre. Such a definition, although convenient and easily applied for census purposes, suffers from the fact that the line between 'urban' and 'rural' must of necessity be drawn arbitrarily, since there is no clear-cut dichotomy between town and country but rather a continuum made up of population clusters ranging in size from the smallest to the largest. There is no point in this continuum at which 'rural' ends and 'urban' begins, so that any line dividing such a graduated distribution must be an arbitrary one.

In Peninsular Malaysia the dividing line between urban and rural was set at 1 000 in both the 1947 and 1957 censuses, and increased to 10 000 in the 1970 census. One thousand was too small a statistical criterion to define an urban centre, for a number of reasons. In the first place there is a large number of settlements of 1 000 and over which are no more than rural villages without any of the cultural, commercial, industrial and administrative activities which are associated with distinctively urban functions. Secondly, the 1 000 minimum population requirement would mean that a good number of the New Villages that were established as a result of the 1950–52 resettlement campaign would be classed as urban centres, when in fact they are groupings of squatters without any of the functional characteristics of towns. Thus the 1 000 criterion would over-emphasize the degree of urbanization, as instanced in the 1947–57 inter-censal period when the total population of Peninsular Malaysia increased by 28 per cent but the urban population, based on the 1 000 criterion, increased by a remarkable 105 per cent mainly due to the resettlement campaign, and only to a small extent to industrialization, building and construction and the extension of administrative activities in urban centres.

While recognizing the arbitrary nature of any threshold or cut-off point, nevertheless in this section central places of 10 000 people or more are defined as urban in order: (*a*) to exclude most of the New Villages and other places which are essentially rural in character; (*b*) to enable a more realistic assessment of the level of urbanization in Peninsular Malaysia to be made. Using this criterion the 1970 census enumerated forty-nine urban centres with a total population of 2 530 000, representing 28.7 per cent of the total population of Peninsular Malaysia. Table 6.3 shows the growth of the urban population in the inter-censal period 1911–70.

The last sixty years have witnessed a steady increase in the level of urbanization in Peninsular Malaysia, with the greatest increase recorded in the 1947–57 inter-censal period. Such a level is higher than that of

Table 6.3   Urban growth, Peninsular Malaysia, 1911–70

Census year	Total population	Percentage of urban to total population	No. of urban centres
1911	2 339 000	10.7	8
1921	2 907 000	14.0	14
1931	3 788 000	15.1	16
1947	4 908 000	15.9	20
1957	6 279 000	26.5	36
1970	8 810 000	28.7	49

any other country in Southeast Asia except Singapore and Brunei, although it is still low when compared with that of Western countries.

The growth in the urban centres of Peninsular Malaysia in the last inter-censal period has led to an overspill outside the gazetted boundaries of these centres, so that the actual urban population was larger than that enumerated in the census. In order to provide a truer indication of the size of the urban population, a study was made by the Federal Department of Statistics of the population overspill outside the gazetted boundaries of all the state capitals in Peninsular Malaysia except Kangar in Perlis. The results are shown in Table 6.4. It will be seen that the difference in population numbers living in the ten gazetted areas and the urban conurbation areas was as much as 400 000 or 15 per cent of the total urban population of Peninsular Malaysia. The largest urban conurbation in the country was Kuala Lumpur which had a total of 255 000 people living in built-up areas outside the gazetted limits, of which 52 per cent were in seven other gazetted areas—Petaling Jaya, Ampang, Salak South, Sungai Way, Sungai Way—Subang, Batu Village and Gombak Setia—and the rest in non-gazetted areas. In the other capital towns the degree of overspill was not as significant as in Kuala Lumpur, and in the case of Kuantan there was no overspill at all as all the built-up areas were within the gazetted limits of the town.

Table 6.4   Population in ten gazetted capital towns compared with the urban conurbation areas

Town	Population in gazetted area	Population in urban conurbation	Population in gazetted area to population in urban conurbation (per cent)
Kuala Lumpur	452 000	707 000 (100*)	63
Georgetown	270 000	332 000 (42)	81
Ipoh	248 000	257 000 (36)	96
Johore Bahru	136 000	145 000 (20)	93
Malacca	86 000	100 000 (14)	86
Seremban	80 000	90 000 (12)	88
Alor Star	66 000	86 000 (12)	76
Kota Bahru	55 000	70 000 (9)	78
Kuala Trengganu	53 000	59 000 (8)	89
Kuantan	43 000	43 000 (6)	—
Total	1 489 000	1 889 000	78

* Kuala Lumpur conurbation has been re-expressed as 100.

Table 6.5   Distribution of the urban population, 1970

State	Total population (000's)	No. of urban centres	Total urban population (000's)	Per cent of urban to total population
Penang and Province Wellesley	775	5	395	50
Selangor	1 631	7	733	44
Perak	1 569	8	432.5	27
Trengganu	406	5	110.5	27
Johore	1 277	7	336	26
Malacca	404	2	101	25
Negri Sembilan	481	3	103.5	21
Pahang	505	4	95	18
Kelantan	686	5	103	15
Kedah	955	3	120.5	12
Perlis	121	0	0	0
Peninsular Malaysia	8 810	49	2 530	29

The level of urbanization and the number of urban centres in each of the states of Peninsular Malaysia are shown in Table 6.5. The level of urbanization varied from nil in the case of Perlis (Kangar, the largest town, had a population of only 8 700 and therefore did not qualify as an urban centre on statistical grounds) to 50 per cent in the case of Penang and Province Wellesley, although this state had only five urban centres. Selangor had the largest number of urban dwellers and was a close second to Penang in its level of urbanization. It is interesting to note that although Perak had the largest number of urban centres its level of urbanization was substantially lower than that of Penang and Selangor. Three-quarters of the total urban population of Peninsular Malaysia lived in the four states of Penang, Selangor, Perak and Johore. In these states were found twenty-seven of the forty-nine urban centres.

Table 6.6 illustrates the increase in the number of settlements with a population of 10 000 or more in the period 1911—70. The number increased from twenty in 1947 to forty-nine in 1970, with four states— Perak, Selangor, Kelantan and Trengganu—recording the largest gain in the last two inter-censal periods. The merger of the two urban-sized New Villages (Pasir Pinji and Guntong) with Ipoh and the growth of Pokok Assam into a settlement of more than 10 000 inhabitants have resulted in Perak suffering a net loss of one urban centre between 1957 and 1970. All the other states have shown gains, the most notable being that of the

Table 6.6   Number of urban centres with a population of 10 000 or more, Peninsular
Malaysia, 1911–70

State	Census year					
	1911	1921	1931	1947	1957	1970
Perak	3	4	4	4	9	8
Selangor	1	2	2	2	5	7
Johore	–	2	3	4	5	7
Penang and Province Wellesley	1	1	2	4	4	5
Trengganu	1	1	1	1	2	5
Kelantan	1	1	1	1	1	5
Pahang	–	–	–	–	4	4
Negri Sembilan	–	1	1	1	2	3
Kedah	–	1	1	2	3	3
Malacca	1	1	1	1	1	2
Perlis	–	–	–	–	–	–
Peninsular Malaysia	8	14	16	20	36	49

two east coast states of Kelantan and Trengganu, each of which had only
one urban centre in 1947 and five in 1970. The growth of these centres
was mainly due to the penetration of modernizing influences—via an
improved communications network, state and federal development
schemes and planned administrative decentralization. In contrast, Perlis
had remained essentially rural throughout the last sixty years, and in
1970 was the only state which had no settlement of more than 10 000
inhabitants.

An analysis of the eight largest (75 000+ population) towns in
Peninsular Malaysia (defined as metropolitan towns in the 1970 census)
reveals some distinctive growth trends. Up to 1947 Georgetown was the
largest town in Peninsular Malaysia, with Kuala Lumpur a close second.
However, the rank order was reversed in 1957. The dominance of Kuala
Lumpur was accentuated between 1957 and 1970 when it experienced a
population increase four times larger than that of Georgetown, resulting
in a marked size differential between the two (Table 6.7). In fact if the
size differential is based on the urban conurbations instead of gazetted
areas, then Kuala Lumpur's primate position becomes quite obvious—it
being more than twice as large as the next largest town (Georgetown),
almost three times as large as the third largest town (Ipoh), and five
times as large as the fourth largest town (Johore Bahru) (Table 6.4). The
dominance of Kuala Lumpur, however, is not as marked as the dominance of the primate cities of Burma, the Khmer Republic, South

Table 6.7   Comparative aspects of metropolitan towns of Peninsular Malaysia

Town	Size (1970)		Increase in population numbers (1957–70)		Average per cent increase in population per annum (1957–70)	
Kuala Lumpur	452 000	(100*)	136 000	(100*)	3.3	(100*)
Georgetown	270 000	(59)	35 000	(25)	1.1	(33)
Ipoh	248 000	(54)	122 000	(89)	7.4	(224)
Johore Bahru	136 000	(30)	61 000	(44)	6.2	(187)
Klang	114 000	(25)	38 000	(27)	3.8	(115)
Petaling Jaya	93 000	(20)	76 000	(55)	35.2	(1 060)
Malacca	86 000	(19)	16 000	(11)	1.8	(54)
Seremban	80 000	(17)	28 000	(20)	5.6	(169)

* Kuala Lumpur has been re-expressed as 100.

Vietnam, Thailand and the Philippines, which have populations more than five times as large as the next largest city. All available evidence points towards the increasing dominance of Kuala Lumpur in the Peninsular Malaysian urban scene, for not only has its area been enlarged from 36 square miles (93 sq km) to 94 square miles (243 sq km) in 1974 but the urban conurbation was growing at about three times the rate of the total population of Peninsular Malaysia, and more rapidly than any other urban conurbation in the country.

The other feature of the growth trend among the metropolitan towns is the rate in which the population of urban conurbations of Ipoh, Johore Bahru and the east coast towns of Kuantan, Kuala Trengganu and Kota Bahru is increasing. All of these showed rates of growth between 1957 and 1970 of more than twice the rate in which the total population of Malaysia was growing, in contrast to Malacca and Georgetown which were growing at about the same pace as the total population (Pryor, 1973). Ipoh, in particular, had a growth rate only slightly lower than that of the Kuala Lumpur urban conurbation and would, at this pace, eventually displace Georgetown as the second ranking urban centre in Peninsular Malaysia.

The distribution of the forty-nine urban centres of Peninsular Malaysia is shown in Fig. 6.4. Thirty-five of them containing 87 per cent of the total urban population fall within the western belt of high population densities, emphasizing the 'heartland' nature of the western belt. The early growth of towns in Peninsular Malaysia was not associated with any process of industrialization as in Western countries. Rather, most of the towns of Peninsular Malaysia originated during the colonial period as

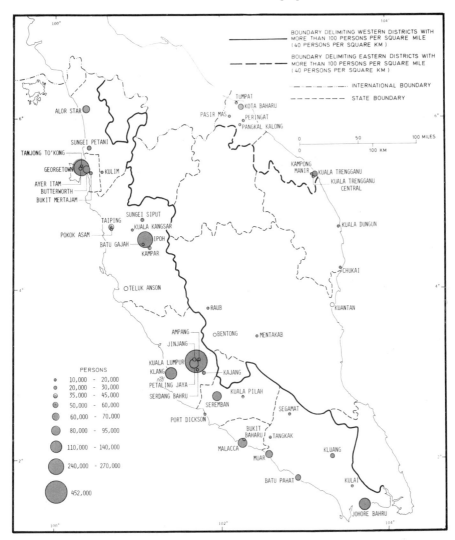

Fig. 6.4   Distribution of towns with a population of 10 000 and over, 1970.

commercial, trading and distributing centres whose growth had been largely associated with the establishment of a modern market economy based on tin and rubber, and the establishment of good transport linkages within the country. Some of these central places eventually grew into towns. The towns were therefore colonial creations linked to the processes of economic development based on the export of a few primary products and to the large-scale immigration of Chinese and Indians, many of whom were attracted by the economic opportunities available in the urban areas.

The success of the tin and rubber industries meant that an increasing number of people was needed to handle the collection, processing and distribution of these exports, as well as the distribution of the essential imports. The overwhelming majority of such people were non-indigenes, both European (and British) as well as Asian. During this phase of the country's economic history most of the Malays remained outside the colonial economy, largely unaffected by the changes being introduced in the towns as well as in the countryside. It is therefore not surprising that up to 1947 92.7 per cent of the population living in settlements of 10 000 and over was made up of non-Malays (Table 6.8).

Table 6.8   Degree of urbanization, Peninsular Malaysia, by race, 1947—70

Race	*Percentage of total population in urban areas*		
	1947 census	1957 census	1970 census
Malays	7.3	11.2	14.9
Chinese	31.1	44.7	47.4
Indians	25.8	30.6	34.7
Others	46.2	49.3	40.8
Total	15.9	26.5	28.7

In the postwar period immigration ceased to be a factor in the growth of towns; rather, it was a combination of political and social forces which was important. No longer were the towns growing as a result of the influx of immigrants, as in the earlier years of the century, but as a result of high rates of population increase (medical facilities, as in most developing countries, are better in the towns) as well as the migration of rural peoples to the urban centres. One of the major reasons for the drift to the towns was the Communist uprising of 1948—60, popularly known as the 'Emergency', which made the towns safer places to live in than the outlying areas, and in particular the resettlement campaign which brought a good proportion of the suburban population into the town boundaries and directly resulted in the formation of two New Villages which had populations of over 10 000, and ten others in the size range 5 000—10 000 (Sandhu, 1964). Many of the rural recruits to the security forces decided to stay on in the towns, thus swelling the urban population.

The postwar growth of the towns was also partly due to rural—urban migration and partly to 'urban—urban' migration; that is, migration upwards through the settlement hierarchy. Apart from the forced migration of rural squatters to the New Villages, rural—urban migration in Peninsular Malaysia also involved other rural dwellers, particularly males in the age group 16—40 years. The causes are both the 'push' factors of poor educational, health and other facilities in the rural areas, rural unemployment and underemployment as well as the 'pull' factors of employment opportunities believed to exist in the towns and the better living conditions there (*see* Hamzah Sendut, 1960/61). An indication of the importance of rural—urban migration in contributing to urban growth is given by Caldwell (1963*b*), who estimated that 62 per cent of the total increase in population living in settlements of 1 000 and over in 1947—57 was due to the influx of rural peoples to these settlements.

In 1970, 71 per cent of the total population of Peninsular Malaysia lived in the rural areas; of this 58 per cent lived in settlements of less than 1 000 inhabitants, and 13 per cent in settlements of between 1 000 and 9 999 inhabitants. During the postwar period, and especially during the 1957—70 inter-censal period urban growth was not only caused by rural—urban migration but also by the migration of people from small settlements to larger settlements, in the process causing changes in the size categories of settlements, the most important of which (on definitional grounds) was the crossing of the size threshold of 10 000 differentiating the urban from the rural population. Thus the thirteen settlements which crossed the rural—urban threshold between 1957 and 1970 (Table 6.6) attained urban status partly as a result of population increase through the upward migration of people from smaller settlements. A distinctive feature of population change during the 1957—70 inter-censal period was the 'urban—urban' migration that took place in five states—Kedah, Pahang, Penang, Perak and Selangor—whereby population living in towns of 10 000 to 19 999 inhabitants moved to larger towns (Pryor, 1973).

The distribution of the urban population by size of the urban centres is shown in Table 6.9. Only one-quarter of the urban population lived in towns having 10 000 to 50 000 inhabitants. The other three-quarters lived in towns of over 50 000 inhabitants; the total number of people in

Table 6.9 Distribution of urban population of Peninsular Malaysia by size of urban centres, 1970

Size of urban centre	No. of centres	Per cent of total urban population
10 000— 20 000	23	12.0
20 000— 50 000	11	13.4
50 000—100 000	10	26.3
100 000—200 000	2	10.0
Over 200 000	3	38.3
Total	49	100.0

such towns was 1 885 000 or 21 per cent of the total population of Peninsular Malaysia. Thus one in every five persons in Peninsular Malaysia lived in a large (50 000+) town in 1970. Even more striking is the dominant position of the three largest towns of Kuala Lumpur, Georgetown and Ipoh, which together had 38 per cent of the total urban population or 11 per cent of the total Peninsular Malaysian population.

The relation of race to urbanization in the postwar inter-censal period 1947–70 is shown in Table 6.8. The Malays have become increasingly urbanized during this period, due to the movement of substantial numbers from the rural areas to the towns (one-quarter of the rural–urban migrants in 1947–57 were Malays; Caldwell, 1963a), as well as the greater rate in which the Malay population in the urban (as well as rural) areas is growing relative to the other races. Urban job opportunities for the Malays have multiplied following political independence and the rise of national consciousness (Hamzah Sendut, 1962). The New Economic Policy of the present government aims at overcoming poverty, un-employment and racial economic imbalance, the latter through the modernization of rural life, a rapid and balanced growth of urban activi-ties and the creation of a Malay commercial and industrial society. The eventual target is a Malay share of at least 30 per cent of the total com-mercial and industrial activities of the country. Such a policy has spatial implications since commercial and industrial activities tend to be concen-trated in central places (many urban-sized), so that in the course of time one would expect the proportion of urban to rural Malays to increase significantly beyond the 14.9 per cent shown in the 1970 census (Table 6.8) as the Malays take on jobs not only in commerce and industry but also in administration, education, transport services, and other urban services.

The Chinese have always been a highly urbanized community in Peninsular Malaysia, mainly because of their immigrant background and the nature of their economic activities. As is apparent from Table 6.8, they have become even more markedly concentrated in the towns in the postwar period, particularly between 1947 and 1957 when nearly half a million Chinese rural squatters were resettled in New Villages, some of which have since crossed the rural–urban size threshold. The urbaniza-tion process slowed down in the last inter-censal period, but even so, nearly half the total Chinese population were living in towns in 1970 (*see* Lam, 1970; McGee, 1964; Hamzah Sendut, 1964).

The Indians (and Pakistanis) have also become more urbanized in the postwar period, the proportion rising from one-quarter of the total Indian population in 1947 to one-third in 1970. The other races experi-enced a decline in the level of urbanization between 1957 and 1970, in part because many expatriates moved out of the country with political independence.

As has been seen, the rate of urbanization in the postwar inter-censal

Plate 6   Low-cost flats at Jalan Pekeliling, Kuala Lumpur. These high-rise low-cost flats were constructed to meet the demand for housing amongst the low income groups in the Federal capital and to alleviate the squatter problem.

years 1947—70 has been markedly rapid. In fact, urbanization has proceeded more rapidly than economic circumstances warranted, in the sense that urban economic opportunities have lagged behind urban population growth, with the result that the urban centres are faced with the problems of unemployment and underemployment. Unemployment was as high as 10.1 per cent in the metropolitan towns and 9.7 per cent in the other urban areas, as compared with only 5.4 per cent in the rural areas of Peninsular Malaysia (Department of Statistics, 1970). Related to the problems of urban unemployment are the problems of overcrowding, the creation and expansion of slums and squatter settlements, and the overloading of public infrastructure and utilities. It is evident that the commercial and service functions of the urban areas cannot expand in step with population growth and the consequent demand for jobs, and that new job opportunities will have to be found, mainly in the manufacturing sector. This would involve a shift in the pattern of urban employment, for up to the 1960s urbanization in Peninsular Malaysia was not related to industrial development but to the movement of rural peoples into towns where they tended to move into low productivity service jobs such as petty trading, taxi-driving, trishaw-peddling, food-hawking and domestic service (Hamzah Sendut, 1964).

Distribution of the main racial groups

The Malays

The term 'Malays' is used here to cover the aborigines (Orang Asli), the indigenous Malays as well as the immigrants from Java, Sumatra and other parts of Indonesia. The distribution of the aboriginal groups has been discussed earlier. The opening up of the country over the last century or so has not materially affected the distribution of the aborigines whose natural habitat is the remote forested interior which has remained almost totally untouched during this period. The greatest changes have occurred in the case of the Jakun who were originally found in the southern part of the Peninsula, many of them in the coastal lowlands. A number of such tribes have been absorbed into the Malay community, others pushed back into the interior and some have died out with contact with modern civilization. The rest of this section will deal with the distribution of the settled Malay (including the immigrant Malay) population.

The basic pattern of the distribution of the Malays on coastal and riverine areas in pre-colonial Peninsular Malaysia has been altered to varying degrees in the different states due to the movement of Malays towards interior sites and into towns. The establishment of British rule and the development of new roads and railways in the country laid the foundations not only for immigrant but also for Malay settlement in the areas thus opened up. These modern transport lines were usually laid in a direction following the grain of the country, cutting across the traditional lanes associated with the rivers. Passing, in the early days, through new territory, the roads and railways quickly attracted new settlement. Land was cleared on either side and cultivated with rubber and other cash crops, by the immigrant population as well as by the Malays, particularly the recent arrivals from Indonesia. Sir Frank Swettenham (1948, p. 238) states that with

> ... the opening of the country ... the opportunity was quickly seized of putting up small native houses in the middle of a few acres of good land, on the side of a track which was almost certain to become a great highway. Malays, Chinese, and Indians, but especially Malays, were thus induced to take a large interest in the earlier stages of development. A bridle road was no sooner completed than small houses, plantations, and fruit and vegetable gardens sprang up along its whole length.

Such ribbon settlements were but repetitions of the usual form of Malay settlements, except that instead of being along the coast or river banks they now followed the line of the roads and railways. This dispersal of population was a gradual one and never assumed the scale of a mass migrational wave of land occupation as in the case of the immigrant population. Nevertheless, it was considerably accelerated through the natural increase of the Malay population as death rates were lowered and birth rates remained high, and through the influx of Indonesians into the country. The creation of points of population pressure on land resources arising from the population increase and local saturation of the land-carrying capacity led in turn to a flow of Malays to areas of lower economic pressure inland from the coast. In addition to this 'push' exerted by population pressure was the 'pull' exerted by the new economy, in particular the attractions of rubber cultivation. Rubber planting quickly found favour among a great many Malays because it involved little labour apart from the initial effort of clearing the land and planting the seedlings. Production techniques were simple and the capital outlay in establishing a smallholding modest. Best of all, the Malay farmer discovered that in times of good prices a few acres of rubber could supply him with the cash needed to provide a standard of living which was higher than could be obtained from padi growing, and with less physical effort. Rubber grows best on well-drained soils, and since such soils are most extensively distributed in the undulating foothill region bordering the western mountain ranges and in the rolling country of central Johore, the rubber-growing Malays moved away from their traditional coastal habitat towards the interior.[1]

The movement into the interior also occurred along the rivers. River or levee settlements in the pre-colonial days rarely penetrated far inland but with the growth of population and the establishment of peaceful conditions there has been a gradual advance up-river. This advance is more noticeable in the eastern states, along the Sungei Pahang, the Sungei Kelantan and the Sungei Trengganu as well as along the lesser rivers. Malay settlements also stretch along most of the length of the Perak River. In many places on the west, however, riverine sites have been rendered valueless by excessive silting of the rivers due to the indiscriminate discharge of tin tailings and to erosion from agricultural clearings.

Not only has there been a spread of Malay ribbon settlements towards the interior, but at the same time there has been a perceptible movement of Malays on a broad front inland from their traditional coastal locations, this movement being conditioned by the character of the soil and the surface relief in different parts of the Peninsula. Over the last half-century Malay settlements, once confined to the coastal strip between the seas and the inland swamps on both sides of the Peninsula, have advanced landwards into the swamps as pressure of population on available padi land increased. This advance has been considerably facilitated by government assistance in swamp clearing, drainage and irrigation, especially on the west where large padi areas have been reclaimed

[1] The term 'interior' is used here in the sense of 'inland from the coast' and does not mean the mountainous forested interior.

Plate 7 Besut, a small town on the east coast near the Trengganu–Kelantan border. Most of the towns on the east coast are sited at the mouths of rivers which are however usually too shallow and also obstructed by shifting sand bars to allow for the movement of large vessels. The fine sandy beaches in this photograph are characteristic features of the east coast and have great potential as a tourist attraction (see p. 161).

from freshwater swampland. Notable among these reclamation schemes are the Krian, the Sungei Manik, the Tanjong Karang, the Kubang Pasu and the Besut Padi Irrigation Areas.

Similar in concept to the planned settlement of Malays in these pre-war irrigation areas is the settlement of Federal citizens, mainly Malays, on agricultural land in both coastal and interior sites, taking place under the direction of the Federal Land Development Authority (FELDA) (Fig. 6.5). Each settler is given 7 to 8 acres (2.8–3.2 ha) of land in the case of a scheme based on rubber as a cash crop, and 10 acres (4 ha) of land in the case of an oil-palm scheme, with a quarter acre as house lot. Up to the beginning of 1972, 23 054 families totalling about 144 000 persons had been settled in the 100 schemes developed by FELDA since its inception. Although only 20 per cent of the placement is reserved for former members of the Malaysian armed forces and the remainder is available to all those who, irrespective of ethnic origins, fulfil the necessary conditions of eligibility, demographic and economic circumstances have worked towards a preponderance of settlers being Malays. Thus, up

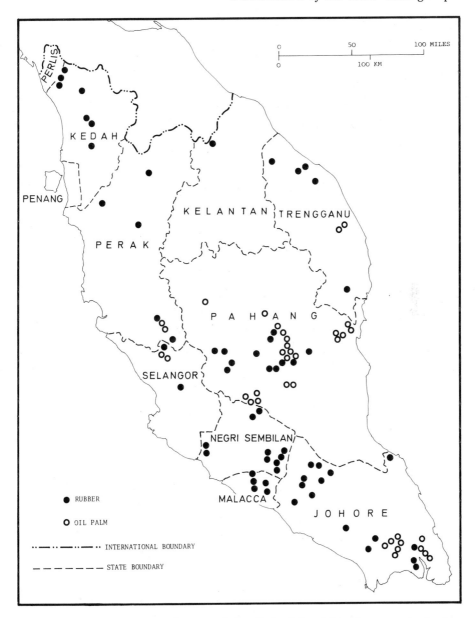

Fig. 6.5   Land settlement schemes of the Federal Land Development Authority, 1970.

to 1970, 94 per cent of the settlers were Malays. In the period since the schemes were first started (in 1957) over 100 000 Malays have been settled, in locations which until recently were sparsely populated. The pattern of population distribution of the Malays will be further modified

157

during the Second Malaysia Plan (1971—75) when FELDA opens up an additional 300 000 acres (121 400 ha) for agricultural development.

In a manner similar to the landward movement along a broad front from the coasts is the expansion of ribbon settlements outwards on both sides of the river banks, roads and railways where these passed through swampland suitable for wet-padi cultivation or through dryland sites suitable for rubber and other cash crops. In a hill and valley environment as exemplified in Negri Sembilan, the spread of population from the valley bottom has not only been outwards but has also occurred in an upward direction along the valley sides. The extent of population dispersion here is therefore restricted and depends on the breadth of the valley floor and the steepness of the valley slopes. There is no indigenous terrace cultivation on hill slopes as in Java and the Philippines.

In a coastal alluvial plain environment, all the large rivers have in the course of time built up levees along both banks. The usual site for a Malay settlement is on the levees away from flood risk. The spread of population has in this case been towards and into the swampland on either side. In contrast to the hill and valley regions where the outward movement has been up-slope, here it has occurred downslope along the outside flanks of the levees and on to the flat land below.

In addition to the gradual spread of Malays inland from their traditional coastal habitat, there has been a small but increasingly significant flow of Malays to the urban centres. Although the Malays are still primarily a rural people, a number of forces have worked over the years to draw them away from the countryside to the towns. The basic cause has been the rapid growth of the Malay population due to both natural increase and the influx of Indonesians. In many localities the increase in population numbers has not been followed by a corresponding increase in economic opportunities, with the result that the excess people had to look elsewhere for work. Most of them moved inland as described earlier, to new farmland. Others became wage-earners in the estates and mines. A small proportion migrated to the towns. Included among these were some of the immigrant Indonesians who also settled in the urban areas. A number of Malays were already in nucleated settlements such as Malacca, Kota Bharu and Dungun, before these grew into towns, so that the Malays in these towns represent part of the original population. In addition, there has been in recent years a general 'drift to the towns' on the part of the rural Malays. This drift to the towns is caused not so much by the economic factors of population pressure and lack of work in the countryside as by a general dissatisfaction with rural life coupled with a desire to live in the town, and enjoy the amenities of urban life. The basic cause is therefore sociological, but the economic implications are serious. On the one hand, the rural community is deprived of many of its able-bodied people, especially young males, with consequent adverse effects on production and, on the other, the uncontrolled

Table 6.10   Distribution of the Malay population by states, 1970

State	Number of Malays	Per cent of total population
Trengganu	381 000	94 (92)*
Kelantan	637 000	93 (91)
Perlis	96 000	79 (78)
Kedah	675 000	71 (68)
Pahang	309 000	61 (57)
Johore	682 500	53 (48)
Malacca	209 500	52 (49)
Negri Sembilan	218 000	45 (41)
Perak	676 000	43 (39)
Selangor	564 000	35 (28)
Penang and Province Wellesley	238 000	31 (29)
Peninsular Malaysia	4 686 000	53 (50)

* Figures in parentheses are for 1957.

addition to the urban population of such rural people leads to unemployment and underemployment in the towns as the number of people begins to outstrip the available economic opportunities.

The above discussion serves as an introductory background to the present-day pattern of the distribution of the Malay population in Peninsular Malaysia. The distribution of the Malays on a state basis is indicated in Table 6.10. The higher rate of population increase of the Malays *vis-à-vis* the other races has resulted in an overall improvement in their positions in the inter-censal period 1957—70, not only in Peninsular Malaysia but also in all the individual states. Thus the number of states with a Malay majority increased from five to seven during this period. Altogether the Malays in these seven states made up 63 per cent of the total Malay population in 1970. It is clear that the Malays have continued to concentrate in the areas least affected by the external influences introduced during the colonial era, namely, in the padi-growing regions of the northeast (Trengganu and Kelantan), the north-west (Perlis and Kedah) and the eastern state of Pahang. In contrast, the states of Negri Sembilan, Perak, Selangor and Penang and Province Wellesley have low proportions of Malays, a reflection of the extent of the penetration of non-indigenous economic interests and people in these areas. In the two contiguous states of Johore and Malacca high rates of population growth in the inter-censal period have moved the Malays into majority positions.

The density of the Malay population on a district basis is illustrated in

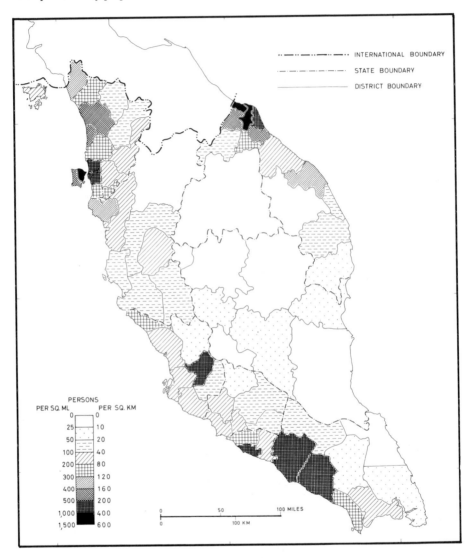

Fig. 6.6   Density of the Malay population, 1970.

Fig. 6.6. There are seven main areas of Malay concentration, six coastal and one inland, where densities are above 200 persons per square mile (80 persons per sq km). These are (*a*) the long coastal strip in the north-west from Perlis to Krian, including coastal Kedah and the state of Penang and Province Wellesley; (*b*) the district of Sabak Bernam; (*c*) the district of Kuala Lumpur; (*d*) central and northern Malacca; (*e*) the west coastal districts of Johore; (*f*) the Trengganu delta; and (*g*) the Kelantan Delta. Within these areas are five clusters where densities are very high, from 500 to 1 500 persons per square mile (200–600 persons per sq

160

km). These are the northern two-thirds of Province Wellesley and north-east Penang (Timor Laut); the district of Kuala Lumpur; central Malacca; the districts of Muar and Batu Pahat in Johore; and the lower Kelantan delta comprising the districts of Tumpat, Kota Bharu and Bachok. The highest Malay densities in Peninsular Malaysia are those of the districts of northeast Penang (Timor Laut 1 279 persons per square mile), Kota Bharu (1 193) and Tumpat (1 008).

Adjoining the seven main areas of Malay concentration are areas of moderate densities—from 50 to 200 persons per square mile (20–80 persons per sq km). These include the neighbouring units of the five main areas of high densities along the western littoral, the coastal districts of Trengganu apart from Kemaman, and all the inland districts of Kelantan except Ulu Kelantan (Fig. 6.6). All the other parts of the country, including the mountainous interior and the eastern coastal districts of Johore and Pahang, are sparsely populated. Malay settlements here are scattered and confined to the more favourable locations—along the coasts in fishing villages, along the banks and levees of rivers as riverine kampongs, in small interior valleys, and in the more accessible regions among roads and railway lines.

The Malays remain predominantly a rural people, although the percentage of Malays living in towns of 10 000+ has increased from 7 to 15 between 1947 and 1970 (Table 6.8). The essentially rural character of the Malays is also reflected in the nature of their economic activities. Table 6.11 shows that of the 1 432 400 Malays in employment two-thirds (66%) were engaged in the primary industries of agriculture, fishing, forestry, hunting, and mining and quarrying. The Malays dominated the industry group 'Agriculture, forestry, hunting and fishing', where they formed about 80 per cent of the total employed. Most of the Malays here were engaged in fishing and smallholder agriculture, mainly padi cultivation. Since the overwhelming majority of the padi planters in Peninsular Malaysia are Malays there is a close correlation between the distribution of padi (Fig. 10.5) and areas of high Malay densities (Fig. 6.6) except in western Johore, where padi is unimportant. In areas where the Malays form a minority of the total population, in west-central Peninsular Malaysia, they are found mainly in the rural areas while the non-Malays are largely urban-distributed.

Although the Malays are not urban dwellers an increasing number of them are beginning to move to the towns, as noted earlier. In 1947 only 7 per cent of the total Malay population were in towns; by 1970 the percentage had increased to 15 (Table 6.8). In 1970, 28 per cent of the total urban population of Peninsular Malaysia were Malays (Table 6.15). Of the forty-nine urban centres in Peninsular Malaysia in 1970, only eleven had a Malay majority. A comparison of Table 6.12 and Table 6.13 will show that (*a*) of the twenty-six major towns (20 000+) in Peninsular Malaysia only three had a Malay majority; (*b*) in contrast, eight of the

161

Table 6.11 Employment by race and sector, Peninsular Malaysia, 1970

Sector	Malays		Chinese		Indians		Others		Total	
	Number in '000	Per cent	Number in '000	Per cent	Number in '000	Per cent	Number in '000	Per cent	Number in '000	Per cent
Primary										
Agriculture, forestry and fisheries	925.4	65	293.0	29	138.3	46	12.3	46	1 369	49
Mining and quarrying	21.1	1	56.1	5.5	7.1	2	0.7	2	85	3
Secondary										
Manufacturing	84.4	6	191.0	19	15.5	5	1.2	5	292.1	11
Construction	16.9	1	56.2	5.5	4.7	2	0.2	1	78	3
Tertiary										
Electricity, water and sanitary services	10.2	1	3.8	—	6.8	2	0.3	1	21.1	—
Transport, storage and communications	49.0	3	45.5	4	19.7	7	0.8	3	115	4
Commerce	69.3	5	192.6	19	31.6	11	1.5	6	295	11
Services	256.1	18	188.5	18	73.9	25	9.5	36	528	19
Total	1 432.4	100	1 026.7	100	297.6	100	26.5	100	2 783.2	100

Source: *Based on Tables 4–4 and 4–5 of the Mid-Term Review of the Second Malaysia Plan, 1971–75.*

Plate 8   Georgetown, Penang, with Swettenham Pier in the foreground (see p. 148).

twenty-three smaller towns (10 000—20 000) had a Malay majority; and
(*c*) all of the eleven towns, except Johore Bahru, with a Malay majority
are distributed in the northeast in Kelantan and Trengganu (Fig. 6.4).
Elsewhere, even in areas that were predominantly Malay, the Malay
proportion of the urban population was less than half. The contrast is
striking in some cases: the Malays formed 97 to 99 per cent of the
population of four towns—Manir, Kuala Trengganu Central, Pangkal
Kalong and Peringat—and only 1 per cent of the population in three
other towns—Serdang Bahru, Ampang, and Jinjang (Tables 6.12 and
6.13).

The Chinese

The main reason for Chinese immigration to Peninsular Malaysia was the
desire to better their economic status. Accordingly from the start they have
not concerned themselves with subsistence agriculture, which was the basis
of their livelihood in China, but have been involved in the occupations
which brought in monetary rewards—initially with tin-mining, trade and
commerce, and later with cash-crop agriculture, and with occupations in
the secondary and tertiary sectors of the new economy.

There is a close correlation between the occupational structure of the

163

Table 6.12   The racial composition of the major towns* of Peninsular Malaysia, 1970

Name of town	Population	Malays	Chinese	Indians	Others
		Racial Composition (per cent)			
1. Kuala Lumpur	452 000	25	55	19	1
2. Georgetown	269 000	14	72	13	1
3. Ipoh	248 000	13	72	14	1
4. Johore Bahru	136 000	50	39	8	3
5. Klang	114 000	21	58	20	1
6. Petaling Jaya	93 000	20	63	14	3
7. Malacca	87 000	15	75	7	3
8. Seremban	81 000	21	59	19	1
9. Alor Star	66 000	40	48	11	1
10. Muar	61 000	37	59	4	—
11. Butterworth	61 000	24	59	16	1
12. Kota Bharu	55 000	68	29	2	1
13. Taiping	55 000	23	58	18	1
14. Kuala Trengganu	53 000	82	16	2	—
15. Batu Pahat	53 000	30	66	4	—
16. Telok Anson	45 000	23	59	18	—
17. Kuantan	43 000	41	49	9	1
18. Kluang	43 000	28	62	10	—
19. Sungei Petani	36 000	28	55	17	—
20. Jinjang	27 000	1	98	1	—
21. Bukit Mertajam	27 000	10	88	12	—
22. Kampar	27 000	9	78	13	—
23. Ayer Hitam	26 000	10	80	10	—
24. Bentong	23 000	15	78	7	—
25. Kajang	22 000	19	67	14	—
26. Sungei Siput North	21 000	10	70	20	—

* 'Major towns' are here defined as those with a population of over 20 000.

Chinese and their distribution. Of the 1 026 700 Chinese in employment in 1970, 34.5 per cent were in the primary sector (agriculture, forestry, fisheries, mining and quarrying), 24.5 per cent in the secondary sector (manufacturing and construction), and the rest in the tertiary sector (Table 6.11). The percentage of gainfully employed Chinese in the secondary and tertiary sectors has therefore increased from 53 to 65.5 between 1957 (census year) and 1970. The employment pattern is a direct reversal of that of the Malays, who in 1970 had 34 per cent in the secondary and tertiary sectors and 66 per cent in the primary sector. The Chinese provided 66 per cent of the Peninsular Malaysian labour force

Table 6.13   The racial composition of the smaller towns* of Peninsular Malaysia, 1970

Name of town	Population	Racial composition (per cent)			
		Malays	Chinese	Indians	Others
1. Kulim	18 000	25	62	13	—
2. Raub	18 000	16	72	12	—
3. Segamat	18 000	18	73	9	—
4. Dungun	18 000	87	12	1	—
5. Kuala Kangsar	15 000	29	47	24	—
6. Manir	15 000	99	1	—	—
7. Pangkal Kalong	14 000	97	3	—	—
8. Bukit Bharu	14 000	32	56	10	2
9. Serdang Bahru	14 000	1	99	—	—
10. Chukai	12 000	76	23	1	—
11. Kuala Pilah	12 000	29	57	14	—
12. Tangkak	12 000	13	81	6	—
13. Tanjong To'kong	12 000	33	49	7	11
14. Kulai	12 000	11	85	4	—
15. Peringat	12 000	97	2	—	1
16. Kuala Trengganu Central	12 000	99	1	—	—
17. Mentakab	11 000	21	67	12	—
18. Pasir Mas	11 000	88	11	1	—
19. Ampang	11 000	1	97	2	—
20. Pokok Asam	11 000	10	76	14	—
21. Batu Gajah	11 000	30	49	21	—
22. Tumpat	11 000	88	9	2	1
23. Port Dickson	10 000	22	47	30	1

* 'Smaller towns' are here defined as those with a population of between 10 000 and 20 000.

employed in the secondary industries—in the manufacture of a variety of goods, mainly food and beverages, metal, wood and cork products, furniture and fixtures, machinery and transport equipment, textiles, clothing and chemical products, and in building and construction. The Chinese, too, dominated the commercial sector, providing 65 per cent of the total Peninsular Malaysian labour force engaged in commerce. In Peninsular Malaysia both secondary production and tertiary activities take place largely in industrial estates and urban centres. The urban character of the Chinese population is therefore a reflection of the high proportion of the economically active Chinese engaged in these two sectors. As Tables 6.12 and 6.13 show, thirty-eight of the forty-nine towns in Peninsular

Plate 9   An aerial view of Kuala Lumpur, the Federal capital. The urban conurbation of Kuala Lumpur–Petaling Jaya is growing more rapidly than other urban conurbations in the country. This rapid growth has given rise to problems of traffic congestion and housing shortage (see p. 147).

Malaysia had a Chinese majority, ranging from 47 per cent to 99 per cent of the total population of individual towns.

The other 34.5 per cent of the gainfully employed Chinese were engaged in primary production. Here again the occupational structure of the Chinese differs from that of the Malays, which in turn results in a different distributional pattern of population. Whereas one-third of the Malays engaged in primary production were padi growers, only 2.5 per cent of the Chinese in this sector of the economy cultivated padi. This disinterest on the part of the Chinese in padi planting is simply due to the fact that it is the most unremunerative of all agricultural occupations. Their interests are directed to growing the better-paying crops, especially rubber. Thus half of the Chinese in primary production were employed in the rubber industry, and nearly one-fifth in mixed agriculture, mainly market-gardening. A further one-tenth were employed in mining, mainly in the tin-mining industry. Most of the rubber areas, nearly all the tin-fields and the Chinese market-gardens are located along the western belt of high population densities. It is along here, too, that most of the rural Chinese are found.

The distribution pattern of the rural Chinese was altered during the

Emergency as a result of the resettlement campaign when some 450 000 Chinese squatters—market-gardeners, rubber smallholders and shop-keepers in the rural areas—were resettled in New Villages. The 'squatter problem' had its origin during the Great Depression of the 1930s when many of the unemployed Chinese turned to growing food, cultivating their plots on the fringes of estates, mining areas, on government and state land, on Malay reservations and forest reserves. None of them had a title to the land they occupied. There was a return flow of these squatters to the towns when trade revived. But a further, and greater, exodus from the towns, mines, estates and other places of employment took place during the Japanese occupation of 1942—45, when thousands of Chinese 'returned to the land' to grow their own food, or to escape from Japanese surveillance, or both. Many of them remained on their farms even after the war was over. These squatters, as well as the Chinese rubber smallholders, were a source of help to the Communist guerillas during the Emergency. Part of the Government campaign against the guerillas included the elimination of this source of help to the Communist war effort. The rural Chinese, as well as some Indians and Malays, were therefore resettled in New Villages located along main roads for easy access to reinforcements in case of attack, and fenced-in for added protection. In all, 580 000 rural dwellers were resettled in 536 New

Plate 10   An aerial view of Petaling Jaya, a satellite residential cum industrial town located southwest of Kuala Lumpur and adjacent to it (see p. 145).

Villages distributed largely along the western belt. The once dispersed Chinese rural population were withdrawn into these planned villages, most of which still remain today. The result of resettlement has been to produce a nucleated Chinese rural population pattern instead of the previously dispersed one (Fig. 6.7). The overall distribution of the rural Chinese, however, remains substantially the same, that is, within the western belt.

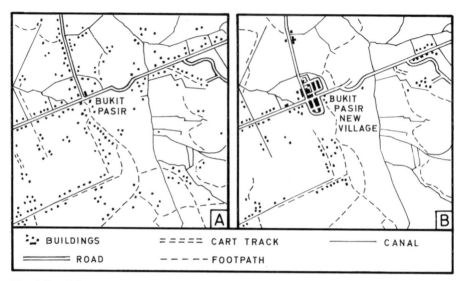

Fig. 6.7   Chinese rural settlement pattern in a rubber growing area, Muar, Johore: (A) before resettlement, and (B) after resettlement.

Table 6.14 shows the present-day distribution of the Chinese population on a state basis. The Chinese constitute the majority in only one state—Penang and Province Wellesley—but in five other states, all in western Peninsular Malaysia, they make up between 38 and 46 per cent of the total state population. The concentration of the Chinese in the more developed western states is evident. In contrast, the proportions of Chinese in the north-western states of Kedah and Perlis and the north-eastern states of Kelantan and Trengganu are small, a reflection of the disinterest of the Chinese in padi cultivation, the main economic occupation in these areas. Pahang occupies an intermediate position, with the Chinese comprising nearly one-third of the state population, and engaged mainly in rubber cultivation, mining, trade and retail shopkeeping.

Table 6.14 also reveals that the percentage of Chinese to other races in all the states as well as in Peninsular Malaysia decreased in the 1957—70 inter-censal period, although the absolute numbers of Chinese increased during this period. The greatest relative decline was in Pahang where the percentage of Chinese decreased from 35 in 1957 to 31 in 1970. This

Table 6.14 Distribution of the Chinese population, by states, 1970

State	Number of Chinese	Per cent of total population
Penang and Province Wellesley	435 000	56 (57)*
Selangor	754 000	46 (48)
Perak	666 000	42.5 (44)
Malacca	160 000	40 (42)
Johore	503 000	39 (42)
Negri Sembilan	184 000	38 (41)
Pahang	158 000	31 (35)
Kedah	184 000	19 (20.5)
Perlis	19 000	16 (17)
Trengganu	22 000	5 (7)
Kelantan	37 000	5 (6)
Peninsular Malaysia	3 122 000	35 (37)

* Figures in parentheses are for 1957.

was probably due not only to the relatively lower rate of natural increase of the Chinese, but also to the influx of Malay settlers to the land settlement schemes established by FELDA (Fig. 6.5).

Figure 6.8 illustrates the density of the Chinese population on a district basis. The extreme localization of the Chinese in the western belt of high densities is evident. Except for the districts of Kota Bharu and Tumpat in Kelantan and three districts in western Pahang, the rest of Peninsular Malaysia have densities of less than 25 Chinese per square mile (less than 10 per sq km). Within the western belt are four main areas of concentration where densities are over 300 per square mile (120+ per sq km). These are (*a*) all of the state of Penang and Province Wellesley, which from the early days has been a focal point for Chinese settlement; (*b*) the Kinta Valley with its large Chinese population engaged in tin-mining and, to a lesser extent, rubber cultivation; (*c*) the district of Kuala Lumpur, which forms part of the Klang Valley, with an economy originally based on tin and rubber, but in recent years expanded to include manufacturing and important service functions; and (*d*) central Malacca, mainly Malacca town. Many of the Chinese here are *Peranakan* Chinese, with a history of settlement going back several centuries.

Elsewhere along the western belt densities vary from 25 to 300 persons per square mile (20–120 persons per sq km), with six areas of greater concentration (100–300 persons per square mile (40–120 persons per sq km)): central Kedah; coastal Perak except Lower Perak; Klang; Seremban, Port Dickson and northern Malacca; Muar; and Pontian

169

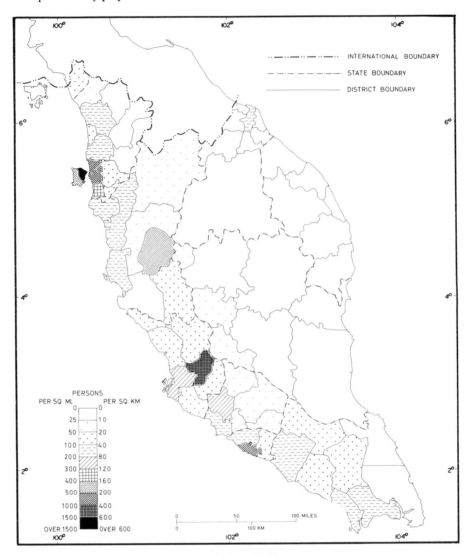

Fig. 6.8   Density of the Chinese population, 1970.

and Johore Bahru districts. The rural Chinese are not dispersed widely over the area of the western belt, but are localized in small nucleations in the rubber and tin-mining districts, in fishing villages along the coast, in a large number of townships and villages with a population of less than 10 000, including New Villages strung out along the main roads.

As noted earlier, the Chinese form the majority of the urban population of Peninsular Malaysia. In 1970, 58 per cent of the total urban population were Chinese (Table 6.15). Although the total urban population of Peninsular Malaysia increased by 52 per cent between 1957 and

Table 6.15   Composition of the urban population, Peninsular Malaysia, 1970

Race	Urban population	Per cent
Chinese	1 479 000	58
Malays	699 000	28
Indians	324 000	13
Others	28 000	1
Total	2 530 000	100

1970, and the total number of Chinese urban dwellers increased from 1 043 000 to 1 479 000 (+41%) during this period, the relative position of the Chinese in the total urban community declined: in 1970 the Chinese made up 58 per cent of the total urban population, as compared with 63 per cent in 1957. The concentration of the Chinese in the three major cities of Peninsular Malaysia—Kuala Lumpur, Georgetown and Ipoh—is very striking: altogether 41 per cent of the urban Chinese and 19 per cent of all the Chinese in Peninsular Malaysia lived in these towns in 1970.

The Indians

The distribution pattern of the Indian population is similar to that of the Chinese in that the Indians are concentrated in the towns and more developed parts of the western belt. The expansion of Indian settlement in Peninsular Malaysia was closely linked with the rise of the plantation economy based largely on rubber. Later groups of Indians settled in the towns and smaller villages as shopkeepers, and as wage-earners in transport and in the urban services. The distribution of the Indians today is, as in the case of the other racial groups, closely related to the nature of their economic activities.

Of the 297 600 gainfully employed Indians in 1970, 48 per cent were engaged in the primary sector, mainly as estate workers in the rubber, oil-palm, coconut and tea plantations (Table 6.11). Their high degree of specialization in this occupation is attested by the fact that they made up nearly half of all the estate workers in the country. Their domination of this occupation is a reflection of the historical circumstances surrounding the establishment and growth of the plantation industries of Peninsular Malaysia, when most of the plantation workers were recruited from South India. Their interest has not widened to include the other types of primary production activities, and up to 1970 less than 2 per cent of the Indians employed were engaged in smallholder agriculture and fishing, and 2 per cent in mining and quarrying.

The secondary sector has also been traditionally of limited interest to the Indians of Peninsular Malaysia, and only 7 per cent of the gainfully employed Indians were engaged in this sector. The remainder (45%) of the employed Indians were in the tertiary sector, mainly in retail trade (as shopkeepers and merchants), in transport, and in the governmental, personal and public utilities services.

The concentration of Indians along the western belt is particularly striking (Fig. 6.9). The highest densities are in the Klang Valley, associated since the early days of development with the cultivation of rubber

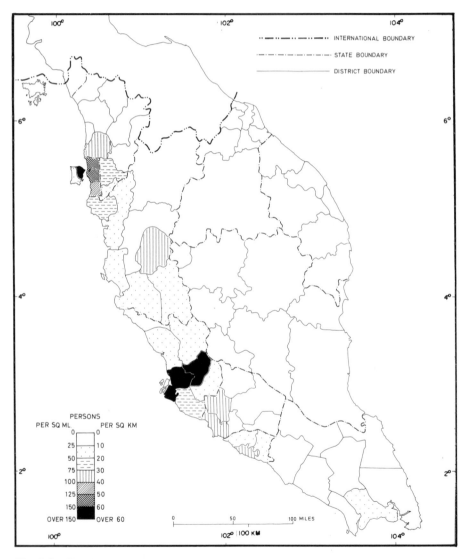

Fig. 6.9   Density of the Indian population, 1970.

under the plantation system. The other area of high densities is in the northwest, namely, the Penang–Province Wellesley–south Kedah area. It was here that the original streams of Indian immigrants entered Peninsular Malaysia and spread along the other parts of the western belt as the country was opened up for rubber cultivation. An average of 20 000 Tamils arrived at Penang annually between 1890 and 1904 to work in the newly established plantations on the mainland–in Province Wellesley, the Kinta Valley and the Klang Valley. These three areas have remained areas of Indian concentration.

About two-thirds of the total Indian population in Peninsular Malaysia are rural. The distribution of the rural Indians is closely correlated with the distribution of the main rubber, oil-palm, coconut and tea plantations of the western belt, with heaviest concentrations in the three areas noted above. Other areas where the rural Indians are found in significant numbers are the coastal strip running from Kuala Langat to central Malacca, and the plantation areas of central Johore, although in the latter case their numbers are small in relation to the land area so that average densities remain low. The postwar phase of estate fragmentation in Peninsular Malaysia, though now controlled, has nevertheless caused the dispersion of many thousands of Indian estate workers to other parts of the country.

Only some 12 000 Indians were moved into New Villages during the resettlement campaign. The majority of the rural Indians were in estates, and instead of being resettled in New Villages at governmental expense, were regrouped at the expense of the estate owners. Regrouping in each estate involved transferring the labourers' settlements to the protection of a defended point within the estate. Apart from the labourers' quarters, the defended area included the plantation offices, factory, smokehouse, engine rooms, etc., as well as the manager's house. Unlike the resettling of Chinese squatters, regrouping of Indian labourers did not result in any significant change in the distributional pattern of the rural Indian population.

Slightly more than one-third of the total Indian population lived in urban centres in 1970. Urbanization amongst the Indians increased significantly in the postwar period: in 1947, 26 per cent of the Indians lived in towns of 10 000 and over; in 1957 this percentage increased to 31, and in 1970 to 35. A further indication of the rate of urbanization among the Indians is the increase in the number of towns with more than 5 000 Indians–from eight in 1947, to eleven in 1957, to thirteen in 1970. The Indians have traditionally occupied an intermediate position between the highly urbanized Chinese and the essentially rural Malays in the proportion of people living in towns.

Most of the 323 000 urban Indians live in the larger towns. In 1970, 92 per cent of the urban Indians lived in towns of more than 20 000 inhabitants, 69 per cent in towns of more than 75 000 inhabitants (metropolitan towns) and 48 per cent in the three largest towns of Kuala Lumpur, Georgetown and Ipoh. The Indians are numerically the smallest of the three main racial groups in Peninsular Malaysia, and only in Klang do they constitute one-fifth of the total urban population; in the seven other metropolitan towns they make up between 7 and 18 per cent of the total urban population. An indication of the trend towards greater urbanization among the Indians is the fact that the number of towns with an Indian population of 10 000 increased from four in 1957 to seven in 1970, with two more (Butterworth and Taiping) just short of the 10 000 mark.

7
Settlement patterns

The history of Malay settlement in the Peninsula and the other parts of the Malay Archipelago goes back many centuries, and while the forms and patterns of their settlements may vary in detail due to differences in local environmental conditions, their broad outlines remain basically similar. Thus the *kampongs* of the Malays in Peninsular Malaysia and the Indonesians in their island world are similar in appearance and pattern, bearing the imprint of a people coming from the same racial stock with much the same cultural background, and living under tropical conditions. In Peninsular Malaysia the settlements that are distinctively Malay have been little modified by the coming of the immigrant peoples during the last century or so. This is to a large degree due to the fact that the immigrants are racially and culturally different from the Malays. They have not been assimilated into the Malay groups, but have remained separate from them, and have also settled in locations removed from the traditional areas of Malay settlement.

The settlements of the immigrant peoples, with their different cultural background, are distinct from those of the Malays. The most distinctive of these are the towns which have sprung up as a result of the economic activities of the immigrants. In the rural areas the Europeans, Chinese and Indians have also established new settlement forms in association with their agricultural and mining activities. In recent years another settlement form has been imposed on the Malaysian landscape—that of the New Villages. The New Villages are an expression of a political and military decision, and the fact that they are generally associated with rural Chinese population is because most of the people resettled happened to be Chinese and not because this settlement pattern is peculiarly Chinese. Since many of the New Villages were built in settings which are unfavourable both physically and from the economic point of view, some settlements have disappeared from the landscape with the ending of the Emergency. On the other hand, many others established in suburban fringes and within the boundaries of existing towns and villages have become permanent features of the landscape.

Malay settlements

The Malays are characteristically a rural people, and Malay settlements predominate in the rural areas of Peninsular Malaysia. The unit of Malay settlements is the village or *kampong*, composed of a number of houses commonly strung along the sides of roads, footpaths, rivers, canals and along beaches. There are no administrative boundaries between *kampongs*, and demarcation is usually based on convention. The houses are usually set well apart from one another, and there is little tendency for Malay *kampongs* to assume a compact form, except in the case of fishing villages occupying sites of limited extent, in which case the houses may be set close together and sometimes one behind the other along a short coastal front. Each individual house in an agricultural *kampong* is set in the midst of a collection of miscellaneous tree and ground crops. The house itself is raised on stilts with a floor and walls of wood, and a roof of atap (a thatch weaved from the leaves of the nipah palm). Since the original foci of Malay settlements were semi-wet locations along coast and river suitable for padi cultivation and fishing, raising the houses on stilts would provide protection against floods. However, Malay houses are also built on stilts even in locations where floods do not occur. There are other advantages in building a house above the ground apart from that of flood protection. In a hot, humid environment stilts help to keep the house free from damp by allowing air to circulate underneath the floor. They also provide protection against wild animals and snakes, especially in newly cleared areas adjacent to the jungle.

Within these general considerations Malay settlements exhibit different forms and patterns due to variations in local physical conditions and differences in the nature, and hence the locale, of economic activities. In general four main Malay settlement types can be easily recognized in the Malaysian landscape: (*a*) fishing villages, (*b*) padi settlements, (*c*) settlements in a cash-cropping area, and (*d*) settlements in a mixed cultivation area.

Fishing villages

Fishing has always been an integral part of the Malay economy, and Malay fishing settlements are found at irregular intervals along both the eastern and western coasts of the Peninsula. The forms which these villages take depend largely on the morphology of the coast. Along the east coast where the beaches are sandy and may stretch uninterruptedly for miles, fishing villages are generally linear in pattern, with the first row of houses only a few yards above the high water mark. In many cases the landward side of the villages for several miles inland is composed of a series of old beach ridges (*permatang*) interspersed with freshwater

Plate 11   A fishing village in Pulau Pangkor, an island off Lumut. The village specializes in *kembong* fishing. Beyond the ridge is the well-known sea resort of Pangkor.

swamps. The villagers may grow some padi in the depressions between the old beach ridges, but on dry land the soil is too sandy for any economic crop other than coconut (Fig. 7.1). The houses of the fishing *kampong* are built in the shade of coconut and casuarina trees. In some cases the individual fisherman may erect a thatch windbreak in front of his house to break the force of the northeast monsoon. Some fishing settlements are located on the southern landward side of northwest— southeast trending ridges so as to obtain natural shelter from the monsoon.

Along western Peninsular Malaysia the coast is usually muddy and mangrove-covered so that suitable sites for settlement are difficult to find. In such circumstances the village may be located on the landward side of the mangrove fringe. Most of the Chinese fishermen are found along this western stretch of coast, and their settlements duplicate in pattern, if not in detail, those of the Malays. Because of the muddy conditions, the Chinese houses are built on stilts, a method of construction not otherwise employed by the Chinese in other parts of the Peninsula. Figure 7.2 shows two typical Chinese fishing villages on the southwest coast of Johore. Each consists of a collection of stilted houses built over the mud flats on the seaward side of the mangroves. Each

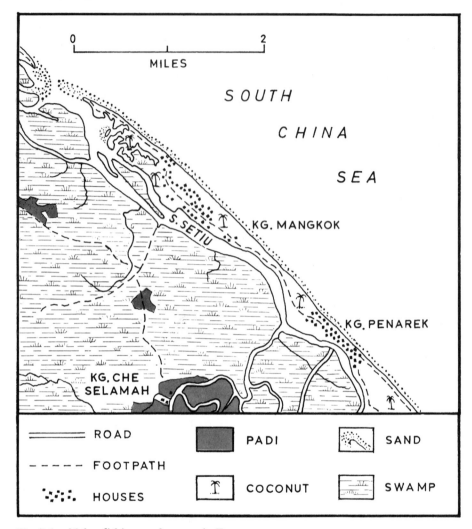

Fig. 7.1   Malay fishing settlements in Trengganu.

house is connected to the neighbouring houses by plank walks. Kukup village is linked to the main road by such a plank walk, but Kangkar Ayer Masin is completely isolated from the land during high tides. Inland from the villages and within the mangrove fringe itself, the villagers have carved out prawn ponds, a method of land-use rarely found in Peninsular Malaysia.

Padi settlements

In the past British colonial policy aimed at making padi lands and padi cultivation a preserve of the Malays. There are a few thousand Chinese

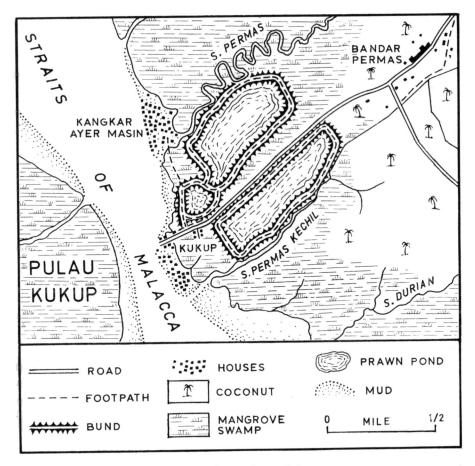

Fig. 7.2 Chinese fishing settlements in southwest Johore.

and Indian padi farmers in Peninsular Malaysia today, but cultivation of the crop is still very much a Malay interest. Padi growing is not only an economic activity, but is also a way of life to the rural Malays. The settlements in most padi areas are typically Malay, and their patterns have not changed over the years except in the new colonization areas where the patterns are determined by the original layout of the lots. In such areas the houses are usually arranged in single rows following the lines of the drainage and irrigation canals, so that the overall pattern is a geometrical one.

Houses in the flat swampy terrain associated with padi growing are built on sites which stand above the general level of the ground. The distribution of the houses is therefore determined by the distribution of available high ground. The lower slopes of hills, the tops of levees and *permatang*, the built-up sides of metalled roads and canals and even small mounds of land standing a few feet above the level of the surrounding

179

Plate 12 Malay settlements at Kaki Bukit, Perlis, with young padi in the foreground, backed by *kampong* land (see p. 179).

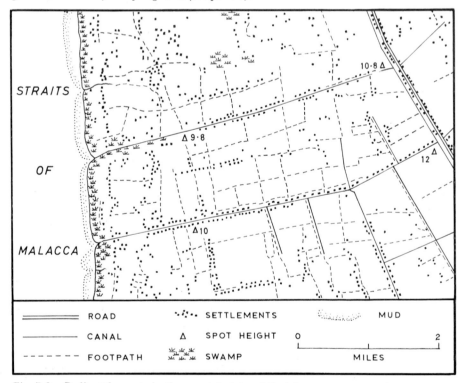

Fig. 7.3 Padi settlements in the coastal plain of Kedah.

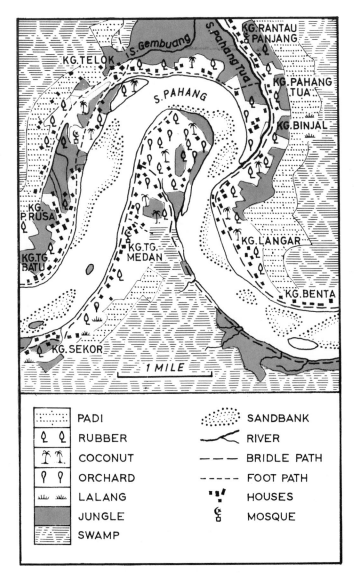

Fig. 7.4   Levee settlements along the Pahang River.

fields offer the best house sites. Such features on the landscape, both natural and cultural, tend to be long and narrow, with the result that most padi settlements assume linear patterns (Figs 7.3 and 7.4).

Settlements in a cash-cropping area

In the pre-colonial days when Malay farmers cultivated those crops that he could eat and not those that he could sell, the typical Malay farm was

181

made up of a few acres of padi and a small plot of kampong land in which some spices, vegetables, coconut and fruit trees grew. The farm was usually set in a riverine coastal area where the best padi lands are found. Today, however, many coastal riverine areas, especially in southern Peninsular Malaysia, are not under padi but under tree crops which are grown for the market and not for consumption. These areas may be settled by Malays working in smallholdings or may be parcelled out in large lots and worked as estates. Such low-lying land is more naturally suited to wet padi than to tree crops, but rubber and to a lesser extent oil-palm and coconut have become such lucrative crops to grow that the Malays, notably those who have migrated from Indonesia, preferred to put their land under these rather than under padi. In order to render it firm enough to support the heavy rubber, oil-palm and coconut trees, the land has to be drained by an efficient system of canals. In such Malay smallholdings the houses are again built alongside the canals, roads and footpaths, so that the patterns of settlements are similar to those in a padi area (Figs 7.5 and 7.6). The only difference in the landscape comes from the nature of the crops grown. In a padi area the general aspect is more open than in a cash-cropping area.

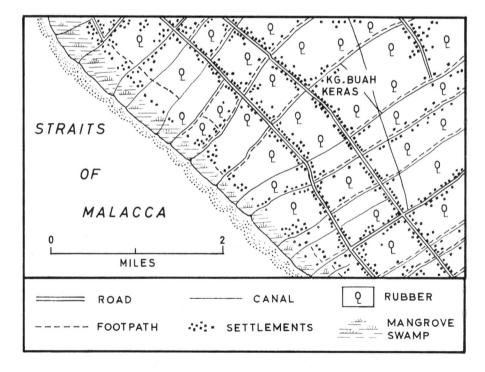

Fig. 7.5 Malay settlements in a rubber growing area.

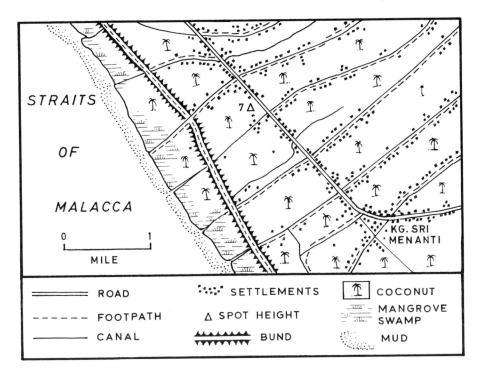

Fig. 7.6   Malay settlements in a coconut growing area.

Settlements in a mixed-cultivation area

An entirely subsistence economy does not exist today among the Malays, who even in the most remote jungle areas participate to some extent in the monetary economy by selling jungle produce and purchasing food, tobacco and other commodities. The introduction of the monetary economy during the colonial era has led to different degrees of specialization of production for the market. There are Malay peasants who specialize in fishing, in padi cultivation and in cash-crop cultivation. On the other end of the scale, there are those who do a little bit of each, and these peasants can be considered to have an economy nearest in characteristics to the subsistence economy. In the small interior valleys of Negri Sembilan, Malacca and other parts of interior Peninsular Malaysia, are settlements associated with the cultivation of padi for home consumption and the cultivation of rubber and coconuts for the market. The settlement patterns in these valleys are distinctive, consisting of a linear arrangement of houses on one or both sides of the break of slope of the valleys, with padi occupying the flat bottom land, and rubber and/or coconut on the well-drained slopes (Fig. 7.7).

183

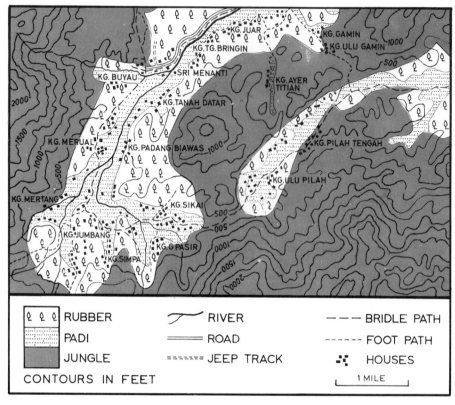

Fig. 7.7   Malay settlements in a mixed cultivation area.

Settlements of immigrant peoples

Mining settlements

The first immigrants to enter the country in large numbers were Chinese tin miners. The earliest immigrant settlements in the Malay States were the mining camps which sprang up along the western tin belt. Most of these disappeared from the landscape when the ore in their vicinity was exhausted or when water flooded the mines and prevented further excavation, but other mining camps grew into villages and a few expanded into permanent towns. The alluvial nature of ore occurrence and methods of mining has given rise to a distinctive form of landscape characterized by stretches of upturned, worked-out ground and mining pools. Because mines are constantly shifting to new locations as the old sites are worked out, mining settlements are usually ephemeral features of the landscape, consisting of a number of temporary buildings and shacks housing the labourers and other mining personnel, all grouped close to the mines. All the Chinese mines employ Chinese labour. The

184

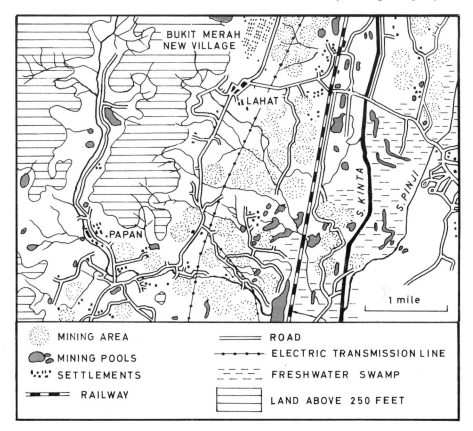

Fig. 7.8   Mining settlements in the Kinta Valley.

European mines may employ labourers from all or any of the main racial groups. The resettlement campaign has changed the patterns of settlements associated with mining. Previous to the campaign mining settlements consisted of a loose agglomeration of huts spread over the mining area. The regrouping and resettlement of mining labourers have altered the dispersed patterns of settlements into tightly nucleated ones, with the workers enclosed either in a small central site near the mines or in New Villages which may be some distance away from the mines (Fig. 7.8).

Estate settlements

Most of the estates in Peninsular Malaysia are rubber and oil-palm estates. A few grow coconut, pineapple and tea. The estate or plantation is an introduced method of growing cash crops in large holdings with a paid labour force. Estates are easily recognized features of the landscape. The boundaries of an estate are well-marked and usually straight, the crops

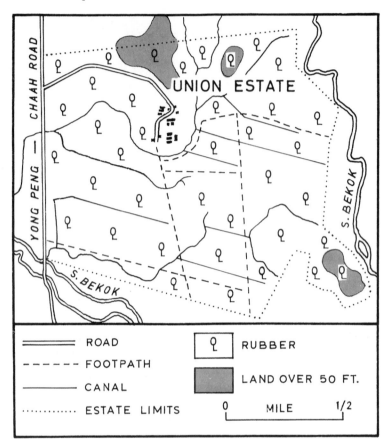

Fig. 7.9   Estate settlements.

are planted in neat, straight rows, with a low undergrowth of cover crops. A system of internal transport lines, usually laterite roads but occasionally light tramways, divides the estate up into a number of rectangular blocks. Occupying a central position in the estate and con-nected to the main road or railway are the labourers' quarters, the processing factory, the smoke house, the store house and the manager's house (Fig. 7.9). The original pattern of settlement was a nucleated one, and the regrouping and resettlement campaign has not altered it, except through the addition of a boundary of barbed wire enclosing the build-ings. In some cases the labourers' quarters and the manager's house have had to be brought in closer to the central nucleus of buildings for easier protection.

Although the estate type of settlement is not indigenous to Peninsular Malaysia, a substantial number of Malays live in such settlements today. These Malays form part of the estate labour force.

186

New Villages

The resettlement of Chinese squatters and other rural dwellers has resulted in the formation of a new settlement type, the New Village. The purpose of resettlement was military, and both the location and pattern of the New Villages reflected this purpose. They were located on easily defended sites by the side of main roads, and in some instances within municipal boundaries. As a further defensive measure, they were surrounded by barbed-wire fences. Watch-towers and flood-lights brought the general appearance of the Villages nearer to that of forts than their names would imply. The usual layout of the houses was in regular grid-like patterns (Fig. 7.10).

The necessity for speed, and the primary consideration for security, resulted in some of the Villages being badly sited from the point of view of the resettled population's economic requirements. Some farmers found themselves so far removed from their farms that they had to abandon them. Early during the resettlement operations an open type of New Village was experimented with, whereby each farming family lived on its own plot of land with the entire area surrounded by barbed wire. Such an arrangement was popular with the Chinese who could then work on their own land even after curfew hours. However, from the security

Plate 13   A New Village in the Gombak Valley of Pahang photographed in 1973. The Village has undergone considerable change since it was established in the 1950s. With the official ending of the state of Emergency in 1960 there has been some dispersion of the settlements (see p. 188).

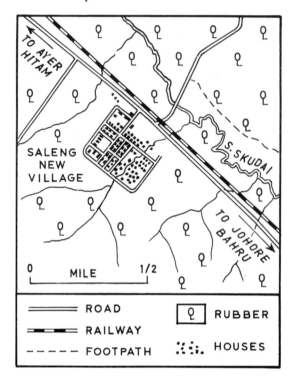

Fig. 7.10   Saleng New Village.

angle the extended perimeter was a handicap as it was difficult to patrol and prevent contact between squatter and terrorist. It was therefore decided to abandon this type of layout. In all agricultural New Villages subsequently established the farms were physically divorced from the Villages. The farmer was obliged to walk a mile or more to his plot of land, and he was not able to work on it after curfew hours. At the same time he was compelled to divide his farming operations into two parts: those connected with crop cultivation which was carried out on the farm itself, and those connected with pig-rearing which had to be performed in, or near, his house. He then had to transport the pig fodder from his farm, and the pig manure to the farm every day, an inefficient and slow operation. Considerable damage too was done to the crops by pests at night. Some New Villages which did not have a firm economic base have been abandoned with the ending of the Emergency. In the past most of the new villagers held land under temporary occupation licences. In 1972 the state governments of Peninsular Malaysia agreed to grant sixty-year leases to those who applied for them, thereby providing them with a degree of security formerly absent.

Urban settlements

In pre-industrial and pre-colonial times there were a number of settlements in the Malay Peninsula which were the seats of power of the Malay sultanates. Most of these were small agglomerations but a few which were located at vantage points controlling trade and agriculture grew in size to the point where it is justifiable to describe them as 'towns'. The most notable of these was Malacca, established in the fourteenth century on a strategic site commanding the sea-borne trade along the Straits of Malacca. At the time of its capture by the Portuguese at the beginning of the sixteenth century Malacca was a busy cosmopolitan port with a population of several thousand. Other smaller nucleated settlements which were established in the pre-British period were Kota Bharu, Kuala Trengganu, Kuala Dungun, Pekan, Johore Lama, Bandar Maharani, Klang, Kuala Selangor, Penang and Kota Star (Hamzah Sendut, 1962).

However, most of the present-day towns have come into existence as a result of the rapid development that took place in the late nineteenth and early twentieth centuries following the establishment of British rule in Peninsular Malaysia. These towns are the creation of the immigrant population, and their immigrant character is reflected in the location, functions, morphology and especially in the racial composition of the urban population. As noted earlier, most of the towns are distributed along the western belt of high population densities. Along this belt are found the main tin fields and the greater part of the rubber, coconut and oil-palm areas of Peninsular Malaysia. Many of the towns such as Ipoh, the other towns of the Kinta Valley, Taiping, Kuala Lumpur and Seremban originated as mining villages. Others such as Georgetown, Butterworth, Port Swettenham and Malacca developed into important towns because their sites were suitable for the discharge of port functions. A large number of towns are sited at river mouths, a reflection of the early importance of river transport in the Peninsula (Figs 7.11 and 7.12).

Although site conditions are important, a settlement can only grow into a town if it is favourably situated in relation to its surroundings. For example, a site which has all the requirements for a good port cannot by itself create a port unless its situation allows relations with a hinterland. All the major towns, with the exceptions of Kota Bharu, Kuala Trengganu, Kuantan and Bentong are distributed along the western belt of greatest economic activities (Table 6.11). Their situations in relation to their surroundings are such that they are the nodal points of the traffic that passes along the belt. Georgetown, for example, has developed to its present size and importance because of its situation in respect to its rich hinterland which includes the northern half of Perak, Penang and Province Wellesley and most of Kedah. Similarly the material bases which govern the growth of Kota Bharu and Kuala Trengganu are external, namely, the resources of the Kelantan and Trengganu deltas respectively.

No two towns have sites or situations that are exactly similar, but all the towns of Peninsular Malaysia, with the exceptions of the few New

189

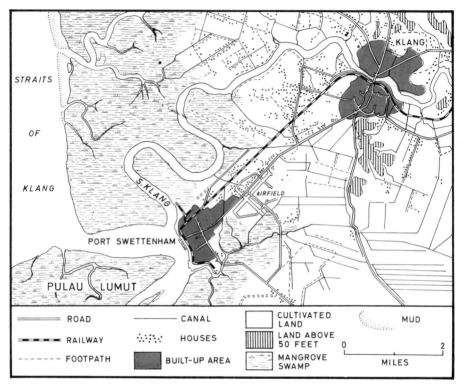

Fig. 7.11   The sites of Port Swettenham (now Port Klang) and Klang.

Villages that fall within the urban category, have basically similar functions. They act as collecting, processing and distributing centres of the tin, rubber, copra, palm-oil and other mineral and agricultural products of the country, and as distributing centres of the food, machinery and other consumer goods imported from overseas. In addition they may also have administrative functions as district or state capitals, and in the case of Kuala Lumpur also as the Federal capital. Kuala Lumpur and some of the larger towns have a manufacturing function of growing importance. The towns are also service centres for the maintenance and repair of transport facilities, and for health, education and entertainment services. The larger towns have shopping centres with a full range of specialized retail services.

Except for the satellite town of Petaling Jaya, the towns of Peninsular Malaysia have grown and have been adapted to perform urban functions without any conscious planning. The unplanned nature of the towns is evident in their layout, which is usually the product of an accumulation of buildings about a pre-urban nucleus (Fig. 7.13). Most towns exhibit similar patterns, each consisting of a kernel of narrow streets lined with shop-

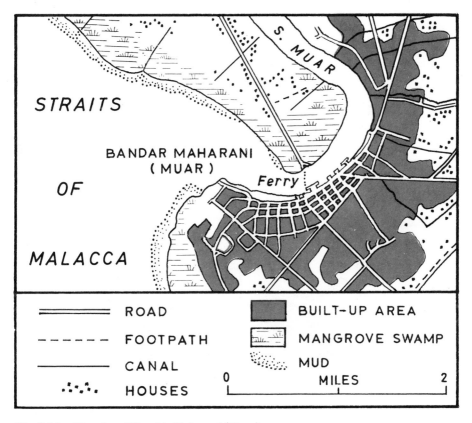

STRAITS

OF

MALACCA

BANDAR MAHARANI
(MUAR)

Ferry

S. MUAR

Fig. 7.12   The site of Bandar Maharani (Muar).

houses and arranged in a simple chequerboard or grid plan and surrounded by irregularly shaped areas with government and residential buildings, and other areas where cultural and recreational activities take place (Fig. 7.14). The roads in this outer zone do not follow any set pattern but are usually winding. The urban core is made up of a series of long blocks of shophouses. The shophouses are of brick and timber and have tiled roofs. They have two storeys, the ground floor being the shop area and the upper floor the dwelling area. Large multi-storey buildings occupied by commercial, insurance and banking concerns are now commonly found within the urban core of the larger towns, in most instances displacing the older shophouses but in some cases built on vacant land where it happened to be available. Around the fringes of the urban core are the government buildings, schools and places of worship, each set in a space by itself. The rapid pace of urbanization in the postwar years has resulted in the outward extension of the boundaries of the urban core in many of the bigger towns, and many of the government

191

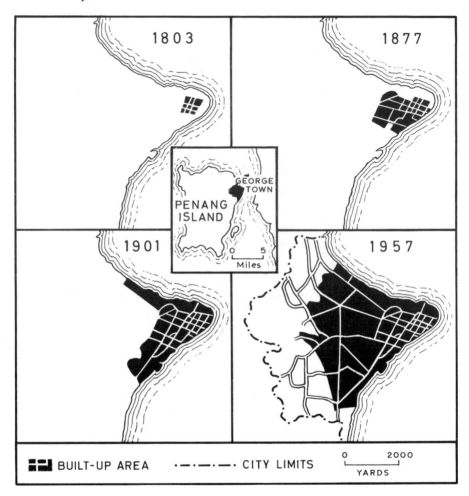

Fig. 7.13   The growth of Georgetown about its pre-urban nucleus.

buildings, schools, temples, mosques and churches are now hemmed in by shops and other commercial establishments. Surrounding the urban core are the main residential areas of the town, the more crowded and smaller houses of the lower-income groups usually being located closer to the town centre while the houses of the wealthier class tend to be on the outskirts. Bus depots are commonly sited within the town centre, but the railway station is usually some distance away.

The non-indigenous character of the towns of Peninsular Malaysia is most evident in the racial composition of the urban population. Except for the towns in the predominantly Malay states of Kelantan and Trengganu, and Johore Bharu, all the other towns have non-indigenous, mainly Chinese, majorities. The long rows of Chinese shophouses are typical urban features, even in towns with a Malay majority. The other

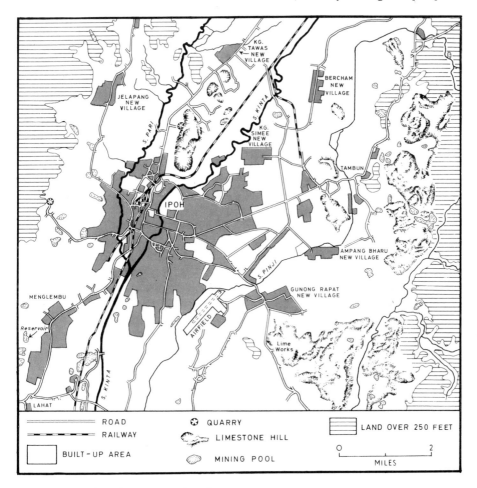

Fig. 7.14   Ipoh: urban core and environs.

racial groups—the Indians, Pakistanis and Europeans—are also town-dwellers. One-third of the Indians in Peninsular Malaysia live in towns, but most of the European population, with the exception of the planters and miners, are concentrated in urban centres, where they are engaged mainly in trade, finance, manufacturing and in the professions.

193

PART THREE

The economy

8

The rudimentary economies of the Orang Asli

The 1970 census returns recorded a total of 52 499 Orang Asli (aborigines) in the Malay Peninsula (Table 8.1). Although there are more than sixty different subgroups most of the Orang Asli belong to one or other of these racial divisions: Negritoes, Senoi and Jakun. The Negritoes constitute 4 per cent of the aboriginal population, the Senoi 82 per cent and the Jakun 14 per cent.

The economies or ways of life of these Orang Asli are varied. A small section of them lived a settled life, following an economy similar to that of the lowland Malays, with permanent settlements, padi fields, domestic animals such as the buffalo, and *kampongs* of fruit and rubber. The rest follow ways of life which are characterized by constant movements from

Table 8.1 Distribution of Orang Asli, by state, 1970

	Negritoes	*Jakun**	*Senoi†*	*Total*
Trengganu	194		9	203
Johore	445	1 283	2 151	3 879
Kedah			123	123
Kelantan	570		4 155	4 725
Negri Sembilan	7	3	2 479	2 489
Pahang	344	5 938	12 049	18 331
Penang and Province				
Wellesley	37	10	36	83
Perak	98	219	16 063	16 380
Perlis	5			5
Selangor	267	139	5 452	5 858
Malacca	2	47	324	373
Peninsular Malaysia	1 969	7 639	42 841	52 449

* Includes the Orang Laut
† Includes the Semai, Semelai, Temiar and other subgroups.

place to place. These wandering Orang Asli can be subdivided into two main classes—the hunters and gatherers and the shifting cultivators.

The hunters and gatherers

Most of the Negritoes are hunters and gatherers practising no agriculture of any sort, except where they have interbred with other agricultural tribes and adopted their habits. They are completely dependent for their subsistence on what they can gather from and hunt in the jungle. The natural produce of any one jungle locality is necessarily limited, so that when this is exhausted the Negrito group will have to migrate to a different locality. For this reason they seldom stay more than a few days in any one place but are more or less continually on the move in search of food. Occasionally, when jungle fruit ripens, they may remain in a particular spot for a longer period in order to gather the fruit harvest. Each community has a tract of jungle which forms its tribal territory, and the wild fruit trees within it belong to its members. Each member may own several fruit trees and one or more Ipoh trees (*Antiaris toxicaria*). The durian is specially prized by the Negritoes.

The limited resources of the jungle cannot support a dense population, so that the Negrito communities are small, consisting of six or seven families totalling perhaps twenty to thirty persons in all. A group may cover 5 or 6 miles daily in search of food, though the rate of movement varies considerably with the luck of the hunters and the availability of food from place to place. Their traditional habitat is the coastal jungle and the swampy terrain that borders the Main Range in upper Perak, Selangor, Kelantan and Trengganu, but their wanderings sometimes lead them south to the forests of Pahang and Johore. With the coming of the lowland Malays and later of immigrant peoples to the Peninsula the Negritoes have gradually been pushed into the interior towards the remote flanks of the central mountain ranges; many small tribes have died out altogether in recent years.

The Negritoes usually hunt with bow and arrows, though some have adopted the blowpipe of the hill Senoi. The arrow tips are poisoned with gum from the Ipoh tree. Rats, squirrels, lizards, birds, monkeys, wild pigs and other small game are hunted, as well as trapped with a variety of snares, pitfalls and noose and spring traps. Birds are caught with birdlime made from *Ficus* sap. The larger and more dangerous animals such as the tiger, the elephant and the *seladang* are normally avoided. Fish may be trapped, speared or poisoned with the juice of the *tuba* root.

On the whole, however, the Negritoes depend largely on vegetable food rather than on meat. Leaves, shoots, berries, nuts, fruit as well as roots and tubers, are gathered by the women and children while the men are out hunting. Crude digging sticks, sharpened at one end with a *parang*, are used to dig out yams and tubers as well as bamboo rats from their underground burrows. Women generally prepare the food. Meat is usually roasted, but sometimes eaten raw. Yams and tubers are grated and baked in banana leaves. Rice, when it is available, is cooked in green bamboo, and is considered a luxury. The Negritoes eat nearly everything that is edible, and many other things which are not considered edible by the other races of Peninsular Malaysia. But days of plenty are not common, while there may be periods when they are reduced to a state of semi-starvation.

The simplicity of their way of life is exemplified by the crudeness of their shelters. These are no more than rough lean-to structures consisting of two or three sticks stuck into the ground at an angle and covered with large leaves such as those of the *bertam* palm, or wild banana or wild ginger. Beneath the shelter is a sleeping platform of bamboo. Each shelter houses a family. The Negrito camp consists of as many shelters as there are families and is arranged in a rough oval. Occasionally caves and overhanging rocks are inhabited instead. The whole community generally stays in the same place for a week to ten days once the shelters are put up. When the available food in the area is exhausted the camp is abandoned and a new one constructed at the next halting place. Their wandering existence precludes the building of more elaborate and permanent houses.

The primitive economy of the Negritoes has not changed over the thousands of years since the little men migrated to the Malay Peninsula. Such a way of life is also followed by Negritoes in other parts of Asia—in the Andaman Islands, in New Guinea, in the Philippines and in Indonesia. In Peninsular Malaysia the growing pressure of other races on the lowlands has resulted in a gradual displacement of the Negritoes into the interior and the highlands. This has brought them into contact with other aboriginal groups such as the Ple-Temiar, Temiar, Semak, Sisek and Semelai. Evidence of such contact is the adoption of the use of the blowpipe by Negrito groups, the blowpipe being traditionally a Senoi weapon. Again, some Negritoes have also benefited from this contact by taking the initial step to an agricultural life by casually planting tapioca and bananas in clearings and returning to them some months later to gather the harvest. However, the main body of the Negritoes still remains on the same very low level of material advancement as their ancestors of thousands of years ago. The total number of hunters and gatherers today is probably about 2 000. Their hunting and gathering economy has made no material impact on the landscape.

The shifting cultivators

The majority of the aborigines of Peninsular Malaysia practise a form of agriculture usually known as shifting cultivation and locally as *ladang* cultivation. Some of the more enterprising communities living on the

Plate 14   An aboriginal (Senoi) family, part of a community occupying only six huts in a *ladang* at the foot of Bukit Chintamani, near Kuala Lipis, Pahang. Besides maize, the main crops cultivated by these shifting cultivators are hill padi, tapioca, banana and sweet potato.

margins of the jungle may have smallholdings of fruit and rubber in addition to their *ladangs*. A few groups have graduated from shifting agriculture and the aboriginal way of life to sedentary agriculture based on the Malay model (padi growing with *kampongs* of fruit, coconut and other tree and bush crops) and have been absorbed into the Malay population.

Both the Senoi and the Jakun are shifting cultivators. Shifting cultivation is a form of agriculture which has been evolved to meet the limitations imposed by infertile tropical soils. The details of this system vary slightly among the different communities but the main features remain the same. The system depends on the clearing of a forest site, the burning of the felled trees and other vegetation, the planting of food crops on the cleared site and the subsequent abandonment of the *ladang* after two or three harvests, by which time the soil would have become too poor to support good crops. A new *ladang* is made in another part of the jungle and the old *ladang* is left to revert to secondary forest and very gradually recover its lost fertility. The aborigines whose natural habitat is the higher slopes of the mountain ranges of the Peninsula usually plant a new *ladang* several miles away from the abandoned one, and this movement is followed by a shift of their dwellings to the new site. Among the aborigines living on the lower slopes the usual procedure is to plant successive *ladangs* adjacent to one another for several years before moving to a new dwelling site. Such a practice differs from that of the hill aborigines in that each new *ladang* is only a few yards from the abandoned one, and the dwellings remain fixed for some time in the same spot while the *ladangs* are rotated.

The technique of *ladang* cultivation has been closely studied by a number of experts in the field. A site of 20 acres (8 ha) or more is selected on the basis of the appearance of the ground and an initial area of 2 to 3 acres (0.8–1.2 ha) is felled with axes and *parangs*. A fairly steep hillside is usually chosen so that there will be a good updraught when firing takes place. The tallest trees at the highest point are cut down and on falling drag down the smaller trees in their paths. In this way a great deal of extra labour is saved. The timber is left to dry for three to six weeks and is then set on fire. When the ashes have cooled, the crops—maize, tapioca, hill padi, banana, chillies and sugar-cane—are planted. The planting holes are made with pointed digging sticks and a few grains of padi or maize tossed into each hole. Tapioca, banana and sweet potato are planted by cuttings. The work may be done communally or by family groups. House building, however, is always a communal effort, with the men doing the heavy work such as cutting the poles, while the women make the thatch for the roofs.

After the houses have been built the main *ladang* is cleared by communal effort and the timber burnt when dry. The burning must be carefully controlled in order that the houses are not set alight or the existing crops destroyed. Planting takes place as soon as the *ladang* has cooled. No further attention is paid to the *ladang* once the crops are in; occasionally the larger weeds are pulled out, but apart from this no serious attempts are made to protect the crops from the depredations of the numerous pests such as elephants, deer, wild boars, rats and birds. A large part of the padi crop may be lost through bird raids.

The 1966 land-use survey of Peninsular Malaysia showed that a total of 19 500 acres (7 900 ha) of land was under shifting cultivation, comprising only 0.1 per cent of the total land area of the country. Most of the land under shifting cultivation was in Pahang (44%), in the districts of Pekan and Lipis; in Perak (31%), in the districts of Ulu Perak, Batang Padang and Kinta; and in Kelantan (18%), in the remote district of Ulu Kelantan.

Table 8.2 illustrates the annual cycle of work and the sources of food of a typical aboriginal community of shifting cultivators. It will be seen that the aborigines rely to some extent on the sale of collected jungle produce such as rattan, various jungle gums, bamboo, and jungle fruit for the money to buy some of their needs, including some food, the useful *parang*, food vessels, matches, etc. This is an indication of the increasing contact between the aborigines and the other lowland races.

Table 8.2 Annual work cycle and sources of food of shifting cultivators in Peninsular Malaysia (after Williams—Hunt)

Period	Agricultural work	Other work	Main sources of food	Subsidiary sources of food
April—May	New *ladang* site selected and initial area of 2 or 3 acres cleared	Some collection of jungle produce— bamboo, rattan and gums	Tapioca from last year's harvest	Purchased food from sale of jungle produce. Also animals, fish and roots
May—June	Initial site burnt and planted to maize, tapioca and banana. Felling of main *ladang* started	Temporary shelters erected, followed by erection of new houses	As above	As above
July— August	Main *ladang* burnt and planted to hill padi, tapioca, maize, yams and sweet potato	Fruit season. *Petai* and *perah* nuts very important	As above, plus jungle fruits	As above, plus food bought through sale of jungle fruit, especially *petai*
September— October	Some weeding	Repair of fish traps. Some fishing	As above, plus maize crop	End of fruit season. Some collection of produce
November— December	Harvest of main padi crop	Durian season	Padi	As above
January— March	None	Fishing and collection of jungle produce	Padi and new tapioca, yams, sweet potatoes, etc.	Sale of jungle produce

Such contact is not always to the advantage of the aborigines, particularly in the case of those groups which have been evacuated to the lowlands because of the Emergency. These resettled aborigines suffered greatly from diseases to which they have no natural or acquired immunity. In cases where the contact with lowland races has been gradual and spread over a number of years and even generations, some of the aborigines have tended to abandon their old way of life and adopt the ways of the lowland Malays, including following the Muslim religion. Some of these people have been absorbed into the Malay community and are practically indistinguishable from the other Malays.

9
The modern economy: Background

Malaysia is one of the richest countries in Southeast Asia, with a gross national product at market prices of M$16 300 million and a *per capita* GNP of M$1 380 in 1973. The Malaysian economy achieved a healthy rate of growth in the 1960s, with output increasing at over 6 per cent annually between 1960 and 1965, rising to over 8 per cent in 1968 and almost 10 per cent in 1969. However, because of stagnant commodity prices the rate of growth declined to an average of only 5 per cent in the period 1970–72. In 1973 strong growth forces generated by the export boom saw output expanding by about 10 per cent during the year.

The states of Malaysia are at markedly different stages of economic development, with Peninsular Malaysia demonstrably the dominant partner, accounting for nearly 90 per cent of the total GNP, while Sarawak and Sabah occupy subsidiary positions. A further indication of this difference is in the proportion of undeveloped land in the states: Peninsular Malaysia has about 75 per cent, while Sarawak and Sabah each has nearly 90 per cent. Moreover the Peninsular Malaysian economy, compared with those of Sarawak and Sabah and indeed most of the other Southeast Asian countries, is relatively advanced in terms of infrastructural facilities (roads, water supplies, power, etc.), institutional patterns, commercial and financial patterns, and management, professional and administrative skills.

The Peninsular Malaysian economy exhibits several distinctive features, a number of which can be regarded as typical of those of a developing country. These include:

1. The export orientation of the economy, with about 40 per cent of the total gross domestic production being derived from exports.
2. A heavy dependence on a few primary commodities (initially rubber and tin, but today rubber, palm-oil, timber and tin) for export earnings.
3. A high (about 50 per cent) but decreasing percentage of the total labour force engaged in primary production, mainly in agriculture.
4. A small but in recent years rapidly growing industrial sector.
5. An infrastructural foundation well developed by most developing countries' standards.

The mainspring of economic development in Peninsular Malaysia since it was opened up to international trade and foreign investment in the last quarter of the nineteenth century was in the export of primary products. The pattern of her resource allocation was based on the principle of comparative advantage, which has led her in those early colonial days to specialize in the production of tin and rubber for the export market. Favourable world market demand conditions for these commodities stimulated their expansion and private foreign investment, attracted by the high rates of return on capital invested in tin and rubber, flowed into the country on an increasingly large scale. This movement, unrestricted because of the *laissez-faire* policy followed by the British administrators, was also responsible for raising the productivity of the natural resources in the primary sector through the introduction of modern technology, organization and management. The capital inflow, however, was channelled towards the export sector only (the mining and plantation sector) while the indigenous sector remained outside the mainstream of the exchange economy—neglected, impoverished and not benefiting directly from the economic growth that was rapidly taking place in the country.

The economic pattern that emerged was that of a modern export-oriented sector functioning side by side with a traditional indigenous rural sector—the 'dual economy' typical of colonial countries in Southeast Asia and elsewhere. In due course however the indigenous rural population began to participate in the new exchange economy by taking to the production of cash crops, notably rubber, for the export market. The stimulus to this move came from the desire to obtain the means to purchase the wide variety of imported consumer goods. The rural population was able to contribute quite substantially to export expansion because of the abundance of virgin and underutilized land in Peninsular Malaysia which could be put to rubber cultivation without encroaching on land under subsistence crops.

The process of export expansion in Peninsular Malaysia depended also on the establishment of a modern infrastructural foundation, especially of transport and communications. The provision of those facilities was an essential precondition for development, and in fact the exploitation of the valuable natural resources in the country and the emergence of the export economy were only made possible by public investment in modern transport and communications.

This period of export expansion was also characterized by the large-scale entry of immigrant labour, both Chinese and Indian, into the country to meet the labour requirements of the rapidly growing primary industries. As seen in earlier chapters, many of these immigrants soon extended their economic activities to include trade, commerce and the services, and eventually came to occupy middlemen positions between the indigenous population and the large British and European trading companies. The postwar problems of economic imbalance and the identification of race with economic function thus have their roots in this early phase of colonial policy.

Up to the period when independence was granted (1957) to the then Federation of Malaya the economic pattern that emerged was the outcome of a free enterprise policy which encouraged the unhindered entry of private foreign investment into the primary export sector; free international trade with low tariff rates; and a free internal market system to provide the stimulus to export expansion from both the modern mining and plantation sector as well as the traditional indigenous sector. However, in pursuing single-mindedly this policy and in basing development on the principle of comparative advantage in resource allocation the country ended up with an unbalanced economy, with an over-concentration on two primary products (rubber and tin); a well-developed export sector; an underdeveloped and largely neglected domestic sector; and a manufacturing sector of embryonic dimensions. In such a situation the prosperity of the country rested almost entirely on her exports, the prices of which depended on external economic factors over which she had no control. The dangers of having so few eggs in her economic basket were dramatically demonstrated during the Great Depression of the 1930s. Nevertheless the country was able to build her economy on this foundation, and in fact enjoyed several decades of prosperity prior to the Second World War.

The relative importance of the three main sectors of the economy up to the period of independence is indicated in Table 9.1, showing the

Table 9.1   Employment by sector, Peninsular Malaysia, 1957 and 1970

Sector	*Total employed ('000)*		*Percentage*	
	1957	1970	1957	1970

Primary
Agriculture, forestry,
   fisheries, mining
   and quarrying
	1 303	1 454	61	52

Secondary Manufacturing, building and construction	204	307	9	14

Tertiary
Transport and communica-
   tions, commerce,
   services, utilities
	619	959	30	34

Total	2 126	2 720	100	100

number and percentage of the workforce engaged in these sectors in 1957. The high percentage (61%) of the workforce engaged in primary production reflects the traditional dependence of the country on agriculture and mining for export earnings. As mentioned earlier, within the primary sector one can differentiate between the 'modern' plantation and mining enterprises and the 'traditional' peasant holdings which collectively were responsible for producing more than 40 per cent of the rubber exported from Peninsular Malaysia. In contrast, the percentage of the workforce engaged in the manufacturing industries was very low (9%); together they made for a lopsided economic structure and a lopsided pattern of development.

The post-independence policy of the Government has been directed towards the promotion of industrialization as a means of economic diversification whilst retaining the established methods of economic development through export expansion. This policy was launched in 1958 with the passage of the Pioneer Industries Ordinance, which was subsequently replaced by the Investment Incentives Act of 1968. The strategy was to create an attractive investment climate in which private enterprise industry would grow; public investment was limited to infrastructure development. Official attention was also focused on the advancement of the poorer peoples and areas of Peninsular Malaysia; this was later to be formalized as part of the New Economic Policy of the Second Malaysia Plan (1971–75).

The approach to industrial development was essentially a *laissez-faire* one, with the Government's role limited to laying the foundations for the private sector to build upon. However, following the racial riots of 13 May 1969 a new policy was promulgated in which the objective was not only to maximize economic growth and eradicate poverty but also to restructure Malaysian society so as to eliminate the identification of race with economic function. In pursuance of this policy a new industrialization strategy was adopted in which the Government would take a more positive role, including participation in the establishment of industries, either by itself or in joint venture with the private sector (Federal Industrial Development Authority (FIDA), 1969).

During the 1960s manufacturing output increased by an average of about 10 per cent annually compared with an average of about 5.5 per cent for the gross domestic product. This sector showed the most vigorous growth of all the sectors during the decade. The increasing importance of manufacturing is seen in Table 9.1, which shows that the employment pattern in the three main sectors changed significantly between 1957 and 1970, with a smaller percentage of the workforce engaged in primary production and a larger percentage in secondary production, mainly manufacturing. To that extent the objective of economic diversification has partially been achieved, though Peninsular Malaysia is still a long way from being an industrial country. The Mid-

Term Review of the Second Malaysia Plan envisages that Malaysia would be transformed from an industrializing country in 1970 to a semi-industrialized country in 1980 and an industrialized one by 1990, by which time manufacturing output would reach 35 per cent of the total for the economy.

At the same time Peninsular Malaysia is fortunate in having the means to promote further growth in the primary sector through bringing undeveloped as well as underutilized land into cultivation. This traditional method of export expansion has served the country well in the past, and, in the context of the New Economic Policy, will be even more important now as a means of increasing indigenous agricultural production and improving their standards of living. Land development expenditure in Peninsular Malaysia increased from $17 million in the First Malaya Plan 1956–60, to $130 million in the Second Malaya Plan 1960–65, to $310 million in the First Malaysia Plan 1965–70, and will be $908 million in the Second Malaysia Plan 1971–75. This growing emphasis on land development is further illustrated by the establishment of the Ministry of Land Development in 1973. The main agencies for land development is the Federal Land Development Authority (FELDA), the Rubber Industry Smallholders Development Authority (RISDA), and the Federal Land Consolidation and Rehabilitation Authority (FELCRA). The largest areas of land potential are in the eastern half of the peninsula, and major land settlement and land development schemes are in various stages of implementation in the Jengka Triangle, Pahang Tenggara, Johore Tenggara and Trengganu Tengah.

The Peninsular Malaysian economy is therefore undergoing change in two respects: first, through the process of economic diversification whereby the country's excessive dependence on export earnings on a few primary commodities is lessened; and second, through the New Economic Policy which seeks to promote national unity by raising the standards of living of the Malaysian population and at the same time correcting the economic imbalance that exists in Malaysian society.

The geographic pattern of economic development will also undergo change as emphasis is laid under the New Economic Policy on reducing the spatial economic imbalance that exists between the different states of Peninsular Malaysia. In 1970 the *per capita* gross domestic product for each of the states expressed as a proportion of the mean for Peninsular Malaysia was as follows: Selangor 1.49, Negri Sembilan 1.16, Perak 1.07, Pahang 1.04, Johore 0.98, Perlis 0.80, Kedah 0.81, Penang 0.78, Malacca 0.69, Trengganu 0.60 and Kelantan 0.52. The contrast between the GDP for Selangor and Kelantan is striking. The contrast is even more striking when the structures of each state's economy is compared: more than 90 per cent of manufacturing output was concentrated in the more developed west coast states of Penang, Perak, Selangor, Negri Sembilan and Johore. These states also accounted for more than 80 per cent of the mining output and, together with Kedah, almost 80 per cent of the agricultural output.

The strategy for regional development is to tap the economic resources and potential of the less developed states; to promote population migration to areas with large economic potential; and to expand the infrastructure and social services in those states and areas which are less developed so as to bring about a better balance between the various regions and their population (Mid-Term Review of the Second Malaysia Plan, 1973). The future will therefore see changes in the spatial patterns of economic development as well as in the distribution of population.

10
Agriculture

The dominant position of agriculture in the Peninsular Malaysian economy is indicated by the fact that it generates about 30 per cent of the gross domestic product and accounts for about 50 per cent of the foreign exchange earnings. Half of the total labour force is engaged in agriculture. The 1966 land-use survey showed that 15.9 million acres (6.4 million ha) of land in Peninsular Malaysia were suitable for agricultural development. This amounts to nearly half (49%) of the total land area of the country. The total area under crops in 1972 was 6.9 million acres (2.8 million ha) or 21 per cent of the total Peninsular Malaysian land area. There are therefore 9 million acres (3.6 million ha) of land still available for agricultural development. Although a proportion of this land would be of marginal value to agriculture because of poverty of soils, poor drainage conditions, inaccessibility and other constraints, and a further proportion would eventually be put to urban and other non-agricultural uses, the fact remains that there will be sufficiently large land resources available in the country for export expansion through the traditional method of bringing more land under cultivation.

Table 10.1 shows the total area under crops of economic importance. It will be seen that most of the crop area (about 80%) is under perennials, of which the most important are rubber, oil-palm and coconut. In the hot wet climate of the Malay Peninsula perennials, because they are in the ground throughout the year, provide the best means of maximizing the use of solar energy. Annuals, in contrast, cannot take advantage of the continuous growing season due to the interruption in the use of solar energy as one crop is harvested and another established. However, padi occupies a substantial acreage in Peninsular Malaysia, not because it yields more than other cereals, but because it is the staple food of the people and is also the only cereal capable of providing sustained yields under continuous cropping even without any conscious input of manures and fertilizers.

The ecological advantage which perennials enjoy in the Malay Peninsula is marred by two serious economic disadvantages. First, perennials suffer markedly from both short-run and long-run price inelasticity of

Table 10.1   Cultivated area under main crops, 1972

Crop	Area (1972)		Percentage	
	Acres	Hectares	1960	1972
Rubber	4 205 000	1 701 000	64	60
Padi*	926 000	375 000	17	13
Oil-palm	887 000	359 000	2	13
Coconut	522 000	211 000	9	8
Food and beverage crops†	177 000	72 000	2	3
Fruit‡	166 000	67 000	4	2
Spices§	17 000	7 000	1	0
Miscellaneous¶	42 000	17 000	1	1
Total	6 942 000	2 809 000	100	100

* Not including the 488 000 acres (197 000 ha) planted as an off-season crop.
† Tapioca, sweet potato, sago, sugar-cane, groundnut, maize, yam, colocasia, ragi, soya bean, pulses, vegetables, tea, coffee and cocoa.
‡ Pineapple, banana, cashew nut, durian, rambutan, mangosteen, citrus and other fruits.
§ Arecanut, chillies, pepper, cardamom, ginger, sireh, nutmeg, clove and tumeric.
¶ Tobacco, derris, nipah, gambier, kapok, ipecacuanha, patchouli, citronella, gutta percha, and other miscellaneous crops.

supply. Second, the long-term commitment involved in perennials results in agricultural resource immobility so that once the decision is taken to plant rubber, oil-palm, coconut or other perennials there is little prospect for changes in the use of the land and other fixed capital during the economic lifespan of the crops (Wharton, 1963). Both these factors have serious economic implications for resource allocation.

Rubber continues to be by far the most important crop, although it has shown a relative decline in area since 1960. The decline was mainly the result of diversification into oil-palm which had in recent years become a more renumerative crop than rubber. However, rubber is still the most important crop not only in terms of planted acreage but also in contributing to about one-quarter of the country's total foreign exchange earnings, one-eighth of the gross domestic product and in engaging about one-quarter of the total labour force. Most of the rubber holdings are distributed along the coastal and foothill belt of western Peninsular Malaysia from Perlis to Johore. There are two main zones of concentration—the first or northern zone includes central and south Kedah, parts of Province Wellesley and north Perak, and the other (southern) zone lies roughly between Sungei Selangor and the southern-most tip of the Peninsula, and includes south Selangor, Negri Sembilan, Malacca and western Johore. The rubber areas of eastern Peninsular

Malaysia are small and scattered. Rubber is grown in the Kelantan delta, in pockets along the southern Trengganu coast, in the Kuantan area, in patches along the Pahang River, the East Coast railway and along the major roads of Pahang as well as in the Johore Bahru—Kota Tinggi area of eastern Johore.

Padi occupied the second largest area of cultivated land in Peninsular Malaysia. Although the padi acreage increased between 1960 and 1972, the relative position of the crop declined during that period (Table 10.1). By 1973 oil-palm had overtaken padi in terms of planted acreage. Most of the padi cultivated is of the wet variety requiring flooded fields, and cultivation is confined to riverine, coastal and deltaic locations which can be easily flooded. In western Peninsular Malaysia the main padi areas are in Perlis, Kedah, Province Wellesley, Perak (Krian, Sungei Manik, Changkat Jong), Selangor (Tanjong Karang), and the coastal plains of Malacca. The largest acreage under padi in eastern Peninsular Malaysia is in the Kelantan delta; other smaller areas are found in the Trengganu delta, the Pahang delta, the interior valleys of Pahang and the Endau delta.

The other major cash crops are oil-palm and coconut. The acreage under oil-palm increased considerably in the period 1960 to 1972 (Table 10.1). It has continued to increase in area since then, as a result of which oil-palm now occupies second position in terms of planted acreage. The crop is grown in all the states except Perlis, but the largest acreages are in Johore, Selangor and Perak. Progress in the cultivation of the crop has been so marked that the country is now the world's largest producer of palm-oil. In contrast to oil-palm, the coconut industry has stagnated in the last decade or so. Most of the large coconut areas are in the coastal parts of Johore, Selangor and Perak, but the crop is cultivated for cash and for subsistence in all the other states.

Apart from the major crops Peninsular Malaysia also produces a great variety of fruits, food and beverage crops, spices and other miscellaneous crops. These crops together occupy 402 000 acres (162 000 ha). Pineapple, sugar-cane, cocoa, tapioca and banana are the most important of the minor crops. Pineapples are ubiquitous in Peninsular Malaysia, but are grown for canning only in Johore and Selangor. The other minor crops which occupy significant areas are sweet potato, vegetables, durian, rambutan, arecanut, tea, coffee and nipah. Many of the minor crops are grown for subsistence purposes in small *kampong* holdings. Some of the produce may go to supplement the income from the major revenue crops of rubber, oil-palm, and coconut in the smallholdings.

Although Peninsular Malaysia's economy hinges largely on agriculture, the emphasis is on revenue crops and the country is not completely self-sufficient in food. Seventeen per cent (by value) of the imports of Peninsular Malaysia in 1972 were foodstuffs, including rice. The Government is trying to counter the over-dependence on outside sources for these essential commodities, especially the staple food—rice—by opening up new padi lands and by encouraging the double-cropping of existing padi lands. By 1972 Peninsular Malaysia had achieved 96 per cent self-sufficiency in rice (Bank Negara, 1973).

Systems of production

Two basic systems of production prevail in the agricultural economy, both based on the continuous cultivation of crops on permanent and well-defined holdings:

Plantation[1] production

The plantation system of agricultural production is a highly specialized one, and has the following characteristic features:

1. It is usually organized on a large scale, that is, the scale of operations, the area per unit holding and the labour force are large. In Peninsular Malaysia the minimum size of an estate or plantation is 100 acres (40 ha).
2. It specializes in the cultivation of a single crop, produced primarily for export. In recent years however multiple cropping based on rubber and oil-palm has become increasingly common.
3. While the labour force may be of local origin the capital is usually of foreign origin, and the managerial staff is also usually expatriate. However, many companies in recent years have recruited local staff to senior management positions.
4. In many instances the crop or crops undergo preliminary processing or preparation before they are exported, as in the case of rubber and oil-palm.

The plantation as an instrument of production is generally efficient, and is in a position to use the latest advances in technological knowledge to solve its problems of production. It is able to command sufficient capital for such requirements as machinery and for the expenses of setting up and carrying out the functions of a large agricultural unit. It also has the resources needed to provide the regularity of supply and the uniformity and high quality of product which world markets demand. But the plantation also has to bear heavy overhead charges which become a serious burden when prices drop below the profit margin. Furthermore, the plantations of Peninsular Malaysia today cannot depend upon unlimited supplies of cheap labour as in the past. Labour, while adequate in quantity, is no longer cheap, and production costs have increased because of the larger wage bills. Mechanization can only

[1] The term 'plantation' is used interchangeably with 'estate' throughout this book.

212

partially solve the problem as much of the work carried out by the labourers cannot be performed by machines.

The first plantation crops established in Peninsular Malaysia were spices and gambier. These were followed by sugar-cane which was fairly extensively cultivated in Province Wellesley in the mid-1850s. Tapioca was also planted on plantations and, in the latter part of the nineteenth century, coconut and coffee were added to the list. Then came rubber in the last decade of the century, and the phenomenal success of rubber led to the decline and abandonment of spices, tapioca, sugar and coffee as plantation crops. Up to 1910 the plantations were only interested in planting rubber, but between 1910 and 1925 many coconut plantations were also opened up in addition to rubber plantations, and after 1926 oil-palm, too, became a plantation crop. Pineapple was not grown on a plantation basis until after the Second World War. The other important plantation crop was tea. During the colonial period it was possible to alienate land on a large scale for plantations because the population was sparse and land was abundant in the Malay Peninsula. There was no encroachment on indigenous Malay land since most of the Malays were settled on riverine and coastal locations where padi could be grown, whereas the plantations were usually established on dry-land sites— foothills and undulating land away from the centres of Malay concentration.

Table 10.2 shows the area under plantation crops in 1960 and 1972. It will be seen that the plantation industry lost some ground in terms of planted acreage during this period. The largest decline was in rubber, due to conversion of old rubber land to oil-palm and other crops and through the subdivision of rubber plantations into smallholdings. All the other

Table 10.2   Area under plantation crops, 1960 and 1972, Peninsular Malaysia

Crop	*Area (acres)*		*Percentage*	
	1960	1972	1960	1972
Rubber	1 942 000	1 508 000 (610 000 ha)	89	68
Oil-palm	135 000	606 000 (245 000 ha)	6	27
Coconut	86 000	51 000 (21 000 ha)	4	2
Sugar-cane	—	28 000*(11 000 ha)	—	1
Cocoa	—	20 000 (8 000 ha)	—	1
Pineapple	15 000	12 000*(5 000 ha)	1	1
Tea	9 000	7 000 (3 000 ha)	—	—
Total	2 187 000	2 232 000 (903 000 ha)	100	100

* Estimated.

plantation crops except oil-palm suffered losses in planted area. The expansion of the oil-palm area has been so large that it was nearly sufficient to compensate for the declines in planted area among the other crops. During this period a new plantation crop—cocoa—was established, displacing pineapple and tea in planted area ranking. In more recent years sugar-cane has also become a plantation crop.

Although the plantation industry has suffered only a very marginal loss in terms of absolute planted area, its relative position in the country's agricultural sector has declined considerably: in 1960 the area under plantation crops comprised 40 per cent of the total planted area; in 1972 it comprised only 32 per cent. The increase of 1 463 000 acres (592 000 ha) in Peninsular Malaysia's total area under crops during this period was therefore due to the growth of the smallholder sector of the agricultural economy, including the land opened up under the land development schemes of the Federal and state governments.

Nevertheless, despite the changed political and social conditions following the achievement of independence in Malaysia, the plantation industry has managed to hold its own in terms of planted acreage. Moreover the plantation industry is the single largest employer in the country, engaging a total of 313 200 people in 1967—68. As noted by Fryer (1970), the main problem which the industry has to face in the independent countries of the developing world is not economic but political. In Peninsular Malaysia the social and political climate has not imposed disabilities on the industry, even though the plantations were originally colonial-creations. Up to 1970, 71 per cent of the total Peninsular Malaysian estate acreage in the corporate sector under oil-palm, coconut and tea was still under foreign ownership (*Mid-term Review*, 1973). In the non-corporate sector however, which made up 30 per cent of the total estate planted acreage, only 6 per cent was under foreign ownership. Thus the overall extent of foreign control in the Peninsular Malaysian plantation industry amounted to 52 per cent of the total planted acreage.

Smallholder production

The smallholder system of production, in contrast to the plantation system, is based on individually small units, each unit being usually run by the farmer and his family without hired labour. The smallholder today cultivates both subsistence and cash-crops, though some may specialize entirely on cash-crops. The range of such crops suitable for cultivation is limited to those which can be marketed without processing or those which require only simple processing within the technical and financial capacity of the farmer. Table 10.3 shows the total area under smallholder crops.

Rubber, again, dominates the sector as it does the plantation sector of

Table 10.3   Area under smallholder crops, Peninsular Malaysia, 1972

Crop	*Area*		*Percentage*
	Acres	Hectares	
Rubber	2 697 000	1 091 000	57
Padi	926 000	375 000	20
Coconut	471 000	191 000	10
Oil-palm	281 000	114 000	6
Fruits	154 000	62 000	3
Food and beverage crops	122 000	49 000	3
Spices	17 000	7 000	—
Miscellaneous	42 000	17 000	1
Total	4 710 000	1 906 000	100

the agricultural economy, and the total rubber area is more than half of the total area under all smallholder crops in Peninsular Malaysia. Padi is grown solely as a smallholder crop. Coconut is next in importance, and is usually grown in conjunction with other crops such as padi and fruit, though some holdings are devoted entirely to coconut. Oil-palm has become an important smallholder crop today, being planted in the land development schemes of the Federal Land Development Authority and other public agencies. Altogether 68 per cent of the total agricultural land in Peninsular Malaysia is smallholder cultivated.

The smallholder economy has undergone considerable changes during the colonial era. The aim of smallholder production in pre-colonial days was to provide the farmer and his family with their subsistence needs, and the farmer produced what he ate and ate what he produced. The farmers were composed of indigenous Malays. The typical Malay farm consisted of a few acres of padi and a small *kampong* in which an assortment of dryland crops were planted—fruit, coconut, spices and some vegetables. There was no incentive to produce beyond subsistence needs because of the insecurity of life and the instability of political conditions.

The advent of British rule inevitably disturbed the foundations of indigenous life. The underlying reason for colonialism was economic gain, and it was in the sphere of economic activities that the greatest changes in indigenous society were brought about. This was not so much due to the deliberate undermining of the economic foundations of traditional village life as to the indirect influence of the money economy on individual members of the village. There was gradually increasing participation in the new economy, arising firstly from the need to raise money to pay taxes and rates, and later given impetus by the desire to buy various consumption goods to satisfy personal needs. Almost every-where the farmer began to produce for the market, secure in the thought that his extra effort would not be seized by the exercise of arbitrary right or by outside raiders.

The first crops sold by the farmer for money were naturally those he normally grew on his farm—padi, coconut, fruit and spices. Later he took to growing crops originally introduced into Peninsular Malaysia as planta-tion crops. The great success of rubber attracted his interest, and since the beginning of the twentieth century rubber has been the outstanding crop in smallholder farms throughout the country. The rapid spread of rubber cultivation among the Malay farmers was the outcome of three factors. Firstly, the tree fitted easily and naturally into the *kampong* setting with its emphasis on tree crops. Secondly, its cultivation made little extra demands on the farmer—as the tree is non-seasonal, the labour involved in its tapping could be spread over the year and there was no clash in labour needs with the seasonal padi crop. (The tree could either be left untapped during the padi sowing and harvest or the tapping rhythm could be adjusted to meet the situation.) There was no necessity for extra draught animals, ploughs or manures, the purchase of which would otherwise be beyond the purse of the peasant. The technique of producing rubber sheet from the latex was simple and required only a little extra investment for the purchase of the tapping knife, coagulant and roller. Thirdly, the farmer soon discovered that in times of good prices an acre or two of rubber could supply his family with the cash necessary to provide a living better than could be obtained from padi planting, with less physical effort and labour. Apart from rubber, the traditional Malay crops are padi (nine-tenths of the padi-farmers are Malays), coconut, fruit, some spices and some food-crops.

The Chinese did not migrate to the Malay Peninsula in large numbers until after the establishment of British rule. Even then the purpose of Chinese migration was not permanent settlement but rather temporary sojournment until such time as they had made enough money to have rendered their stay profitable. Farming was therefore not taken up for subsistence purposes but as a means to raise money, in direct contrast to the normal set-up in their villages in China. Farming methods as practised in Peninsular Malaysia by the Chinese in the early years were not far removed from that of shifting cultivation, a destructive system of 'land-mining' tolerated if not actively encouraged by the authorities, in a country where land was plentiful. Padi cultivation, the traditional agricultural backbone of South China, did not attract the Chinese as it was the least paying of all agricultural occupations in Peninsular Malaysia. Instead the Chinese took to growing those crops which were in great demand in local and export markets and which brought in the highest returns, and they grew them in large estates as well as small farms.

Amongst the earliest crops cultivated by the Chinese farmer were vegetables, grown in market-gardens. Market-gardening as practised by the Chinese is a highly intensive form of agriculture based on a closely-knit and interdependent relationship between the growing of short-term crops and vegetables, the rearing of pigs and the utilization of both pig and human excreta as manure. There were Chinese market-gardeners in Malacca as early as the mid-seventeenth century. Their number increased greatly during the initial phase of Peninsular Malaysia's economic development when large numbers of immigrants entered the country and the demand for food increased correspondingly. There were 50 000 market-gardeners in 1931; by 1947 their numbers had increased to 86 000, mainly as a result of the Japanese occupation when thousands of Chinese 'returned to the land' to grow their own food. But the disruption created by the resettlement campaign caused their numbers to fall to 38 700 in 1957. The Chinese also cultivated pepper and gambier, clove and nutmeg, sugar-cane, coffee, coconut and pineapple during the nineteenth century. Most of these crops, however, had become unimportant by the end of the century because of plant disease or low prices, or both, and when rubber came into the scene the Chinese began to cultivate it as enthusiastically as did the Europeans and the Malays. The Chinese planted rubber in estates as well as in smallholdings, unlike the Europeans who grew it exclusively in estates, or the Malays who grew it mainly in smallholdings. Rubber again takes first place among the crops grown by Chinese farmers. Other crops of importance in the Chinese smallholder economy, apart from rubber and vegetables, are coconut, pineapple, most of the food-crops, some spices, fruit and miscellaneous other crops such as tobacco and coffee. The Indians, Pakistanis and other races do not contribute much to the smallholder economy, except as rubber smallholders.

The peninsula-wide census of agriculture conducted by the Ministry of Agriculture and co-operatives in 1960 revealed that there was a total of 449 510 farms in Peninsular Malaysia larger than a quarter of an acre but smaller than 100 acres in size. Ninety-six per cent of these farms were small farms, that is, consisting of less than 15 acres (6 ha) of land. Such small farms are worked by the farmer with the aid of his family but normally without hired labour. The distribution of these farms is shown in Table 10.4. Forty-five per cent of the smallholder farms are located in the north-eastern states of Kelantan and Trengganu, and the north-western states of Perlis and Kedah, where there is a long history of Malay settlement based largely on the cultivation of padi. The other two states where smallholder farming is important are Perak, where padi, rubber, coconut and mixed cultivation are the bases of the smallholders' economy, and Johore, where padi cultivation is unimportant as compared with cash-cropping based on rubber, coconut and pineapple.

The third preliminary report of the census contains statistical data on

Table 10.4   Distribution of smallholder farms in Peninsular Malaysia, 1960

State	*Number of farms*		*Total*	*Percentage*
	Below 15 acres (6 ha) in size	15—99¾ acres (6—40 ha) in size		
Kedah	79 734	3 768	83 502	19
Perak	70 346	2 270	72 616	16
Kelantan	68 908	1 514	70 422	16
Johore	51 688	4 406	56 094	12
Selangor	33 062	966	34 028	8
Trengganu	29 292	1 024	30 316	7
Pahang	26 062	1 846	27 908	6
Negri Sembilan	23 124	640	23 764	5
Penang and Province Wellesley	19 044	626	19 670	4
Malacca	17 994	558	18 552	4
Perlis	12 494	144	12 638	3
Total	431 748	17 762	449 510	100

the size of the farms. Table 10.5 shows the sizes of the farms within the small farm category. Several significant features of the smallholder economy are brought to light by the table above. Most of the farms (90%) are less than 10 acres in size, and 67 per cent are less than 5 acres in size. The minimum economic holding, that is, one which can give the farmer a fair to good standard of living, is between 8 to 10 acres (3—4 ha) according to the Federal Land Development Authority. It is therefore evident that a very high percentage of Peninsular Malaysia's smallholders cultivate holdings which fall below this minimum, although the position is generally better than that which obtains in many other parts of tropical Asia, where a farmer does not have more than 2 to 3 acres of land. That Peninsular Malaysia is fast approaching this situation is indicated by the fact that 45 per cent of the total number of small farms are holdings of less than 3 acres (1 ha).

Of the 45 892 farms that are less than 1 acre in size, about 9 000 are in Kelantan, 7 900 in Perak, 6 900 in Kedah, 3 700 in Malacca, 3 900 in Trengganu and 3 300 in Negri Sembilan. It is significant that all of them are located in states which have a long history of Malay settlement and where the twin processes of population increase and land subdivision have worked to reduce the average size of the individual farm and family

Table 10.5   Size of smallholder farms in Peninsular Malaysia, 1960

Size group (acres)	Number of farms	Percentage
Below 1	45 892	10
1–1¾	79 666	18
2–2¾	78 014	17
3–3¾	57 426	13
4–4¾	41 726	9
5–7¼	72 074	16
7½–9¾	28 678	7
10–14¾	28 272	6
15–99¾	17 762	4

holding. The division of agricultural land into minute parcels of less than an acre each is the result both of a congested rural population exerting a heavy pressure on available land and of the prevailing laws of inheritance and succession which demand the splitting up of land.

Thus in many localized parts of Peninsular Malaysia the problem of uneconomic holdings has become acute. The size of a holding which can provide minimum subsistence cannot be assessed without taking into account the soil fertility, rainfall and water conditions, the intensity of cultivation and types of crops. Nevertheless, the process of physical subdivision, if continued long enough, must necessarily lead to a stage when the unit holding cannot by itself yield enough to support the farmer and his family. Up to a certain level the reduction in size may encourage a more intensive form of cultivation, but beyond that the law of diminishing returns begins to operate, and no amount of extra labour or capital will succeed in increasing production. Except in the case of intensive market-gardening, an acre or less of land under any other form of cultivation in Peninsular Malaysia cannot yield even the bare minimum for sustenance.

Allied with this problem of uneconomic holdings due to excessive subdivision is the problem of excessive fragmentation, which arises when a single farm is made up of several fragmented parcels of land scattered over a wide area. The dispersal of fields entails extra expense and effort in moving seeds, implements, animals and workers from one plot to another. Efforts to improve conditions of farming on any piece of land are held up unnecessarily because such improvements require the close co-operation of many individual and often individualistic farmers. They become even more difficult when radical changes, such as soil conservation measures, mechanization and major drainage and irrigation schemes are projected, for then reorganization of the farms, and perhaps of ownership, becomes essential.

As an instrument of agricultural production the smallholder system of small farms suffers from a number of defects which collectively manifest themselves in low standards of production and inferior qualities. These defects are not so much inherent in the system as being due to the lack of education and of scientific, technical, financial and administrative assistance. During the colonial era most of agricultural services provided by the governmental and semi-governmental organizations, such as the Rubber Research Institute and the Department of Agriculture, have benefited the plantations, except in the case of the Drainage and Irrigation Department which provided water control facilities to padi areas.

In spite of the defects of the smallholder system, practical experience in Peninsular Malaysia and other tropical countries has shown that a well-organized system of peasant farming, because of its greater flexibility, is better able to withstand crisis conditions than an economy based on plantation agriculture. For example, during the Great Depression of the 1930s the rubber plantations were very badly hit while the rubber smallholders simply left off tapping and turned to other alternative occupations without having to worry about heavy overhead costs. Again, an economy based on peasant farming gives greater stability to the country during a major depression because the farmers can always turn from growing cash-crops to growing food-crops. No mass unemployment need follow such a depression, unlike the position in a country which is mainly dependent on plantation agriculture. However, it should be borne in mind that such stability may have to be bought at a high price—in terms of lower technical efficiency, while also, in the view of some writers, jeopardizing the country's chances of achieving sustained economic growth (see Fryer, 1970).

The agricultural economy in Peninsular Malaysia today is made up of a stagnant (in terms of planted acreage) plantation sector and a rapidly growing smallholder sector. The increase in total planted area in the last decade has all been in the smallholder sector, including land opened up by the Federal Land Development Authority and other public agencies in their large block-planting schemes. Under the New Economic Policy it is envisaged that the growth in foreign investment between 1970 and 1990 will be mainly in the industrial and commercial sectors of the economy. Foreign private investment in plantation agriculture and in mining will decline during this period. In rubber production, for example, three-quarters of the new planting and replanting will be in the smallholder sector so that by 1990 this sector will account for about 60 per cent of the total production and 66 per cent of the total acreage (*Mid-term Review*, 1973).

With the increasing importance attached to smallholder agriculture it is therefore vital to ensure that the efficiency of the farmer is raised to as high a level as possible. At the same time the problems of marketing, indebtedness, credit facilities, tenancy, land subdivision and fragmentation will have to be solved in order to achieve the objective of providing the smallholder the maximum returns for his produce and to raise his standards of living.

Rubber

The history of rubber in Peninsular Malaysia has its beginnings in the latter part of the nineteenth century. The rubber that is exported from Peninsular Malaysia comes from the latex of the tree *Hevea brasiliensis*, native of the Amazon Valley. In 1876 Sir Henry Wickham collected some 70 000 Hevea seeds from the Tapajos region of the Amazon and sent them to Kew Gardens in England. Peninsular Malaysia received its first consignment of seedlings from Kew in the same year, but these soon died. Another consignment was received in 1877, and the plants were successfully raised in the Botanic Gardens of Singapore.

Until the end of the nineteenth century *Hevea* was planted only on an experimental basis, and in conjunction with similar experiments using other rubber-yielding plants such as *Ficus elastica* and the Malayan species of *Wilughbeia*, to determine which of the several varieties was best suited to plantation agriculture. But by about 1895 the superiority of *Hevea* was established beyond doubt when it was found that it was easier to grow, and that it yielded a greater quantity and a better quality of latex than the other varieties. The year 1895 coincided with the advent of the first pneumatic automobile tyres. The rapid development of the motor car industry greatly increased the demand for rubber, causing prices to rise to levels which made it highly profitable to grow the crop.

The first commercial attempt at rubber planting in Peninsular Malaysia was made by a Chinese who established an estate in the north-eastern section of Malacca in 1898. His example was followed by other planters, mainly European, who started a number of small estates in several localities in western Peninsular Malaysia. From this tentative beginning rubber soon became firmly established as the major revenue crop of the country. The successful introduction of *Hevea* into the agricultural economy marked the end of the search for a tropical crop that could be profitably grown in the Malay Peninsula.

The earliest plantation crops grown on a commercial scale were spices and gambier, which were cultivated on Singapore Island, Penang and the adjoining mainland. Of these, pepper was the most important, but its place in the economy declined until, by the middle of the nineteenth century, it became only a minor export crop. There was a similar decline in the export of cloves and nutmegs from Penang when plant diseases devastated large areas under these crops. Meanwhile the 1830s saw the introduction of another revenue crop, namely sugar-cane, in Penang and Province Wellesley. Sugar-cane cultivation was given an impetus in 1846 when the British sugar import duty was reduced. There was an immediate and rapid expansion of sugar-cane estates, to such an extent that planters in Province Wellesley began to encroach on land in the Krian area of Perak. By 1899 there were about forty sugar-cane estates in Perak, occupying a total area of more than 50 000 acres (20 000 ha) and employing between 8 000 and 9 000 labourers. But sugar-cane did not last very long as a major revenue crop. It has never been a very profitable industry, and severe competition from sugar-beet soon reduced prices to levels which forced the sugar growers of Peninsular Malaysia to stop production. The industry, however, lingered on until 1913 when the last refinery closed down.

The last important revenue crop to be grown before the introduction of rubber was coffee. *Coffea arabica* was planted on a small scale in many parts of the Peninsula, but it was not until the 1870s that it became a plantation crop, cultivated chiefly in Perak. In 1879 a fungus disease, which had decimated the coffee plantations of Ceylon, attacked the holdings and destroyed all hopes of establishing Arabian coffee as a major crop. A different species, *Coffea liberica*, was then tried in the hope that it would not succumb to the fungus. Planting on a fairly wide scale took place in the 1880s in Perak, Selangor and Negri Sembilan, and the Malays began to cultivate it as a peasant crop. At the end of 1896 there were seventy-two European-owned coffee estates in Selangor alone, occupying a total area of some 47 000 acres (19 000 ha) and with a labour force of about 4 000 Indians and Javanese. After an initial period of success the price became unremunerative as Brazilian coffee beans flooded world markets, and by 1901 all the European-owned estates of Liberian coffee had been interplanted with the new crop—rubber. Although prices improved after 1912, coffee never regained its status as a principal export crop.

The failure of coffee coincided with the discovery that *Hevea* would grow readily in the country. Between 1896 and 1899, as the price of coffee fell and pests and diseases took their toll of the coffee trees, some of the planters began inter-cultivating *Hevea* with coffee. Rubber planting was pursued most vigorously in the area between Klang and Kuala Lumpur, where a number of coffee estates supplied land suitable for rapid planting. Later, as more seeds became available, areas of jungle were cleared and planted with rubber. The average price for rubber between 1890 and 1900 was from Malaysian $1.30 and $1.70 per lb. The decline of coffee and the high prices for rubber acted in conjunction to stimulate rubber cultivation on an ever-increasing scale. The rubber areas increased from a meagre 345 acres (140 ha) in 1897 to about 50 000 acres (20 000 ha) in 1905. Coffee and sugar-cane were then being grown mainly as catch crops interplanted with young rubber trees. In the same year the export of rubber from the Federated Malay States was 105 tons, an insignificant figure compared with the 62 000 tons of wild rubber from South

America and other tropical areas. But a large percentage of the Peninsular Malaysia rubber acreage was composed of trees which had not yet attained the tapping age of six to seven years. After 1905, as more trees reached maturity, there was a corresponding increase in rubber output from the Peninsular Malaysian plantations.

Planting was further stimulated when the demand for rubber forced prices to rise above $2.50 per lb in 1906 and 1909, and to a record of nearly $5.50 per lb in 1910. Boom prices prevailed from 1910 to 1912. The rubber acreage in Peninsular Malaysia leaped from 50 000 (20 000 ha) in 1905 to over 290 000 (117 000 ha) in 1909. The spectacular profits realized by the rubber estates during the boom of 1910 to 1912 encouraged investors to put their capital into the large number of new rubber companies being formed in London. Although prices dropped steadily from the record of $5.50 per lb in 1910 to an average of 80 cents per lb in 1920, the rubber acreage and production continued to expand. In 1919 the net exports of rubber from Peninsular Malaysia reached nearly 200 000 tons, exactly half the total world exports of rubber. The pioneers in rubber were the Europeans and Chinese, but from 1910 onwards there was a rush by Malay smallholders to grow the crop. In some cases they cut down their fruit trees and even planted their padi fields with rubber; in others, especially where immigrant Malays were concerned, they cleared and opened up new land. Planting was greatly facilitated by the ease with which land could be obtained.

The first setback to the industry came in the years 1920 to 1922 when prices dropped to depression levels, averaging 33 cents in 1921 and 1922. The slump was due to overproduction, aggravated by the postwar depression and by extravagant methods of cultivation. The Stevenson Committee of Inquiry was appointed in 1921 to study the situation. The final report of the Committee recommended that the production and export of rubber in Ceylon (Sri Lanka) and Peninsular Malaysia be restricted and controlled by the Government. The decision to impose restrictions was made on the strength of the fact that Peninsular Malaysia and Ceylon together produced more than 70 per cent of the world's rubber, and in spite of the refusal of the Netherlands East Indies to co-operate in the Scheme. The object of the Stevenson Scheme was to raise prices above slump level, and to stabilize them at about 54 cents per lb by curtailing production and imposing a system of variable export quotas. The Scheme was adopted in 1922 and restriction remained in force for six years until November 1928.

The immediate effect of restriction was to raise average prices to 54 cents per lb in 1923, and 47 cents in 1924. The recovery of the motor car industry in the United States and the growing demand for rubber boosted average rubber prices to $1.25 per lb in 1925. The price increases which resulted from restriction in Peninsular Malaysia and Ceylon benefited all the other rubber-producing countries of the world, especially the former Netherlands East Indies. Because they were not partners in the Scheme, they were able to take advantage of the rise in rubber prices by increasing production and planting new areas with rubber. The result was that, while the share of Peninsular Malaysia and Ceylon in the total world exports of rubber fell from 70 per cent in 1922 to 52 per cent in 1927, the Netherlands East Indies' share over the same period rose from 25 per cent to more than 40 per cent, while their total planted area of rubber increased from 934 000 acres (378 000 ha) in 1922 to 1 299 000 acres (526 000 ha) in 1928. At the same time, restriction in Peninsular Malaysia and Ceylon encouraged the use of reclaimed rubber in the United States, so that the demand for natural rubber dropped and the accumulated stocks of rubber on the market could not be cleared.

The effect of increased production in the Netherlands East Indies and the drop in demand in the United States was to lower the price of rubber to 85 cents per lb in 1926. In spite of the Stevenson Scheme, the prices of rubber continued to fall steadily until they reached about 36 cents per lb in 1928 and 1929. By then it was apparent that the Scheme was no longer effective because of Dutch competition, and it was therefore abandoned in 1928. During the six years of the Scheme the local government had followed a policy of refusing to alienate land for new planting, with the result that Peninsular Malaysia lost its place to the Netherlands East Indies as the territory with the world's largest planted area of rubber. By 1929 the total planted area in the Netherlands East Indies was 3 155 000 acres (1 277 000 ha) and that in Peninsular Malaysia was 2 945 000 acres (1 192 000 ha) but a much larger percentage of the acreage in the Netherlands East Indies consisted of immature rubber so that its production remained less than that of Peninsular Malaysia.

With the end of restriction, rubber production increased greatly and surplus stocks began to accumulate as more and more rubber came into the market than could be consumed. In 1930 the market for rubber collapsed due to the world depression, and prices slumped to the lowest so far recorded. Average world prices during the Great Depression were 19 cents per lb in 1930, 10 cents in 1931, 7 cents in 1932, 10 cents in 1933 and 22 cents in 1934. The effects of the Depression in Peninsular Malaysia were serious. A very large percentage of the rubber smallholders discontinued tapping and turned to growing food crops. Some of the estates stopped production and there was widespread unemployment as the estate labourers were discharged. The other estates managed to survive the crisis by practising the strictest economies, and greatly reducing their costs of production to the levels where they could avoid loss at the current prices.

It became clear to all the rubber producers, including the Dutch in the Netherlands East Indies, that some form of restriction had to be imposed on production if the industry was to survive. Accordingly, a committee was appointed for the purpose of formulating a plan to regulate production from the rubber-growing countries of Southeast Asia, India and Ceylon. The new agreement was signed by all the countries concerned and came into effect in May 1934. From then until the outbreak of the Second World War rubber production in Southeast Asia, India and Ceylon was controlled by the International Rubber Regulation Committee. A definite quota was assigned to each producing country for each year. The basic quota for Peninsular Malaysia in 1935 was fixed at 504 000 tons. At the same time the Government stopped the alienation of land for rubber planting and prohibited new planting, although it permitted replanting of old rubber land. This law was relaxed for 1939 and 1940, when producers were permitted to engage in new planting on an area equivalent to 5 per cent of their 1938 acreage.

With the curtailment of exports rubber prices began to improve. The average prices increased gradually from about 21 cents per lb in 1934—35 to about 43 cents in 1941, the improvement being due as much to the armaments race and stockpiling as to export restrictions.

The 1920—22 depression, the Great Depression and the restriction schemes of 1922—28 and 1934—41 put a check to rubber planting in Peninsular Malaysia. In fact the official policy over this period was to discourage new planting by refusing to alienate land for rubber. In spite of this, the rubber acreage increased from 2 945 000 acres (1 192 000 ha) in 1929 to 3 481 000 acres (1 409 000 ha) of which 60 per cent were in estates and 40 per cent in smallholdings, that is, holdings of less than 100 acres. The increase in planted area was due to new planting on land already alienated but not yet planted with rubber. Such land had been held either in reserve and unplanted, or for the cultivation of other crops. Many of the larger estates had reserved land which could be used for the purpose, but most smallholders did not have unplanted reserve land. The only alternative was to grow the rubber on land which was under some other crops, such as coconuts, fruit and even padi. That many of them were willing to do this and sacrifice a source of income indicates the great attraction rubber growing had for the smallholders. Some of them ignored the planting ban during the Stevenson Scheme and grew rubber on land which had been alienated for other crops, while others went even further and established holdings on untitled land.

The rubber industry, in common with the other sectors of production in Peninsular Malaysia, suffered a reversal during the Japanese occupation. Planting and production came to a standstill. The occupation period saw the destruction of about 8 per cent of the estate acreage and about 4 per cent of the smallholding acreage of the country. In addition, there was widespread destruction of factories and other buildings as well as machinery. Many of the rubber areas suffered badly from general neglect, and were unkempt and overgrown with *lalang* and other growth. The estate labour force was scattered: some of the labourers turned to food growing, others to wage earning in the towns, whilst a large number of them were sent by the Japanese to help build the Burma—Siam railway. When the war ended only about a third of the pre-war labour force remained, so that the estates were greatly handicapped in their efforts to resume production.

The smallholders, on the other hand, relied mainly on family labour, and this, coupled with the fact that only the simplest equipment was required in their manufacturing processes, enabled them as a group to recover more quickly from the neglect of the war years. They were thus able to produce nearly 57 per cent of the total output for 1946, although owning only 44 per cent of the total acreage. By 1947, however, estate efficiency had been restored and estate production exceeded that of the smallholders.

The rubber industry suffered another set-back when the Communist uprising broke out in 1948. One of the major aims of the Communists was to disrupt the national economy by armed attacks on the rubber estates and the intimidation of workers. Whilst they did not succeed in attaining their objective, the attacks, nevertheless, seriously hampered production in some of the remote estates. In addition, the estate sector of the industry had to bear part of the heavy expenditure involved in providing protection for the plantations. This financial burden cut deeply into the profits for 1948 and 1949, when the profit margin for estates was already poor because of low average prices. However, the overall production remained high.

When the Korean War broke out prices soared high as the United States began to build up her stockpile of rubber. Prices rose to $1.08 in 1950 and later to a postwar record of $1.69 per lb. However, the boom petered out quickly and by 1953 average prices had fallen to 67 cents per lb. In the decade 1953 to 1962 average prices fluctuated between 67 cents (1953) and 114 cents (1955) per lb. Prices drifted lower in the decade 1963—72, from an average of 72 cents in 1963 to a new low of 42 cents in 1972. September 1972 saw the average price falling to its lowest level in twenty-three years. It was only towards the end of 1973 that prices began to improve, and for the first time in the decade rose beyond the $1 a lb level ($2.20/kilo). Prices in 1973 averaged 75 cents a lb. The four-fold increase in crude oil prices imposed by the Organization of Petroleum Exporting Countries (OPEC) in 1973—74 will inevitably raise the cost of producing synthetic rubber (which derives its raw materials from petroleum) and put natural rubber in a better competitive position against its synthetic rival.

The total planted area during the decade 1963—72 has remained at about 4.2 million acres (1.7 million ha). However, the area under estates declined from 1.9 million acres (770 000 ha) in 1963 to 1.5 million acres (600 000 ha) in 1972, whilst the area under smallholdings increased from 2.3 million acres (930 000 ha) to 2.7 million acres (1.09 million ha) during the same period. The fall in estate acreage was due to the subdivision and break-up of some estates and to the decisions of many estates to replant their old rubber land to oil-palm rather than to rubber. The increase in the smallholding acreage was due mainly to extensive new planting on land development schemes throughout the country.

Malaysia (Peninsular Malaysia, Sabah, Sarawak) today has the world's largest planted area under rubber, amounting to 4.9 million acres (2 million ha) or 35 per cent of the total world planted area of 14.6 million acres (5.95 million ha). Indonesia has a planted area almost equal to that of Malaysia, while Thailand has the third largest area with 12 per cent of the world total. Although some thirty countries in the tropical world grow rubber, these three Southeast Asian countries together account for 82 per cent of the world's acreage.

Methods of cultivation and production

The rubber tree, *Hevea brasiliensis*, is a hardy plant and in its native habitat in the Amazon Valley can survive the fiercest competition from other jungle species. It is a large tree with a straight trunk and high branching limbs. The smooth dark green oval leaves are shed once a year between January and April, but all the trees are never devoid of leaves at the same time. During this 'wintering' period there is a temporary drop in yield. Observations over a number of years have shown that the monthly production of rubber in both estates and smallholdings is lowest in April—May when refoliation takes place. The tree grows best in an equatorial climate with constantly high temperatures and a heavy, evenly distributed rainfall of 60 to 100 inches (1 500–2 500 mm) or more a year. As far as climatic conditions are concerned, the tree will thrive in any part of the Malay Peninsula below an elevation of about 1 000 ft (304 m); its growth becomes stunted at elevations above 1 500 ft (457 m).

It is also undemanding in its soil requirements but grows best in soils which are friable, deep, well-oxidized and acid in reaction (pH 4 to 6.5). Rubber is planted on a wide variety of soils. The value of the alluvial soils, most of which contain large amounts of impervious clay, depends on adequate drainage. They are suitable for rubber if the water table lies at an average depth of more than 42 in (100 cm). The soils derived from acid igneous rocks (granite) support good stands of rubber, but the sides of most of the granitic mountains are too steep for agriculture. However, rubber is planted where such soils occur in the foothills. Soils derived from basic igneous rocks are the most fertile of the inland residual soils, and rubber trees grow to a large size and give high yields when planted in them. Sedimentary rocks cover a large proportion of the foothills and undulating land between the coastal plains and mountain ranges of western Peninsular Malaysia. Soils derived from such parent materials are

227

of variable value for rubber cultivation. Soils derived from sandstones can be cultivated with *Hevea*, but those developed from shales and phyllites usually contain a lateritic hardpan which is highly resistant to root penetration. Rubber trees planted in areas where the hardpan lies near the surface become stunted and give very poor yields.

Hevea will not grow well in areas of impeded drainage. Good drainage is necessary to maintain a sufficient concentration of oxygen in the soil

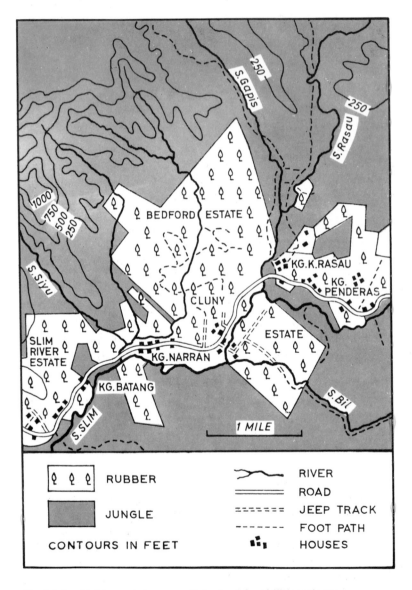

Fig. 10.1   Rubber estates on well-drained foothill locations.

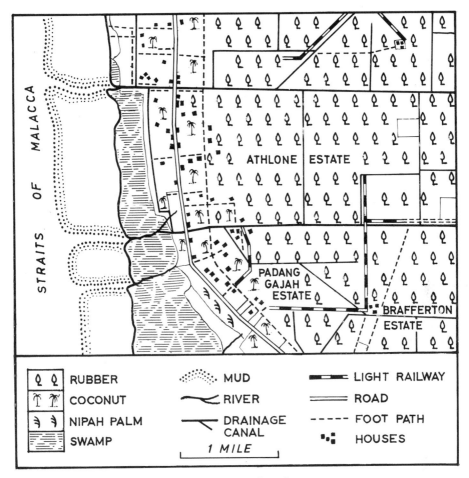

Fig. 10.2   Rubber estates on coastal, swampy locations.

atmosphere, to allow excess carbon dioxide to diffuse away from the root zone and to assist in the removal of toxic hydrogen sulphide from the soil. The best sites are undulating land with good natural drainage (Fig. 10.1), but flat swampy areas can be converted into good rubber land by an efficient drainage system. Much of the swampland along the west coast has been rendered suitable for rubber cultivation by careful drainage (Fig. 10.2). However, rubber trees planted on recently drained peat soils may have their roots exposed through progressive subsidence of the land as the peat dries, and are liable to fall over in a strong wind.

Most of the rubber holdings have been established on land formerly under jungle, though some of the oldest estates are on land previously under other crops such as sugar-cane, gambier, coffee or tapioca. Some of the Malay smallholdings, too, are planted on land formerly under subsistence crops such as padi, coconut or fruit.

229

The processes involved in establishing a rubber holding have remained substantially the same since the early days of rubber cultivation. The selected site is cleared of its jungle cover and the felled timber left to dry for two or three months. The timber is then set on fire. The requirements for a successful burn are (a) a period of three consecutive days without rain immediately prior to the day of the burn; (b) several hours of sunshine on the day of the burn, to dry off the dew; and (c) at least a slight breeze to help spread the fire. Burning causes a great loss of organic matter and nitrogen from the soil, although it is the cheapest and most efficient way of clearing the jungle. Soil exposure may be reduced by clearing the site of its vegetative cover without burning. But the advantage of conserving the humic matter is more than offset by the difficulty of movement of labour, the problem of controlling root disease and weeds and the dangers of pest damage which result from this method.

In the early phase of rubber planting the land was clean-cleared after burning, and the rubber seedlings planted on the bare land. In recent years it has been recognized that cover crops are necessary to protect the soil from excessive exposure and erosion. Apart from affording such protection, cover crops help to aerate and drain the soil, preserve its structure and enrich it with mineral nutrients taken up from below, or, in the case of leguminous covers, through the fixation of atmospheric nitrogen by bacterial action. There are two types of cover crops planted in estates: leguminous creepers such as *Centrosema pubescens* or *Pueraria javanica*; indigenous plants, except such undesirable weeds as *lalang* (*Imperata cylindrica*), bracken, stagmoss and Straits rhododendron. Creeping leguminous covers have the most marked effects on poor soils, by the improvement of the soil, enhancement of tree growth, advancement and improvement of early yields and reduction of root disease incidence (Gray, 1969). However, no cover crops are planted in many of the Chinese and Indian smallholdings. Instead, the spaces between the rubber trees are inter-planted with revenue crops such as gambier, tapioca, pineapple and banana. They are usually grown for two or three years until the rubber trees branch out and form too dense a shade for further successful intercultivation. Apart from cover crops, other methods of soil conservation may be necessary. On steep slopes terracing may be required as well as cover crops, and on moderately steep slopes contour bunding with a cover crop planted on the bunds is common. The cover crops are put in as early as possible after clearing, and after they are established the planting of rubber begins. Another method of soil conservation on slopes is to dig silt-pits. The soil from the pits is placed on the upper edge to check the force of the water running down the slope.

In the first few decades of rubber planting most of the estates and practically all the smallholdings were planted with unselected seedlings.

The seeds were either raised initially in nurseries, or in baskets, and then transplanted to the field when they reached a height of about 18 in (45 cm). Some were planted directly in the field. Two or three seeds were planted per hole and the weaker seedlings removed after six to nine months, leaving only the most vigorous seedling. But the trees raised from such seed gave highly variable yields. The modern practice is to plant only selected material which has been proved to be capable of high yields. A number of such high-yielding varieties or clones[1] have been developed by the Rubber Research Institute and by similar organizations in the other rubber-growing countries of the world (notably Indonesia). There are two ways in which high-yielding material may be propagated—through clonal seedlings or through budded stumps. By the first method the seeds from clones which have been proved to be high yielders are planted and the seedlings used to stock the holding. In the second, a high-yielding clone is grafted on to an ordinary seedling (called the root-stock) to produce a budded stump. This is done in a nursery and the budded stumps are then transplanted into the field.

The policy in the large European estates is to maintain a limited number of trees per acre. The pre-war practice was to plant an initial stand of 120 to 180 trees per acre, and subsequently to thin them out until a final stand of 80 to 100 trees per acre was obtained. The optimum density for high-yielding trees is about 120 per acre, with initial stands of 180 trees per acre for a budded stand, and 200 per acre for clonal seedlings. However, there is no hard and fast rule about the most profitable planting density. In contrast to estate practice, planting on smallholdings is very dense. Initial stands on smallholdings are between 300 and 500 trees per acre, with final stands of between 200 and 400 per acre; in Government block-planting areas the density is 160 trees per acre. The aim of the smallholders is to obtain a high yield per acre through dense planting, while the estates aim at high yields per tree. In most estates the extra revenue from yield increases that can be obtained from densities higher than the usual 120 to 130 trees per acre would be offset by increased tapping and collection costs.

The smallholder does not normally apply any manure or fertilizer to the growing plants. The general practice in estates is to add fertilizers to most soils at different stages in the growth of the trees. Fertilizers are thoroughly mixed with the top 6 to 8 in of soil in the planting hole at the time of transplanting the seedling or budded stump from the nursery, rock phosphate or an organic manure being used. Experimental work at the Rubber Research Institute has indicated that a mixture of phosphate, potash and nitrogen should be given at regular intervals during the growth of the young rubber plants in order to ensure against deficiencies of these elements. With some soils, however, one or more of these

[1] A clone is a group of plants, all the individuals of which are obtained by vegetative propagation from a single parent tree, whether directly or by multiplication.

mineral elements can safely be omitted without impairing the growth of the trees. Sulphate of ammonia or mixtures containing nitrogen and phosphate are most commonly used in mature rubber holdings. Potash is added to the mixture in areas with very sandy soils. Recent systematic studies of the soil series of Peninsular Malaysia on which rubber is grown have established the nutrient status of most of these soils. The specific fertilizer requirements of an area can now be assessed accurately by taking into account its nutrient status and other relevant field data, and, where one soil series is fairly uniform in nutrient status, a single fertilizer recommendation would be sufficient for rubber cultivated on that series (Guha, 1969; Chan *et al.*, 1973).

It takes from five to seven years from planting for a rubber tree to attain its tapping age. Tapping is the controlled wounding of the bark of the rubber tree so that the latex vessels are opened and the liquid latex flows out. Latex itself consists of about 60 per cent water, 35 per cent rubber hydrocarbon, and the remainder small percentages of mineral constituents. One of the main steps to the successful introduction of rubber into tropical Asia was the discovery of the proper method of tapping, a discovery made by H. N. Ridley and other pioneers at the turn of the century. The modern method of tapping is to cut a thin shaving of

Plate 15 Tapping rubber in a rubber plantation. Note the light undergrowth in this plantation. This photograph was taken at a time when the rubber trees were experiencing their annual 'winter', hence the unusually light canopy (see text above).

bark (bark excision) from the trunk at regular intervals, the cut being made at an angle so that the latex flows down into a cup placed to receive it. The cut is made with a special tapping knife. The tree is tapped once daily, or once in two, three or four days, by reopening the cut with the tapping knife. There are many different tapping systems practised in Malaysia, depending upon the type of tree (whether grown from unselected seedlings, clonal seedlings or budded stumps), the method of cultivation (whether estate or smallholding), the prevailing rubber prices and on individual preference. The ideal system is one which gives the highest yields at lowest tapping costs with the best growth and bark renewal, and the lowest incidence of brown bast (a disease of the tapping panel). Modern tapping systems are aimed not only at maximizing yields in areas planted with high-yielding clones but also at optimizing the usage of labour since in the estates tapping and collection costs represent more than 50 per cent of the total production costs (*see* de Jonge, 1969; Ng Eng Kok, 1969; Ng *et al.*, 1969).

The yield of latex varies considerably with the type of planted material. Figure 10.3 shows the average yields for estates in Peninsular

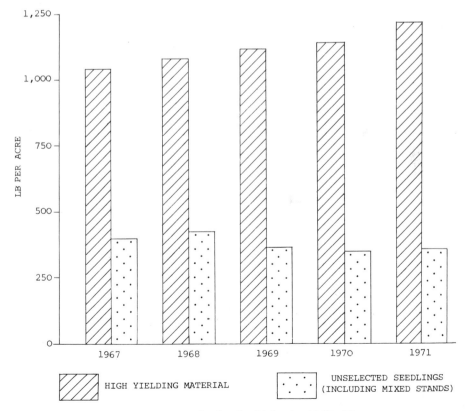

Fig. 10.3   Yield on rubber estates, Peninsular Malaysia, 1967—71.

Malaysia as a whole. The difference in yield between unselected seedlings and high-yielding material is considerable. An acre of high-yielding rubber can produce more than three times as much latex as an acre of rubber grown from unselected seedlings. The raising of yield levels by breeding and selection has been one of the major factors responsible for maintaining the competitive position of natural rubber. The average yields of unselected seedlings have seldom exceeded 50 lb/acre/year even in the best areas. In contrast, the average yields in areas planted with high-yielding material have increased from 450 lb/acre in 1951 to 1 214 lb in 1971. This increase in yields has enabled Peninsular Malaysia to expand its total production of rubber quite substantially during the last two decades in spite of the slight fall in total planted area. Experiments conducted by the Rubber Research Institute (RRI) have shown a peak yield of 3 855 lb/acre in one year from the clone RRIM 600, indicating the great potential for further improvements in yields in commercial plantings (Wycherley, 1969*b*).

The estate sector has always been ready to implement research findings as soon as they have been proved to be commercially feasible, and as a result of a vigorous policy of replanting with high-yielding material carried on over a period of years, 93 per cent of the total estate area is now planted to high-yielding trees. The smallholding sector, on the other hand, has lagged behind, and has only 62.5 per cent of its total area planted to high-yielders (Bank Negara, 1972). Since rubber trees have an average economic life of thirty years the smallholding sector is adversely affected through the immobilization of valuable rubber land for a lengthy period under low-yielding trees.

Latex is prepared for export by two basic processes, both of which involve the removal of unwanted water (latex from the tree contains 60 per cent water). The first is simple concentration by centrifuging, the end product being concentrated latex. This is then preserved by the addition of ammonia, and exported to consumers without any further preparation. Production of concentrated latex in 1972 amounted to 15 per cent of the total Peninsular Malaysian production of 1 258 000 tons of all types of rubber.

Latex is also prepared into dry forms by coagulating the latex particles by the addition of a small quantity of acid. Until recently the conventional method of treating the coagulum was to pass it through specially ribbed rollers to squeeze out the surplus water, and to dry the sheets in a smoke house. The rubber so produced is ribbed smoked sheet. Alternatively the coagulum may be passed through a creping machine and air-dried in a drying shed, the final product being crepe rubber.

In the 1950s and early 1960s intensive research was conducted on the methods of processing, packing and grading of rubber so as to enhance the competitive position of natural rubber and to meet the discriminating requirements of consumers. New methods were evolved of converting latex into rubber that is easy to handle, dry and compress while retaining the excellence of the polymer. The main objective was to convert liquid latex into solid rubber by the shortest and most economical route. The new forms of rubber have been given different trade names by the manufacturing companies and organizations, but all of them are blocked-baled, technically specified rubbers. One of the most widely used processes is the Heveacrumb process in which the wet rubber coagulum is milled between a series of grooved steel rolls which exert strong shearing forces on the coagulum. A small quantity of castor oil is added, allowing the rubber to break into crumbs. These are then dried in a special dryer (Morris, 1969). Rubbers produced by this and other new processing methods have excellent physical properties, including a uniformity which

Plate 16 SMR crumb rubber, a technically specified rubber which carries a guarantee of quality, presentation and technical specifications. Much of the rubber exported today is in this sophisticated form rather than as a purely agricultural product (see p. 236).

is much desired by the consumers and which is difficult to achieve by conventional methods.

With the advent of these new technically specified rubbers it was necessary to rationalize the classification of the types of rubber marketed. Accordingly Malaysia introduced the Standard Malaysian Rubber (SMR) scheme in 1965 which set technical specifications of rubber exported in conventional as well as new forms. SMR can only be produced by a producer registered with the Malaysian Rubber Exchange and Licensing Board, and punitive action can be taken against a producer who does not conform to the requirements of the scheme. All SMR rubbers carry a guarantee of standards of quality, presentation and technical specifications, and one tailored to meet the requirements of the consumers (Graham, 1969; Nair and Abdul Kadir, 1973). The scheme has now made it possible to market natural rubber as a sophisticated raw material rather than a purely agricultural product; its success can be seen in the increasing amount of rubber produced which bears the SMR trademark—from 8 000 tons in 1966 to 367 000 tons in 1972, representing 29 per cent of the total rubber production in Peninsular Malaysia for that year. The smallholder sector has also benefited from this development by selling its latex to central processing factories which process it into SMR. It is anticipated that SMR production would reach 50 per cent of total rubber production by 1975 (Bank Negara, 1972).

The types and distribution of rubber holdings

The rubber industry is stratified according to size of holdings and nationality of ownership. The situation with regard to the estates is summarized in Tables 10.6 and 10.7. Although Malaysians own three-quarters of the 2 014 estates covering 44 per cent of the total planted

Table 10.6   Nationality of ownership of rubber estates in Peninsular Malaysia, 1971

Nationality	Number of estates	Planted Area		Per-centage	Average size	
		Acres	Hectares		Acres	Hectares
Malaysian	1 480	694 000	282 000	44	469	190
Non-Malaysian:						
British	273	623 000	252 000	40	2 282	924
Singaporean	153	139 000	56 000	9	908	368
American	6	28 000	11 000	2	4 667	1 890
Indian	83	23 000	9 000	2	277	112
Europeans, etc.	19	54 000	22 000	3	2 842	1 151
Total	2 014	1 561 000	632 000	100	775	314

Source: *Rubber Statistics Handbook, 1971.*

Table 10.7   Nationality of ownership of rubber estates by size group, Peninsular Malaysia, 1971

Size group (acres)	Malaysian		Non-Malaysian	
	No. of estates	Per-centage	No. of estates	Per-centage
0–499 (0.202 ha)	1 149	78	175	33
500–999 (202–405 ha)	158	11	86	16
1 000–1 999 (405–809 ha)	111	7	120	22
2 000–2 999 (809–1 214 ha)	34	2	59	11
3 000–4 999 (1 214–2 023 ha)	18	1	57	11
5 000 and over (2 023 ha and over)	10	1	37	7
Total	1 480	100	534	100

Source: *Rubber Statistics Handbook, 1971.*

area, most of their estates are small, averaging less than 500 acres (200 ha) in size. Most of the larger estates are owned by non-Malaysians. The British, in particular, continue to be the dominant group in the estate sector, controlling 40 per cent of the total planted area. Fifty-one per cent of the non-Malaysian estates are larger than 1 000 acres (400 ha); in contrast, only 11 per cent of the Malaysian estates belong to the larger size groups (Table 10.7).

Table 10.8 shows the distribution of the rubber estates. Eighty-eight per cent of the estates are concentrated in western Peninsular Malaysia,

Table 10.8   Distribution of rubber estates in Peninsular Malaysia, 1971

State	No. of estates	Total planted area		Percentage of planted area
		Acres	Hectares	
Johore	396	399 000	162 000	26
Negri Sembilan	245	238 000	96 000	15
Selangor	262	227 000	92 000	14
Perak	340	205 000	83 000	13
Kedah	303	195 000	79 000	12
Pahang	177	118 000	48 000	8
Malacca	126	97 000	39 000	6
Kelantan	73	40 000	16 000	3
Penang and Province Wellesley	51	23 000	9 000	2
Trengganu	36	17 000	7 000	1
Perlis	5	2 000	1 000	—
Total	2 014	1 561 000	633 000	100

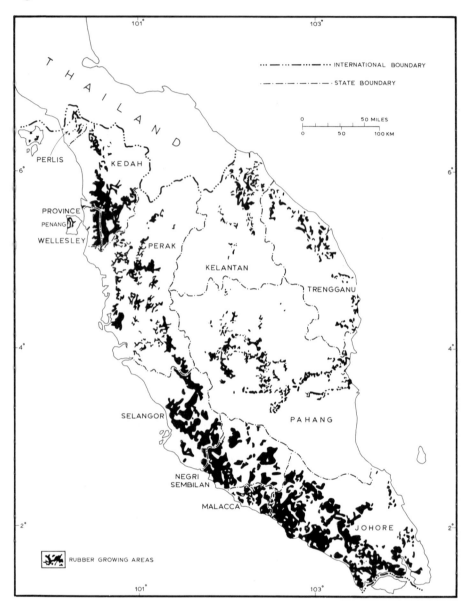

Fig. 10.4 Distribution of rubber (based on Wong, 1971).

from Kedah in the north to Johore in the south (Fig. 10.4). This zone or belt, sometimes referred to as the Tin and Rubber Belt, varies in width from 5 to 40 miles, and covers the coastal plain, inland freshwater swamps and the foothills up to an altitude of about 500 ft (152 m). The earliest rubber holdings were developed on the drier sites of the undulating lowlands and the slopes of the foothills. But the great demand for

Table 10.9   Distribution of rubber smallholdings in Peninsular Malaysia, 1966

State	Total planted area		Percentage
	Acres	Hectares	
Johore	666 000	269 000	26
Perak	390 000	158 000	15
Pahang	346 000	140 000	13
Kedah	244 000	99 000	10
Negri Sembilan	221 000	89 000	9
Selangor	187 000	76 000	7
Kelantan	179 000	72 000	7
Malacca	140 000	57 000	5
Trengganu	131 000	53 000	5
Penang and Province Wellesley	51 000	21 000	2
Perlis	17 000	7 000	1
Total	2 572 000	1 041 000	100

Source: *Land-use survey, 1966.*

rubber soon led to the reclamation of extensive areas of swampland, especially on the coastal plains of west Johore.

A smallholding is defined as 'an area, contiguous or non-contiguous, aggregating less than 100 acres, planted with rubber or on which the planting of rubber is permitted, and under a single legal ownership'. The land-use survey of 1966 showed that the total smallholding area was 2 572 000 acres (1 042 000 ha). The area was estimated to have increased to 2 703 000 acres (1 094 000 ha) by 1972 due largely to new planting and the fragmentation of estates into smallholdings. The distribution of smallholdings is shown in Table 10.9. It will be seen that although three-quarters of the total acreage is in the Tin and Rubber Belt, the degree of concentration in this Belt is not as marked as in the case of the estates. The east coast states of Kelantan, Trengganu and Pahang have substantial areas under smallholding rubber although this is not visually apparent because of the small size of the holdings and their dispersed distribution. Much of the rubber in Kelantan and Trengganu (and Kedah on the west) is poorly managed and has become rubber scrubland. The 1966 land-use survey enumerated a total area of 139 000 acres (57 000 ha) of scrub forest/scrub grassland/rubber in these three states. The average size of a smallholding is 6.6 acres (2.6 ha) (Barlow and Chan, 1969).

The marked concentration of rubber holdings along the western littoral of the Peninsula, as illustrated in Fig. 10.4 is the result of a fortuitous combination of circumstances. Given the demand for rubber and its products in world markets, the successful establishment of *Hevea* depended upon three other main factors, namely, (*a*) suitable conditions of climate and soil; (*b*) a cheap and abundant supply of labour; and (*c*) cheap and efficient means of transport. The natural conditions of climate and soil were found to be well suited for the growth of *Hevea*, especially along the well-drained gentle slopes of the foothills on both sides of the mountainous backbone of the Peninsula, and the undulating land of southern Peninsular Malaysia. Cheap and plentiful labour was available from South India. But the special attraction of western Peninsular Malaysia for the rubber planters was provided by the skeleton network of roads and railways already laid out to serve the tin mining industry of the western foothills. The combination of a good transport system, well-drained sites and proximity to the deep-water ports of Penang and Port Swettenham (now Port Klang) as points of entry and exit for labour, materials and processed rubber, probably accounts, more than anything else, for the concentration of rubber cultivation in this part of the country. In addition, many of the earliest rubber estates were planted in the western states on land which had once been under sugar-cane or coffee. Another factor which attracted the planters to the west was the early establishment of political stability in the tin-rich states of Perak, Selangor and Negri Sembilan. The success attending the first ventures at rubber growing gave further impetus to agriculturalists to open up more land for the crop. All these influences have worked to establish the greatest concentration of rubber in the west.

The distinction between the two main types of holdings—estates and smallholdings—does not lie in differences in size alone. The limits of an estate are usually well defined. It generally presents a picture of orderliness, with the rubber trees growing in neat rows and the undergrowth kept down by constant cutting. Some estates have little or no undergrowth and in this respect resemble the orchards of temperate lands in appearance. Each estate is served by an internal system of roads or laterite tracks radiating from a focal point (marked by the processing factory) to all parts of the holding, with pathways from tree to tree. There is also direct connection between the processing factory and the nearest main road or railway line. Occupying a central position in the estate is a group of buildings composed of the processing factory and smokehouse, the labourers' quarters and the manager's house. One of the main differences in the functioning of an estate as opposed to a smallholding is the source of labour. Labour is hired, either directly or by contract. There is also a division of labour within an estate—one group being engaged in tapping and latex collection, another in the preparation and processing of latex, a third in packing the finished rubber and minor groups in weeding and the general upkeep of the estate. Forty per cent of the 199 000 labourers employed in estates in 1971 were Indians, 37 per cent were Chinese and 32 per cent Malays.

The smallholding has a very different external appearance from that of the estate. The rubber trees are often interplanted with fruit, coconut or other trees and bushes. The rubber trees do not always form continuous stands but may be in isolated clumps separated by other vegetation. Beyond the environs of the farmer's house, the mixed stand of rubber and other tree crops usually gives way to a pure stand of rubber growing in the midst of tall undergrowth and rubber seedlings which have taken root from fallen seed. This pattern of mixed stands facing the road, river or railway and pure stands in the interior is a common one. Smallholdings of this kind may stretch for many miles on both sides of a line of communication, with no clear boundaries between individual holdings. The processing shed is usually near the house and consists of nothing more than an open-sided thatched hut housing a mangle or roller. There is no division of labour, the farmer and his family performing all the tasks of tapping, collecting, processing and drying the rolled sheets. The dried sheets are transported by bicycle and sold as low grade rubber to the nearest rubber dealer, who is usually also the local shopkeeper. Some farmers now sell their latex direct to a central processing factory.

From the post-1950 period the smallholding sector has expanded to include two other types of smallholdings. The first was the result of the subdivision of estates, whereby for a variety of economic and other reasons large estates were broken up into smallholdings, mainly on the west coast states and affecting largely the European-owned estates (Federation of Malaya, 1963). The average size of these smallholdings was 10 acres (4 ha) (Barlow and Chan, 1969). The second was the result of the block planting schemes established by the state and federal governments. These involve the new-planting of jungle land to provide farms for the landless, or in the case of fringe alienation and unsubsidised schemes, to supplement the area of existing smallholdings. The most important agency for block planting is the Federal Land Development Authority (FELDA), established in 1956, which up to 1970 was responsible for opening up about 150 000 acres (607 000 ha) of rubber smallholdings in all the states except Perlis and Penang. The average planted area per holding in the FELDA schemes was 7.5 acres (3 ha) and that in the state and unsubsidised schemes was 6 acres (2.4 ha) (Barlow and Chan, 1969), but the average planted area in the FELDA schemes will increase as FELDA now provides a 12 acre (4.8 ha) instead of a 10 acre (4 ha) lot to each settler in its rubber schemes.

Problems and prospects

It is difficult to over-emphasize the importance of rubber in the national economy. Peninsular Malaysia now produces about two-fifths of the world production of natural rubber.

In the seventy-five years since *Hevea* was first introduced into the Peninsula, Peninsular Malaysia has emerged from economic obscurity to occupy the position of a leading supplier of rubber to the international commodity markets. The industry has attracted overseas capital and given impetus to the development of all the states. The attendant benefits of prosperity have in their turn permeated all spheres of life. Public services in the form of roads, railways and harbours, and social welfare amenities including health and education, have expanded accordingly to cover a large section of the population.

But the prosperity of the rubber industry was not achieved without a struggle. In the course of attaining its pre-eminent position in the country, the industry had to overcome a number of problems which at times threatened to overwhelm it. These problems were not connected with the actual growing of *Hevea*, for in the Peninsula there is no disease that threatens the rubber plant in the way that the South American leaf blight devastates rubber holdings in tropical America. One of the most serious obstacles to rubber cultivation in Peninsular Malaysia was malaria. Most of the estates which were started in the early years of the industry were on the gentle slopes of the western foothills. The main and most dangerous malaria vector of the Peninsula—*Anopheles maculatus*—has its natural habitat in the clear, sunlit waters of small running streams. This vector was responsible for very high death-rates among rubber estate workers. The clearing of the forest and its undergrowth for rubber created favourable conditions for the multiplication of *maculatus*. The result was an extremely high malarial infection rate among the susceptible labour force recruited from South India. In 1911, for example, 9 000 out of a total estate labour force of 143 000 died from malaria. Individual estates suffered regular heavy losses from the disease. For instance, the Highlands and Lowlands Para Rubber Limited had a mortality rate of 20 per cent every year during its pioneering phase. Nearly half the labourers of the Midlands Estate died in the three years 1910 to 1912.

The problem of malaria was overcome through the efforts of Ross, Watson and Strickland, who evolved various methods of controlling the vectors by the destruction of their larvae. One very successful method was subsoil drainage, whereby all running water was led into underground drainage pipes out of the reach of the anophelines. Such a method, however, was too expensive for estate application. It was later discovered that a mixture of crude oil and kerosene poured over the breeding locations completely destroyed the mosquito larvae, and this method was widely adopted by the estates. Oiling, together with the increasing use of drug prophylaxis, led to a spectacular fall in the incidence of malaria and by 1935 malaria had ceased to be a major problem both in the estates and in the towns.

As seen earlier, rubber is especially liable to violent fluctuations in price. The rubber planters of Peninsular Malaysia have experienced periods when the price of rubber has fallen far below the cost of producing it, whilst at other times boom prices have prevailed. In seeking the advantages of crop specialization, rubber planters, as well as the country as a whole, have to face the liability of price instability. The problem is one over which the planters have little control, for the price levels are determined by the interplay of international market forces, and are tied in with the general economic as well as political conditions of the world. In some tropical countries, such as those of West Africa, semi-governmental organizations called Produce Marketing Boards help to smooth out the ups and downs of commodity prices by guaranteeing prices for any one season, and taking up all the produce that local growers can supply. The Marketing Boards then sell the produce at the prevailing world prices in the commodity markets, profiting or losing by the transaction as the case may be. There are no such marketing boards in Peninsular Malaysia, and all rubber growers, estates as well as smallholders, are fully exposed to price risks.

The economic instability arising from price fluctuations of the degree common in the rubber industry produces many undesirable consequences. The balance of payments and government revenues which are dependent largely on export duties and taxes fluctuate in sympathy with price changes, with the result that planning at the national level becomes difficult. On the individual level such instability generates income instability amongst the farmers, affecting their patterns of savings, investments and resource allocations, and ultimately their standards of living.

The rubber planters of Malaysia as well as the natural rubber producers in other parts of the world are faced with serious competition from the synthetic product (*see* Thomas and Allen, 1973). Synthetic rubber production expanded considerably during the Second World War. The Japanese conquest of Southeast Asia deprived the Allies of most of their natural rubber, and forced them to manufacture the synthetic product on a large scale in order to continue the war effort. The total production increased from a mere 2 560 tons in 1940 to 820 350 tons in 1945. In 1971 the total world output of synthetic rubber was 5 000 000 metric tons compared with the total output of 3 000 000 metric tons of natural rubber. Synthetic rubber is now manufactured in seventeen countries. The Western industrial countries account for most of the production; the most important Asian producer is Japan, with 15 per cent of total world production. New types of synthetic rubber are being manufactured to meet the demand by consumers for special purposes rubber. With the advent of synthetic cis-1,4-polyisoprene, a very near duplicate of natural rubber, the latter no longer enjoys the advantage of being a unique material. Furthermore, to this technological advantage must be added the economic advantage which synthetic rubber has over

243

its natural rubber competitor in requiring less processing steps, a smaller factory area and fewer inventory stations in factory handling (Bekema, 1969).

The growth of the synthetic rubber industry in the last twenty years has been stimulated by the availability of cheap feedstocks (which are oil-derived) and by cost economies of scale. But even before the oil crisis of 1973 feedstock prices were already rising due to increases in crude oil prices (Bateman, 1974). The steep increases in crude oil prices following the oil crisis of 1973—74 have resulted in a deterioration of the competitive position of synthetic *vis-à-vis* natural rubber. This highlights the greatest advantage of natural rubber over synthetic rubber—that is, a biologically derived raw material that can be produced on a renewable basis—whereas synthetic rubber must depend for feedstocks on a non-renewable resource which today is not only highly priced but which is also rapidly being depleted.

In the local sector the Malaysian rubber planters have been meeting the synthetic challenge by raising their operating efficiency, reducing costs, improving the quality of their product, and especially by raising yields from the rubber tree. In so far as costs are concerned, a survey of 312 estates has shown that 56 per cent of the total operating costs are for tapping and collection, 13 per cent for management, 12 per cent for processing, 5 per cent for weeding, 3 per cent for manuring and 13 per cent for sundry items such as transport, field maintenance, pest and disease control, etc. (Ng *et al.*, 1969). The most likely area for cost reduction therefore lies in tapping and collection, which in view of the rising expectations of labour appears to be possible not through a reduction in wage costs but through increasing yield levels (*see* Ng *et al.*, 1969).

The smallholding sector has traditionally suffered from high production costs while producing a lower quality rubber, both of which are features characteristic of low-volume producers. Their poor quality product can only command correspondingly low prices. The fact that in 1966 about 70 per cent of the smallholders' latex was in the form of unsmoked sheet (Lim, 1969) is an indication of the scope that exists for improving the quality of smallholder rubber. The first attempt to produce higher quality smallholder rubber was made before the Second World War when local businessmen established group processing centres where smallholders could process their latex into smoked and unsmoked sheet for a small charge. A large number of such processing centres were established in the postwar period, especially after independence when the Government and the Rubber Research Institute (RRI) made a concerted effort to better the livelihood of the hitherto neglected smallholder sector of the rubber industry. More recently the RRI developed new central processing factories which can process smallholder rubber into top quality rubber as well as SMR rubber. The establishment and operations of these new factories have been taken over by the Malaysian Rubber Development Corporation (MRDC). These factories not only enable the smallholders to upgrade the quality of their rubber which is then sold for a higher price, but they also provide competition to the dealers in the neighbourhood so that those smallholders who have not contracted to sell their latex to the factories have also benefited from the improved prices which the dealers are now willing to pay (Barlow and Chan, 1969). Moreover the smallholders who sell their latex to the factories no longer have to spend their afternoons processing sheet rubber but could use them for other remunerative work.

By 1973 the MRDC had set up eleven heveacrumb and three latex concentrate factories. The MRDC expects to have twenty-eight factories in operation by 1975; in addition fifteen factories would be built by FELDA, the State Economic Development Corporations and the private sector (Bank Negara, 1972) so that the outlook for upgrading the quality of smallholder rubber appears promising.

Another important problem facing the rubber industry is the replacement of old uneconomic trees with high yielders. The productive life of a rubber tree is about thirty years. The tree is not tapped until it is six or seven years old. The yield from the seventh year onwards increases rapidly until a peak is reached between the fifteenth and seventeenth year, after which there is a steady decline until the tree ceases to be economic to tap. For this reason a rubber holding must be replanted with new stock about once every thirty years in order to maintain continuous production. Unfortunately, because of the Great Depression of the 1930s followed by the Second World War, and because of a lack of foresight, especially on the part of the smallholders, a position was reached in 1952 in which more than half of the total planted acreage, both estates and smallholdings, was composed of trees which were more than thirty-three years old. The backlog of replanting in 1952 has been estimated at 1 500 000 acres (600 000 ha), and in order to counter the combined threat of over-aged trees and competition from synthetic rubber it was necessary to accelerate the rate of replanting.

In order to assist the rubber industry in its replanting programme a special tax was imposed on all rubber exported from Peninsular Malaysia, and funds thus acquired were used to subsidize the cost of replanting in both estates and smallholdings. The smallholders were in a far worse position than the estates as a greater percentage of their acreage consisted of over-aged trees. The Government therefore set a target of 480 300 acres (194 000 ha) to be replanted by the smallholders between 1953 and 1959. The actual acreage replanted up to 1959 was 310 000 (125 000 ha). The estates, aided by the Replanting Scheme and reserve funds of their own put aside for the purpose, had replanted at a much faster rate than the smallholders. The slow progress in the smallholdings was due to a number of factors. In the first years of the Scheme many smallholders were not aware of their eligibility for a replanting grant, while others were hesitant about applying for assistance until they were fully satisfied that it did not involve governmental control of their holdings. But the main reason for the slow rate of replanting was the reluctance on the part of the farmers to cut down their old trees and thus lose their major source of income for the next six or seven years before the new trees could mature. This reluctance became more pronounced as the price of rubber increased, since the income lost through cutting down the trees would be correspondingly greater.

Table 10.10   Acreage replanted on estates and smallholdings, Peninsular Malaysia, 1947—71

Period		Estates	Smallholdings	Total
1947—50		167 100	12 300	179 400
1951—55		236 300	85 400	321 700
1956—60		362 900	294 600	657 500
1961—65		304 100	381 000	685 100
1966—71		179 600	311 800	491 400
Total	Acres	1 250 000	1 085 100	2 335 100
	Hectares	505 800	439 100	944 900

Source: *Rubber Statistics Handbook*, various years.

Table 10.10 shows the area of rubber replanted by estates and smallholdings in the postwar period. Although the total area replanted in the smallholding sector is more than 1 million acres (400 000 ha), the rate of replanting has been slower than that of the estate sector, and by 1972 only 62.5 per cent of the smallholdings have been planted with high-yielding material as compared with 93 per cent of the estates. The present rate of smallholder replanting per annum is about 69 000 acres (28 000 ha), which means that it would take a further nineteen years from 1972 to replace the entire smallholding stock with high-yielders. But since rubber trees have to be replanted on a thirty-year cycle, the area first replanted in 1952 would have to be replanted in 1982. To clear the backlog by 1982 the rate of replanting would have to be accelerated from 69 000 acres (27 600 ha) to 133 400 acres (54 000 ha) per annum (Bank Negara, 1972).

In order to achieve this objective and to modernize the smallholding sector a new authority—the Rubber Industry Smallholders Development Authority (RISDA)—was established in 1973. Smallholders are being encouraged to replant under a new policy of full replanting grants for holdings of up to 15 acres (6 ha) compared with the former policy of limiting full replanting grants to holdings of up to 5 acres (2 ha). Holdings larger than 15 acres would be entitled to grants covering two-thirds of their area.

The slower replanting rate of smallholdings as compared with that of the estates has meant that a higher proportion of the smallholding area remains under poor stock, mainly unselected seedlings, thereby serving to depress average yields. Thus in 1972 the average yield in the smallholding sector was only 608 lb/acre (681 kg/ha) as compared with the estate yield of 1 099 lb/acre (1 232 kg/ha) (Bank Negara, 1972).

One of the most promising methods of increasing the competitive position of natural rubber is through increasing the yield and thereby productivity per unit area. This is in fact the policy followed in the estate sector so that although the estate acreage decreased from 2 030 000 (494 000 ha) in 1953 to 1 508 000 (609 000 ha) in 1972, production increased from 341 000 tons to 669 000 tons in the same period. In contrast, the smallholders have increased their acreage from 1 606 000 (647 000 ha) in 1953 to 2 698 000 (1 089 000 ha) in 1972 but their production has only increased from 232 000 tons to 589 000 tons. In brief, the smallholders, while having 64 per cent of the total planted acreage, accounted for only 47 per cent of the total production in 1972. Their low productivity is due to their poorer receptivity to research innovations, which manifests itself mainly in their lower rate of response to the benefits that can be derived from replanting their low-yielding stands with the best modern clones.[1] Not only will the modern clones provide substantially higher yields than unselected seedlings, but they are also less prone to disease and require less attention to thinning.

Apart from the planting of high-yielding clones the rubber producers, mainly the estate sector, have also been able to increase yields through the use of chemical stimulants such as 2,4,5T and Ethrel. The application of Ethrel once in two or three months to scrapped bark below the tapping cut is now an established estate practise. However the yield increase is concentrated in the first few weeks after each application, while experience has shown that the tapping intensity must be reduced in order to prevent a rapid fall-off in response. The greatest gains have been through the use of stimulants to maximize yields of rubber stands due to be cut down for replanting, in estates as well as smallholdings.

On the research frontier today the RRIM is conducting experiments which aim at improving the yields of rubber from 3 000 lb/acre, which some estates are already achieving, to as high as 6 000 lb/acre; perfecting the technique of crown-budding whereby a clone with a light disease-free crown is grafted on to a high-yielding trunk clone; and overcoming two inherent shortcomings of the rubber tree, namely, the lengthy period of

[1] A survey of rubber smallholders showed that lack of up-to-date knowledge of rubber cultivation was one of their major problems, the others being low prices and lack of working capital (Selvadurai, 1972*a*).

immaturity (six to seven years) and the slowness with which maximum yield levels are reached. Reducing the period of immaturity, maximizing early yields and shortening the current rate of exploitation to twenty instead of the normal thirty years appear not only to hold promise of increased returns and profits but have these additional attractions: (*a*) capital investments can be recovered earlier; (*b*) the long-run inelasticity of supply characteristic of a long-life perennial such as rubber is reduced; (*c*) the 'time-lag' between availability and commercial planting of the latest high-yielding material is reduced; (*d*) accelerating the rate of replanting from 3 to 5 per cent per annum will provide an increased flow of rubber wood for wood-based industries; and (*e*) the rubber producer is able to reduce the length of time his land is immobilized under one crop (*see* Lim *et al.*, 1973).

Padi

Padi was the second most important crop in terms of area, occupying 14 per cent of the total cultivated area of Peninsular Malaysia in 1971. By 1973 it had become the third most important crop, after rubber and oil-palm. Padi cultivation is entirely a smallholder occupation and almost entirely a Malay interest. An estimated 97 per cent of the padi farmers are Malay. There are some Chinese padi farmers in Sekinchan (Selangor), Changkat Jong (Perak) and the Central district of Malacca. A few Thai farmers grow the crop in the border states of Kelantan, Perlis and Kedah, while the Indian padi farmers are confined mainly to the Tanjong Karang area of Selangor. The padi that is grown in Peninsular Malaysia is mainly of the 'wet' variety, cultivated in flooded fields.

The history of wet-padi cultivation in Peninsular Malaysia is a comparatively recent one, and this may account for the lack of adjustment of planting techniques to the physical environment in some parts of the Peninsula. Although the crop has long been planted in the Peninsula, the varieties grown before the fifteenth century were cultivated in the *ladang* manner without the use of irrigation water. Malay tradition has it that the techniques of ploughing and flooding the fields were introduced from Thailand into the northern Malay States during the fifteenth century. The new method spread slowly along the coast to the southern states during the course of the next century. The Minangkabau who migrated from Sumatra and settled in large numbers in Negri Sembilan also grew wet-padi and worked the land with the methods they brought over from across the Straits of Malacca. From the beginning of the nineteenth century wet-padi cultivation was increasingly adopted by the Malays but did not entirely supersede hill or dry-padi cultivation until the beginning of the present century when the Government discouraged dry-padi cultivation because it led to serious erosion of the hillsides and slopes. Today, in consequence, wet-padi is the dominant form of padi

Table 10.11   Area, distribution and types of padi land in Peninsular Malaysia, 1972–73 season

| State | Area | | | | Percentage of total area |
	Wet padi (acres)	Dry padi (acres)	Total (acres)	(hectares)	
Kedah	293 000	4 000	297 000	120 000	32
Kelantan	174 000	6 000	180 000	73 000	19
Perak	124 000	4 000	128 000	52 000	14
Trengganu	70 000	4 000	74 000	30 000	8
Perlis	66 000	—	66 000	27 000	7
Selangor	49 000	—	49 000	20 000	5
Pahang	41 000	7 000	48 000	19 000	5
Penang and Province Wellesley	39 000	—	39 000	16 000	4
Malacca	27 000	—	27 000	11 000	3
Negri Sembilan	23 000	—	23 000	9 000	2
Johore	7 000	—	7 000	3 000	1
Total	913 000	25 000	938 000*	380 000	100

* Does not include the 525 000 acres (212 000 ha) of wet-padi planted as an off-season crop.

cultivation, and hill or dry-padi occupies significant areas only in five states (Table 10.11).

Although padi is a cereal capable of giving sustained yields without exhausting the fugitive fertility of tropical soils, its cultivation in the Peninsula is at best a risky occupation because of the unfavourable climate, which is more suited to the growing of tree crops than of annuals, the lack of water control over wide areas and the depredations of pests and diseases. Crop failures are common. The process of pioneering for padi is an arduous one, involving the clearing and draining of swamps, the construction of irrigation and drainage works, and often the preliminary burning off of the peat layer over-lying the soil. All such work has to be done under water-logged conditions and in mosquito-infested country. The labour of preparing the land for planting, especially where draught animals cannot be used because of excessively soft soils, and of transplanting and weeding by hand, demand considerable physical effort under the hot and saturated atmosphere of the flooded fields.

Moreover the low economic returns from padi growing compare unfavourably with the returns from almost every other form of agriculture, particularly with rubber cultivation. The smallholder can obtain more rice by purchasing it with the proceeds from an acre of rubber than by growing the rice directly from an acre of land. For this reason padi planting has never been a popular occupation with the Chinese, in spite

249

of the fact that many of them were padi growers in China before they migrated to Peninsular Malaysia. An indication of this disinterest is seen in the Changkat Jong Irrigation Area of Lower Perak, where the Chinese padi farmers prefer to cultivate vegetables in the off-season rather than grow a second padi crop (Selvadurai, 1972a). Even among the Malays padi is no longer planted as a matter of course. Because of the hard work involved, the higher earnings from other occupations and the attractions and amenities of town life, many of the younger Malays are drifting from the padi areas and rural *kampongs* in search of other work.

Yet on the whole the padi acreage has increased from an average of 662 000 acres in 1926–30 to 938 000 acres (380 000 ha) in 1972–73. This represents a net expansion of more than 250 000 acres (100 000 ha) since the 1920s. The increase has come about mainly through the efforts of the Government to lessen the country's dependence on rice imports from other parts of Southeast Asia. Up to the end of the First World War the large profits from rubber were responsible for the general disinterest in the growing of other crops. The demand for rice by the rapidly increasing population was met by imports from the rice-granaries of Burma and Thailand. Between 1917 and 1921, however, failures of the rice harvests in Burma and India doubled the price of rice; at the same time rubber prices slumped, and the then Malayan Government had to spend one-third of the accumulated financial surplus balance of earlier years on subsidizing rice imports. Home growing of padi was stimulated and production which had stood at 178 000 tons in 1918–19 rose to 309 000 tons in 1925–26 and to 440 000 tons in 1930–31.

The Great Depression of the 1930s brought home with renewed force the vulnerable position of Peninsular Malaysia with regard to her staple food supply and to the overdependence on rubber and tin for her economic wealth. A new policy of self-sufficiency was adopted at this critical period. Following the recommendations of the Rice Cultivation Committee of 1931, the Drainage and Irrigation Department (DID) was established in 1932, and its activities in providing controlled water supplies, in draining swampy coastal lands and in opening up new land as padi settlement areas up to the beginning of the Second World War did much to turn governmental hopes to partial reality. Production of padi increased to 570 000 tons in 1935–36.

The threat of war and the emergencies that might arise as a result of the rice supplies being cut off induced the Government to adopt a new attitude towards padi cultivation by non-Malays. Up to the 1940s it was the British policy to reserve all potential padi land for the Malays. In 1939 the Government announced that, in view of the dangerous position of the country with regard to its food supplies, non-Malays would be allowed to take up new padi land. But in order to safeguard Malay interests short leases were issued, and occupancy by non-Malays was to be confined to newly opened padi land only. A minimum price of

M$2.50 per *picul* was fixed and guaranteed for all padi produced. Various other measures, such as the distribution of fertilizers and waiving of the water rate, were planned as additional inducements. But these measures were taken too late to be of practical value. Besides, the high prices of rubber and tin lured all available Chinese and Indian labour to these industries, and no one wanted to leave his work for the hard life of padi planting. Not surprisingly, the production of padi fell from 570 000 tons in 1935–36 to 540 000 tons in 1940–41.

The Japanese occupation and the cessation of rice imports coupled with steadily falling home production lowered the nutritional standards of the people to near the danger line by the end of the war. In 1946 padi production was only 375 000 tons and net imports of rice had fallen from 659 000 tons in 1939 to 141 000 tons. With the restoration of normal conditions in 1948 production returned to its pre-war level. The policy of the Government up to 1973 was to make Peninsular Malaysia 90 per cent self-sufficient in rice. The concerted efforts made to increase rice production in the 1960s, mainly through the provision of better irrigation facilities and double cropping, have resulted in the attainment of this objective as early as 1971. Imports of rice, which stood at 400 000 tons in 1964, have fallen in consequence, and in 1973 were only 157 000 tons. In 1973 the Government, because of the world food situation, decided that the country should be fully self-sufficient in rice. This target was to be achieved through the extension of irrigation facilities and double cropping to cover the existing areas under wet-padi cultivation and through the opening up of new padi lands, particularly in the Trans–Perak and Rompin–Endau areas. The emphasis in governmental policy is also to enhance the economic status of the padi farmers through increasing yields per acre, reducing costs of production, providing a guaranteed minimum price and through the establishment of an integrated authority—the National Padi and Rice Authority—which will co-ordinate the production, milling and marketing of padi and rice in all the padi producing areas.

The colonization of padi lands

The reclamation of an undeveloped piece of swamp land is only the preliminary, though vital, step in the colonization of that area. The past settlement schemes in Peninsular Malaysia were from the start only moderately successful because of a marked lack of response on the part of the population to take up new land for padi cultivation. This was partly due to the fact that pressure of population on padi land was confined to only a few localized regions such as the Kelantan delta, and there was therefore no large surplus agricultural population ready and eager to settle in the newly opened lands. Then again, pioneer settlement in the humid tropics is always a laborious and difficult process, and the

Plate 17   Pioneer cultivation in a swampy valley in Pahang. The forest has been cut down and partially cleared. It is not possible to clean-burn the clearing because of the waterlogged conditions. The felled vegetation is therefore being left to rot. The first crop of padi is already in the ground (see p. 251).

pioneer settler in Peninsular Malaysia has to face several years of hard work with poor returns before his fields can begin to produce a reasonable income. It takes a minimum of three years before the settler and his family can start to plant padi in the fields, for he has first to clear the land, build his house and construct the sawahs (wet or flooded fields). During this period he has to find work elsewhere to support his family.

The area of land issued to each settler varied from region to region. In Sungei Manik experience had proved that a Malay family could gain a fair livelihood by cultivating 6 acres (2.4 ha) of padi and planting *kampong* produce (e.g. fruit, coconut and vegetables) in another 2 acres (0.8 ha) of non-irrigated land. In many of the other areas, however, the settler was given only 2 acres of padi land, an area too small to provide any surplus above the farmer's bare subsistence needs. In Tanjong Karang the 3 acres (1.2 ha) of padi land and 1 acre of *kampong* land allotted to each settler were insufficient for a good livelihood.

Many of the colonization schemes, including large ones such as Sungei Manik and Tanjong Karang, provided only the most rudimentary facilities for the colonists. Up to 1939, settlers were offered no facilities other than a free survey and free irrigation water. After the war the shortage of food led the Government to promise more liberal terms in order to encourage settlement. These included free transport to the colonization area, temporary housing, a $33 to $50 subsidy for each acre of land cultivated, loan of saws, axes, *parangs* (long-handled knives), *changkols* (hoes), free seed for the first two years and a guaranteed minimum price for padi. The planter, in trying to provide for his family during the first few years before his crops could be harvested, often had no option but to borrow money from professional money-lenders or shopkeepers at high rates of interest, thus getting early into debt.

Today, land for padi cultivation has become a scarce resource. The Economic Planning Unit has projected that only 42 000 acres (17 000 ha) of land would be cleared for padi between 1966 and 1985. In view of the limited extent of potential padi land and the high cost of developing land for padi, it would appear that the best prospects of increasing the production of padi lie in increasing yields in existing padi areas rather than in the opening up of new areas. This indeed is the intention of the Government—to concentrate padi production in the rice bowl areas where double cropping can be practised and yields increased, and to encourage padi farmers in the single crop and marginal areas to put their land to alternative uses where possible or to move out altogether from these areas to more remunerative occupations (Selvadurai, 1972*b*).

Areas, farm size and average yields

The main padi areas are located in the northern part of the Peninsula, north of latitude 4° 30′ N (Fig. 10.5 and Table 10.11). There is a small but distinct climatic seasonality here which makes it more suitable for padi cultivation than areas lying nearer the Equator. More than 70 per cent of the total production of padi comes from these two northern regions:

1. The northeast coastal plains centred round the Kelantan delta where padi growing is the main occupation and padi occupies the largest crop areas. This is largely a subsistence region, and little of the padi produced goes beyond the state boundaries. Padi has long been grown here, and up to the beginning of the present century the region had been self-sufficient, producing enough to feed the population. But the increase of population in the last seventy-five years and the shortage of land for conversion into padi fields have turned it into a rice-deficient area, and a small amount has to be imported annually to supplement the rice produced within Kelantan.

2. The north-western coastal zone running from Perlis southwards to the Krian district of Perak. The extension of modern drainage and irrigation facilities to a large part of the region, and the opening up of new lands, notably the Krian Irrigation Area, have made this into a rice-surplus area,

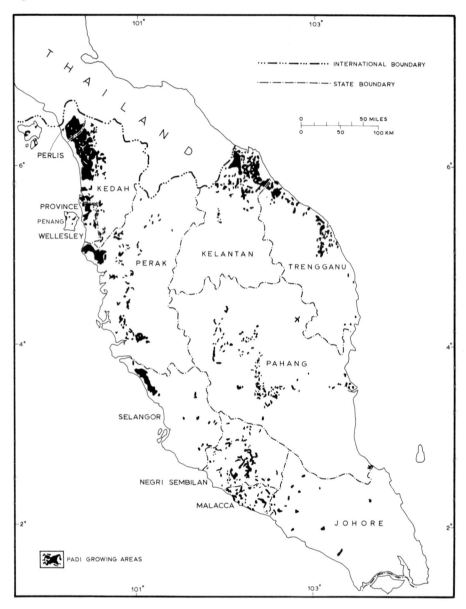

Fig. 10.5   Distribution of padi (based on Wong, 1971).

and the annual surplus goes to supplement the requirements of a part of the non padi-growing population.

Of the large coastal plains lying south of the rice bowl areas of Perlis, Kedah and Province Wellesley and Krian on the west, those of Perak and Selangor cover substantial areas, but only part of these areas have been

254

developed for padi. The Sungei Manik Irrigation Scheme, located between the Batang Padang and Kinta rivers in Lower Perak, was started in the 1930s when investigations by the Drainage and Irrigation Department indicated that about 25 000 acres (10 000 ha) of land could be opened up for padi. Development was planned to cover five stages; to date four stages totalling 16 000 acres (6 500 ha) have been completed. Adjacent to this scheme is the Changkat Jong Irrigation Scheme lying in the triangle formed by the Telok Anson—Bidor and Telok Anson—Degong roads. The scheme aimed at converting 6 000 acres (2 400 ha) of jungle into irrigated padi lands for Chinese settlers. Work was started in 1940, the original plan being to develop the land in three stages. Two stages covering 5 000 acres (2 000 ha) have been completed; the Second Malaysia Plan has provision for the development of the third stage.

In Selangor part of the 500 square miles (1 295 sq km) of swamp which lie between the Bernam and Selangor rivers has been converted into padi fields. This developed section, known as Tanjong Karang, is a coastal strip some 3 miles wide and about 27 miles long, and is bounded by a coastal bund on the west and the main irrigation canal on the east. In eastern Peninsular Malaysia the Pahang and Rompin—Endau deltas remain undeveloped except for small widely scattered fields and *kampongs*.

In addition to the contiguous tracts found on the large coastal plains, padi is also grown in inland valleys throughout the Peninsula, in small widely scattered fields in rolling country and foothill regions. A typical landscape is one of padi fields occupying the flat, narrow valley bottom on either side of a river, with smallholder houses strung out along the break of slope, and tree crops of rubber, coconut and fruit occupying the slopes (Fig. 7.7). The padi is grown entirely for subsistence, while the tree crops are grown partly for consumption (in the case of coconut and fruit) and partly for sale. This form of land-use is common in the hill and valley regions of Negri Sembilan, in upper Malacca, parts of inland Selangor, upper Perak and in many parts of central Pahang and Trengganu. The other common type of padi landscape is a variation of the inland valley type, with the difference that the padi fields are generally on both sides of a river, and the houses and tree crops on the drier sites on the levees and river banks. Such a pattern is a typical one along the lower courses of the larger rivers, best exemplified by the Pahang River (Fig. 7.4). In places the fields and *kampongs* are contiguous with one another and may stretch for several miles to form a linear belt of riverine settlements.

The majority of the padi farms are less than 5 acres in size, and more than half of them are less than 3 acres. There are approximately 296 000 padi farmers in Peninsular Malaysia cultivating a total of 938 000 acres (380 000 ha) of land; the average padi farm area is therefore 3 acres (1.2 ha). Of the 132 276 individual farms recorded in the 1960 Census of Agriculture in which wet-padi was the main crop, 97 per cent were under

255

Table 10.12 Number and size of padi farms in Peninsular Malaysia, 1960

State	Total number of farms	Percentage						
		Below 1 acre	1–1¾ acres	2–2¾ acres	3–3¾ acres	4–4¾ acres	5–9¾ acres	10 acres and over
Kedah	44 910	8	19	19	12	10	26	6
Perak	20 772	14	26	19	12	9	19	1
Kelantan	20 554	8	26	32	16	10	8	0
Penang and Province Wellesley	11 290	9	31	23	13	11	13	0
Perlis	8 540	3	11	19	16	13	33	5
Selangor	7 996	3	14	5	40	13	23	2
Trengganu	6 966	14	23	29	11	10	13	0
Pahang	3 940	16	38	26	11	5	4	0
Malacca	3 128	21	32	24	7	6	9	1
Negri Sembilan	2 980	38	36	19	4	3	0	0
Johore	1 200	5	60	27	3	3	2	0
Federation	132 276	10	23	21	14	10	19	3

10 acres in size, 78 per cent under 5 acres in size and 54 per cent under 3 acres in size (Table 10.12).

Eighty per cent or more of all the padi farms in all the states except Kedah, Perlis and Selangor were less than 5 acres in size. More than half of all the farms in all the states except Kedah, Perlis and Selangor were less than 3 acres in size, while more than half of the farms in Negri Sembilan, Johore, Pahang and Malacca were even smaller (less than 2 acres each). The highest percentage of small farms was found in Negri Sembilan: 74 per cent of the farms in that state were less than 2 acres in size, and 93 per cent less than 3 acres in size. In contrast, the highest percentage of large farms was found in Kedah and Perlis, with 32 and 38 per cent of the farms 5 acres or larger. The general overall pattern of small farm size may be due to a number of factors such as the pressure of population on padi land and the lack of suitable areas for expansion, the shortage of draught animals which prevents the farmers from cultivating a larger acreage, the excessively soft nature of the soils in some of the padi areas which prevents the use of the plough, and the subdivision and fragmentation of the land.

Experimental research carried out by the Department of Agriculture indicated that over all the padi lands of Peninsular Malaysia there was a 'bar' beyond which padi yields could not be raised in spite of liberal applications of manure and fertilizers and of good drainage and irrigation. This bar varied from 400 to 500 *gantangs* per acre (or 2 200–3 025 lb per acre). These maximum potential yields, however, were low compared with those actually attained in sub-tropical warm-temperate regions. Italy, for example, had an average yield of 3 750 lb per acre in 1949–51, and Spain of over 4 000 lb per acre. Yields in Australia, reputed to be the highest in the world, averaged 4 250 lb per acre in a normal year, and may be as high as 6 720 lb per acre in exceptionally good years. In contrast, the actual yields in Peninsular Malaysia (Table 10.13) while among the highest in Southeast Asia, are still low when compared to those in the extra-tropical countries. The average

Table 10.13   Average yields of wet-padi (main-season crop), Peninsular Malaysia, 1925–71

Season	Average yield per acre (lb)	Season	Average yield per acre (lb)
1925–26	1 089	1950–51	1 842
1930–31	1 545	1955–56	1 754
1935–36	1 787	1960–61	2 391
1940–41	1 512	1965–66	2 285
1945–46	1 155	1972–73	2 498

yields have shown a modest rate of annual increase of 1.6 per cent between 1952 and 1973. There is still clearly room for improving yields, and because of the limited acreages of potential padi land, the country will have to depend for part of its food supply in the long run on increased yields as a means of increasing rice production rather than on the opening up of new padi lands. The new rice variety 'Mahsuri Bahagia' which can yield 600 *gantang*/acre with moderate fertilizer application could play a key role in the realization of this target.[1]

The average yield for any one year is computed by dividing the estimated annual production by the acreage planted. These average yields, however, vary greatly from region to region and from season to season, depending on the degree of water control, the planting techniques, the ravages of pests and diseases and the fertility of the soils. The crop in any one season may be totally or partially destroyed because of late planting, drought, floods or the depredations of pests and diseases. The consequences of the loss of a season's harvest on the padi planter are far-reaching. Although actual starvation seldom occurs, the planter will have to find a means of supporting himself and his family until the next harvest. The usual way out is to obtain an advance in cash and/or in kind from the village shopkeeper-cum-moneylender at an exorbitant rate of interest. The loan is given on the security of the next season's harvest or the mortgage of the planter's land. Since, in view of the small size of the farm, a season's harvest is barely sufficient to cover the subsistence needs of the planter and his family, there is great difficulty in repaying even the interest accumulated on the loan, and the entire debt may never be repaid during the farmer's lifetime.

The cycle of padi cultivation

The overwhelming majority of the padi farmers are Malays. The 1957 census enumerated 381 593 Malay padi planters, and only 16 702 Chinese, Indian and other farmers. The number of padi farmers today is estimated to be 296 000 (Selvadurai, 1972*b*). In the northeast and northwest, the cultivation methods employed have been evolved over a long period of time and show an intimate adaptation to local conditions. While the principles are essentially similar throughout the Peninsula, customary methods vary in detail from region to region, due mainly to variations in local conditions. The main factors which influence the methods of cultivation are the nature of the soil, the nature of the water-supply (whether from direct rainfall or from an irrigation canal), the surface relief and the extent to which the planters of one area are able or willing to modify their techniques to suit the environmental conditions existing in their area.

[1] A new, as yet unnamed, variety that can yield 1 200 *gantang*/acre is being developed by MARDI.

The cycle of cultivation activities is geared primarily to the annual cycle of rainfall, in Kedah and Perlis and in Kelantan and Trengganu to the northeast monsoon and in the Port Dickson—Malacca coast to the southwest monsoon. The rainfall in the other padi-growing areas is of the equatorial type, without any distinct seasons. The onset of the rains in most parts of the Peninsula is so uncertain, however, that crop losses through late planting are common in those regions without the advantage of a controlled drainage and irrigation system. In general the work cycle commences a little earlier in the north and then moves southwards. The main phases of the cultivation cycle are:

1. Preparation of the land. The padi season opens with the farmer clearing and cleaning the canals and waterways and repairing the bunds that separate the fields from one another. The bunds are constructed of a mixture of clay, mud and weeds, and are necessary to retain the water in the fields during the growing season. The methods and implements used to prepare the land for the padi seedlings depend mainly on the nature of the soil, the water supply and local custom. The land is usually ploughed in most areas with drainage and irrigation facilities, and ploughing is commonly done in Kedah, Perlis, Penang and Province Wellesley, Malacca and Kelantan. A wooden, single-furrow plough with an iron-shod share is used, and may be drawn by one buffalo or two oxen. The land is flooded to a depth of 1 or 2 in to render the soil soft enough for the light plough. Cultivation is usually to a depth of 3 or 4 in. The fields may be ploughed two or three times. The weeds are then left to rot for three weeks to a month. The land is then raked and harrowed until the soil is left in a soft, puddled condition. Raking continues until all weeds are destroyed.

A different method of preparing the land is employed in those areas where the soils are too soft to permit the use of the plough, or where poverty prevents the farmers from hiring buffaloes for ploughing. The fallow vegetation is cut down a little below ground level by means of a scythe-like implement known as a *tajak*. The cut vegetation is left to rot for about two weeks, and is then raked into heaps for a further two to four weeks of decomposition. The rotted growth is subsequently plastered on to the bunds or scattered throughout the fields. This method is practised in Krian, Tanjong Karang, Negri Sembilan, Pahang and parts of Province Wellesley and Kedah.

In the double cropping areas of Province Wellesley and the Muda Irrigation Area the farmers have to harvest their main season crop and plant their second crop within a period of six to eight weeks. The traditional methods of field preparation have to be replaced by mechanical methods, using two- and four-wheeled tractors, in order to cope with the tight schedule of work. An estimated 70 per cent of the farmers in these areas make use of the hired tractor service to plough their fields.

Plate 18   Tractor ploughing in a padi field in Tanjong Karang, Selangor. The tractor has replaced the buffalo in many of the padi areas of Peninsular Malaysia especially those areas which are double-cropped (see p. 259).

2. Sowing.   The usual method employed is to sow the seeds in carefully prepared nurseries and to transplant the seedlings when they have reached the right stage of development. The nursery beds are located on dry land in those areas where the water supply is uncertain and the farmer has to rely on direct rainfall. The advantage of a dry nursery is that the seedlings can remain as long as three months before transplanting, so that the farmer is able to delay transplanting, if necessary, until field conditions are suitable. In areas with a controlled water supply the nurseries are of the 'wet' type. The seedlings in this case must be transplanted after forty days or they become too mature for the purpose.

3. Transplanting.   Transplanting takes place as soon as possible after the final preparation of the fields in order to check weed growth. This phase of padi cultivation is done by the women. The seedlings are pulled from the nursery and tied in small bunches. The roots are washed to remove the soil, and the top few inches of leaves are cut off in order to reduce water loss through evaporation. Transplanting may be entirely by hand, or may be made less laborious by using a two-pronged implement known as a *kuku kambing*. Two to six seedlings are planted in the mud

260

at intervals of between 12 and 15 in per 'hill', the actual spacing depending upon the variety of seeds used, the local conditions of soil and on custom. The plants are spaced closer in fields where the irrigation water is more than 12 or 18 in deep, as deep water inhibits tillering. Transplanting is labour-intensive, needing six to ten man-days to complete an acre. The large labour requirements for this phase of the cultivation cycle can be a limiting factor in the size of farm operated by the padi farmer (Selvadurai, 1972*b*). A more complex system of multiple transplanting is carried out in Krian. The injury to the root system through frequent transplanting acts as a stimulus to the subaerial section of the plants, resulting in increased tillering and higher yields.

4. After-cultivation. This consists mainly of weeding by hand. In richer soils the plants grow rapidly to form a thick canopy. Weed growth is thus inhibited, and one thorough weeding some six to eight weeks after transplanting is usually sufficient for the season. In poorer soils the land may have to be weeded twice or even three times in order to control excessive weed growth and encourage tillering. The plants begin to tiller about a month after transplanting, each plant sending up anything from two to fifty tillers, depending on the fertility of the soil, the depth of water and the distance of planting.

5. Harvesting. The fields are gradually drained of water as flowering becomes general, and should be completely dry by the time the grain has 'set' and begins to ripen. The varieties traditionally planted take from five to eight months to mature, and short-maturation varieties are sown only in the lighter soils where retention of water presents a difficult problem. Because of the different maturation periods and different planting dates, harvesting is generally going on in some part of Peninsular Malaysia between November and May. The threshing methods employed are simple but laborious. By far the most common method is to harvest each ear separately by means of a small knife known as *pisau menuai* or, in Selangor, as *tuai*. The other method is to harvest by means of a sickle (*sabit*). The grain together with about 2 ft of straw is cut in armfuls and laid on top of the stubble to dry before threshing. The crop is threshed by treading on the ears (in the case of padi reaped by the *pisau menuai* method), or by beating the sheaves against a wooden tub (in the case of padi reaped by the *sabit* method). Winnowing is also done by hand.

The cycle ends with the harvest and the land is laid fallow until the beginning of the next season. In some areas the land is put to some other use after the harvest. In Province Wellesley and the Muda Irrigation Area where double-cropping is practised, the farmers grow short maturation varieties in order to fit two padi crops in one year. A widespread practice in other areas is to plant off-season crops such as vegetables and other food crops after the padi harvest. In Kelantan short-term crops such as maize, tapioca, peppers, chillies, beans, sweet potato and vegetables are planted in fields close to the farmer's house. However, the total area thus utilized is less than 10 per cent of the total padi acreage of the state. The practice of off-season cropping is best developed in the *mukims* of Tranquerah and Lorong Pandan in Malacca. The farmers here grow vegetables for the Singapore and Kuala Lumpur markets and have been doing so for the past thirty years. A short-term padi strain is used so as to leave sufficient time after the harvest for the vegetable crop. Most of the farmers are Chinese, although there are also some Malays who grow off-season crops during the fallow period. But for best results and high yields the land must be heavily manured, and while the Chinese are able to use the droppings from pigs, the Malays do not do so for religious reasons. Apart from pig manure, the Chinese farmers also employ prawn dust, rotted fish and buffalo dung. The main crops grown are leafy vegetables, radish, tomato, beans, gourds, cucumber, ginger, sweet potato, yam, onion and tapioca.

Some major problems of padi cultivation

1. Water control and double cropping.   The distinguishing feature of wet-padi cultivation is the fact that the plants grow in a field of standing water. The basic need of wet-padi is a large and assured supply of water during the greater part of the growing season. There is a definite relationship between water supply and crop yields, and within the tropics yields are higher in artificially irrigated lands than in lands which are rain-fed. The quantity of water necessary for optimum yields depends on the soil characteristics, the evaporation rate, the variety of seed planted, the method of planting and the level of the water table. The minimum quantity necessary has been estimated to be about 143 000 cubic ft per planted acre. About 2 in of water should cover the field immediately after transplanting in order to check weed growth. This is later increased to 4 in, and, in the final stages of growth, to about 8 in.

Drainage is as important to high yields as irrigation. Excess water must be drained from the fields if the grains are to ripen properly. There must be provision for getting rid of unwanted water which may flood the fields as a result of unusually heavy rainfall or through the encroachment and infiltration of water from adjoining swamps. Lack of drainage in peaty lands causes the soils to become waterlogged and excessively sour. Padi planted on such soils cannot retain a firm hold and the plants are liable to fall over with the first heavy windstorm, especially after they have flowered. A period of drainage between the harvest and the next planting is essential for soil aeration. Drainage also affects the nitrogen supply of the soil. In adequately drained fields the nitrogen is released by anaerobic decomposition and becomes available to the growing plants during the early and middle stages of growth when it is most needed. In poorly drained areas the nitrogen becomes available only late in the growing season when it causes grain lodging, late ripening and renders the plants more susceptible to disease.

Water control is therefore essential to successful padi cultivation. The Malay padi planters in historical times used various ingenious means of regulating the water supply. The most common system employed for fields which bordered streams was to raise the water level of the stream by means of dams constructed of brushwood, tree trunks, bamboos and boulders. Such dams were small and weak, and often gave way at a critical period and ruined the crops. Where the river was large and the banks too high to allow for dams, water-wheels were used to lift the irrigation water to the fields on one or both banks. The water was conducted by troughs to the fields, but the water-wheels could not rise or fall with the river levels, and were easily destroyed in floods. They were capable of lifting 1 500 gallons of water per hour, sufficient to irrigate 3 acres of land. In the largest rivers with well-developed levees such as the Perak and Pahang rivers, irrigation by gravitation presented considerable difficulties as the river levels in many parts were lower than the levels of the fields and the levees were too high to permit the efficient working of the water-wheels. The farmers had to rely entirely on local rainfall for their water supply in swampy locations, and the areas they were able to plant each year varied with the amount and incidence of rain that season.

The successful cultivation of padi under such conditions was difficult. While they were effective under ordinary conditions, dams and water-wheels were small and capable of irrigating only small acreages. They could not act as reservoirs when the rainfall was deficient, and were liable to be destroyed during floods. Failures of crops through floods or drought were therefore common.

The development of modern methods of water control based on concrete reservoirs, dams, weirs, canals, pumps, etc., began in Peninsular Malaysia soon after the establishment of British rule. The first major attempt was the Krian Irrigation Scheme, which was completed in 1906 and brought adequate water control facilities to some 56 000 acres (23 000 ha) of land on the northwest coast of Perak. But governmental interest in padi flagged as rubber came into the agricultural scene, and for the next twenty-five years no attempts were made to extend modern drainage and irrigation facilities to other parts of the Peninsula.

The Great Depression revived governmental interest in increasing the home production of rice. A Rice Investigation Committee was set up. Its report stated that the basic need of padi farmers in all the states was for better water control facilities, pointing out that, apart from the Krian Scheme, no such facilities existed anywhere else in the country. The Committee recommended that the work of water control should be pan-Malayan and accordingly recommended the formation of a new department to be called the Drainage and Irrigation Department (DID).

263

Between the formation of the DID in 1932 and the outbreak of the war, the department set about restoring padi lands that had been abandoned because of silting, and also initiated the development of two large padi colonization schemes—the Pachang Bedina Scheme in Selangor and the Sungei Manik Scheme in Lower Perak. A number of small riverine areas were also provided with proper water control facilities. In the ten years of its existence up to the Second World War, the DID provided modern methods of drainage and irrigation to some 120 000 acres (49 000 ha) of existing padi land, and opened up an additional 53 000 acres (21 000 ha) of new padi land. Altogether about 23 per cent of the total padi acreage in 1940 was provided with some form of water control.

Considerable damage was done to irrigation and especially to drainage works during the Japanese occupation. The DID had to repair this damage and at the same time increase the tempo of its activities because of the serious shortage of rice in the postwar period. The padi acreage was expanded to 803 000 (197 000 ha) in the 1947—48 season, but only 30 per cent of the total acreage had proper drainage and irrigation facilities. Between 1949 and 1954 the area of padi increased to 846 000 acres (210 000 ha) of which 37 per cent had water control facilities. The programme of the DID for the period 1955—59 planned for the construction of thirty-four irrigation projects to affect an estimated 206 000 acres (50 000 ha) of existing padi land and bring into cultivation an additional 70 000 acres (17 000 ha) of new land. Owing to the shortage of experienced engineers, among other factors, the target was not realized, and at the end of 1960 the total area with proper drainage and irrigation facilities increased by only 80 000 acres over that in 1954.

The need for modern drainage and irrigation facilities remains as great as ever, although the situation has improved substantially since the pre-1930s. Damage to crops because of floods or drought is common in those areas without a controlled water supply. It is estimated that an increase of at least 25 per cent in yields can be achieved in Peninsular Malaysia by just guaranteeing the water requirements of the padi plants. But more than increasing the yield of the main season, crop irrigation enables farmers to grow two crops per year instead of only one. Since double-cropping is the main instrument whereby rice production can be increased substantially, the Government has made massive efforts to extend the area served by modern irrigation facilities. By 1971 the area with such facilities amounted to two-thirds of the total padi acreage of 926 000 (228 000 ha). Slightly less than half of the irrigated area had water supplies for double-cropping; while the remainder of the irrigated area had supplies which were inadequate for more than one crop a year.

As one-third of the total padi area in Peninsular Malaysia is still either rainfed or dependent on traditional means of irrigation, there is considerable scope for the extension of modern irrigation facilities to these areas.

Under the Second Malaysia Plan an additional 165 000 acres will be provided with modern irrigation facilities, so that by the end of 1975, when the total padi acreage is expected to be 1 million acres (405 000 ha), the total irrigated area will be 785 000 acres (320 000 ha) or 78.5 per cent. It is also expected that the double-cropped area will then increase to 600 000 acres (243 000 ha).

Double-cropping brings in its train a number of problems other than the provision of an adequate supply of water. Firstly, farmers who have been used to growing only one crop a year will have to adjust their work cycle in order to maintain the tight planting and harvesting schedule necessary for successful cropping. This involves carrying out a large number of farm operations in the six- to eight-week interval between the main season crop and the second crop. Secondly, harvesting of the off-season crop will have to be carried out during the rainy season. This in turn poses the problems of drying the harvested padi and transporting it from the farm to the mill. The National Padi and Rice Authority (NPRA) plans to provide half the drying capacity needed in the double-cropped area, while leaving the other half to the private sector. So far seven of the sixteen drying complexes have been built by the NPRA. All-weather roads are being constructed in the Muda and Kemubu (Kelantan) Irrigation Areas as a solution to the transportation problem.

2. Manuring of padi soils.   Manuring of padi land, whether for the main crop, for off-season crops, or for double-cropping, is influenced by the type and characteristics of the padi soils, and these in turn have an important bearing on yields. Padi soils are generally classified according to the percentage of clay they contain. In Peninsular Malaysia wet-padi grows best on clay loams (containing 15−25% clay), clay soils (25−30% clay) and heavy clay soils (more than 35% clay). The critical factor affecting yields is the sand component—the higher the percentage of sand, the less valuable is the soil because plant growth on such soils tends to be retarded. Yield variations of padi are determined more by the mechanical composition of the soils and their physical structure than by their chemical and nutrient content which is satisfactory for normal plant requirements. The composition and quality of some common padi soils as worked out by Jack are shown in Table 10.14.

The first-class soils have an organic matter content of 2 to 8 per cent, clay content of 25 to 65 per cent, fine silt 10 to 25 per cent and sand 2 to 10 per cent. The quality of the soils deteriorates where the sand content increases to 20 to 40 per cent, and such soils are classified as second class. Where the sand content is above 40 per cent, the soil is very poor and produces very poor crops, as exemplified in Soil Sample No. 9 (Table 10.14). Soil Sample No. 10 has first-class qualities but its peaty nature with toxic humic and other acids is detrimental to the padi plants. Three or four inches of peat are sufficient to reduce good padi land to

Table 10.14 Mechanical composition and quality of representative padi soils in Peninsular Malaysia

Locality	Organic matter (per cent)	Clay (per cent)	Fine silt (per cent)	Silt (per cent)	Sand (per cent)	Class of land
1. Krian	4.0	57.7	20.9	15.3	2.1	First
2. Kedah	nil	28.2	58.1	10.5	3.2	First
3. Kedah	nil	31.1	31.7	27.2	10.0	First
4. Kuala Kangsar	nil	26.2	50.4	16.3	7.1	First
5. Jelebu	4.0	17.5	32.8	16.3	29.4	Second
6. Kuala Pilah	nil	17.6	28.1	16.6	37.7	Second
7. Kuala Kangsar	nil	18.6	27.4	14.0	40.0	Second
8. Jelebu	1.6	19.1	30.2	7.3	41.8	Second
9. Kuala Kangsar	nil	6.9	10.2	14.0	68.9	Third
10. Krian	12.8	28.9	34.6	15.6	8.1	Third

Source: *Jack (1923)*.

very poor land. Soils with a peat layer composed of organic matter derived from the *gelam* tree (*Melaleuca leucadendron*) occur widely in low-lying swampy riverine and alluvial lands in Malacca, Perlis, Kelantan and Trengganu, and are avoided by the padi farmers because of their excessive acidity.

Most of the padi lands are cultivated year after year without any systematic manuring. Regular manuring is practised only in Kedah, and to a lesser extent in Province Wellesley, where the farmers apply heavy dressings of bat guano to their fields. The average rate of dressing is equivalent to 50 lb of phosphorus per acre per annum, and the resultant increase in yields is about 186 lb per acre. In Kelantan and Malacca the farmers dip the padi seedlings into a mixture of cow manure and wood ash before transplanting.

Experiments conducted by the Department of Agriculture have shown that manuring will increase yields significantly in those acres where normal yields are considerably below the average because of poor soils. In eastern Peninsular Malaysia where there are about 200 000 acres (81 000 ha) of light soils which are deficient in soluble phosphates and nitrogen, systematic applications of the correct mixture of fertilizers have resulted in yield increases of 30 to 400 per cent. However, governmental attempts to popularize the use of fertilizers in Kelantan in the early 1950s drew poor responses, mainly because of the farmers' lack of capital and their unfamiliarity with chemical fertilizer use. In more recent years the Kelantan farmers have become more conscious of the benefits that could be derived from regular fertilization of their fields: a 1968 survey of the Kemubu padi area showed that 70 per cent of the farmers there used fertilizers, most of them obtaining the fertilizers under the government fertilizer subsidy scheme.

Over Peninsular Malaysia as a whole fertilizer use in padi cultivation has become increasingly important for two main reasons: (*a*) the successful implementation of the double-cropping programme depends on the ability of the farmers to grow padi on a sustained yield basis, which in turn implies maintaining the productivity of the soils through fertilization; and (*b*) the introduction of fertilizer responsive varieties of padi which are also high yielders. Selvadurai (1972*b*) has found that in the double-cropping areas nearly all the farmers regularly apply fertilizers to their fields, although the amount used is usually about half of the quantity recommended by the Department of Agriculture. Up to 1971 the Government provided a 30 per cent subsidy on fertilizers for padi cultivation, but this has now been withdrawn to farmers in irrigated areas. Credit for the purchase of fertilizers, among other inputs, will now be provided by the Agricultural Bank (Bank Pertanian).

3. Socio-economic problems.   Tenancy has become a major problem in the padi-growing areas of Peninsular Malaysia. The position is summarized in Table 10.15. It will be seen that only 48 per cent of the farmers own all the land they operate; the rest are either full tenants or owner-tenants. Tenant farmers either lease their land from the owners or else pay rental in the form of a fixed cash sum; padi equivalent; or crop-sharing. Tenancy can be a disincentive to double-cropping if the tenants

Table 10.15   Tenure status of padi farmers, Peninsular Malaysia

State	*Total padi farms*	*Padi farmers by tenure status* (per cent)		
		Full owners	Part owners Part tenants	Tenants
Johore	4 000	70	20	10
Kedah	81 000	45	20	35
Kelantan	56 000	25	55	20
Malacca	12 000	52	18	30
Negri Sembilan	19 000	87	7	6
Pahang	20 000	70	14	16
Penang and Province Wellesley	16 000	44	17	39
Perak	44 000	50	13	37
Perlis	12 000	45	24	31
Selangor	13 000	60	25	15
Trengganu	19 000	55	23	22
Total	296 000	48	25	27

Based on Selvadurai (1972b).

are not protected against excessively high rentals. The Padi Cultivators (Control of Rent and Security of Tenure) Act of 1967 seeks to provide this protection to the tenant farmers by setting the maximum rentals for various classes of land.

Indebtedness and lack of capital are serious constraints to the development of smallholder agriculture throughout Peninsular Malaysia. Within the padi-growing sector indebtedness is very high: for example, surveys undertaken by the Ministry of Agriculture have shown indebtedness rates of 85 per cent in Malacca and Selangor (Selvadurai, 1972b). Debts were incurred for non-productive purposes, mainly to finance living expenses. The main sources of credit are the rural provision shops which may charge interest rates as high as 60 per cent per annum. In the rice bowl areas of the northwest the padi-kuncha system is commonly practised whereby seasonal loans are given to farmers who repay them at harvest time in padi in units of the kuncha (160 *gantangs* or 8 960 lb).

The need to provide alternative sources of credit at reasonable interest rates has become more acute with the introduction of the double-cropping programme. Institutional credit facilities provided by the co-operative societies and farmers' associations and supplemented by the co-operative bank have not been adequate. In 1969 the Government established the Agricultural Bank (Bank Pertanian) to co-ordinate and provide credit for agricultural purposes, giving priority to the credit needs of farmers in the double-cropping padi lands of the Muda and Kemubu Irrigation Areas. Up to 1973 some 22 500 padi farmers have obtained credit from the bank.

The traditional padi marketing system has also become inadequate. It does not provide the padi farmer with the stimulus for increasing production, mainly because of malpractices by the dealer-cum-shopkeepers who make excessive deductions from the Government guaranteed minimum price, often manipulate the weighing scales to their advantage, and may purchase padi by volume rather than by weight whenever it is more profitable to do so (FAMA, 1967). The Federal Agricultural Marketing Authority (FAMA) was established in 1965 to solve this problem. It in turn formed a separate body in 1967 called the Padi and Rice Marketing Board to control the marketing of padi at farm level (including the direct buying and selling of padi) and to ensure that fair and stable prices are paid to the farmers. The functions of this Board were taken over by the National Padi and Rice Authority in 1972.

Oil-palm

The oil-palm (*Elaeis guineensis*) was introduced into Peninsular Malaysia in the 1850s but the palm was cultivated only as an ornamental plant until 1917 when the first plantation was started in Kuala Selangor. Very little progress in the cultivation of the crop was made until 1926 when the area under oil-palm increased by nearly 2 000 acres over that of the previous year, to 12 000 acres (5 000 ha). The acreage after 1926 steadily expanded as more planters began to take an interest in the crop in response to attractive prices for palm-oil. In 1933 the total area was 63 646 acres (26 000 ha) and by 1940 it had increased to 78 300 acres (32 000 ha). The postwar period was spent in extensive rehabilitation of the estates and the total acreage remained unchanged until after 1948 when slow but steady increases were recorded. In 1953 the total area under oil-palm was 108 000 acres, and in 1960 135 000 acres.

The declining trend in rubber prices in the 1960s made oil-palm an attractive alternative to rubber, and decisions were therefore made by both the private sector and the Government to plant oil-palm on newly cleared land as well as on old rubber land due for replanting. The result was an unprecedented increase in both the area and the production of the crop (Table 10.16). In the decade 1960–70 the area increased by an average annual rate of 24 per cent while the production increased by an average annual rate of 34 per cent. By 1966 Malaysia had become the world's leading producer of palm-oil, a position she continues to maintain today.

Table 10.16   Area, production and yield of oil-palm, 1960–72

Year	Area in production		Production of palm-oil (tons)	Yields (lb/acre)
	Acres	Hectares		
1960	99 000	40 000	90 000	2 045
1961	107 000	43 000	93 000	1 951
1962	114 000	46 000	106 500	1 090
1963	121 000	49 000	124 000	2 278
1964	128 000	52 000	120 000	2 099
1965	147 000	59 000	146 000	2 229
1966	162 000	66 000	183 000	2 527
1967	184 000	74 000	213 000	2 598
1968	210 000	85 000	261 000	2 784
1969	267 000	108 000	321 000	2 686
1970	331 000	134 000	396 000	2 648
1971	421 000	170 000	542 000	2 890
1972	887 000	359 000	649 000	3 061

The area under oil-palm has continued to increase since 1970. In 1971 the total area of mature and immature oil-palm was 769 000 acres (310 000 ha). This has since increased to 1 182 000 acres (478 000 ha) in 1973. Thus between 1960 and 1973 the planted area has multiplied nine times, a rate of expansion that could be regarded as almost parallel to that of rubber during the early years of this century. As a consequence oil-palm has now become the second most important crop in Peninsular Malaysia in terms of planted acreage.

The increase has come from two directions—the private sector and the Federal Land Development Authority (FELDA), and to a lesser extent the other governmental agencies. In making their decision to invest in oil-palm both the private sector and the Government had to take a number of factors into consideration. Unlike rubber, palm-oil has no synthetic competitor. However, it is only one of many varieties of edible oils and fats which are to some extent interchangeable. Of these soya bean oil is perhaps the most serious competitor to palm-oil. But soya bean oil supplies are seasonal whereas palm-oil offers its consumers the advantage of year-round availability. In contrast to rubber which has to defend an established position, palm-oil has to move into markets long held by other oils and fats, a task made more difficult because these are usually in ample supply. From the employment point of view oil-palm is not as labour intensive as rubber as the number of workers needed per acre is only seven, or half that of rubber. Also oil-palm cultivation is more capital intensive, and the plants are more prone to disease and weed problems. But the high yields per acre and the shorter gestation period of the crop make it an attractive economic alternative to rubber. Indeed, careful analyses have shown that under the most favourable demand conditions as well as the least favourable demand conditions the returns from oil-palm would be substantially greater than those from rubber (Bevan and Goering, 1968).

The private estates began their switchover to oil-palm in the 1960s, planting an average of 15 000 acres (6 000 ha) per annum between 1960 and 1965. The average annual rate of increase in oil-palm acreage in this period was 9 per cent. The second half of the decade (including the year 1971) saw an acceleration in the planting rate when the estates began to move into oil-palm in earnest, planting an average of 53 500 acres (21 000 ha) per annum. The average annual rate of increase during this period was 17 per cent. In all the estate area increased by 394 000 acres (159 000 ha), from 135 000 acres (54 000 ha) in 1960 to 529 000 acres (214 000 ha) in 1971. The crop was cultivated either on newly cleared land or on land previously under old rubber. Many estates which had stands of old low-yielding rubber due for replanting did not replace them with high-yielding rubber but chose instead to convert to oil-palm. Today, in consequence, a good percentage of the large estates have holdings consisting of high-yielding rubber as well as oil-palm.

The most dramatic change in the oil-palm industry was brought about by the governmental decision to participate in the cultivation of the crop, using FELDA as its main agent. Up to then (1960) several factors have contributed to keep oil-palm an estate monopoly. When the crop was taken up seriously by the estates in 1926 rubber was already firmly

Plate 19   A newly planted oil-palm estate in Kulai, Johore. This estate has been established on the old rubber land. Many of the rubber estates in Peninsular Malaysia are being replanted with oil-palm.

established as a cash-crop in both the estate and the smallholder sectors. None of the smallholders were interested in oil-palm, not even as a source of cooking oil (for which they already had the coconut). Moreover the crop demanded more complex harvesting and processing methods while the machinery for extracting the oil from the fruit was expensive. It was estimated that the fruit from at least 2 000 acres (800 ha) was needed to keep one factory going; optimally a factory should process fruit from an area of 5 000 acres (2 000 ha) (Khoo, 1964). All these called for a large labour force, heavy equipment, a good network of internal roads and light railways and for heavy capital investment, none of which the smallholder, with his limited resources, could provide.

The establishment of FELDA in 1956 provided the Government with an agency for the opening up of new land for land settlement based on the cultivation of cash-crops. Up to 1960 FELDA land settlement schemes were devoted primarily to rubber, but the declining trend in rubber prices coupled with the desire for agricultural diversification led to a change in governmental policy on crop emphasis—from rubber to oil-palm. Thus in the eleven years between 1961 and 1971 FELDA developed forty new oil-palm schemes covering 189 000 acres (76 000 ha), compared with thirty-eight rubber schemes covering 153 000 acres (62 000 ha). In addition 52 000 acres (21 000 ha) of oil-palm were also developed by other governmental agencies. The total area

271

of oil-palm opened up by the public sector during this period amounted to 31 per cent of the total oil-palm acreage in Peninsular Malaysia in 1971. By 1976 FELDA expects to have 350 000 acres (142 000 ha) of land under oil-palm.

It is expected that future increases in the oil-palm acreage would be from FELDA and other public sector schemes as estate plantings will slow down sharply because most of the old rubber lands suitable for oil-palm have already been replanted with oil-palm (Bank Negara, 1971). New planting by individual smallholders on isolated farms is not economically viable, and the main impetus will continue to be from FELDA and the other public agencies. Already by 1973 this sector had expanded its share of the oil-palm acreage in Malaysia to 50 per cent. Moreover yields per acre were not greatly different from those of the private estates, mainly because the schemes were operated on lines similar to those of the estates.

Table 10.17 shows the area and distribution of oil-palms in Peninsular Malaysia in 1971. Most of the crop areas are in coastal and inland locations along the west, from Johore to Province Wellesley (Fig. 10.6), but in the last decade the east coast states—Pahang, Trengganu and Kelantan —have become important in oil-palm cultivation, with 29 per cent of the total area. Pahang in particular has now the second largest oil-palm acreage in Peninsular Malaysia due largely to the development of FELDA schemes. The Johore plantations are in rolling country, concentrated in three main areas—the Kluang area, Labis and Layang Layang. There is one large estate near Semana Halt in the Kuala Pilah district of Negri Sembilan. In Selangor the main areas are along the coast between Batu Laut and Kuala Sepang, to the southeast of Port Klang, north of Batu Tiga between Klang and Kuala Lumpur, at Merbau Sepak, and on the upper reaches of Sungei Selangor. The Perak estates are on the right bank of the middle and upper reaches of Sungei Bernam, with part of these estates in Selangor territory, and south of the Perak River mouth.

The private estates vary considerably in size, but most of them (85%) are larger than 1 000 acres (400 ha). Fifty-three per cent of the estate acreage in 1971 were British-owned, while Malaysians owned 27 per cent. There were altogether 393 estates but only 303 of them were in production. The largest number of estates (125) were in Selangor but Johore, with 120 estates, had a larger area under the crop. The average size of a FELDA estate was 4 725 acres (1 900 ha).

The palm requires a warm climate, abundant sunshine and an annual rainfall of 60 in (1 524 mm) or more. It is sensitive to drought and the rainfall must be evenly distributed throughout the year with no marked dry season. Most parts of the country are climatically suitable for the crops, although it grows best at altitudes below 1 000 ft (300 m). In addition the oil-palm in the Peninsula is relatively free from major diseases. In general the climate is more favourable to good palm growth than those in most

Table 10.17 Area and distribution of oil-palm, 1971

State	Estates (acres)		FELDA* (acres)	Others† (acres)	Total		Per cent
	Malaysian	Non-Malaysian			Acres	Hectares	
Johore	29 000	169 000	43 000	10 000	251 000	102 000	33
Pahang	39 000	6 000	106 000	10 000	161 000	65 000	21
Selangor	19 000	114 000	14 000	7 000	154 000	62 000	20
Perak	8 000	58 000	11 000	7 000	84 000	34 000	11
Trengganu	24 000	4 000	12 000	13 000	53 000	21 000	7
Negri Sembilan	7 000	22 000	3 000	1 000	33 000	13 000	4
Kelantan	7 000	3 000	—	1 000	11 000	5 000	1
Kedah	1 000	6 000	—	1 000	8 000	3 000	1
Penang	4 000	1 000	—	2 000	7 000	3 000	1
Malacca	3 000	4 000	—	—	7 000	3 000	1
Total	141 000	387 000	189 000	52 000	769 000	311 000	100

* Federal Land Development Authority.
† Rubber Replanting Board and State Government Schemes.

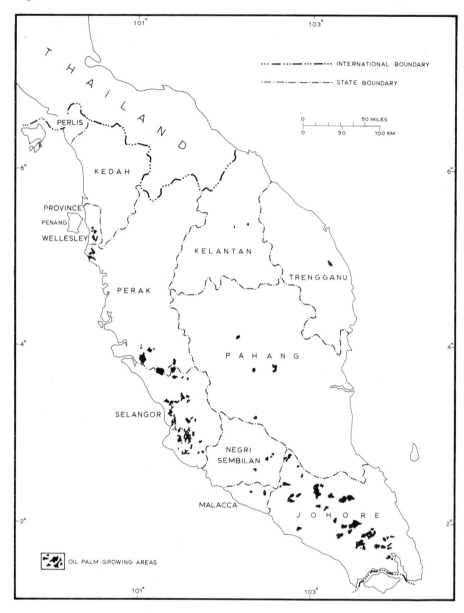

Fig. 10.6   Distribution of oil-palm in 1966 (based on Wong, 1971).

African countries so that yields attain levels seldom achieved in Africa.

The palm grows in a variety of soils, from moist, peaty coastal alluvium to the drier inland soils derived from sandstone and granite. Good drainage is essential in all cases. The best soil for the palm in Peninsular Malaysia is alluvial loam overlying a friable clay subsoil which will allow for easy root penetration and at the same time retain soil moisture. Coastal and riverine alluvial soils such as the Telemong, Briah, Kangkong and Selangor soil series which are properly drained support very good stands of the oil-palm. The palm will not grow well on deep peat, on soils with impervious hardpan layers, on very sandy soils, and on black soils with a high percentage of carbonaceous matter. In general the physical properties of a soil are more critical to oil-palm development than the chemical properties since deficiencies in the latter can be rectified by good management techniques. The best soils should have the following properties: be on flat or gently sloping terrain with slopes of less than 12°; have a soil depth of more than 30 in with no lateritic hardpan; a loamy texture; a strongly developed structure and be friable to moderately firm; a pH value of 4 to 6; a peat layer, if present, of less than 2 ft; be of moderate permeability (Ng, 1968*a*). Such soils, under proper management, should yield between 8 to 12 tons of fresh fruit bunches per acre.

The majority of the common soil types of Peninsular Malaysia can support oil-palm. Ng (1968*a*) has estimated that about 8 million acres (3.2 million ha) of land can be developed for the crop. Of this 2.8 million acres (1.1 million ha) are in Pahang and 2 million acres (800 000 ha) in Johore. There is therefore a very large potential for future development in so far as land availability and suitability are concerned.

There are four main varieties of *Elaeis guineensis*: (*a*) the Congo type (var. *macrocarya*) from the former Belgian Congo, is thick-shelled; (*b*) the Lisombe type (var. *tenera*) has fruit with a thick shell and 80 per cent pericarp; (*c*) the Pisifera type (var. *pisifera*) has fruit with no nut shell but a very well-developed pericarp with a high oil content; and (*d*) the Deli type (var. *dura*) which has fruit with a medium-thick shell and 35 to 55 per cent pericarp by weight. The Deli type is normally tall, but a short-stemmed 'dumpy' or dwarf palm has been developed in Peninsular Malaysia. The tenera variety, which is obtained by crossing *dura* with *pisifera*, produces about 30 per cent more oil per acre than the *Deli dura*. Up to 1958 most of the plantings in Peninsular Malaysia were of *Deli dura*, but from 1958 to 1961 *dura* and *tenera* material was used. A switchover to *tenera* material was made in 1961, and the hybrid variety is now cultivated on a large scale.

The palms are raised from seed in a nursery until they are from twelve to fourteen months old, when they are transplanted to the field. Occasionally, plantings may be deferred for a few months. However, the older the plant the more expensive it is to transplant. The usual planting distance is 32 x 32 ft, which gives a density of forty-nine palms per acre. Some estates adopt planting densities of fifty-six or sixty palms per acre. Recent research indicates that the optimal densities per acre are sixty-one palms for the coastal soils, sixty-four palms for the good inland soils and sixty-seven palms for the poorer inland soils (Corley *et al.*, 1973). The period of transplanting is timed to coincide with a period of adequate rainfall. It is usual to plant a leguminous cover-crop in order to suppress the growth of weeds, prevent soil erosion and to keep the soil temperatures down. Local soils except some fertile coastal clays cannot meet the heavy requirements for plant food made by the crop, and some form of manuring is necessary in order to obtain high yields over a sustained period.

The palm begins to fruit during its third year in the field, but regular harvesting is normally postponed until the end of the fourth year. Full production is reached when the palms are about nine or ten years old; the productive life of the palm is about twenty-five years. The yields depend on the genetic constitution of the palm, on drainage, manuring, planting distance, rainfall and soil conditions, and the incidence of pests and diseases. There is a close relationship between rainfall and yields, low yields usually following on spells of dry weather. There are also annual variations in yields caused by rainfall variations. Maximum yields occur during April, May and June in Johore, but during November and December in other parts of Peninsular Malaysia. The highest yields are from the coastal clays of the west coast. Table 10.18 sets out the average yields of oil-palm in Malaysian estates.

Table 10.18   Average yields of *deli* oil-palm on coastal soils

Age of palm (years)	Fresh fruit bunches (tons/acre/year)	Age of palm (years)	Fresh fruit bunches (tons/acre/year)
3—4	3.0	11—12	8.5
5—6	5.8	13—14	8.0
7—8	8.0	15—20	7.5
9—10	9.0	21—25	6.0

The quality and price of palm-oil decrease with increases in the free fatty-acid content, which may be caused by cracking, bruising or over-ripening of the fruits. In order to produce high quality oil, the fruit bunches must be harvested when they are just ripe and transported to the factory for immediate processing. The harvesting intervals are from five to fifteen days. On an average, the palms increase in height at the rate of 1 ft a year, and harvesting becomes more difficult and expensive as the palms grow taller. Harvesting 25 to 30 ft palms may cost several times as much as harvesting 10 ft palms.

Accessibility to all parts of an estate is important as the fruit bunches must be transported quickly to the factory for processing. Delay in processing bruised fruit increases the acidity of the oil. Transport systems in an oil-palm estate are therefore elaborate and are based on laterite roads or, if the estate is on suitable flat land, on light tramways. The running costs are lower in the case of the rail system, which has the additional advantage in that the rail trucks can be run directly into the factory for processing, with minimum handling and consequently reducing oil acidity to a minimum.

On entering the factory the fruit bunches are initially steam-sterilized to arrest enzymic degradation of the oil into free fatty acid. The oil is then extracted by a centrifuge or hydraulic press, the usual recovery rate being about 90 per cent. The oil is purified before it reaches the market. After oil extraction, the nuts are separated from the pulp, cracked and the kernels separated from the shell. The kernels are processed into palm kernel oil before being exported.

The oil produced in Malaysian estates is of high quality with a free fatty-acid content of less than 5 per cent. The large-scale expansion of the oil-palm acreage since the mid-1960s has resulted in a corresponding increase in the production of both palm-oil and palm kernel oil. Malaysia today contributes nearly two-thirds of the world's exports of palm-oil. Production in 1973 was at 810 000 metric tons of which 90 per cent was from Peninsular Malaysia. The production of palm kernels in Peninsular Malaysia was 154 700 metric tons in that year. It is anticipated that by 1975 the production of palm-oil will increase by over 50 per cent as the present immature areas reach maturity.

Coconut

The coconut palm (*Cocos Nucifera*) is ubiquitous in the Malay *kampongs* of the Peninsula. A few coconut trees are planted as a matter of course wherever the Malays have settled. The palm has played an important part in the domestic economy of the Malays since early historical times, providing them with food, drink and many of the necessities of life. The palm was widely distributed in the Malay Archipelago long before the first Europeans came to this part of the world. Coconuts were originally planted in locations near the sea, but experience has shown that they will grow and fruit successfully in areas remote from the sea.

Coconuts were cultivated in plantations in Penang and Malacca at the beginning of the nineteenth century. The nuts were sold for domestic use, and it was not until about 1850 that copra from Peninsular Malaysia was exported to Europe. The failure of the nutmeg industry in Penang in 1846 and the expansion of the export markets for copra and coconut oil brought about an increase in coconut planting in the island and, later, in Province Wellesley. Planting was extended into the Federated Malay States at the end of the nineteenth century, and was greatly stimulated when the price of nuts doubled. The Malays, too, began to plant the palm as the main crop in smallholdings, and smallholder interest in coconut cultivation increased to such an extent that, by 1917, 61 per cent of the 180 000 acres (73 000 ha) under coconuts in the Federated Malay States were in smallholdings of less than 100 acres (42 ha) each. The rapid rate of extension of the coconut acreage was checked temporarily during the First World War, but the Western industrial demand for vegetable oils for the manufacture of margarine, lard substitutes, cooking and edible oils, and soap and toilet preparations stimulated further planting at the end of the war. By 1935 the total area under coconut had increased to 606 000 acres (243 000 ha).

Some areas of coconut were cut down during the Japanese occupation of 1941—45, and many of the larger estates suffered badly from neglect and had to be rehabilitated before normal production could be resumed.

By 1961 the total planted area under coconut was 520 000 acres (210 000 ha) of which 85 per cent were in smallholdings and the remainder in seventy-seven estates of varying sizes. The estate sector has been undergoing a continuous decline since the 1960s, the number of estates decreasing from seventy-nine in 1963 to only forty-eight in 1971 and the planted area from 80 000 acres (32 000 ha) to 53 000 acres (21 000 ha) in that period. The smallholding sector has stagnated, the planted area increasing by only 28 000 acres (11 000 ha) in the period 1961—72. On the whole therefore the coconut industry, the fourth most important in Peninsular Malaysia in terms of planted acreage, has suffered a slow slide into relative insignificance, and has not shown either the vigour or the strength of rubber or oil-palm. Today its contribution to the national economy is less than 2 per cent of the total foreign exchange earnings.

The main reason for the decline in the estate sector was the replacement of coconut by oil-palm. Although the total capital investment for coconut is about half that for oil-palm, the returns per acre from the best managed coconut estate are only about one-third those obtainable from a good oil-palm estate (McCulloch, 1968). However, it has been found that inter-cropping coconut with cocoa would give as good returns per acre as from oil-palm. Such inter-cropping would also lead to better yields from the coconut trees (Fernando and Grimwood, 1973). Inter-cropping holds promise of arresting the decline in estate acreage.

Of the forty-eight estates in 1971, thirty-one were Malaysian-owned and nine British. Thirty-one of these estates (65%) were smaller than 1 000 acres (400 ha), nine were between 1 000 to 2 000 acres in size, six between 2 000 and 5 000 acres in size and two were estates of over 5 000 acres in size. Coconut was cultivated on an estate basis in only four states: Perak, Selangor, and Penang and Province Wellesley on the west coast and Trengganu on the east coast (Table 10.19).

Yields varied widely: the average yield was 2 351 nuts per acre but yields in all the coconut-producing states were lower than this except Perak, which had yields of 2 824 nuts/acre. It has been established that with improved planting materials and better use of fertilizers yields could

278

Plate 20   A coconut plantation in Sabak Bernam. The coconuts in the drainage canal are tied with rattan and are hauled in a long string to the nearest collecting point. Many of the coconut plantations are being interplanted with cocoa (see p. 281).

be improved to levels two to three times as high as those presently obtained. However, to double the yields would take twenty years or more and even doubling the yields would not make coconut monoculture as paying as high-yielding oil-palm (McCulloch, 1968).

As Table 10.19 shows, in 1972 90 per cent of the total area under coconut was in smallholdings of less than 100 acres (40 ha). The average size of a coconut smallholding varies widely. A sample survey of coconut smallholdings in Peninsular Malaysia showed the average size to be 11.6 acres in Selangor—Perak, 9.5 acres in Johore and 2.7 acres in Kelantan (Selvadurai, 1968). Coconut may be cultivated in pure stands where it is the sole crop, in mixed stands where it is interplanted with perennials such as rubber, coffee, fruit, etc., or as scattered palms. The holdings in the survey area were mainly (83%) in pure stands. Coconut cultivated as scattered palms is ubiquitous in the *kampongs* of Peninsular Malaysia. Although individually insignificant, such palms go far to satisfy the domestic requirements for the nut and its products.

The distribution of coconut is shown in Fig. 10.7 and Table 10.19. The largest areas are in the coastal strips of west Johore, Selangor, Perak and Penang and Province Wellesley. Along the east coast the palm is

279

Table 10.19   Area under coconut, by states, 1972

State	Area (acres)		Total		Per cent
	Estates	Smallholdings	Acres	Hectares	
Johore	–	124 000	124 000	50 000	24
Selangor	13 000	99 000	112 000	45 000	21
Perak	32 000	75 000	107 000	44 000	21
Kelantan	–	44 000	44 000	17 000	9
Penang and Province Wellesley	2 000	37 000	39 000	16 000	8
Kedah	–	29 000	29 000	12 000	6
Trengganu	4 000	24 000	28 000	11 000	5
Pahang	–	17 000	17 000	7 000	3
Malacca	–	12 000	12 000	5 000	2
Negri Sembilan	–	7 000	7 000	3 000	1
Perlis	–	3 000	3 000	1 000	–
Total	51 000	471 000	522 000	211 000	100

cultivated in a narrow coastal strip in northern Trengganu and Kelantan, as well as along the banks of the Trengganu River. There are also fairly extensive but scattered smallholdings along the banks of all the larger rivers in the Peninsula.

The coconut palm is a tropical plant which requires a mean annual temperature of about 75 to 85° F for successful growth. It can be cultivated anywhere in the Peninsula up to an altitude of about 2 000 ft, but it will not fruit when cultivated on steep slopes with gradients of more than one in fifteen. It requires moisture at the crown such as afforded by sea breezes, but proximity to the sea itself is not a necessary requirement for growth, though the largest coconut areas are near the coast. The palm grows best in localities with heavy (over 75 in (188 mm) a year) and evenly distributed rainfall and high humidities. It is usually cultivated on light, well-drained soils in South India, Ceylon and the Philippines. In Peninsular Malaysia most of the commercial cultivation has been on the western coastal alluvial soils developed over recent deposits of marine clay. However, the palm can grow well on a very wide range of soils except soils which have a thick peat layer. Along the east coast coconut is grown on sandy soils (*bris*) which are very free-draining and highly leached. Yields here are poor because of soil nutrient deficiencies.

The successful cultivation of coconut on the heavy clay soils of the coastal plains of Peninsular Malaysia depends to a large extent on careful drainage which must be so arranged that there is free movement of water in the soil, and that the water table is not lowered more than 3 ft from the soil surface as the main feeding roots of the palm are in this 3 ft zone. Apart from the usual drainage canals, estates near the sea must be

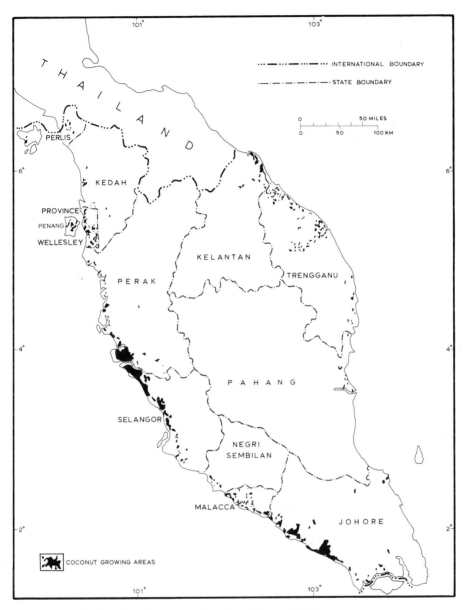

Fig. 10.7   Distribution of coconut (based on Wong, 1971).

protected from brackish tidal water by water-gates and sea-bunds. Many of the smallholdings along the Johore and Selangor coast have deteriorated considerably because of inadequate drainage. The high costs of drainage construction and upkeep are lowered in those estates which use the drainage canals as transport lines by which the nuts are moved from the field to the factory.

281

Today one of the major problems of coconut cultivation on the west coast is drainage. Low-lying and swampland with standing water does not provide good physical conditions for the coconut although it grows well on locations where there is free movement of water, such as the margins of well-drained padi fields, the edges of sandy beaches and the banks of rivers, lagoons and estuaries. Waterlogging, either through fresh water or sea water inundation or through inadequate drainage is a seasonal problem on the west coast coconut areas, and is a perennial problem in parts of the districts of Pontian and Batu Pahat in Johore. The Drainage and Irrigation Department has been engaged in the construction of a series of drainage schemes along the west coast in an effort to solve this problem. Each scheme consists of a coastal bund to prevent the ingress of sea water, a high level drain and a system of internal drainage to prevent fresh water inundation. While the estates have benefited from these schemes by constructing their own systems of internal drainage to link up with those of the DID schemes, the smallholders have not always done so, and have consequently failed to take full advantage of the DID drainage programme.

Two main types of coconuts are cultivated in Peninsular Malaysia—the talls and the dwarfs. The dwarfs can further be subdivided into three varieties—the green, the red and the yellow. The dwarf coconut (Malay: *nyor gading*) was introduced into Peninsular Malaysia from Indonesia in the nineteenth century or earlier, but was not grown commercially for copra until 1912. It is more sensitive to unfavourable conditions than the tall palm and requires a heavy clay soil with good drainage and a regular water supply for high returns. The talls, however, still form the foundation of the coconut industry being planted in most smallholdings and estates. They are much more hardy and tolerant of poor growing conditions, although they show much diversity in their growth and fruiting characteristics.

The seedlings are raised in nursery beds until they are between five and seven months old, when they are transplanted to the fields. The planting density is usually 50 palms per acre for the tall varieties and 108 palms per acre for the dwarfs. Smallholders generally adopt a closer planting density of about 70 palms per acre, although individual small-holders may adopt densities as high as 200 palms or as low as 20 palms per acre. Some smallholdings have densities considerably above that of the optimum recommended by the Department of Agriculture. A dwarf palm reaches fruiting age in its fourth year and produces its best yields towards its fifteenth year, while the tall variety begins to fruit in its fifth year and reaches its best towards the thirtieth year. Most trees produce good yields up to their sixtieth year. Yields vary considerably according to site and care of cultivation. On the whole yields have declined in both the estate and the smallholder sectors. In 1931 a high percentage of the estates averaged 1 470 lb of copra per acre per annum; in 1968 the mean yield of six estates representing about one-quarter of the estate acreage was only 1 300 lb per acre. The yields in the smallholder sector are even lower: the 1964—65 coconut smallholdings survey showed the average yield to be 674 lb per acre (Selvadurai, 1968). The ideal harvesting procedure is to collect the nuts as they fall from the trees, when the highest yield of copra and oil is obtained. But most estates harvest the nuts once a month, every six weeks, or every two months, while small-holders generally harvest once a week. The excessive frequency of small-holder harvesting leads to the collection of a high percentage of unripe nuts. Smallholders often sell their crop forward and the buyer then gathers every nut visible, including the very unripe ones. Because of the high percentage of unripe nuts and the poor methods of preparation, smallholder copra is usually of low quality, with a moisture content of 12 to 15 per cent as compared with the 6 per cent of the estates.

The marketable products are fresh nuts, copra, coconut oil, copra cake, coir, toddy and coconut shell by-products. The most important of these is copra, the dried kernel of the nut. Smallholders usually prepare copra by sun-drying the kernel, but kiln-drying is the normal method of preparation in estates. Kiln-drying, being independent of weather condi-tions, is a more reliable process than sun-drying, and enables the estates to produce a standard quality product. The total drying period varies between one and seven days, and averages three days. In favourable weather the kernel may also be sun-dried either before or after kiln-drying. An average of about 4 500 nuts is required to yield 1 ton of copra.

The coconut industry in Peninsular Malaysia has been in decline for some time, due to the fragmentation of estates and the switchover from coconut to oil-palm as well as the stagnant condition in the smallholder sector. Production of copra has consequently dropped from about 180 000 tons in 1960 to only 130 500 tons in 1973, of which 20 800 tons were from the estates. Nearly all the copra produced in the country is processed locally into coconut oil.

The poor condition of the smallholder sector was recognized by the Federal Government in 1961 when it set up a Working Party to investi-gate the reasons for the decline and recommend ways and means of reviving the industry. As a result of the findings and recommendations of the Working Party, the Coconut Rehabilitation and Replanting Scheme was launched in 1963. A pilot project was started in the Minyak Baku area of Johore (Selvadurai and Othman Lela, 1967), and, based on the experience gained there, the Scheme was implemented on a national scale under the First Malaysia Plan.

Under the Scheme compact blocks of 4 000 acres (1 600 ha), with adequate drainage facilities and where the response from the small-holders has been tested, are selected for replanting and rehabilitation. The total replanting grant is M$500 and the rehabilitation grant M$300 per acre. In order to maximize returns as well as the use of land resources the Scheme stipulates that all participating smallholders must intercrop their holdings with pineapple, banana, coffee or cocoa. They are also encouraged to plant other cash crops such as maize, vegetables and sweet potato. Under the Second Malaysia Plan it is proposed to intercrop about 20 000 acres (8 000 ha) with cocoa in the more fertile coastal alluvial soils of the west coast.

The target acreage for the Scheme in the period 1963—70 was 63 700 acres (26 000 ha). By 1972 about 63 000 acres (25 600 ha) had been replanted and rehabilitated. The projected area to be replanted and rehabilitated under the Second Malaysia Plan (1971—75) is 50 000 acres (20 000 ha). In addition tó this Scheme the Federal Agricultural Marketing Authority set up a Coconut Marketing Scheme in 1973 to secure maximum returns to the coconut smallholders in the marketing of their crop. The Authority will also set up twenty-five copra processing centres by 1976 which will purchase coconuts and copra from the smallholders and process them into high grade copra.

Pineapple

The pineapple, *Ananas comusus*, indigenous to South America, was introduced to the Far East by the Portuguese and the Spaniards, and was a common fruit by the end of the sixteenth century. It was widely cultivated in the Malay Peninsula but only for the local market. In 1890 some Chinese in Singapore began canning the pineapple as a 'shop-house' industry. The Malaysian pineapple canning industry has grown from this humble beginning to be one of the largest fruit-canning industries in the Commonwealth.

The rise of the pineapple industry was closely linked with the expansion of rubber cultivation in the Peninsula. Pineapple was interplanted with young rubber to provide a cash income until the rubber reached maturity. As the rubber acreages increased large surpluses of cheap pineapples were available for canning, and canning factories sprang up in Singapore, Johore and Selangor. By 1930 the export of canned pineapples was 57 960 tons. Paradoxically, the Great Depression of the 1930s marked the real beginning of the modern pineapple industry. Pineapple could no longer be cultivated as a catch-crop because the Depression put a stop to further rubber planting, and the fruit had to be grown as a sole crop if the canning industry were to survive. Large areas of land were therefore opened up for pineapple growing, and the area under pineapple as a sole crop increased from 3 000 acres (1 200 ha) in 1929 to about 40 000 acres (16 000 ha) in 1941.

The industry suffered heavy losses and damage during the Japanese occupation. Out of seventeen pre-war canneries only one remained intact, and only 6 000 acres (2 400 ha) of land were under pineapple at the end of the war. The rehabilitation of the industry was slow due to difficulties in the supply and marketing of the fruit.

In the postwar period the total area under pineapple has fluctuated markedly, due mainly to the changing fortunes of the pineapple canning industry. The area under canning pineapple increased from 14 000 acres (5 600 ha) in 1948 to a peak of 38 000 acres (15 000 ha) in 1956. Thereafter the area has remained below this peak until 1970, when it reached 38 500 acres.

Table 10.20   Area and distribution of pineapple, 1972

State	*Area* (acres)		*Total*	
	Fresh fruit	For canning	Acres	Hectares
Johore	3 200	44 200	47 400	19 200
Perak	1 100	—	1 100	440
Selangor	300	2 200	2 500	1 000
Kelantan	1 400	—	1 400	570
Penang and Province Wellesley	1 000	—	1 000	400
Trengganu	900	—	900	360
Pahang	400	—	400	160
Negri Sembilan	200	—	200	80
Kedah	100	—	100	40
Total	8 600	46 400	55 000	22 250

Note: *areas with less than 100 acres have been excluded.*

Table 10.20 shows the area and distribution of pineapple in 1972. About 80 per cent of the area is devoted to pineapple grown for the canning industry; the remainder is for the fresh fruit market. Only two states—Johore and Selangor—cultivate pineapple for the canning industry (Fig. 10.8). The largest acreage of canning pineapple is in the peat swamps of Pontian, Johore. Kluang and Batu Pahat too have substantial areas under the crop.

Pineapple for canning is grown on estates and smallholdings although smallholdings were the original source of fruit supply when the canning industry was established before the Second World War. In the postwar period canners were required to have a minimum of 1 500 acres (600 ha) of land under pineapple before they could operate a cannery. Eighteen thousand acres (7 000 ha) of peat land was set aside in Johore and Selangor for the canners to establish their pineapple estates. By 1956 half of the canning pineapple acreage of 38 000 (15 000 ha) was in estates. The estates' share subsequently declined, and is now about one-third of the total canning acreage.

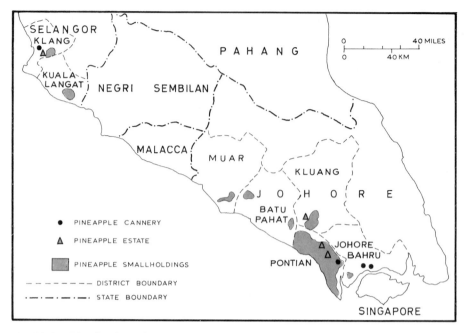

Fig. 10.8   Distribution of canning pineapple.

There are three main varieties of pine grown in Peninsular Malaysia—
the Singapore Spanish, the Mauritius and the Sarawak. Each variety has
various strains. The principal canning variety is the Singapore Spanish
and its mutant, the Selangor Green. The fruit is golden yellow when ripe
and weighs from 2 to 4 lb. The Mauritius and the Sarawak pines are cultivated for the fresh fruit market. The ideal pineapple for canning is one
which has eyes as shallow as possible to reduce loss in cutting; a diameter
of 4–5 in; a fairly long fruit with a small core; a fair degree of acidity;
low fibrous texture; as few air cells (flecks) as possible; a good colour;
and a tendency to have some flavour as the colour changes over before
the final ripening stage. The Singapore Spanish and the Selangor Green
fulfil enough of these requirements to satisfy the canneries.

The climatic conditions under which the plant is cultivated vary.
In Hawaii pineapple is grown in areas with about 30 in (762 mm) of
rainfall and a mean shade temperature of between 70° and 75° F
(21°–24° C). The equatorial climate in Peninsular Malaysia appears to be
more favourable to pineapple cultivation, since two fairly large crops are
harvested a year, in contrast to the one large and one small crop a year
common in higher latitudes.

Good drainage is essential for pineapple cultivation, and open, free-
draining soils on slopes as found on the inland quartzite and granite areas
of the Peninsula were used extensively for the crop until 1938, when

286

legislation was passed restricting pineapple cultivation on hilly land because of the widespread erosion caused by the growers. As a result the growers migrated to the peat lands of west Johore. Pineapple has been grown successfully on peat soils for many years. The present policy is to restrict pineapple cultivation to the peat lands, and all the major pine-apple areas are today found on deep peat. There are 2 million acres (800 000 ha) of peat in Peninsular Malaysia, most of which are in Pahang, west Johore, Selangor, Perak and Trengganu. The peat layer may be a few inches to 18 ft or more thick, and, apart from shallow rooted vegetables, pineapple is the only crop that is grown on a commercial scale on deep peat.

Preparation of the land for cultivation consists of clearing and burning the swamp forest, and the laying down of a drainage system. The land is then cleaned and levelled and the pineapple slips planted in rows. The planting density in estates today can be as high as 30 000 plants per acre. In contrast the smallholdings have much lower densities: a survey in Pontian showed densities of between 6 000 and 25 000 per acre (Tan, 1969). The area is kept clear of weeds. The crown that develops after flowering is removed to increase the fruit size. The best quality canned

Plate 21   Harvesting pineapples in the Pontian district of Johore. Pineapples are cultivated on peat lands. The present policy is to restrict pineapple cultivation to such peat lands, as apart from shallow-rooted vegetables, pineapple is the only crop that can be grown on a commercial scale on deep peat.

287

pineapple is produced from fully ripe pines, which have to be handled and transported carefully to the factory and canned immediately. Careful and frequent harvesting is therefore necessary. Proximity of cannery to growing area is also an added advantage.

The pineapple industry today faces a number of problems. Output was stagnant in 1971 and declined by over 12 per cent in 1972 to about 300 000 tons, and to 260 000 tons in 1973. This decline in fresh fruit production was due mainly to low yields, a result of the peaty nature of the soils as well as the over-aged plants in many smallholdings. It has been found that about 40 per cent of the smallholders do not fertilize their fields at all (Wee, 1970). Moreover, about 35 per cent of the small-holdings acreage have plants which are more than ten years old, and some have plants as old as twenty years. The proper practice is to replant every five years. Plants which are too old become more susceptible to disease. They bear fruit which progressively becomes smaller so that the recovery rate, after skinning and coring, drops to as low as 17 per cent. This increases the cost of canning. To meet this problem the Government established a seven-year replanting scheme whereby smallholders are provided with a replanting grant of M$400 per acre.

Seasonal gluts continue to hamper progress in the industry. Although the pineapple can be induced to flower through the application of calcium carbide solution, thereby evening out fruit production, a high percentage of the smallholders still do not use this method. In the small-holder sector therefore the production of fruit reaches a peak twice a year, with adverse effects on the canneries as well as on the smallholders themselves. The canneries cannot cope with the over-supply of fruit, and will stop accepting fruit once they reach their maximum capacity, so that the farmers are unable to sell their excess crop. At other times of the year when fruit supply slackens, canning operations may slow down considerably. Some farmers cut their fruit when it is still green so as to escape the seasonal gluts.

There are five canneries in operation at present. Only 20 per cent of the total output is sold in tins with the cannery brand names. The remainder is sold under a multiplicity of brands so that they have no established identity. Apart from this, the industry has to face severe competition from other producing countries, as well as tariff barriers in Japan and the European Economic Community which now includes the United Kingdom, traditionally the major consumer of Malaysian pineapple.

Costs of production have also increased due to the higher costs of fruit, sugar and packing materials. But the industry is unable to raise export prices to offset the higher production costs because the appreciation of the Malaysian dollar against the pound sterling and the US dollar has reduced the price competitiveness of Malaysian canned pineapples (Bank Negara, 1973).

288

Secondary and minor crops

Apart from the major crops of rubber, padi, oil-palm, coconut and pine-apple, a very large variety of secondary and minor crops are cultivated in Peninsular Malaysia. These can be classified under four main categories: food and beverage crops; fruit; spices; and miscellaneous crops.

Food and beverage crops

Table 10.21 shows the area and distribution of these crops. The largest areas are occupied by tapioca, sugar-cane and vegetables, and the beverage crops of cocoa, tea and coffee. The other food crops together occupy about one-fifth of the total area under food and beverage crops. Except for cocoa, tea and tapioca all the crops are produced for home consumption only and do not enter the export market.

The vegetables that enter the local market are from Chinese market-gardens. The Malay farmer does not cultivate vegetables for sale but may have a small vegetable plot in his *kampong* for his home supplies. The vegetables cultivated by the Malays are usually herbaceous plants such as *Basella rubra* (Malay: remayong), *Amaranthus gangeticus* (bayam merah) and *Sauropus androgynus* (asin asin). In addition, the Malay may have a few trees such as *Morinda citrifolia* (mengkudu), *Claoxylon longifolium* (salang) and *Phaeomeria speciosa* (kantan) which supply him with green foodstuffs. These home-grown vegetables may be supplemented by wild vegetables such as *Athyrium esculentum* (puchok paku), *Polygonum minus* (kesom), *Centella asiatica* (pegaga) and *Portulaca oleracea* (gelang pasir), gathered from the neighbourhood. It is also customary among the Malay padi growers in Kedah, Penang, Selangor, Malacca and the east coast states of Kelantan and Trengganu to cultivate small selected areas of the padi fields with food crops such as maize and groundnut and vegetables such as chili, cucumber, beans and Chinese radish during the annual fallow.

Chinese market-gardens are of two types: (*a*) the ordinary mixed farm, raising pigs, chickens and some crops, including vegetables, for sale, and other crops such as tapioca, for stock-feed, and (*b*) the vegetable farm specializing in the intensive cultivation of vegetables for sale. The techniques and principles of intensive market-gardening are similar to those practised in ordinary market-gardening. The vegetable farm is common only in Penang, and is a response to the great demand for leafy vegetables generated by the large urban population on the island.

Chinese market-gardens are usually located on the outskirts of towns and villages, most of them being found in western Peninsular Malaysia where the demand among the urban population for fresh vegetables, pork, freshwater fish, chickens and ducks is greatest. During the Second World War a large number of Chinese from the urban centres migrated to

Table 10.21   Acreage under food and beverage crops, 1972

State	Tapioca	Sugar-cane	Cocoa	Vegetables	Coffee	Tea	Other food-crops*	Total	
								Acres	Hectares
Perlis	100	10 000	—	—	—	—	700	10 800	4 400
Kedah	1 000	100	—	100	500	—	500	2 200	900
Kelantan	1 000	400	—	2 800	—	—	9 800	14 000	5 700
Trengganu	600	200	2 600	1 100	100	—	5 000	9 600	3 900
Penang and Province Wellesley	400	100	600	900	—	—	500	2 500	1 000
Perak	18 900	12 900	16 300	5 700	400	—	8 600	62 800	25 400
Selangor	3 900	200	7 900	1 300	9 400	500	1 400	24 600	9 900
Pahang	3 700	200	200	6 800	100	5 900	4 000	20 900	8 400
Negri Sembilan	300	2 000	—	300	200	—	800	3 600	1 500
Malacca	400	—	—	800	200	—	1 000	2 400	1 000
Johore	2 100	6 100	1 900	1 600	2 400	—	7 700	21 800	8 800
Total	32 400	32 200	29 500	21 400	13 300	6 400	40 000	175 200	70 900

* Sago, sweet potato, groundnut, maize, colocasia, sugar-palm, yam, water-melon, soya bean, pulses, ragi, rock melon, ubi kemili.

the outlying rural areas to grow their own food. Some of these squatters remained on as market-gardeners after the war, but all of them have now been resettled in New Villages along the main roads.

The principles and methods of market-gardening as practised by the Chinese in Peninsular Malaysia are basically similar to those of farmers in China, and they appear to be as suited to the tropical conditions of the Peninsula as to the temperate regions where they were evolved. These techniques enable the farmers to cultivate vegetables successfully in an environment where natural soil fertility is low, soil aeration inadequate, rainfall irregular and sometimes insufficient, insolation often too intense, and harmful organisms too numerous to allow anything more than a low yield. The efforts of the farmers are directed towards overcoming these unfavourable conditions, and making the most of the favourable ones. The extent to which they succeed is reflected by the yields they obtain: in the highly efficient farm yields of 17 tons of leafy vegetables per annum are not uncommon.

Water is the essential factor in the production cycle, and in the selection of a suitable site for his garden the Chinese farmer is more concerned with obtaining a flat, low-lying piece of land near a water body (usually a stream) than with the natural fertility of the land. For optimum growth and to prevent wilting, the vegetables must have adequate soil moisture at all times. Rainfall alone, high as it is in Peninsular Malaysia, cannot provide this, being too irregular, and coming in too brief and violent showers. The deficit is supplied by hand-watering, and it has been calculated that hand-watering supplies the equivalent of 36 in (914 mm) of rainfall per annum for every acre devoted to intensive market-gardening. For this reason, a farm that is too far away from a suitable stream always has one or more ponds as a source of water. The ponds are usually stocked with fish, thereby serving two purposes—as a source of water and a source of income from fish.

The Chinese market-gardener can grow vegetables successfully on a variety of soils, and even on mined-over land which has no nutrient content and provides little more than the physical medium for plant roots. However, a well-balanced alluvial soil is considered best for vegetable cultivation, and very light or very heavy clay soils less suitable. Generally the best soils are those that are well aerated and at the same time have sufficient water-retaining properties to facilitate the intake of moisture by the shallow-rooted vegetables. The farmer ensures that the soil is well aerated by careful and frequent cultivation and through the use of raised beds.

The nutrient content of local soils is usually low. Vegetables need considerable quantities of plant foods, and the farmer must apply large amounts of manure, both solid and liquid, in order to obtain high yields. The Chinese market-gardener uses organic manures, the most common being pig dung, sometimes mixed with night soil to form a liquid manure. The farmer who specializes in the intensive cultivation of vegetables utilizes prawn dust or cattle dung as primary manure, with supplementary liquid dressings of groundnut cake, soya bean cake, stale fish and sometimes, in spite of Government regulations banning its use, night soil. Pigs are an essential complement of the farm economy in an ordinary market-garden, their droppings being used to fertilize the vegetable beds and fish ponds. The pigs are fed on mash prepared from vegetable waste, chopped banana trunks and sometimes also on cooked water-hyacinths from the ponds. A pig–vegetable nutrient cycle is thus established, and the symbiosis of soil, plant and animal is so balanced that the whole system can be carried on indefinitely without soil exhaustion or deterioration.

The vegetables commonly cultivated are the green leafy vegetables such as Chinese cabbage, spinach, cress, lettuce, mustard leaf, Chinese kale, vegetable fruits such as cucumber, bitter gourd, snake gourd, tomato, brinjal, pumpkin, root vegetables such as potato, sweet potato, carrot, lobak and the beans and nuts such as four-angled bean, French bean, string bean and groundnut. Chinese market-gardens in Cameron Highlands are run on the same lines as those in the lowlands, the manures used being prawn dust and fish waste. The vegetables cultivated are those which cannot be produced commercially in the lowlands, and include green peas, beetroot, parsnip, radish, turnip, vegetable marrow, celery, lettuce, mustard, watercress, capsicum, asparagus, cabbage, cauliflower, shallot, spinach, horse-radish, mint, parsley, sage and thyme. These grow well in the cooler environment of the highlands.

Production from the market-gardens in the lowlands as well as Cameron Highlands is insufficient to satisfy the needs of the country, and large quantities of vegetables are imported each year. These consist of fresh vegetables such as Chinese cabbage, potatoes, onions and garlic as well as dried and preserved vegetables such as canned vegetables, pickled cabbage, dried mushrooms, lily roots, turnips, bamboo shoots and radish.

Tapioca occupies the largest area under food crops. Although now grown in every state, *Manihot utilissima* (Malay: ubi kayu) is indigenous to South America, and was introduced into Peninsular Malaysia a little more than a century ago. Many varieties are cultivated, but all contain prussic acid in all parts of the plant. The varieties in which the acid occurs mainly in the rind of the tuber are classed as 'sweet' and those in which it is more evenly distributed throughout the root are classed as 'bitter'. Tapioca is a tropical plant that will grow on almost any soil, provided it is well drained. Because of its drainage requirements, it is usually cultivated on undulating or hilly land. Before the war, it was widely grown as a catch-crop with young rubber, but Government legislation stipulated that no more than two crops of tapioca could be planted on land alienated for rubber or other permanent forms of cultivation.

Plate 22   Market gardens on terraced hillside, Cameron Highlands. Vegetables such as cabbage, lettuce and spinach can be successfully cultivated in the cooler climate of these highlands. The output from the market gardens is sent to the main towns of the west coast and as far south as Singapore.

This restriction was necessary as tapioca on undulating or hilly land caused considerable soil erosion, not because it was an extremely exhausting crop but because no soil conservation measures were taken. Moreover Chinese planters often dug drainage trenches up and down hill, and this, coupled with the disturbance of the soil when cultivating and lifting the crop, led to serious soil erosion during heavy rain.

The main areas of tapioca are in Perak, Johore, Pahang, Selangor, Kedah and Kelantan. The crop is widely cultivated by the Chinese as pig-food, while the lower income groups of all races use it occasionally as a rice-substitute, or in the preparation of cakes. A feature of the tapioca industry is that a high percentage (up to 75%) of the tapioca acreage is illegally planted (FAMA, 1969). The crop supports a significant process-ing industry which converts the tapioca into starch, pearl, flakes and

293

chips. With the end of the Emergency in 1960 the tapioca industry expanded rapidly as farmers could again move into the countryside to grow tapioca, largely on an illegal basis. The industry was given an additional boost when the local feedmill industry was established. The feedmills use locally processed tapioca chips as a component for animal feed. As a result a large number of tapioca processing factories, each employing less than twenty-five people, were started in the 1960s, mainly in Perak. Factories are also being built by a MARA-sponsored company, in Perak as well as in Pahang and Trengganu.

The only tapioca products exported are flakes, pearls and starch. The export potential appears to be promising. Production of starch, pearls and chips in 1973 was only 57 000 tons, and at present Malaysia's contribution to world tapioca exports is less than 5 per cent. Local demand would depend on the growth of the livestock industry. To meet part of this demand the Perak State Economic Development Corporation will be opening up 3 000 acres (1 200 ha) of land in the Dindings to cultivate and process tapioca for animal feed.

In recent years the cultivation of sugar-cane has attracted the attention of a number of commercial enterprises. The scope for developing sugar-cane as a plantation crop is indicated by the fact that Peninsular Malaysia imports about a quarter of a million tons of raw sugar annually, and the successful and large-scale production of the crop will not only save a considerable amount of foreign exchange but will also assist the Government in meeting its declared objective of diversifying the agricultural economy of the country.

Sugar-cane was cultivated on a commercial basis in Province Wellesley as long ago as the 1820s, by Chinese and later by European interests. Yields of 3 tons per acre were recorded, but labour requirements were very high. By 1860 the area under sugar-cane was 9 000 acres (3 600 ha), the Europeans owning a larger percentage than the Chinese. But the collapse of world sugar prices and the meteoric rise of rubber at the turn of the century eventually forced the sugar planters to stop production, the last refinery closing down in 1913.

In 1964 the Government's Department of Agriculture began investigations into the agricultural and economic possibilities of developing a sugar-cane industry in Malaysia. As far as the plant is concerned it has been established that it grows best on coarse-textured soils which are freely drained. The cane will not do well on heavy clay soils unless they are aerated by deep cultivation and drainage. The climatic requirements of the plant are more demanding in that a period of moisture stress is desirable to build up the sugar levels in the cane prior to harvesting. In this respect the Malaysian climate, which lacks a cool dry season, is not ideal for sugar-cane, but the northern, western and north-eastern parts of the Peninsula which experience a marked dry season and the 'dry' zone of the inland districts of Negri Sembilan with less than 70 in (1 778 mm) of rain a year (see Fig. 2.11) are considered suitable for cane growth.

In 1968–69 four companies indicated their intention to establish a total of about 100 000 acres (40 000 ha) of sugar-cane in Perlis, Perak, Negri Sembilan and Johore. The plantations have to be large as each sugar mill, for economic operation, should have about 20 000 acres (8 000 ha) of cane to support it. At present plantations and mills have been established in south Johore near Ayer Hitam, in northeast Negri Sembilan, Pantai Remis in the Dindings district of Perak and in Perlis. Another plantation is being developed in the Padang Terap district of Kedah. The Kelantan State Economic Development Corporation has plans to open up 20 000 acres (8 000 ha) of land for sugar-cane, half for a plantation and the other half for smallholdings (*Malaysian Business*, May 1973). By 1973, 28 500 acres (11 500 ha) of cane had been planted, and 11 700 tons of refined sugar produced from the factories.

These large-scale ventures have encountered a number of problems: one plantation achieved an effective cane yield of 25 tons per acre instead of the projected 30 tons because it could harvest only 70 per cent of the crop. There was a shortage of harvesters, and local labour was inexperienced in harvesting a full crop under exacting conditions. Difficulties were also encountered in transporting the cane from the field to

Plate 23   Harvesting sugar-cane in a smallholding at Nibong Tebal, Province Wellesley. Sugar-cane, once a major crop in Peninsular Malaysia is now being cultivated on an increasingly large scale for the new sugar factories established in the country.

the mill. But the most serious problem is in the selection of a suitable cane species that would fit in well with local soil and climatic conditions, be high yielding and pest and disease resistant and pose minimal harvesting difficulties. Nevertheless, once these problems are solved, sugar-cane holds promise of becoming a significant contributor to the agricultural economy of Peninsular Malaysia.

Of the other important food crops, sweet potato is cultivated in Chinese market-gardens for pig food and to meet a small local demand for a cheap rice-substitute. The main areas under the crop are in Perak and Johore. Maize occupies the largest areas in Pahang and Perak and is grown mainly for the animal feed industry, with a small percentage going to meet local demand for corn-on-the-cob or as a vegetable in curries.

All the other food crops are of minor importance and occupy only small areas: sago (6 600 acres in 1972), groundnut (11 400 acres), water-melon (5 200 acres), colocasia (700 acres), yam (900 acres), pulses (200 acres), and sugar-palm (200 acres). Sago is obtained from two species of the sago palm, *Metroxylon sagu*, common in western Peninsular Malaysia, and *M. Rumphii*, found more abundantly along the east coast. The palms grow in a half-wild state in swampland along river banks and low-lying riverine areas. They are harvested when about twelve years old, when they are cut into 4 ft logs and floated to the processing shed where the raw sago is extracted from the logs. The yield of raw sago varies with the size of the palm, averaging between 250 and 650 lb (113–295 kg) per palm. The raw sago is sent to factories, where it is processed into 'pearl' sago or flour, similar to tapioca flour. Each 100 lb (45 kg) of raw sago yields about 58 lb (26 kg) of sago flour. The main sago areas are in Johore (Batu Pahat), Perak, Malacca and Kelantan.

Groundnut or peanut is cultivated on a small scale in every state, with Perak and Kelantan having the largest acreages. The nuts are either eaten whole after roasting or frying, or expressed to produce oil. Groundnut oil is used extensively by the Chinese as a cooking oil, and as local production is insignificant large quantities are imported to meet the demand. Water-melon is an important seasonal crop in the northern states experiencing monsoonal conditions. Most of the planted acreage is in Kelantan and Trengganu. Colocasia (Malay: *keladi*) is a herbaceous plant with edible tubers. It is cultivated mainly by the Chinese, who use it for feeding pigs. The tubers are eaten boiled or fried and the large leaves may be used locally for wrapping packets. Yams (Malay: *ubi*) are of minor importance, except in Kelantan and Perak where a few hundred acres are cultivated. Pulses are planted as off-season crops in the padi areas of Kedah and Perlis. The sugar-palm, *Arenga pinnata*, grows semi-wild in Malay *kampongs*, and provides a local source of sugar.

The beverage crops—coffee, tea and cocoa—are cultivated on a small scale. Coffee is mainly a smallholder crop. The variety planted is

'Liberica' coffee (*Coffea liberica*); the robusta variety is of minor import-ance. The plant grows best in alluvial clay soils which are well-drained. It is grown without shade, and gives high yields—from 650 to 800 lb (294–363 kg) of prepared beans per acre per annum from well-maintained holdings. The bushes flower in their second year, and a small crop is obtained during the third and fourth years, the size of the crop increasing with the age of the plant. The bushes will live from twenty to thirty years when cultivated on coastal clays. Coffee is grown both as a sole crop and as a mixed crop, mainly under coconut. The main coffee areas in the country are in Selangor, in the coastal districts of Kuala Selangor, Kuala Langat and Klang. Johore too has substantial acreages under the crop, most of them in the district of Batu Pahat. The total cultivated area in 1972 was 13 300 acres (5 300 ha).

Tea (*Thea sinensis*) or *Camellia sinensis* had long been planted on a small scale by the Chinese in Peninsular Malaysia, and there were several estates growing tea on a commercial scale in 1893. However, interest in the crop waned as rubber began to dominate the agricultural scene, and by 1936 only 3 000 acres (1 200 ha) of tea had been planted. In the postwar period the area has fluctuated from about 9 000 acres (3 600 ha) in 1949 to 16 000 acres (6 500 ha) in 1959. However, low tea prices in the 1960s induced some tea estates to change over to oil-palm and other cash crops; the area under tea has consequently declined to 7 700 acres (3 000 ha) in 1972. Three-quarters of this acreage are under highland tea, cultivated exclusively in the Cameron Highlands, while low-land tea is grown mainly in Selangor, and on a minor scale, in Perak. Tea cultivation is highly labour-intensive, from five to ten times more than rubber or oil-palm cultivation. Yields of tea are much higher in the low-lands than in the highlands. Average yields for lowland tea vary from 800 to 1 600 lb (294–726 kg) of made tea per acre per annum, and for upland tea from 250 to 1 000 lb (113–453 kg) per acre. The quality of upland tea, however, is better. In general, yields of both upland and low-land tea are higher than those obtained in India and Sri Lanka (Ceylon), as the heavy rainfall, which is fairly evenly distributed throughout the year, leads to frequent and heavy 'flushes' of leaves. Production of tea in 1973 was 7 400 000 lb.

Cocoa has become the third beverage crop to be cultivated on a commercial scale in Peninsular Malaysia. Isolated cocoa trees were reported in Malacca as early as 1778 but the crop was not grown for the market until recently. After the Second World War considerable interest was aroused in Malaysia by the potentialities of cocoa as an alternative to rubber, partly because of the greater world demand and the decreased production from West Africa and the West Indies. A cocoa expert from the Colonial Office reported that Peninsular Malaysia (then Malaya) was capable of producing 100 000 tons of cocoa per annum, and that the development of cocoa was unlikely to interfere with either padi or

Plate 24   Picking tea in the Cameron Highlands. Highland tea is grown only in this hill resort and is labour intensive (see p. 297).

rubber cultivation as the requirements of the cocoa tree were different from those of the other two crops. The Peninsula also had the advantage of being free from the deadly 'swollen shoot' disease. The hot humid climate of the Peninsula differed from that in established cocoa areas in its higher total rainfall and absence of a pronounced dry season but was otherwise not unfavourable.

Following his recommendations trial blocks of seedlings imported from Sri Lanka and Ghana were made in 1949, and experiments on locally available material were also conducted. A pilot commercial planting of 50 acres (20 ha) of the well-tried Amelonado variety from Ghana was established on the Jerangau (granitic) soils of Trengganu. The area was increased to about 1 000 acres (400 ha) in the next three years but subsequently a serious disease known as 'die-back' attacked the trees and became so widespread that cocoa ceased to be an officially recommended crop.

However, it was discovered that cocoa varieties planted experimentally under mature coconut on the marine clay soils of the west coast were more healthy than those planted on the granitic soils of the east coast. It would appear that soils derived from basalt (e.g. the Kuantan series), from andesite (e.g. the Segamat series) and from limestone (e.g. the Langkawi series) are better for cocoa than those derived from granite and granodiorite (Kanapathy and Thamboo, 1970). Soils which have a high moisture-retaining capacity and do not have rooting impediments to a depth of 5 ft or more are best for cocoa. These include the marine alluvial soils of the Selangor, Kangkong and Briah series; the riverine alluvial soils of the Telemong and Akob series; and sedentary soils of the Segamat, Kampong Kolam and Kuantan series (Wong, 1972). Attention was also shifted from the Amelonado variety to the Upper Amazon and hybrid varieties, which although lower yielding were more resistant to dieback and better able to withstand local climatic and soil conditions.

As a result of these developments cocoa became an important commercial crop in the late 1960s, being found particularly suitable for interplanting with coconut. The area under the crop increased from 2 000 acres (800 ha) in 1967 to 30 000 acres (12 000 ha) in 1972. Most of the

Plate 25   A cocoa tree in fruit. Cocoa has become an increasingly popular beverage crop and is now cultivated on a commercial scale mainly in the district of Lower Perak. It is usually interplanted with coconut.

cocoa area is in Perak, mainly in the Bagan Datoh delta of Lower Perak covering Bagan Datoh, Hutan Melintang, Rungkup, Teluk Baru and Kota Setia.

Although the estates have so far been the main planters of cocoa interplanted with coconut, smallholders are showing increasing interest in the crop, especially now that FELDA has accepted it as a crop next in importance to rubber and oil-palm in its agricultural diversification programme. The Coconut Rehabilitation Scheme authorities have also placed cocoa as one of the crops suitable for interplanting in coconut smallholdings. The average income of the smallholders intercropping cocoa with coconut in the Bagan Datoh delta was M$250 a month per acre for the first half of 1974 as compared with M$112 a month from coconut planted as a sole crop. The Selangor Agriculture Department initiated a programme in 1974 to encourage smallholders to plant cocoa as a cash crop as well as interplant cocoa with coconut. The future for cocoa as an estate and smallholder crop thus appears to be a promising one.

Fruit

Tropical fruit in great variety grow well in the Malay Peninsula. Many of these are indigenous while others are varieties introduced from other tropical countries. Indigenous fruit may be wild or cultivated. A catalogue of local fruit lists thirty-nine principal varieties commonly cultivated, forty-seven varieties of lesser importance, forty-four indigenous varieties not commonly cultivated but collected and eaten by the local population, and five varieties which only grow at high altitudes. In spite of this great variety of fruit, cultivation is only of local importance, and canned pineapple is the only fruit regularly exported in large quantities. Local production of fruit is insufficient to meet demand, and large quantities of fresh, preserved and canned fruit are imported each year.

Table 10.22 shows the area and distribution of cultivated fruit, most of which are grown in mixed stands in Malay *kampongs*. Only a small percentage of the fruit area in the country is devoted to sole crop cultivation, the fruit so cultivated being banana, rambutan, citrus and durian. In the areas of commercial monocultivation, fruit forms the main source of income. In contrast, fruit in the *kampong* holdings is grown for home consumption, and the income from the sale of any excess is supplementary to that from the main crop, usually rubber, padi or coconut.

Practically all Malay smallholdings have some fruit trees. The characteristic feature of the dusun (fruit) areas in the *kampongs* is the haphazard and casual way in which the trees are planted. There is no systematic cultivation, manuring or selection and the trees are usually

Table 10.22 Area under fruit, 1972 (acres)*

State	Banana	Durian	Rambutan	Mangosteen	Citrus†	Other fruit‡	Total	
							Acres	Hectares
Johore	4 600	2 800	3 500	600	500	2 600	14 600	5 900
Kedah	1 600	4 100	3 900	400	2 500	2 900	15 400	6 200
Kelantan	3 000	1 400	2 500	200	1 600	1 700	10 400	4 200
Malacca	200	600	1 200	200	—	500	2 700	1 100
Negri Sembilan	1 700	600	700	200	100	600	3 900	1 600
Pahang	10 500	1 400	2 200	300	1 400	2 200	18 000	7 300
Penang and Province Wellesley	700	900	1 100	200	—	400	3 300	1 300
Perak	6 300	4 000	4 800	1 100	1 100	3 000	20 300	8 200
Perlis	500	400	300	—	100	200	1 500	600
Selangor	2 600	1 500	1 500	600	300	700	7 200	2 900
Trengganu	2 900	2 800	2 300	300	900	4 000	13 200	5 400
Total	34 600	20 500	24 000	4 100	8 500	18 800	110 500	44 700

* Excluding pineapple.
† Mandarin orange, lime, pomelo and other citrus.
‡ Duku and langsat, mango, rambai, chempedak, chiku, jackfruit and other fruit.

301

self-sown. Seedlings once established are left to grow as best as they can, the only assistance provided by the smallholder being that of cutting back excessive undergrowth. Sporadic attempts are made to limit the ravages of pests such as squirrels and flying foxes. Some fruit, mainly for home consumption, is also grown in Chinese market-gardens, the popular varieties being banana, papaya, lime, pomelo and jackfruit.

In general, the best soils for fruit are alluvial soils which are well-drained and do not contain too much clay. Heavy, impermeable clay soils restrict root growth, but some varieties such as the mangosteen can tolerate such soils. Peat lands can only support pineapple. In spite of the equatorial climate, the principal varieties, except the banana, are markedly seasonal and come into the market at well defined periods of the year.

Banana is the most widely cultivated fruit in the country, and almost every smallholding, whether Chinese, Malay or Indian, has a few plants to supply fruit for home consumption. A large number of varieties are grown, some of which bear large coarse fruit which are only eaten cooked. But most of the bananas planted are dessert varieties for which there is a greater demand. The principal commercial dessert varieties are Pisang Embun, Pisang Mas and Pisang Rastali. Pisang Embun is identical with the Jamaican or Gros Michel banana, and the best variety established in Peninsular Malaysia. Banana is sometimes grown as a catch-crop in young rubber areas. It is common in all Chinese market-gardens as the Chinese use banana stems as pig fodder. Bananas are exported in small quantities to Singapore.

Durian enters the home and Singapore markets in larger quantities than any other seasonal fruit. The durian tree, *Durio zibethinus*, is probably indigenous to Borneo, but has spread in its cultivated form throughout the Malay Peninsula. It grows to a height of 80 to 100 ft (24–30 m), and fruits in its seventh to eighth year. There are two fruiting seasons a year, the main crop being produced in June to August, and a subsidiary crop towards the end of the year. In the northwest and northeast, however, where monsoonal influence is more pronounced, only one crop is produced, around August. Durian is found in most *kampong* areas and also some aboriginal jungle clearings.

The rambutan tree, *Nephelium lappaceum*, is indigenous to Malaysia, and cultivated throughout the Malay Peninsula. It is second in importance to the banana as a commercial crop under monocultivation. The fruits are variable in quantity and flavour, ripening in August and September, with a secondary crop towards the end of the year. The mangosteen, *Garcinia mangostana*, comes into bearing only after its fifteenth year, but in spite of the long period between planting and fruiting, it is widely distributed throughout the rural areas. It is usually interplanted with other fruit trees in the *kampongs*, and grows best in low-lying, well-drained alluvial soils.

The *Citrus* genus as cultivated in Peninsular Malaysia includes the lime *Citrus acida*, lemon *C. limon*, orange *C. aurantium*, mandarin orange *C. nobilis*, and pomelo *C. maxima*. Of these the mandarin orange is the most important, occupying approximately 40 per cent of the total acreage under citrus. The pomelo is the largest of the citrus fruit, and grows well in districts with low-lying alluvial soils, those from Ipoh being particularly well known. The lime, too, is fairly widely distributed.

Of the other *kampong* fruit, duku and langsat (*Lansium domesticum*) occupy the largest area with smaller areas under champedak (*Artocarpus champeden*), rambai (*Baccaurea motleyana*), mango (*Mangifera indica*), chiku (*Achras sapota*), jackfruit (*Artocarpus integra*), papaya (*Carica papaya*) and a great number of minor varieties which are planted mainly for home and local consumption.

In the 1960s official attention was focused on the possibilities of cultivating cashew on the 'bris' soils of the east coast. There are extensive areas of these sandy, very freely draining, poorly structured, highly leached soils which have developed along the *permatang* of the east coast. The agricultural potential of such soils is poor, being limited to pasture, livestock rearing, coconut and cashew.

The cashew tree (*Anacardium occidentale*) was introduced into the Peninsula about a century ago, and is today ubiquitous along the east coast, growing in hedges, among coconut or semi-wild. However, each household has only a few trees from which it derives some food (fresh fruit and nuts) and a little income. In 1963 the Government initiated a development scheme for the cultivation of cashew on a commercial scale,

Plate 26   A cashew plantation in Pahang. Cashew is being cultivated on a modest scale on the *bris* soils of the east coast. These sand and highly leached soils have a poor agricultural potential and cashew is one of the few crops that can be grown on such soils.

through planting on vacant state land and through subsidizing small-holders to grow it on their land. The proposed target under the First Malaysia Plan (1966—70) was to plant 1 500 acres (600 ha) in each of the states of Kelantan, Trengganu, Pahang, Johore and Kedah. By 1971 however only 3 900 acres had been planted, mainly in Trengganu, Pahang and Kelantan. The smallholders have not responded well to the scheme, and most of the cultivation has been on state land (Osman Noor, 1972).

Spices and miscellaneous other crops

Table 10.23 shows the area and distribution of these crops. Arecanut and pepper are the only spices exported. The betel-palm, *Areca catechu*, is grown everywhere in the lowlands, with the largest acreage in Johore and the northern states of Kedah and Kelantan. Chillies, *Capsicum annuum*, are grown in Chinese market-gardens and Malay *kampongs* for home and local consumption. The sireh plant, *Piper betle*, is grown on a small scale in most Malay *kampongs*, the leaves being used for chewing. Pepper, *Piper nigrum*, is the most important of the other spices. It has been cultivated since the nineteenth century, although only on a minor

Plate 27   A pepper farm in Johore. Pepper, once a major crop in the nineteenth century is now only cultivated on a minor scale and mainly in the State of Johore (see p. 306).

Table 10.23 Area under spices and miscellaneous other crops, 1972 (acres)

State	Spices							Miscellaneous other crops					
	Arecanut	Chillies	Pepper	Sireh	Others*	Total		Nipah	Tobacco	Gutta-percha	Others†	Total	
						Acres	Hectares					Acres	Hectares
Johore	2 600	200	2 200	—	200	5 200	2 100	1 600	—	—	—	1 600	600
Kedah	1 900	100	—	200	100	2 300	900	2 400	—	—	100	2 500	1 000
Kelantan	500	300	—	400	200	1 400	600	700	14 800	—	—	15 500	6 300
Malacca	—	—	—	—	—	—	—	400	—	—	—	400	100
Negri Sembilan	—	—	—	—	—	—	—	—	—	—	—	—	—
Pahang	200	200	—	100	200	700	300	4 100	100	1 600	100	5 900	2 400
Penang and Province Wellesley	400	100	—	—	1 300	1 800	700	1 500	—	—	—	1 500	600
Perak	500	1 100	—	100	100	1 800	700	6 500	1 300	—	100	7 900	3 200
Perlis	400	100	—	300	100	900	400	500	200	—	—	700	300
Selangor	—	100	—	—	500	600	200	400	—	—	—	400	200
Trengganu	1 100	300	—	100	500	2 000	800	3 900	1 300	—	—	5 200	2 100
Total	7 600	2 500	2 200	1 200	3 200	16 700	6 700	22 000	17 700	1 600	300	41 600	16 800

* Ginger, tumeric, nutmeg and cloves.
† Kapoh, gambier, derrio, patchouli, citronella and manila hemp.

scale. Pepper cultivation was responsible for much of the soil erosion in Johore in the past, due to the clean-weeding practised by the Chinese farmers on the hill sites in which the crop was grown. In recent years the high prices for pepper have stimulated some expansion in acreage. Practically all of the area under the crop is in Johore. Clove and nutmeg were once export crops, but are only of local importance today, most of the area under these spices being in Penang and Province Wellesley. Tumeric and ginger are also grown only for the home market.

The Nipah palm, *Nipa fruticans*, grows wild in tidal locations along the coast of the Peninsula, mainly in estuaries where there is the brackish water necessary for its growth. The leaves are much used as thatching material (atap) by the Malays for the roofs as well as walls of their houses. The leaves are also used for making baskets and mats, and the young leaves as cigarette-wrappers. Supplies from the wild palm are limited, and supplementary supplies are obtained from palms planted along the coasts of all the states, except Negri Sembilan.

Tobacco is usually grown in rotation with market-garden vegetables or as an off-season cash-crop in padi areas, mainly in Kelantan. The variety commonly planted is the large-leaved Deli type which yields a low quality tobacco. Yields are about 650 lb per acre. Home-grown tobacco finds a ready sale, and planting has been stimulated as a result of increases in duty on imported manufactured tobacco. Gutta-percha is obtained from the sap of a forest tree, *Palaquium gutta*, indigenous to the Peninsula. Pahang is the main source of the gum.

In the period 1962–72 the total cultivated area of Peninsular Malaysia increased by 13 per cent, from 6 131 000 acres (2 477 000 ha) to 6 942 000 acres (2 805 000 ha). This increase was not confined to only the major crops but was extended to cover the secondary and minor crops. The latter showed an increase in cultivated area of about 18 per cent over the same period. This contrasts sharply with the trend during the period 1952–62 when the area under secondary and minor crops decreased by 4 per cent, and is an indication of the success of the Government's agriculture diversification policy as well as the growing awareness among planters and smallholders that there are attractive alternatives to rubber, oil-palm and the other dominant crops.

11
Livestock rearing, fishing and forest production

Livestock rearing

As in other parts of the wet tropics, climatic conditions in the Malay Peninsula are not conducive to pastoralism, and there is no tradition of cattle-rearing amongst the indigenous aboriginal groups or amongst the lowland Malays. The Malays, however, use the buffalo for ploughing padi fields, but the animal does not play more than this subsidiary role in their predominantly agricultural economy. Buffaloes are occasionally slaughtered for meat, but milking is not general except in parts of Kedah and Province Wellesley.

Available evidence indicates that the tropical environment is not suited to cattle rearing. The hot, wet climate induces hyperthermy in cattle and causes them to lose their appetite. Cattle are not indigenous to Peninsular Malaysia, and those that are reared in this country have been introduced from India, Thailand and other neighbouring territories. Indiscriminate breeding and the general lack of interest in quality have resulted in a cattle population that is undersized, weedy and degenerate. Although Peninsular Malaysia remains free from the major cattle diseases of rinderpest, foot-and-mouth, anthrax, blackwater and tuberculosis, many other diseases, especially those caused by parasites and nutritional deficiencies, are common among the livestock population.

The potentialities of livestock rearing are limited by the fact that there are no natural pastures in the Peninsula. Grass of one kind or another is the basic foodstuff of the local swamp buffalo, cattle and sheep, but the natural vegetation is deeply shaded forest where the sun-loving grasses cannot grow. Grasses can only be established where the forest has been felled, and the development of pastures from primary and secondary jungle is a costly affair in a region where climatic and other environmental conditions are continually working towards the reversion of these cleared areas to jungle. Furthermore, noxious and rapidly-growing weeds such as *lalang* (*Imperata cylindrica*) and *pokok kapal terbang* (*Eupatorium oderatum*) soon invade any pasturage or grazing area that is not continuously tended. The conversion of forested land into pastures therefore requires a fairly substantial outlay of capital, for not only are they expensive to develop but they are also expensive to maintain.

Tropical pastures are of poor nutritive value, with a crude protein content of only 2 to 4 per cent. The highly nutritious leguminous plants used for feeding livestock in temperate lands cannot be established in the tropics because of the low fertility of the soils. It has been established that the higher rate of photosynthesis under tropical conditions tends to produce rapidly growing herbage with low protein and mineral content, the content becoming progressively poorer during growth because of a dilution effect. The poor quality of tropical pastures causes grass-eating livestock to grow slowly. In Peninsular Malaysia the growth rate of cattle is only half that in Britain. The poverty of tropical grasses is such that a larger area is needed to support one head of cattle than is necessary in temperate lands. For example, an acre of tropical pasture can feed only 48 lb (22 kg) of live weight, whilst the same area in Europe can feed 480 lb (218 kg).

All ruminant livestock in Peninsular Malaysia depend to a large extent on such pasturage as is available on grazing reserves, forest clearings, vacant and waste land, roadsides and bunds, and on padi land during the fallow period. Much of the grazing land is ill-kept and inadequate, often reverting to scrub. There is no deliberate or planned attempts at pasture management. The grass common to all grazing lands except padi land under fallow is *lalang*. Although *lalang* is tough and of low nutritive value, young *lalang* (up to a month old) is palatable, and because of its ubiquity it forms the basic feedstuff of much of the livestock population. Grasses superior to *lalang* which are established on some grazing lands are mixtures of indigenous pasture grasses such as cow grass (*Paspalum conjugatum*), carpet grass (*Axonopus affinis*) and savannah grass (*A. compressus*). But the yields of such grasses vary from only 2 to 4 tons per acre per annum, and are inadequate to maintain cattle efficiently (Lim, 1968). Far higher yields can be obtained from fodder grasses such as guinea grass, elephant grass, *Stylosanthes gracilis*, *Brachiaria mutica*, Napier grass, etc. Guinea grass can yield up to 30 tons/acre/annum, the local Napier grass 43 tons, and *Stylosanthes* on good soil 60 tons.

Apart from the above, a combination of economic and cultural factors has been responsible for the relatively poorly developed state of the livestock industry as compared with the other sectors of the agricultural economy. As pointed out by Crotty (1967), livestock in Peninsular Malaysia are competitive rather than complementary to crop production. Livestock do not contribute to the maximization of crop production, either as draught animals or as a source of manure, in a country such as Peninsular Malaysia where tree crops rather than cereals predominate; on the contrary, livestock compete against these crops for land, labour and capital. Since the returns from these tree crops, especially rubber, have so far been higher than could be obtained from livestock rearing, the latter has not attracted either public or private investment. The opportunity cost of livestock production is therefore quite high.

Secondly the availability of a wide variety of protein and plant foods such as fish, fruits, vegetables and spices which are cheaper than livestock products has also tended to depress the demand for such products. Thirdly the demand pattern among the culturally diverse peoples of the country is complex. Thus the Malays, being Muslims, do not rear pigs or eat pork but only mutton and beef. Those Indians who are Hindus do not eat beef, while only the Indians among the various races have milk as part of their regular diet. The only protein foods acceptable to all races are poultry, mutton and fish. This complexity in demand pattern tends to fragment a market which is already small. Collectively the combination of physical, economic and cultural factors has worked against the large-scale development of a livestock industry. However, as standards of living improve, the demand for livestock products will also increase, thereby paving the way for an expansion of the livestock industry.

Up to very recent years Peninsular Malaysia had only an embryonic livestock industry based on the full-time raising of milch cattle and buffaloes by Indian herdsmen, and the part-time rearing of pigs and poultry in Chinese market gardens and farm backyards. Buffaloes and oxen in the padi lands formed part of the agricultural landscape, being kept mainly as draught animals. Goats were reared on a casual and very minor basis for meat. The situation has changed to a certain extent— through the pig and poultry industry becoming more commercialized and specialized and through the setting up of cattle farms by the newly established National Livestock Industry Development Corporation (NLIDC) to produce beef and milk. So far six farms of 3 000 acres (1 200 ha) each have been opened up in Johore, Negri Sembilan, Perak, Pahang and Trengganu.

Table 11.1 shows the livestock population in 1972. There are more than half a million buffaloes and oxen in the country, of which more than half are in the padi-growing states of Kedah and Kelantan. The number of buffaloes has decreased by 9 per cent since 1952, but that of cattle has increased by 20 per cent. It is evident that on the whole this section of the livestock industry has stagnated in the last twenty years. Most of them are work animals, beef and milk being produced only on a very small scale. Cattle dung as a manure is only of minor and local importance in the agricultural economy of the Malays. Most of the work done by the draught animals is in the cultivation of padi land, the ploughing period lasting for two months. A few are also used by the Chinese for hauling timber. In Kelantan buffaloes are preferred for ploughing the wetter and more clayey lands, while oxen are used on the less soggy fields.

These draught animals are a problem to feed. There is abundant grazing in the padi fields during the four or five months fallow, but once

309

Table 11.1   Distribution of livestock population, 1972 (per cent)

State	Buffaloes (total population 204 898)	Oxen (total population 330 137)	Goats (total population 310 230)	Sheep (total population 39 774)	Pigs (total population 732 975)	Total (1 618 014)
Kedah	32	19	23	6	4	14
Negri Sembilan	4	7	8	25	22	14
Penang and Province Wellesley	2	2	4	0	23	12
Kelantan	22	28	8	43	1	12
Selangor	2	6	6	0	18	11
Johore	1	5	19	1	12	10
Perak	5	8	12	3	12	10
Pahang	10	6	8	12	4	6
Malacca	9	3	7	1	4	5
Trengganu	10	14	3	8	0	5
Perlis	3	2	2	1	0	1
	100	100	100	100	100	100

the padi seedlings are planted grazing is restricted to vacant, waste and village grass-lands, to roadsides and the sides of irrigation canals and drains. During the six or seven months between planting and harvesting of the padi crop the cattle cannot obtain sufficient feed and consequently lose condition. This hunger season occurs regularly each year, and is a major problem in the more densely settled padi areas such as Kelantan and Kedah. Moreover the extension of double-cropping in the major padi producing states of Kedah and Kelantan would result in the further decrease in the buffalo population because of the growing use of tractors for ploughing, and the shortening or elimination of the fallow period which would mean that the fields would no longer be available to the animals for off season grazing.

There are two types of buffaloes in Peninsular Malaysia, the wide-horned Kerbau or swamp water-buffalo and the curly-horned Indian Surti or Murrah buffalo. The Malay farmer may own a few swamp water-buffaloes, using them mainly for ploughing the padi fields, and only occasionally for meat and milk. They are water-loving animals and are therefore well suited to working in the soft ground of the padi fields. They are also used to haul timber in the jungle; such buffaloes are usually better cared for by their owners. The swamp water-buffalo make up 98 per cent of the buffalo population in Peninsular Malaysia and are distributed in the main padi areas.

The Indian buffaloes are exclusively dairy animals kept by Sikhs in the vicinity of the larger towns of Perak and Selangor. There are only 3 000 of these buffaloes. In contrast to the water-buffalo, the Indian type requires dry grazing grounds. In addition to grasses, the buffaloes are fed on concentrates made up of rice bran, broken rice, sesame cake and salt. Yields of milk average from 20 to 30 pints (11—17 litres) per day, these gradually diminishing as lactation advances. Surplus milk is converted into ghee, and a small supplementary income is derived from the sale of manure.

There are also two main types of cattle, the common draught cattle bred from Thai—Kedah stock, and milch cattle of mixed Indian Zebu breeds. The draught cattle are, as in the case of the swamp water-buffalo, used mainly for ploughing, only occasionally for meat, and still more rarely for milk. They form the majority (80%) of the cattle in the country. Their distribution is closely related to that of the padi-growing areas, most of them being found in the north-western and north-eastern states of Perak, Kedah, Perlis, Kelantan and Trengganu. In the Kelantan delta pressure of population and the long history of land subdivision have resulted in a large number of individually small padi holdings. Ploughing is commonly practised, and cattle are used in preference over the water-buffalo in all areas except low-lying swampland. Although the cattle are hardy and well adapted to local conditions, they suffer from a seasonal lack of forage during the period when the padi plants are growing in the fields. Overstocking here, as in Kedah, contributes to the problem of pasture shortage.

Milch cattle are mainly of mixed Zebu breeds originally imported from India and known as Local Indian Dairy (LID) cattle in Peninsular Malaysia. There are about 64 000 such cattle distributed in the neighbourhood of towns, largely along western Peninsular Malaysia. They are reared by Indian diarymen chiefly for milk, with surplus animals, especially males and culls, sold for beef and sometimes for draught purposes. Some cattle are also reared by Indian labourers in the rubber and coconut estates. Cattle in the suburban areas are fed on such fodder as is available on waste and vacant land, and only cows in milk are supplied with additional foodstuffs in the form of concentrates. Inadequate feeding and indiscriminate breeding methods have resulted in cattle that are poor milk producers, and the average lactation yields is only about 1 000 lb (454 kg) or 10 per cent that of cattle in temperate countries. Yields are increased to 3 000 lb (1 361 kg) in well-managed herds.

It is clear that the local dairy industry is very poorly developed while there is no beef industry as yet. Such beef as is produced within the country comes from surplus draught or dairy animals. Productivity is low because of poor nutrition, low levels of management and the indifferent quality of the animals. The National Livestock Industry Development Corporation is engaged in a multiplication programme in its farms in order to provide sufficiently good breeding stock. Research is also being conducted on problems of pasture development, livestock diseases and locally produced animal feed. At present there are only two dairy farms run on modern lines in the country—a 2 000 acre (800 ha) farm at the Central Animal Husbandry Station near Kluang producing a few thousand gallons of milk a day from cross-bred cows, and a 40 acre (16 ha) one at Kempas Tebrau where imported Australian cows produced a few hundred gallons of milk a day for the Singapore market. New beef and dairy farms, ranging in size from 2 500 to 5 000 acres (1 000—2 000 ha) are being implemented or planned in Pahang, Perak, Negri Sembilan and Trengganu.

The local goat is bred by Malay smallholders and Tamil labourers for meat, and by the latter for milk also. The local population prefers goat flesh to mutton, and there is a constant demand for goats. The majority of the herds are small and large herds are seldom encountered. The goats are fed exclusively on the natural herbage and foliage of the neighbourhood. As a browsing animal, the goat appears to be better suited to the bush and tree setting of the Peninsula than the grazing animals. It can survive on the very poor feed from waste land and *belukar*, and from scavenging in the *kampongs* and villages. Malacca has 47 per cent of the total goat population in Peninsular Malaysia (Table 11.1).

Sheep rearing on a large scale is impracticable because of the unfavourable climatic conditions, but small flocks of sheep are found in those areas with a long dry season—Kelantan, Trengganu and Pahang—and also in parts of Negri Sembilan where the average rainfall is the lowest in the Peninsula (Table 11.1). The sheep are well adapted to the unfavourable environment and low-level nutrition. They are bred for meat only.

Pig rearing is an integral part of the Chinese market-gardening economy. The pigs consume the waste products from the gardens and in turn contribute manure. Most of the market gardens and, therefore, the pig population are distributed in the suburban areas and New Villages in western Peninsular Malaysia. Pig rearing is also frequently associated with coconut and fishing districts along the coast, the pigs being fed on copra and fish waste. The industry received a severe setback during the resettlement campaign when thousands of Chinese squatter farmers were evicted from their farms and resettled in New Villages. But conditions returned to normal almost as soon as the resettlement campaign was completed. The pig industry has expanded considerably since then, and is now no longer a backyard industry carried on at a subsistence level but a highly specialized and commercialized one. Farms with a few thousand pigs each are now common. The number of pigs increased by 155 per cent in the twenty-year period between 1952 and 1972, and Peninsular Malaysia is now not only self-sufficient in pork but has become a net exporter of pigs. Eighty-two per cent of the pig population is distributed in the western states of Penang, Negri Sembilan, Selangor, Perak and Johore (Table 11.1).

The quality and size of the local pigs have been improved by crossbreeding with imported purebreds. The pigs which are now reared in the specialized farms are bigger and faster maturing than the local Chinese pig, reaching a marketable age in only six months.

In the Chinese market-gardens the pigs are fed on a soft diet composed of boiled succulent vegetable foods—sweet potato haulms and tubers, tapioca leaves and tubers, keladi (*Colocasia*) leaves and tubers, banana stems, kangkong (*Ipomea reptans*) and yams (*Dioscorea*). Concentrated foods are included in the diet when the pigs reach a marketable age, the most common foods being rice bran and broken rice, coconut cake and some fish meal. However, with the intensification and specialization of pig rearing the animals in the pig farms are fed on scientifically balanced rations. This aspect of pig rearing is especially important since the cost of feeding accounts for 70 to 80 per cent of the total cost of production.

Poultry is the only livestock raised by all the peoples of Peninsular Malaysia, in rural as well as in urban areas. The discovery and widespread use of an anti-Ranikhet vaccine after the Second World War enabled the poultry farmers to control this major disease effectively, thereby paving the way for the large-scale development of the poultry industry. By the 1950s poultry farming had started to move out from its backyard industry background towards commercial specialization, and by the

1960s the poultry industry was sufficiently well established to supply most of the country's needs for eggs and poultry meat. Large farms with several thousand birds now specialize in the production of eggs and of table birds, mainly for the home market. As a consequence the total number of eggs produced increased from 77 million in 1956 to 1 345 million in 1972 while the production of poultry meat increased from 27 million pounds to 154 million pounds. The *per capita* consumption of eggs and poultry meat has also increased steadily and is now 145 and 16.7 pounds respectively.

This rapid expansion in the industry was due to the adoption of modern large-scale production methods and to raising the quality and productivity of the fowls. For example the average output of meat per bird in 1956 was only 1.7 lb (0.8 kg); by 1964 the output had been raised to 5 lb (2.2 kg). Similarly the output of eggs was raised from 4.8 to 40 per bird (Crotty, 1967).

In contrast to this modernized industry is the raising of poultry on a small family scale in backyards and *kampongs*. Here the birds are usually underfed and badly housed. Poultry in rural areas are allowed free range, scavenging such food as they can in the form of insects, grass, seeds, household refuse. Occasionally the owner may throw them a handful of broken rice or padi. Ducks are bred extensively by the Chinese in some coastal areas where large amounts of fish refuse are available. They are also common in some localities where irrigated padi is cultivated. Geese, turkeys and pigeons are reared only on a minor scale.

Fishing

Part-time fishing and the main occupation of padi cultivation have always formed the traditional bases of the subsistence economy of the coastal Malays. Living in an environment which does not encourage livestock rearing, the diet of the Malays is essentially vegetarian. The main source of animal protein is fish. Fish—fresh, dried or salted—forms the second staple food not only of the Malays, but also of the immigrant Chinese and Indian population. Although fish is the cheapest of the animal protein foods, the *per capita* consumption is only between 60 and 70 lb (27–31 kg) per annum, an amount insufficient to maintain a balanced diet in the absence of other protein food intake.

Its cheapness, relative abundance compared with meat and acceptability to all religions have made fish a popular food in the country. The influx of the immigrant population earlier in the century generated an increasing demand for fish. In response to this demand, the fishing communities along the 1 200 miles (1 931 km) of coasts began to specialize in catching fish for the local markets, and fishing became a regular full-time occupation. The number of people engaged in fishing has increased steadily over the years, reaching a peak of 77 700 in 1950, but declining to 69 200 in 1972. Of these 56 per cent were Malays, 43 per cent Chinese and the rest Indians and other races. Thirty-six per cent of the fishermen are in the east coast states of Kelantan, Trengganu, Pahang and east Johore. There are some 350 fishing villages strung out along the coasts of the Peninsula. Most of these are small and many are in isolated locations.

The importance of the fishing industry is illustrated by the fact that its contribution to the gross domestic product was higher than that from forestry, amounting to M$224 million in 1970. After an initial period of postwar rehabilitation, production of marine fish rose to 109 000 tons in 1949, 139 000 tons in 1960, 294 000 tons in 1970 and 367 000 tons in 1973. In addition, about 25 000 tons of freshwater fish are produced annually, mainly for local consumption. Catches are affected by seasonal weather conditions, among other factors, and the high seas and the heavy weather of the northeast monsoon result in low landings in the months of November, December and January along the entire east coast. However, the monsoon months are no longer a completely 'dead' period as mechanization of the fishing boats has enabled many fishermen to go out during the monsoon. Peak production usually occurs from April to September along the east coast. Production along the sheltered waters of the west coast is less seasonal in pattern.

Marine fishing

The fishing industry of Peninsular Malaysia is based largely on the intensive fishing of shallow inshore waters, centred around the South China Sea, the Straits of Malacca and the eastern-most parts of the Indian Ocean. The Malay Peninsula forms part of the Sunda Platform, a drowned plateau linking the Peninsula to Borneo and Sumatra. The seas around the Peninsula are shallow, seldom exceeding 200 ft (60 m) in depth. The nutrient level and hence the productivity of these seas is low, for a number of reasons:

1. In an equatorial environment where solar radiation and temperatures are high throughout the year, the metabolic rates also tend to be high, with the result that there is no seasonal check to growth which might permit the accumulation of nutrients. The utilization of nutrients goes on as fast as they are produced. Such nutrients, mainly phosphates and nitrates, are essential for the growth and maintenance of the plankton pastures which are the bases of fish food.

2. Oceanographical research has shown that the surface waters of tropical seas are generally poorer in phosphates and nitrates than the surface waters of temperate and arctic seas. However, it is also known that the deeper layers of tropical seas contain large amounts of nutrients released through the processes of decomposition of waste matter. In temperate seas, where the surface layers may be colder than the

underlying layers in winter, such nutrient accumulations are brought up to the surface by convection currents, but in tropical seas the surface water is always warmer than the underlying layers, so that the nutrients are locked up in the lower layers.

3. In other parts of the tropics such as the western South American coast and the west coast of Africa, the stocks of nutrients locked up in the deeper layers are brought up to the surface by the process of up-welling of deep sea-water. Such a process does not occur in the shallow Malaysian seas. However, research has suggested that a process similar to upwelling takes place during the intermonsoon periods when the current drifts of the South China Sea and the Singapore Straits are reversed in direction. These intermonsoon periods have been found to be periods when large numbers of diatoms (microscopic algae) prevail in the Singapore Straits.

4. The movements of water around Peninsular Malaysia are largely conditioned by winds, tides and currents from neighbouring seas. No high latitude cold currents intrude into this region to displace the lower layers of water and enrich the seas.

Under such circumstances the richest areas are those fertilized by drainage water from the land carrying terrestrial detritus of all types as well as dissolved mineral salts. Here, again, the value of this discharge depends upon the physical composition of the land from which it comes. For example, the water which drains off the volcanic rocks of Java and Sumatra is richer in dissolved salts than that which drains off the old sedimentaries and granite of the Malay Peninsula.

Thus the physiography of the coasts and the nature of the tropical waters around Peninsular Malaysia account largely for the importance of inshore fisheries, and the major catches are taken from the narrow Straits of Malacca and a narrow belt bordering the east coast. But the form and nature of fishing activities are also conditioned by climate, technology and tradition. In many parts of the Peninsula where winds provide the main motive power for fishing boats, the daily cycle of fishing activities relates closely to the incidence of land and sea breezes. Superimposed upon this is the seasonal cycle along the east as influenced by the north-east monsoon, and along the west coast as influenced by the southwest monsoon, although the southwest monsoon is not strong enough to hamper fishing to any great extent except in the north-western part which lies unprotected by the Sumatran landmass. There is also a close correlation between tides and fishing. The largest catches are made when the tidal rise and fall is greatest, during the spring tides which occur at the periods when the moon is new or full. At neap tides (first and last quarter of the moon) the tidal flow is small, and fish shoal movements are reduced, with the result that fishing activity is also reduced. Still less fishing takes place during the few days between each tide when tidal flow is practically absent.

The use of traditional craft propelled by oars and sails restricts fishing to a narrow zone and reduces the quantity and variety of fish caught. But in recent years mechanization of fishing boats has become important. In 1960, 61 per cent of the 14 608 boats were powered; in 1972, 78 per cent of the 21 612 boats were powered. Mechanization has reduced the dependence upon sails and made the fishermen more mobile. However, for the majority of fishermen it has not extended the range of fishing operations to any significant extent. In general they do not operate more than 50 miles (80 km) from the coasts in their small boats. Moreover most of the catches are the pelagic fish of the inshore waters, and with the increased intensity of fishing in the postwar period the pelagic fish stocks in these waters are rapidly being depleted. In fact most of the increased production in recent years have come from tapping the fish resources of the benthic zone, through trawling for the demersal fish in inshore as well as deeper waters.

Trawl fishing was introduced in the 1960s during the Indonesian confrontation against Malaysia when, with the (temporary) cessation of the Malaysian—Indonesian barter trade, the barter-boat owners converted their boats into trawlers. The effectiveness of this fishing method is seen in the earnings of the trawler fishermen, which average two to three times more than those of the inshore fishermen using traditional methods. Since then trawling has become an increasingly important contributor to total fish landings; in 1972, for example, it contributed 36 per cent to the total. The number of licensed trawl nets has increased very rapidly, to over 4 000 in 1974. Today trawl fishing is carried on in all the states except Negri Sembilan and Malacca, both of which have been found to be unsuitable for trawler operations. However, the rapid advance of trawling is seen by some as posing a challenge to the livelihood of the traditional inshore fishermen (Bank Negara, 1971), although in fact trawling harvests bottom fish resources which up to recently have been little exploited. The potentialities for trawling are good, as the fishing area of less than 25 fathoms totals about 50 000 square miles (129 500 sq km). The Trawling Exploratory Survey of 1970 indicated that the exploitable fish resources for trawlers are better off the east coast than off the west coast of Peninsular Malaysia.

The number of species of fish so far recorded in this region exceeds 1 000, but only some 250 are food fish, and only twenty main varieties are commonly caught and enter the market. The fish that are commonly found in Malaysian markets are catfish (Malay: *keli, bagok, bakap*), sea bream (*batu*), pomfret (*bawal*), grey mullet (*belanak*), anchovy (*bilis*), whiting (*bulus bulus*), horse mackerel (*kembong, chincharu, selikor*), jewfish (*gelama*), grunters (*gerus gerut*), sea perch (*kerapu*), snappers (*kerisi*), thread-fins (*senangin, kurau*), red snapper (*ikan merah*), stingrays and skates (*pari*), sprats, pilchards and herrings (*tamban*), Spanish mackerel (*tenggiri*), sharks (*yu*) and the Malaysian shad (*terubok*). The

317

greater part of the fish population in Malaysian waters consists of small fish. But such fish, which would be regarded as being too small for food in some countries, are widely consumed by the population, and even those that are not normally eaten by the population are used as duck food. On an average, the non-edible fish make up 40 per cent of the annual catch.

A wide range of fishing methods is employed by Malaysian fishermen to catch the great variety of fish in these waters. To the indigenous methods have been added methods introduced by Chinese as well as Japanese fishermen. The Japanese drive-in net or *moro-ami* is especially useful for fishing in coral reefs where the more usual nets cannot be used. For each of the main methods—line, nets and traps—there is multiplicity of equipment, and the fishermen display great ingenuity in the construction of such equipment from locally available material such as wood and bamboo. The most important traps employed in the shallow coastal waters are the fixed fishing stakes. There are several types of stakes, but the commonest are the *kelongs*, constructed of nibong palms and erected in waters up to 7 fathoms deep. These stakes were once widely employed in the fishing industry and used to contribute as much as one-third of the total catches in Peninsular Malaysia (in 1957). But today there are just over 400 fishing stakes in the country, most of them off the coasts of Johore, and together they contribute less than 2 per cent of the total fish catches per annum. The most important fishing gears employed at present are the purse seives (*pukat jerut*) and the trawl nets (*pukat tunda*). They are responsible for over 60 per cent of the fish production, and are also widely used in the major fishing countries of the world. They have displaced many of the traditional fishing gears such as the stationary *belats, pompangs* and *gombangs*, the small sieves and the fish traps.

The output of the Malayan fisherman is low. Firth estimated a prewar annual average of 1.5 tons, a very low figure when compared with the output of the British fisherman, which was six to eight times larger in bulk and twelve to fifteen times higher in value. Production per fisherman was 2½ tons in 1960, with wide differences in output in the different states. In the period since 1960 the productivity of the fishermen has increased significantly, being 4.42 tons per fisherman in 1972 (Table 11.2). This was due to three main factors: (*a*) the progressive mechanization of the fishing fleet (in 1960 only 38 per cent of the fleet was powered; in 1972 the percentage was 79), providing the advantages of greater reliability, mobility and the ability to go out to sea in all but the worst weather; (*b*) the greater efficiency of the fishing gears employed by the fishermen, in particular the replacement of natural fibre by synthetic fibre nets, and the use of purse seive and trawl fishing techniques; and (*c*) the tapping of new fishing grounds, including those in the benthic zone.

318

Plate 28   A *belat* fish trap constructed from bamboo, Sabak, Kota Baharu (see p. 318).

Although the motorized boats could maintain a high and steady rate of production which could only be achieved by the non-motorized traditional oar-and-sail craft at peak periods, there is no clear correlation between productivity and use of motorized boats, as Table 11.2 shows. It is evident that the output of the fishermen also depends on other factors such as weather conditions, tides, the presence of fish shoals and the skill and efficiency of the fishermen themselves. Fishing has always been an uncertain occupation, and production fluctuates from day to day, season to season, and year to year.

There are more than 300 landing points for fish along the entire coastline of Peninsular Malaysia. Apart from what is retained by the individual fisherman for his own consumption, the catch goes to the nearest market. Spoilage takes place very rapidly in the tropics, and some form of preservation is necessary while the fish are being transported to market. Ice is commonly used to preserve fresh fish, at sea as well as in transit from the landing points to the distribution centres. The demand for ice is relatively inelastic, so that where the ice manufacturers are in a monopolistic position and are able to set the price, ice is relatively expensive to use. In addition there may be locational or regional inadequacies in supplies, so that the only alternative would be to process the fish into dried or salted forms.

Table 11.2   Production of fish per fisherman, 1972

States	*Total production* (tons)	*Number of fishermen*	*Production per fisherman* (tons)	*Percentage of powered to non-powered boats*
West coast				
Selangor	58 200	7 050	8.25	88
Perak	78 000	14 020	5.56	93
Penang	31 700	6 280	5.05	88
Kedah	37 600	6 630	5.67	71
Perlis	5 400	1 370	3.94	62
Johore (west)	14 200	7 140	1.99	64
Malacca	1 500	1 390	1.08	85
Negri Sembilan	300	370	0.81	80
Average			(5.13)	
East coast				
Johore (east)	29 800	5 250	5.68	60
Pahang	8 100	3 010	2.69	80
Trengganu	30 200	10 870	2.78	72
Kelantan	11 200	5 870	1.91	77
Average			(3.17)	
Total and average	306 200	69 250	4.42	79

Fish which are processed into boiled, salted or dried fish are those which cannot find a market as fresh fish because of inadequate transport facilities, distance from markets and insufficient supplies or prohibitive prices of ice. Some fish (e.g. *terubok* and *kembong*) are also processed due to an overabundance of supplies at certain seasons, or to a deterioration in freshness on landing. In 1972 about one-third of the total fish catches in Peninsular Malaysia was processed into salted, dried or boiled fish, into fish meal, manure fish, prawn dust, fish paste (*belachan*), fish and prawn crackers, and a variety of other products. The two states which had a higher proportion of their fish production converted into processed products were Selangor (63%) and Penang (43%). The east coast states, which used to be the main centres for dried and salted fish, had lower percentages: 34 in Trengganu, 28 in Pahang and only 18 in Kelantan. The main reasons for the decline in the proportion of processed to fresh fish are the improved transport facilities along the east coast, and the greater availability and use of ice for preservation.

The marine fishing industry of Peninsular Malaysia has expanded

Plate 29   Drying *ikan merah* in a fishing village at Tumpat, Kelantan. Dried and salted fish are a regular item in the diet of the major communities in the country and most of the fishing villages convert part of their catches into these dried forms.

considerably in the last fifteen years, but it continues to face a number of problems such as the regional disparity between the well-developed west coast fishing areas and the poorer east coast areas (except east Johore), where productivity and therefore incomes are low. In addition there is also a marked disparity in returns obtained from inshore fishing using traditional methods and those from trawling using modern methods. In order to meet these problems the Government has instituted a number of measures, including the establishment of the Fisheries Development Authority (FDA) and the Fish Marketing Board (FMB) in 1971, and the formation of fishermen's associations. The FDA is concerned with the commercialization and modernization of the fishing industry, to which end it has formulated a programme consisting of construction of boats for sale to fishermen, the development of fish processing industries and the construction of fishing complexes complete with jetties, cold storage facilities and wholesale marketing facilities. Five complexes would be built by 1975: in Kuala Trengganu, Lumut, Kuala Kedah, Batu Maung (Penang) and Kuantan. The FDA will also engage directly in trawl fishing on the east coast with a trawler fleet which is expected to grow to 300 by 1975 (Bank Negara, 1971).

Plate 30   Frozen tuna caught in the Indian Ocean being unloaded at Penang. The fish will be canned in a factory and will eventually be exported to different parts of the world (see p. 321).

The Fish Marketing Board's aim is to establish an efficient marketing and distribution network which would provide better returns to the fishermen. To complement the work of these institutions the Government has given high priority to the formation of fishermen's associations, of which fifty-three would be set up under the Second Malaysia Plan.

Freshwater fishing

Whereas marine fishing is a self-contained industry providing full-time work for a large number of people, freshwater fishing is only a complementary facet of the rural economy of Peninsular Malaysia, providing part-time employment for smallholders and estate workers. Throughout the country padi fields, rivers, ponds, lakes, catchment areas, freshwater swamps, lagoons and abandoned mining pools are fished regularly by Malay agriculturalists, Chinese market-gardeners and Indian estate workers. The catch seldom goes beyond the home or the nearest village market. The largest single source of freshwater fish is from flooded padi fields, but considerable potentialities exist for the extension of aquaculture to the other areas of freshwater. An estimated 500 000 acres (200 000 ha) of inland waters including natural and man-made lakes, rivers, streams, irrigation canals and disused mining pools are available for aquaculture development (FAO, 1965). In addition many other thousands of acres of mangrove and freshwater swamps, which at present are only casually fished, can be converted for coastal and inland aquaculture.

The brackish-water zone along the west coast, corresponding roughly with the mangrove belt, is being utilized on a small scale for the culture of the cockle, *Anadara gravosa*, and for prawn culture. Cockle culture was started experimentally in 1948 and has proved to be a success in the mangrove areas of Perak and Selangor. About 5 000 acres (2 000 ha) of foreshore, four-fifths of them in Perak, produce between 25 000 to 30 000 tons of cockles per annum, sufficient to meet the demand from the local and Singapore markets.

Prawn culture on embanked mangrove swamps is a fairly recent introduction and at present is confined to an area of 830 acres (330 ha) along the west coast of Johore. The most critical environmental factor in the successful establishment of prawn culture in the mangrove swamps of the west coast is the tidal range: the range must be such as to cover the land to a depth of 2 to 8 ft (0.94–3.78 m) at high tide and to expose the land at ebb tide. In the prawn ponds sluice gates at strategic locations are used to regulate the flow of water according to the tidal cycle. No supplementary feed is provided to the prawns which are let into the ponds. Harvesting is carried out once a night for a period of fifteen to twenty nights a month.

The potentialities for the extension of prawn culture are good, especially as local and export demand for prawn continues to exceed supply, and large areas of mangrove-covered foreshores remain under-utilized. However, as seen earlier, only those with the correct tidal range can be converted to prawn ponds, and in some areas there may be conflict with the need to keep the mangroves as forest reserves. Another problem is the high capital cost of developing the ponds.

The flooded padi fields of Monsoon Asia have always been the source of home-table fish for the farmers. In Peninsular Malaysia freshwater fish for the home and for the market are caught in the fields, irrigation canals and drains of the padi-growing areas. In general fish from the small and discontinuous fields characteristic of the south Malaysian padi landscape are for the subsistence only, and it is only in the large extended plains of the northwest that there are substantial surpluses above subsistence needs. The four most important varieties of padi field fish are *Trichogaster pectoralis* (Malay: sepat siam), *Anabas testudineus* (ikan puyu), *Ophiosephalus striatus* (aruan) and *Claricas batachus* (keli). All are labyrinth fish, capable of absorbing atmospheric oxygen when their gills are wet and of surviving extremes of temperature and oxygen availability. These qualities of hardiness are necessary for the fish to survive in fields which are flooded for only part of the year. There is always a sufficient number of fish left in the drains and canals to supply the next season's fry, so that no restocking is necessary. No deliberate efforts are made by the padi planter to encourage the growth of these fish, which are left to forage for themselves.

Except for the *sepat siam*, the padi field fish are consumed locally as fresh fish. A prolific and hardy fish, the *sepat siam* was introduced from Thailand into the Krian Irrigation Area in about 1921 and has since spread to other padi areas. Feeding on silt, algae and other vegetable matter, the fish enter the fields when these are flooded for transplanting, and they mature there after four months. When the irrigation water is drained off before the harvest, the fish collect in the specially dug sump-ponds at the lowest part of the fields. Each pond may drain 2 or 3 acres, and in rich localities may yield from 700 to 1 300 lb (318–590 kg) of fish, though in fields where there is poor growth of the fish's main food—algae—the catch may be as low as 40 lb (18 kg) per pond. There are about 14 500 sump-ponds in Krian, and the area produces most of the *sepat siam* sold each year. The surplus fish sold are an important source of extra income to the padi planters. In a 3 acre padi field the income from fish would be about one-quarter of the total annual income from padi (Tan, 1973). But the production of *sepat siam* has been decreasing rapidly in recent years because the chemical insecticides used to control padi pests have proved to be deadly to the fish.

As part of its overall programme for the development of the inland water fisheries the Fisheries Division has been engaged in assessing the suitability of indigenous and imported species for stocking and culturing or natural development. In the early 1940s *Tilapia mossambica* was introduced as a possible fish, but it has not become popular because it tends to over-breed so that individuals become stunted. Experiments conducted on the *lampam jawa* (*Puntius javanicus*) as a pond-fish proved to be successful, and in 1959 a large-scale programme of stocking rivers, lakes and irrigation canals was initiated. It has since become the most important pond fish in the country, especially for mixed culturing, and over 3½ million fish fry are produced annually by the fish-breeding stations to meet the demand for the fish. It is a popular table fish and fetches a price similar to that of the Chinese carp.

Among the more popular items of food from inland and brackish waters is the giant freshwater prawn or *udang galah* (*Macrobrachium rosenbergii*). It occurs in most of the rivers, especially the lower reaches, as well as in lakes, reservoirs, mining pools and in some padi fields. The most important production areas for the prawn are Telok Anson, Tanjong Tualang, Parit Buntar, Nibong Tebal, Alor Star and Sabak Bernam. An omnivorous feeder, it can be cultured in ponds and flooded padi fields which have a depth of water of at least 6 in (15 cm) throughout the growing period. However, prawn culture so far is being practised on only a very small scale.

Chinese participation in freshwater fishing is concentrated mainly in carp-rearing in artificially constructed ponds. Fish culture here forms an integral part of the Chinese market-gardening-cum-fish-rearing landscape. This form of pisciculture which had its origins in the warm temperate environment of South China was introduced successfully into the tropical setting of Peninsular Malaysia without substantial modifications. Carp rearing depends on the careful division of the available food resources among the different species. Usually the grass carp make up half or more of the total in a pond. Their food is any succulent grass that may be placed in the pond. The droppings from these fish help to raise the fertility of the waters, thereby encouraging the growth of the algae and plankton upon which the big head and the silver carp feed. The mud carp depends on food at the bottom of the pond, while the common carp is a general scavenger. Where intensive methods are employed, the yields may be as high as 4 000 lb per acre (1 300 kg per ha) of fish, but the average is low because most of the farmers rear carp only on a part-time basis, in conjunction with market gardening.

As the demand for pond fish increases new ponds are constructed each year for fish culture, and today there are over 8 000 ponds covering over 8 000 acres (3 200 ha) in Peninsular Malaysia, mainly in Perak and Negri Sembilan, compared with only 1 900 acres (780 ha) in 1963.

Forest production

The land-use survey of 1966 showed that about 22.3 million acres (9 million ha) or 68 per cent of the total land area of Peninsular Malaysia were under primary forest cover (Fig. 11.1). Of this total 19.4 million acres (7.8 million ha) consisted of dryland forest and the remainder of swamp and wetland forest. The land capability classification survey indicated that 14.3 million acres (5.8 million ha) of forested land consisted of forest above the steepland line (i.e. with slopes exceeding 20°) and peat swamps, and were therefore unlikely to be developed for agriculture. The remaining 8 million acres (3.2 million ha) of forest were classed as being suitable for agricultural development, providing the country with a substantial agricultural land potential.

The rate of land development in Peninsular Malaysia under the Second Malaysia Plan totals about 1 million acres (0.4 million ha) over the five-year period. This implies that at the present rate of conversion of forested land to agricultural land some forty years would elapse before the conversion process is completed. When forest is cleared for permanent agriculture the forest yields a certain quantity of timber and other forest products. But this is a once-and-for-all yield because the land is subsequently put to agricultural use. In this respect the forest can be regarded as a wasting asset and a non-renewable resource.

In contrast, the permanently forested land under proper management

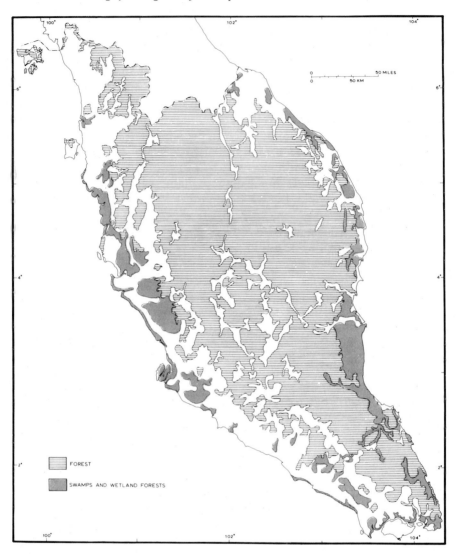

Fig. 11.1 Distribution of dryland and wetland forests.

will provide the country with a steady flow of forest products, and therefore fall into the renewable natural resource category. However, not all of the 14.3 million acres of permanently forested land have this productive potential. The montane forests, covering about one-third of the permanently forested land, do not have a productive function but are nevertheless important for watershed protection. The productive forests are the mangrove swamps, peat swamps and lowland and hill forests on steepland. Lee (1973) has estimated that Peninsular Malaysia's timber requirements for a projected future population of 20 million can be met from intensively managed forest covering about 4 million acres (1.6 million ha), consisting mainly of hill forest. There therefore appears to be sufficient reserves of permanent forest to meet the country's timber requirements for a long time.

However, up to the present forest products are derived mainly from inland forests up to an elevation of 1 000 to 1 500 ft (305–457 m). These include areas gazetted as forest reserves as well as forested areas which are being cleared for land development schemes. In 1973 the total forested area of Peninsular Malaysia was 20.6 million acres (8.35 million ha), as compared with 22.3 million acres (9.15 million ha) in 1966. The commercially accessible forest land available for exploitation was estimated to cover 5.8 million acres (2.36 million ha); in addition 9.8 million acres (3.99 million ha) of logged-over forest with some commercial timber were also available for exploitation.

The importance of forest production in the country's economy is seen in the fact that in 1973 the net exports of sawn logs and sawn timber from Peninsular Malaysia amounted to M$528 million. Only 30 000 people are employed directly in the forest industry, while over 120 000 are employed in the wood-based industries.

Forest exploitation in Peninsular Malaysia has followed the usual historical phases of highly selective logging of the few most valuable species in the initial phase to the almost full utilization of a greater number of species as occurs today. As a consequence although the total wood volume per acre of climax rain forest may be 150 tons or more, the yield of commercial timber in the early phase was only about 2 to 3 tons per acre (Flemmish, 1959). Since then the yields have increased considerably, as seen in Table 11.3.

Table 11.3 Yield of timber, by state

State	Yield (tons/acre)
Johore	16.0
Negri Sembilan	12.7
Perak	12.5
Trengganu	11.5
Pahang	10.3
Kedah	8.9
Selangor	6.6
Kelantan	5.4
Average	10.5

Source: *Based on Pelinck (1970).*

Nevertheless the yields today compare poorly with the yields of 100 tons or more from the coniferous forests of Europe and America. This disparity in yields may appear surprising in view of the greater luxuriance of the tropical rain forests when compared with the coniferous forests. However, although there are more than 2 500 species of trees in Peninsular Malaysia, only a few of these produce timber which is commercially acceptable.[1] Again, the commercially valuable trees are the large, top-storey dominants, and there are fewer such trees per unit area in the rain forest than in the temperate forests, and these are also generally smaller in size and produce less timber than the conifers. Another cause of low yields is the greater susceptibility of tropical timbers to decay and insect depredations in the living trees, so that the final recovery of saleable wood is significantly lower.

The exploitation of timber in Malaysian forests is difficult because of the great number of different species of trees of various sizes scattered over a wide area. It is not unusual to find an average of only one tree of commercial value in several acres of forest. This is particularly so where the heavy hardwoods are concerned; patches of 20 to 100 acres (8–40 ha) in extent in eastern Peninsular Malaysia may have only two or three trees of marketable size in them. There are also some species that yield second-class timber which could be sold locally if they could be extracted without too much expense. Most of the remaining trees have wood so soft as to be worthless even for firewood or pulp. The practical exploitation of such forests is therefore very much dependent upon accessibility and cheap transport. The more remote areas will be un-economical to exploit because of excessive transport costs. Nor is it always possible to reduce costs by floating logs down-river as the working areas may not be near a suitable river, and also because many tropical hardwoods are not buoyant. In eastern Peninsular Malaysia logs are floated down in large rafts, but the rivers of the western states are little used for log transport. Poles are floated down in large quantities.

The main forest products are timber, poles, firewood and charcoal. Table 11.4 shows that the production of timber has increased steadily over the ten-year period 1964–73, but the production of poles has remained constant, that of charcoal has decreased since 1971 and that of firewood has decreased substantially over this period.

The exploitation of the forests is under the charge of state governments, which altogether have exploitation rights covering a total area of 2.34 million acres (948 000 ha). The Federal Government established a National Forestry Council in 1971 to co-ordinate the implementation of the forest policies of the individual states so as to allow for the better use of the country's forest resources. A master plan for the forest industries of Peninsular Malaysia, Sabah and Sarawak is being drawn up by the

---

[1] See Chapter 4 on Vegetation.

Table 11.4   Production of timber, poles and fuel, 1964–73

Year	Timber	Poles	Charcoal	Firewood
	(million solid cubic feet)			
1964	105	3.3	11.1	5.9
1965	114	3.6	10.7	5.9
1966	135	3.6	10.5	6.1
1967	148	4.1	12.3	5.5
1968	179	3.4	16.7	4.8
1969	189	2.8	17.6	5.5
1970	231	2.9	16.4	4.7
1971	253	3.2	21.1	4.8
1972	308	3.4	18.9	3.5
1973	321	3.5	17.8	3.4

Government with the assistance of the United Nations Development Programme and the UN Food and Agriculture Organization. This Forest Industries Development Project was completed at the end of 1975.

Plate 31   A forest tree being felled for timber. Peninsular Malaysia has greatly increased its output of timber and timber products in recent years. Much of this timber is obtained from forests being cleared for agricultural land development (see p. 327).

One of the main problems of the logging industry is timber wastage and the under-utilization of the forest resources. Log extraction is confined to easily marketable varieties in the forest concession areas outside the forest reserves where logging is not strictly controlled. Wastage in the more inaccessible areas can be up to 50 per cent. Another cause of wastage is the failure to develop better end uses for timber left-overs (Bank Negara, 1970). In order to reduce these timber losses the Government is encouraging the establishment of integrated timber complexes.

Peninsular Malaysia in principle prohibits the export of logs overseas in order to stimulate the establishment of timber-based industries, thereby providing more employment opportunities and increasing the value added from the timber industry. As a consequence both the number and the variety of such timber-based industries have increased in the decade 1963—72, sawmills from 411 to 477, and veneer and plywood factories from six to thirty-three. In addition there were four match-making factories and one pencil-making factory in 1972. The distribution of these industries is shown in Table 11.5.

Table 11.5   Timber-based industries, 1972

State	Sawmills	Veneer/ plywood mills	Pencil factory	Match factory
Perak	90	7	—	2
Pahang	89	7	—	—
Selangor	79	5	—	1
Johore	45	7	1	—
Negri Sembilan	38	2	—	—
Kedah	32	2	—	—
Kelantan	32	1	—	1
Penang	32	—	—	—
Trengganu	24	1	—	—
Malacca	12	1	—	—
Perlis	4	—	—	—
Total	477	33	1	4

The first sawmills were established in the 1920s, and by 1940 there were eighty mills. The postwar period has seen a very rapid expansion of the industry, and there are now 477 mills. Expansion has in fact been over-rapid, with the result that some mills are as far as 100 miles (160 km) away from the source of logs. As a general rule sawmills should be sited nearer their source of raw material (i.e. the forests) than their markets since it takes about two tons of greenwood to make one ton of green lumber. The Emergency has also had adverse effects on the industry, and security considerations have led to the siting of mills in towns rather than near forests, with resultant increase in costs. There have also been fluctuating and regional shortages of logs. Many of the mills are undersized, and there was no increase in efficiency in terms of output per labourer or per horsepower until recently when new modern sawmills including timber drying kilns were established. The output of sawn timber from all mills in 1973 was 2 493 000 tons of 50 cubic ft (1.4 cu m), and the net exports of sawn timber totalled 1 340 000 tons of 50 cubic ft.

The mangrove forests are intensively worked to produce firewood, charcoal and poles. There are 440 square miles (1 140 sq km) of mangrove reserves. Small areas are clear-felled each year on a rotation of twenty years. Felled areas are naturally regenerated and are ready for further felling at the end of the rotation period. There has been a marked decline in the demand for the production of firewood and poles in recent years. Poles are used mainly in the tin mines, but due to changes in mining methods and restrictions on tin production the demand has fallen. Firewood production has declined steadily in face of competition from more efficient fuels, especially bottled gas, kerosine and electrical power. There is, however, still a substantial demand for charcoal. Charcoal production has increased partly because of the use of charcoal from rubber wood for smelting at the steelmills in Prai.

Apart from the major products of timber and fuel, the forests also yield a number of minor forest products which are collected in small amounts and sold or bartered. The most important of these in terms of value are nipah (the leaves of which are used in the manufacture of *atap* thatch), rattan (used for making baskets, mats, rattan furniture, etc.) jelutong, gutta-percha and other gums and resins collected by tapping species of trees of the families *Sapotaceae* and *Dipterocarpaceae*, and a large number of miscellaneous products such as incense wood, tanning and dyeing material, fibres, derris, medicinal plants, and a variety of food plants. The total annual revenue from such minor forest produce forms a very small part of the total revenue from all forest products.

12
Mining

Gold, tin and iron-ore have been mined in Peninsular Malaysia for centuries, though on a small scale, and mostly for local use. As in many other parts of the tropics, mining provided the initial impetus to the development of Peninsular Malaysia, and was in one way or another responsible for the evolution of the economic and social landscapes of the country. Mining has been and still is centred largely on tin, and it was the discovery of rich deposits of alluvial tin in the Larut Valley of Perak during the middle of the nineteenth century which led to the first 'tin rush'. New tin fields were subsequently discovered in the Kinta Valley and in the Klang Valley of Selangor. The exploitation of these fields was largely in the hands of the Chinese who streamed into Peninsular Malaysia from South China.

Mining operations gained momentum with the establishment of British rule and production rose to 40 000 tons in 1898 and then to over 50 000 tons in 1913. The pioneers of the tin industry were the Chinese, but towards the end of the nineteenth century European capital entered the field. The Chinese tin monopoly was gradually broken: in 1910, 78 per cent of the total production came from Chinese mines, and the rest from European mines. By 1930 European mines were producing 63 per cent and the Chinese only 27 per cent. Non-Malaysians have continued to dominate the mining sector in the postwar period and up to the present day; in 1970 the non-Malaysians owned 72 per cent of the total share capital in mining companies.

Tin has long been one of the major sources of the Government's revenue. In 1899 the export duty on tin provided nearly 46 per cent of the total revenue, and although the relative contribution of tin has since fallen with the rise of the agricultural sector of the Malaysian economy, its absolute contribution remains significant. Thus while tin contributed about 12 to 15 per cent of Government revenue in the postwar period, the absolute contributions in the boom years of 1951 and 1952 alone came to over $76 million and $69 million respectively.

The mining economy of the Federation of Malaysia is based on the production of tin, petroleum, natural gas, copper, iron-ore, bauxite,

332

Table 12.1   Mineral production, 1973

Mineral	*Production*	
	Tons	Metric tons
Tin-in-concentrates	71 100	72 200
Iron-ore	509 000	517 100
Bauxite	1 124 700	1 142 700
Ilmenite concentrate (exports)	182 400	185 300
China clay	104 300	106 000
Raw gold (in Troy oz)	2 800	—

ilmenite, gold and china clay (kaolin). Copper, petroleum and natural gas are produced in Sarawak and Sabah, but with the recent discovery of petroleum and natural gas off the east coast, Peninsular Malaysia will soon be also an oil producer. Table 12.1 shows the main types of minerals produced in Peninsular Malaysia in 1973. The outstanding position of tin in the mining economy is clearly revealed by the fact that the value of the exports of tin metal amounted to nearly $900 million in 1973, and also by the fact that the tin mining industry employed 97 per cent of the total mining labour force of 43 300 in that year. The total area of land alienated for mining has declined from 512 000 acres (207 000 ha) in 1964 to 395 500 acres (160 000 ha) in 1972. The growth area in the mining industry in the future is likely to be in oil and natural gas, although tin will continue to be dominant for many more years.

Tin

The tin fields of the Malay Peninsula belong to the large metallogenetic tin province of Southeast Asia, which includes Burma, Thailand, the Malay Peninsula and parts of Indonesia. This tin province, centred in Peninsular Malaysia and extending for hundreds of miles northwards into Thailand and lower Burma, and southwards to the islands of Singkep, Banka and Billiton, is the richest and most extensive in the world, contributing for the last half-century the bulk of the world's supply of the metal. Primary tin deposits always occur in, or near to, an acid igneous rock, usually granite or granitic rocks, although only a small fraction of the world's granite masses are stanniferous. Thus, for example, while the Main Range of Peninsular Malaysia is highly stanniferous, tin has not been found in the neighbouring granite range—the Benom.

Hosking (1973a) has postulated that there were four widely separated periods of tin deposition in the Malay Peninsula, of which three were important and one was relatively minor. This tin mineralization was genetically related to the emplacement of the granitic bodies at geologically different times in the evolution of the Peninsula. The first period occurred in Upper Carboniferous times when granites were emplaced during the conversion of the existing geosyncline into a folded belt, mainly along the eastern part of the Peninsula but also in some parts of the west. The primary tin deposits that were genetically related to those granites occur today as the Pahang Consolidated lodes of Pahang and the tin—niobium—tantalum pegmatites of Bakri and Kedah Perak on the west coast. This was followed, probably in Permian times, by a relatively minor phase of tin deposition, when the Manson Lode of Kelantan was formed.

The third and most important phase of tin deposition was in Triassic times, associated with the emplacement of most of the Main Range granite, the Kledang and other granite ranges in Perak and the Damansara granite mass in Selangor. During this phase of igneous activity the primary tin deposits of greatest economic value were developed. Known as hydrothermal deposits, they were developed as a result of hot fluids ascending from the Earth's interior along cracks and fissures and depositing minerals, including cassiterite, in them. Most of the deposits however were developed by replacement of the wall rock as well as of earlier deposits, resulting in mineralized veins, lodes, stringers, stockworks and disseminations.

After this main phase of igneous activity and mountain building, a final phase of tin deposition occurred in Upper Cretaceous times, when Mount Ophia and other neighbouring granite masses were emplaced. The tin in this case were xenothermal deposits, that is, deposits formed at high temperature but at shallow to moderate depth. Such xenothermal tin deposits are found today in Perak and Selangor.

While the cassiterite mined had its origin in the primary deposits that were genetically connected with the granites, the actual modes of occurrence of the mineral are varied, as seen in Table 12.2.

Most of the tin-ore mined today occurs as secondary deposits in alluvial flats in the river valleys, coastal plains and shallow offshore areas, or as eluvial deposits on the slopes of hills.[1] Existing evidence points to the fact that during the Pleistocene sea-level was several hundred feet lower than at present. Fluvial erosion went on rapidly, stripping weathered materials from the ridges and highlands and laying them down in the valleys and plains. In the process the rocks containing the primary tin deposits were also eroded away and subsequently laid down as

---

[1] Eluvial deposits are those formed by the weathering and decomposition of stanniferous rocks and lodes *in situ*. No mechanical transport except soil creep is involved, so that the detrital deposits overlie the rocks from which they are derived. When such deposits are transported and redeposited by water they become alluvial deposits. The same methods of mining are applied for both types.

Table 12.2   Modes of occurrence of cassiterite (after Scrivenor)

Containing formation	Mode of occurrence
1. Granite	In veins, pipes and disseminated throughout the granite
2. Limestone hills	In caves and fault-fissures. Often cemented by calcite to form a hard rock
3. Limestone beds and valley floors	In pipes, veins, and as detrital ore in caves
4. Shales, schists and quartzites	Near the junction with the granite, and in veins connected with it
5. Recent deposits	Derived from 1, 2, 3 and 4 as a result of weathering, erosion and deposition

alluvial material with a high percentage of cassiterite. Most of the alluvial tin were deposited during the very long period of time between the Pleistocene and comparatively recent times. The tin-bearing zone varies in depth from a few feet to over 100 ft (30 m), with some of the alluvium lying too deep to be mined economically by present-day methods.

Another type of secondary tin deposit is found where limestone containing veins and pipes of cassiterite adjoins granite. Such limestone commonly underlies the alluvium. Percolating ground-water easily dissolves the limestone, especially when it is fissured by fault planes, bedding planes and cleavage planes. The effect of solution is to hollow out and enlarge such fissures to form cups and cavities. Over a period of time deep solution troughs and innumerable pinnacles develop, with rich eluvial and sometimes alluvial tin-ore accumulating in the troughs. Such preferential weathering has occurred to a depth of 300 ft (91 m) below the limestone floor, in the case of the famous Lahat Pipe. The nature of the limestone surface poses a problem in the extraction of the ore, the only practical solution being gravel-pump mining using water pressure to flush out the hidden deposits.

An indication of the wide distribution of tin in Peninsular Malaysia is the fact that every one of the major geological formations is stanniferous to a greater or lesser extent. Tin mining takes place over a vertical range extending from well below sea-level to (at one time) heights of 4 000 ft (1 219 m), although there are now no highland mines. Scrivenor has divided the tin areas into two zones—the western tin-belt and the eastern

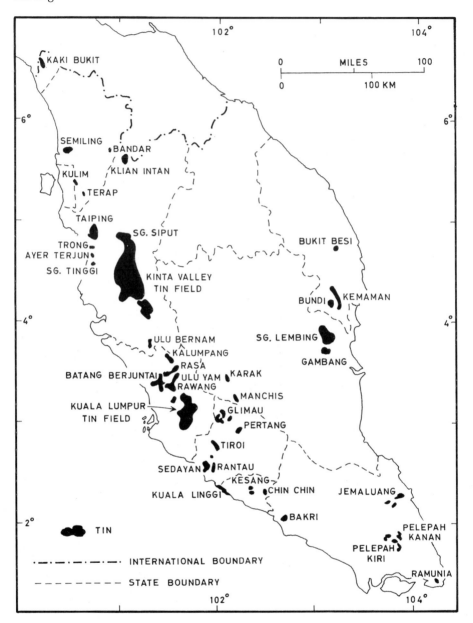

Fig. 12.1   Distribution of tin fields.

tin-belt. The western tin-belt lies along the flanks of the Main Range and on either side of the subsidiary granite ranges west of the Main Range. The largest and most famous of the tin fields along this belt is the Kinta Valley (Fig. 12.1). It has been estimated that about 50 per cent of Malaysia's past production of tin has been derived from the Valley. Most of the rich alluvial deposits in the Valley occur along the valley margins close to the granite contact zone. The floor of the Valley is of limestone of Carboniferous age, and has been extensively metamorphosed by the granite of the Main and Kledang Ranges. Interbedded with the limestone are schists, phyllites, quartzites and indurated shales, all also metamorphosed by the granite, and occasionally carrying tin-ore. The granite and the metamorphosed sedimentary rocks have been weathered and decomposed to considerable depths, and are the source of the tin-ore which is found as residual and eluvial deposits.

The second major area of mineralization occurs south of the Kinta Valley, mainly in Selangor and Negri Sembilan, and parts of southwestern Pahang. Here, primary and secondary tin deposits are scattered over an area nearly 90 miles (144 km) long by 50 miles (80 km) wide, covering the Main Range and its flanks. Most of the present-day production comes from alluvial deposits in Selangor.

Deposits are found in numerous other localities along the western tin-belt. The limestone caves of northern Perlis contain residual and alluvial deposits, now being mined by underground methods. Minor deposits of tin occur in shallow water along the sea coast of the Dindings area of Perak and in Malacca. These deposits extend beyond the low-water mark, the ore being derived from local granitic rocks and concentrated by wave and tidal action. In all, more than 90 per cent of the tin produced in Peninsular Malaysia comes from the western belt. Most of the surface mines and all of the dredges in the country are located there.

The eastern tin-belt is less continuous and less rich than the western. It includes the deposits in the eastern parts of Kelantan, Trengganu, Pahang and Johore (Fig. 12.1). The richest field is in eastern Pahang, where the primary deposits of the Pahang Consolidated Lode are mined by underground methods. This area of mineralization extends northwards for about 50 miles (80 km), covering part of southern Trengganu. Two extensive areas of mineralization occur in eastern Johore, one northwest of Kota Tinggi and the other south of Jemaluang. Minor deposits are also found in northern Trengganu and Kelantan.

Methods of mining

Three main stages are involved in all forms of tin mining: (*a*) excavation of the *karang* (ore-bearing ground); (*b*) separation of the ore from the waste material, with water as the separating agent; (*c*) and concentration of the crude ore. About 95 per cent of the total output of tin is from alluvial and eluvial deposits, but because of the different modes of occurrence of the deposits, a variety of mining methods is employed. The principal methods are dredging and gravel-pumping, normally accounting for more than 80 per cent of the total output. Other methods include open-cast mining, underground mining, and *dulang* washing. Hydraulic

Table 12.3   Number of tin-mining units and production by methods of mining, 1973

Method	Mining units	Production (tons of tin content)	Percentage
Gravel-pumping	873	38 300	54
Dredging	58	22 100	31
Open-cast mining	12	3 600	5
Dulang washing	—	3 000	4
Underground mining	26	2 300	3
Small workings, etc.	5	1 800	3
Total	974	71 100	100

mining, whereby the *karang* is broken down by water issued from a monitor under natural pressure obtained by damming a stream above the mine, was used with success for a long time, but the last hydraulic mine closed down in 1973. Table 12.3 shows the number of mining units and production by methods of mining.

Dredging lends itself to the systematic and thorough exploitation of large areas of suitable mining land, with little loss of tin in the mining process. It is the only practical method of working deposits in swampy or very wet ground, and it has the decided advantage of being able to treat low-grade ground at a lower cost per cubic yard than is possible by any other method. As a result of the introduction of dredging in 1912, extensive areas of land formerly considered too poor in tin to be worth working, or which had previously been mined by other methods but still contained sufficient ore for profitable dredging, were opened up. But the capital cost of installing a dredge is very high, so that a dredging property must be extensive and have a working life long enough for costs to be recovered as well as profits made. Depending on the grade of ground and the capacity of the dredge, the mining company must have sufficient land for mining operations to be carried on for a period of fifteen to twenty years to make dredging worthwhile.

A dredge consists of an excavator and a concentrating plant mounted on a floating platform in an artificial pond or paddock formed by the dredge itself as it digs up the ore-bearing ground. The excavator is made up of buckets mounted on an endless band, the ground being excavated by successive 'bites' of the buckets. The digging capacity of dredges vary from 90 000 to 480 000 cubic yards per month,[1] and the depths to which they can dig vary from 40 to 135 ft (12–41 m), although the

[1] A new generation of million cubic-yard-capacity dredges is being built to mine deposits in the Kinta Valley and in Kuala Langat.

latest dredges can dig to depths of 170 ft (52 m). The excavated material is washed and screened, and the crude ore recovered by means of *palongs* (see below) and/or jigs. The ore is then further washed and cleaned to a marketable product in a treatment plant on shore. The waste material (tailings) is passed to slimes-retention areas behind the dredge. The dredge is continuously moving forward as it digs and extends the area of its paddock. Most of the dredges are electrically-powered, the rest being driven by steam using coal, oil or wood as fuel.

Dredges operate best over level areas with soft bedrock which permit the total excavation of the tin-bearing ground. The rate of ore recovery today can be as low as 0.25 lb of tin concentrate per cubic yard. Treating such low grade ground has been made possible by the increasing efficiency of the dredges, and the use of improved methods of ore recovery. The use of hydro-cyclones, for example, has resulted in the recovery of very fine ones that previously were lost in the treatment process. As a consequence the average quantity of tin produced per dredge has increased from 372 tons in 1964 to 381 tons in 1973. The recovery rates are lowered in cases where the deposits are clayey, while the efficiency of the dredge is still further reduced where the bedrock is of limestone and pinnacly in nature, and the ore inaccessible in pockets between the pinnacles. As the richer deposits are rapidly being exhausted the future of the dredging section of the industry would appear to lie in treating the lower grade deeper ground which constitutes the bulk of the reserves.

In general the economic cut-off grade of ground treated in tin-mining is dependent on four factors: (*a*) the metal price, (*b*) the depth of the deposit, (*c*) the nature of the ground, and (*d*) the nature of the minerals present. In 1893, when records of production were first kept, the average grade of ground treated was phenomenally high, and there were cases recorded when ore was dug and sent for smelting with little or no treatment or separation being necessary, so rich and pure were the deposits. In 1906 the Tronoh mines in the Kinta Valley were mining ground containing 32 lb of casseterite per cubic yard, and it was doubtful if any mine was working on ground containing less than 3 lb per cubic yard.

As mining and recovery methods improved, it became possible, at any given metal price, to mine ground previously considered uneconomical to work. Dredging in particular can recover ore from ground regarded as low grade by other miners. Technological progress in dredging is reflected in these figures on the average value of ground treated by individual dredges:

Year	Dredging company	Average value (lb/cu/yd)
1915	Ipoh Tin Dredging	0.82
1926	Austral Amalgamated	0.67
1936	Rawang Concessions	0.38

1946	Rawang Concessions	0.48
1951	All Malaya	0.36
1966	Taiping Consolidated	0.27
1970	Sungei Way (Dredge No. 1)	0.24

Some companies are today mining land with 0.25 to 0.24 lb per cubic yard.

Gravel-pumping is the method most commonly used to mine all types of alluvial deposits, particularly by the Chinese section of the industry. Its scale of operations is small compared with dredging, but it is well adapted to recovering ore lying in hard, uneven bedrock such as pinnacly limestone where dredging is not practicable. In this form of mining, the ore-bearing ground is broken down by a high-pressure jet of water from a monitor nozzle. The slurry bearing the tin-ore flows down to the bottom of the mine or mine sump, and is then sucked up by a gravel pump to the head of a *palong* or sluice. The slope and flow of the *palong* allow the waste material to pass over the baffles which trap the heavier tin-ore. When a sufficient amount has been trapped, the low-grade concentrate is cleaned against an inflowing stream of clean water, and the product taken to a treatment shed for final dressing. The waste is discharged from the lower end of the *palong* to the tailings area.

Owing to their short life and the large number of workers employed, the costs of production of gravel-pump mines are higher than those of dredging. Capital costs however, are a fraction of those of dredging. Gravel-pump mines employ more than half the total labour force engaged in tin mining. The high cost of equipment and labour, and the progressive deterioration in the yield of tin concentrate per cubic yard of ground due to the exhaustion of the richer deposits, have contributed in recent years to the closing down of many gravel-pump mines, while a substantial number are working on a very narrow margin of profit. In some cases the small producer continues to operate even at a loss because complete closing down would lead to flooding of the mine and the dispersal of the specialized labour forces. Once a mine has closed down, subsequent reopening would be a very costly affair, and would only be economically feasible if prices were high enough.

In open-cast mining the ground is excavated in the dry state by mechanical means. The material is then mixed with water in puddling machines for separation in the treatment plant. The Sungei Besi mine near Kuala Lumpur is the largest open-cast tin mine in the world.

Underground mining includes small-scale alluvial shafting operations, and cave workings in the limestone hills of Kaki Bukit, Perlis, for the ore in pockets of detrital alluvium. The only conventional underground mine is the large mine at Sungei Lembing, Pahang. Tin has been worked in the lode mines of the Pahang Consolidated Co. at Sungei Lembing, since 1888. Up to 1950, 80 000 tons of tin concentrates had been produced

Plate 32   An open-cast tin mine, one of the largest in Peninsular Malaysia.

from this mine, the production since the First World War amounting to 5 per cent of Peninsular Malaysia's total output. The lodes are in sedimentary rocks near a granite mass, and all the lode mines are within an area of about 6 square miles (16 sq km). Mining takes place at depths of a few hundred feet to 2 000 ft (600 m); there are altogether 200 miles (320 km) of underground tunnels in the mine.

The other miscellaneous methods of mining include ground sluicing and open-cast mining, but with little or no machinery. *Dulang* washing is a method of recovery rather than of mining. It is similar to gold-panning and is carried out by individual operators, always women. The tin concentrates produced are smelted in Penang and Butterworth. The ore is mixed with limestone and anthracite and smelted at high temperatures in furnaces. The resultant metal is then refined and moulded into 100 lb ingots of 99.9 per cent purity.

Problems facing the tin-mining industry

1. Market instability.   The market prices for tin, in common with those of other primary raw materials, are subject to violent fluctuations. Changes in price levels reflect changes in supply and demand. Since Peninsular Malaysia consumes only a fraction of its output, it must face competition from other producers at prices determined in the open market. From the beginning of the present century to 1929 the annual world production of tin rose from 85 400 tons to 193 600 tons. Consumption of tin also increased during the period as a result of the general industrialization of the world and, in particular, the development of the use of tinplate for canning. Then the Great Depression of 1930—34 brought about a serious drop in consumption with the result that large stocks of surplus tin accumulated, leading in turn to low prices. The average price of tin fell from £227 per ton in 1928 to £118 in 1931, while stocks rose simultaneously to 55 000 tons.

A voluntary restriction scheme failed to check the fall in prices and in 1931 an international tin control scheme was brought into force, the object being 'to regulate the production ... with a view to adjusting production to consumption, preventing rapid and severe oscillations of price, and maintaining reasonable stock'. The scheme was implemented in three Agreements: 1931—33, 1934—36 and 1937—41. An International Tin Committee allotted to each tin-producing country a standard tonnage of possible production, and decided the percentage of this tonnage which it was permitted to export each quarter. But while the restriction scheme was successful in raising the price levels, it was unable to check violent short-term fluctuations caused by rapid increases and decreases in consumption. To correct these fluctuations, the Buffer Stock Agreement was brought into force in 1938 as an adjunct to the restriction scheme. The Buffer Stock operated effectively, buying and selling tin in the market and keeping prices between £200 and £230 per ton.

The overall effect of these schemes on the Malaysian industry was an adverse one. Restriction benefited the high-cost producers more than it did low-cost producers such as Peninsular Malaysia. It was also widely held that Peninsular Malaysia's international standard tonnage was under-assessed, being only three-quarters of its actual productive capacity. Restriction also raised the average costs of mining and discouraged capital investment in the industry. Another effect of restriction was to discourage prospecting for new tin areas at a time when many of the known reserves were being exhausted.

The postwar market for tin has remained uncertain for a number of reasons. The tin shortages during and after the war have forced the tin-plating and other tin-consuming industries to cut down their consumption of tin, and at the same time stimulated the use of tin substitutes such as aluminium, plastics and cellophane. The introduction of electrolytic tinning, which only requires about half the tin to produce the same amount of tinplate as in the older process, has meant a corresponding decrease in world tin consumption. The cumulative result has been a drop in world consumption of tin, from an average of 165 000 tons in the period 1935—39 to 136 000 tons in 1954.

Although world production has exceeded consumption since 1948, the surplus stocks were absorbed by the United States stockpiling programme. The buying of tin for strategic stockpiling resulted in boom prices during the Korean War, peaking at £964 per ton in 1952, but subsequently dropping to £731 in 1953. The boost to prices during the Korean War was only temporary, and with the sharp reduction in stockpiling purchases, a surplus of tin began to accumulate. A new International Tin Agreement was signed in 1953 by six major producing countries—Peninsular Malaysia, Indonesia, Bolivia, the former Belgian Congo and the former Ruanda Urundi, Thailand and Nigeria—with the objectives of preventing or alleviating excessive fluctuations in the price of tin and of ensuring adequate supplies at reasonable prices at all times. The Agreement called for the creation of a Buffer Stock of 25 000 tons to act as a damping agent. The Buffer Stock Manager was authorized to buy tin when prices fell below a set minimum, and sell when prices rose above a set maximum.

In addition to the Buffer Stock, the production and export of tin was brought under control with effect from December 1957. The initial effects of the Tin Agreement on the Malaysian industry was serious. In the first year of control (1958), Malaysian producers were permitted to operate at only 43 per cent of their assessed productive capacity. When control came into force in December 1957 there were 738 tin mines operating with a labour force of 36 585. By December 1959 the number of active mines had dropped to 483, and the number of labourers to 23 778. Production of tin fell from 59 293 tons in 1957 to 38 458 tons in 1958 and to 37 525 tons in 1959. Thus by the end of 1959, 255 mines had been closed, and 12 807 labourers laid off, and total production of tin was 11 768 tons less than when restriction came into force in 1957.

This period of restriction ended in June 1961, but was succeeded by the second postwar scheme of international tin control which came into force in July 1961. This scheme was essentially the same as the first one, and when it expired in 1966 the third (similar) scheme came into force that same year. At present Malaysia and other tin-producing countries are operating under the Fourth International Tin Agreement, signed in mid-1971.

The history of the tin-mining industry in Peninsular Malaysia has been a turbulent one since the 1930s. Market and price instability has always been a major problem over which Peninsular Malaysia has had little control. Excessive price fluctuations have tended to create an unfavourable climate for capital investment. Many mines working marginal land suffered heavy losses when the price ruling at the time dropped below current costs. The various international tin control schemes are attempts to reduce this problem to manageable proportions.

2. *Exhaustion of reserves.* There is increasing difficulty of finding

343

commercial deposits of tin-ore to replace those that are being worked out. Tin-ore, like all other mineral resources, is a wasting asset and, once exhausted, cannot be replaced. It is necessary that Peninsular Malaysia continues to be a low-cost producer in order to meet competition from overseas. To achieve this end there must be a continuing process of replacing exhausted mining land with new and proved reserves.

Prospecting for new deposits has been severely restricted from the 1930s as a result of an unfortunate combination of circumstances. During the Great Depression restrictions were placed on the alienation of land for mining. Restrictions continued until just before the outbreak of war in 1941, when every effort was made to maximize production, but from existing fields and reserves rather than by prospecting for new ones. The three-and-a-half years of the Japanese occupation were years of stagnation, with only limited mining activity and no prospecting. Post-war attention was focused on rehabilitation, and mining companies were not in a position to undertake any long-term prospecting. The alienation of land up to September 1947 was limited to that required for the main-tenance of existing undertakings, or to the granting of pre-war applica-tions. Only at the close of this period of rehabilitation was prospecting attempted, but the declaration of a State of Emergency throughout Peninsular Malaysia in 1948 brought such activities to an abrupt end. It was only after the Emergency ended, in 1960, that the search for new deposits was able to continue. A major problem is that existing mining regulations do not encourage investment in prospecting because success-ful prospectors are not assured of mining leases (Bank Negara, 1972). Thus in 1972 only one licence was issued for prospecting. The indica-tions to date have been disappointing, with no new large deposits being discovered. The opinion of the Mines Department is that 'unless and until evidence to the contrary is produced . . . the discovery of further, extensive, tin fields is unlikely'.

The problem is an acute one. The average grade of ground now being mined has deteriorated, and many mines are now falling back on marginal land containing low-grade ore. Almost all the new mining units since 1964 have been worked on mined-over land (some more than once) or on land previously considered too low-grade to be economic. However, the position is not entirely irrecoverable, for although major fields in non-reserved land are unlikely to be discovered, the prospects of commercial deposits in Malay Reservations and in offshore areas appear to be promising. Within the Kinta Valley the search for tin has been extended to the sites of small towns and villages such as Papan and Kopisan, where the deposits are rich enough to justify the resettlement of the inhabitants to adjoining areas so as to free the land for mining. In addition, miners are looking into the feasibility of mining riverbeds for tin.

The exploitation of tin and other minerals in Malay Reservations is

344

financed by a revolving fund. Prospecting is carried out by the Department of Mines and by 1969 about 270 000 acres (109 000 ha) of land in sixty-seven Reservations had been prospected. Payable deposits totalling 30 000 acres (12 000 ha) of land have been discovered. In 1972 four areas in Perak and one in Selangor were opened up for mining, with fifteen mines operating, either with sole Malay ownership or on a joint-venture basis. It is likely that tin mining in Malay Reservations will become increasingly important in future years.

Offshore deposits of tin have been mined for many years off the Indonesian islands of Singkep, Banka and Billiton and the Thai island of Phuket. Up to the present no similar deposits have been mined in Peninsular Malaysia on a systematic basis, although some years ago illegal mining was carried out in the sea off Tanjong Mengkudu in the Dindings. Some cassiterite has been mined from the beach sands in Malacca and Perak, but only on a very minor scale. Apart from the Dindings coast, some cassiterite occurs on some small islands west of Kedah Perak, while traces of the ore have been found in the Langkawi beaches. It may be possible that offshore tin deposits of commercial dimensions occur in the seabed between the mainland and these islands. In 1973 the national trading company, Pernas, through a joint venture company called Malaysia Offshore Mining Sdn. Bhd. signed a thirty-five year agreement with the Government to carry out offshore tin exploration, prospecting and mining in a 15 713 square mile (40 697 sq km) concession off the coasts of Penang, Perak and Selangor. The company has recently (in 1974) discovered offshore deposits near Malacca. Initial proven ore reserves are estimated to total 11 900 tons. Along the east coast there are no onshore deposits near the sea nor have there been indications of any deposits within 5 miles (8 km) of the sea, so that the prospects of offshore deposits here are poor.

Tin mining in Peninsular Malaysia has been concentrated mainly on the mining of the rich alluvial deposits along both the western and the eastern tin belts, and on an average less than 5 per cent of the tin mined each year is from lode mining. Nevertheless as the alluvial deposits are worked out and no large new deposits are likely to replace them, greater attention will be paid by the miners to lodes and other types of bedrock ores. The potentialities are not fully known, and certainly no organized exploration has been made of the eastern tin belt. But lode mining involves a large capital outlay on exploration and development work, experienced personnel and greater financial risks and will usually only provide profits which are modest in comparison with alluvial mining in its pioneer years. It is therefore likely that lode mining will initially focus on the reworking of known underground deposits which have not been mined out. A number of such deposits occur in the Kinta Valley and Ulu Selangor (Chand and Singh, 1970).

From time to time various authorities have attempted to estimate the tin reserves of Peninsular Malaysia. Fermor in 1939 put the total reserves at about 1 million tons of tin metal, but between then and 1964 about 1.2 million tons of tin metal had been recovered, and the industry is still producing about 70 000 tons of tin concentrates a year today. The Paley Report of 1953 placed Peninsular Malaysia's reserves at 1.5 million tons of tin metal, which would give the industry about thirty years of life at the present rate of output. The latest estimates are from Sainsbury (1969), based on official figures from the International Tin Council, and shown in Table 12.4.

Table 12.4   Tin reserves and known resources, Malaysia

Reserves: (i) measured and indicated	600 000 tons
(ii) in Malay Reservations (first indications)	170 000 tons
Resources (known)*: submarginal; old tailings and residual areas; and areas within which mining is prohibited or restricted	230 000 tons
Total	1 000 000 tons

* Defined as deposits not currently mineable because of low price, low grade and beneficiation problems.

These estimates are in reality nothing more than informed guesses, as the exhaustion of a deposit of tin, like that of any other mineral deposit, depends on two main factors: (*a*) the average cost of production, which in turn is determined by, among other factors, mining techniques; and (*b*) the metal price. Thus as the deposit is being mined the recovery rate decreases until finally the average cost of production becomes too high in relation to the metal price to justify continued operations. The mine subsequently closes down, but the deposit itself is not necessarily fully mined out or 'exhausted'. An improvement in mining techniques and/or a substantial increase in the metal price may lead to the rejuvenation of that deposit by lifting it out from the non-payable to the payable category, thereby giving new life to the industry. As seen earlier, the continued viability of the tin mining industry in Peninsular Malaysia has been due in large part to the remining of mined-over deposits as well as the mining of deposits previously considered non-payable, both largely a consequence of improvements in mining techniques.

3. Land competition.   The difficulties and slow progress of prospecting arise in part from the conflict between mining and other forms of land-use, especially agriculture and forestry. Mining is a destructive form of land-use, and in Peninsular Malaysia where alluvial mining is the general rule, not only are the mining sites laid waste after the ore has been extracted from the ground, but in the past before the Mining Enactment was passed requiring proper control schemes, large expanses of agricultural land were damaged, either directly through the encroachment of the tin tailings, or indirectly through flooding as a result of silted rivers. Deforestation of the mining sites is also a natural corollary of mining. The problem is made more acute by the fact that most of the land alienated for mining is also suitable for agriculture and forestry.

Experiments have been conducted on the rehabilitation of mined-over land. The difficulties of reconditioning mined land depend upon the type of mining methods used. Where land has been worked at the surface, whether for gravel-pumping or hydraulicking, the resultant landscape consists of a series of abandoned mining pits filled with water. It is economically impracticable to restore such land to its original level by filling up the pits. Where dredging has been employed, the slimes are accumulated in separate paddocks, and the final result after mining is a series of small, flat terraces of varying levels. Such land contains very little vegetable matter and no humus, and is therefore agriculturally useless unless intensively manured. Thorough drainage is also a necessary prerequisite to reconditioning. Experiments at rehabilitation of such land by reafforestation have shown that it is both expensive and difficult. So far the only practical use to which mined-over land has occasionally been put is for Chinese market-gardening. In the Kinta and Klang Valleys however mined-over land is being used for housing development.

For all practical purposes, then, land which is alienated for mining will be land lost to agriculture and forestry. The problem is whether mining should take precedence over all other forms of productive land-use, and whether such precedence will be in the interests of the country as a whole. The argument in favour is that tin mining brings in greater revenue than can be derived from any other alternative use to which the land can be put. The argument against is that tin is a wasting asset, and the revenue derived from mining a piece of land accrues once only, whereas the same piece of land if cultivated or under productive forest will continue to accrue revenue for the country in perpetuity. Again, mining may cause pollution of streams and rivers used for irrigation as well as soil erosion.

O'Reilly (1963) has attempted to show that, although the revenue from tin mining is non-recurrent, the revenue yield from 1 acre of tin land if invested at the current rate of interest would produce an annual income almost five times higher than could be obtained from an acre of rubber (at the prices then prevailing). The present policy of the Government is to allow an area to be cleared for agricultural development only after the Mines Department and the Geological Survey Department have jointly certified that no economic minerals exist in that area, the rationale being that it would be false economy to allow mineral deposits to be blanketed by other development.

Iron

The iron-ore deposits of Peninsular Malaysia have been classified by Hill (1964) into three types. The first consists of contact-metamorphic deposits which are scattered along a well defined belt extending from Bukit Besi to Bukit Bangkong in Trengganu (Fig. 12.2). The deposits here occur in close association with tin ore, as do the deposits in Pelapah Kanan in Johore. The second type consists of replacement bodies in volcanic rocks, schists, quartz porphyries and limestones. These magnetite deposits are distributed in a number of isolated localities along the central part of the Peninsula but they are too small to be of economic importance. The third consists of haematitic replacements controlled by extensive fault zones. These deposits are located within a 70 mile (113 km) belt from Sungei Siput south to Chenderoh Lake. The iron-ore is of high grade haematite with no trace of tin contamination. In addition to these there are large occurrencies of limonitic oxides that have been formed above the water table in a manner similar to that of bauxite, as well as ferruginous laterite, a product of tropical laterization, which however is unlikely to be of economic value because of its superficial mode of occurrence.

The economic exploitation of iron-ore dates from 1921, when 74 250 tons were produced and exported. Iron mining has since its start been closely associated with the iron and steel industry of Japan, with Japan providing the capital for the development of the iron-ore resources of Peninsular Malaysia, and absorbing most of the ore produced. In 1921 the Ishihara Sangyo Company started mining operations in Johore, extending them a few years later to Trengganu. Other Japanese companies began mining deposits in Johore, Trengganu and Kelantan. Production of ore increased steadily and reached the highest pre-war total of 1 962 000 tons in 1940. During the Japanese occupation only the Bukit Besi mine was worked until shipping difficulties forced it to shut down in 1943. After the war the mines were taken over by the Custodian of Enemy Property and later sold to other companies. In the immediate postwar years some 462 000 tons of ore stockpiled by the Japanese were exported, but large-scale mining operations did not take place until 1950 when the revival of the Japanese heavy industries created a demand for Malaysian ore. The Bukit Besi mine at Dungun, bought over by the Eastern Mining and Metals Company, resumed operations in that year, and by the end of 1950 its production was 498 530 tons. Production since then has steadily increased as other mines came into operation, in particular that at Ulu Rompin. By 1963 production reached a record total of over 7 million tons. Over the next decade, however, production declined progressively until 1970 when it totalled 4.4 million tons. At the end of 1970 the two largest mines—at Dungun and Ulu Rompin—which together accounted for 80 per cent of

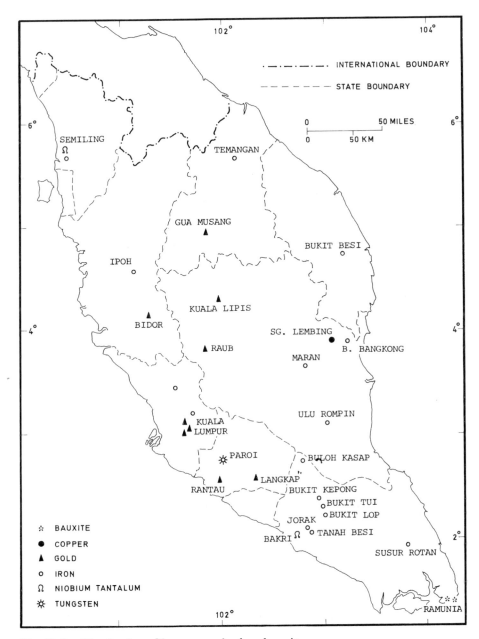

Fig. 12.2 Distribution of iron-ore and other deposits.

the total output in the country, ceased operations because of the exhaustion of their deposits. Production thereafter fell to 935 000 tons in 1971 and to only 509 000 tons in 1973. It is clear that iron-ore mining is no longer of major importance in Peninsular Malaysia, and as

349

the remaining small mines reach the end of their economic life, and new large deposits are unlikely to be discovered, the industry may cease to exist altogether.

Coal

Coal, intermediate in properties between typical lignite and sub-bituminous coal, is the only solid mineral fuel of economic importance in Peninsular Malaysia. Coal seams have been found in five localities—at Bukit Arang on the Perlis—Thai border, at Enggor in Perak, Batu Arang in Selangor, and at two other localities in Johore—but only the Perak and Selangor deposits have proved workable. All of the deposits are associated with Tertiary rocks believed to be of Miocene or younger age. The Enggor coalfield contained two seams, an upper seam 3 ft (0.9 m) thick separated by a thick bed of shales from the 4 ft (1.2 m) thick lower seam. Mining started in 1925 but the deposit proved to be uneconomical to work, and operations ceased in 1928 after a total of only 28 500 tons of coal had been extracted. There are about 180 000 tons of coal left in the Enggor coalfield, but it is unlikely that these will prove economically profitable to exploit.

The Batu Arang coalfield was developed by the Malayan Collieries Ltd in 1915. The coal measures consist of two main coal seams, the upper seam averaging 30 ft (9 m) in thickness but attaining a thickness of up to 45 ft (14 m) in places, and separated by about 200 ft (61 m) of shale from the lower seam which averages 25 ft (8 m) in thickness. The upper seam extends for 3½ miles (5.6 km), and the lower for almost 1½ miles (2.4 km). The seams are worked by both open-cast and underground methods. The quality of the coal is poor, being non-coking and very friable. The coal is liable to spontaneous combustion, and one of the main problems of mining underground is to dissipate the heat through air circulation in order to prevent the coal igniting. The heating value of typical Batu Arang coal is only 9 000 BTU.

From its modest beginnings in 1915, coal-mining at Batu Arang developed into a large-scale enterprise, employing a large labour force. Production increased steadily, reaching a maximum of 781 509 tons in 1940. Between 1915 and 1948 nearly 13 million tons of coal were obtained from this field. The output was sold locally, the Malaysian Railways, power stations and tin-mines being the main consumers. Postwar production reached a peak of 416 000 tons in 1950, but declined rapidly in subsequent years to 206 000 tons in 1955, and 75 600 tons in 1959. Part of the decline in output was due to labour troubles, but the main cause was the reduction in demand for coal in competition with imported fuel oil. On the basis of calorific values, fuel oil was cheaper than Batu Arang coal, and the latter lost its main consumers when the Malaysian Railways and the Central Electricity

Board switched to oil. The mine finally ceased operations in 1960.

There are still extensive reserves of coal at Batu Arang. A Government geologist estimates that there are about 32 million tons of coal remaining in the field in seams 3 ft and over in thickness, of which about 16 million tons are probably extractable and another 5 million might possibly be extractable. Production, however, depends entirely upon demand, and present indications are that there is little likelihood of the mine being reopened, although the high prices of oil may in time bring about a revival of the coal industry as consumers turn to alternative sources of energy.

Other minerals

Bauxite, an hydrated aluminium oxide, is the only commercial source of aluminium. It occurs widely in Peninsular Malaysia, notably in the southern half of the Peninsula (Fig. 12.2). The ore is a product of tropical weathering of a variety of rocks, ranging from shale and acid volcanic rocks (Johore), to basic volcanic rocks (Pahang), granite (Trengganu) and possibly also pegmatitic rocks (Malacca). The best conditions for its development are prolonged stability of the area, low rates of denudation and marked seasonal variations in rainfall. Ore developed from acid rocks tends to have too high a silica content to be commercially acceptable. Bauxite deposits are generally superficial, and occur as a mantle up to 25 ft thick covering the tops and slopes of small hills.

Bauxite was first mined at Bukit Pasir near Batu Pahat in 1936. Two other mines were opened before the war—one at Perigi Achih, east of Johore Bahru, and the other at Sri Medan, the latter associated with iron-ore. Both these ceased operations in 1941, but the Bukit Pasir mine produced an estimated 150 000 tons during the Japanese occupation. The Japanese also worked the deposit at Telok Mas, Malacca (estimated production, 1942–45, 100 000 tons), and started mining at Telok Ramunia on the southeast coast of Johore. The total production of bauxite from all mines up to 1952 was only about 580 000 tons, of which an estimated 10 000 tons came from the Telok Ramunia mine. All of Malaysia's production of bauxite today is from the deposits in southeast Johore (Fig. 12.2). There are two major companies—Southeast Asia Bauxite and Ramunia Bauxite—and one smaller company mining the ore in Telok Ramunia. After the overburden has been removed the ore is excavated by mechanical shovels and transported by trucks to the washing plant where it is washed and screened. The production from the larger mines of Southeast Asia Bauxite is twice that of Ramunia Bauxite, while the third company, Johore Kimm Kimm, produces only a few thousand tons a month. With the decline of iron-ore production bauxite has become the second most important mineral in Peninsular Malaysia in terms of value. Production of bauxite in the decade 1964–73 increased from 463 800 tons to 1 124 700 tons. Most of the ore is exported to Japan.

Gold has been mined in Peninsular Malaysia for several centuries. There is evidence of the Chinese mining gold as early as the sixteenth century. European participation did not begin until the 1890s, but except for the Raub Australian Gold Mining Company's underground mines all the European workings failed. The Raub mine was the only important gold-mine in Peninsular Malaysia, having produced 700 000 ounces of gold in fifty years since production started in 1899. Other lode deposits that have been worked in the past include those at Selensing, Buffalo Reef, Kechau, Punjum and Sungei Muntan in Pahang, Batu Bersawah and Sungei Luit in Negri Sembilan, and the Kedana mine at Mount Ophir in Johore. However, as with the tin deposits, most of the gold deposits are alluvial. Again, the primary deposits of gold are about the same age of those of tin, and are also derived from granite. But the two minerals have different distribution patterns. Most of the gold is irregularly distributed in a belt extending from southeast Thailand, Kelantan, Pahang, Negri Sembilan to Mount Ophir in Johore. But the deposits are neither extensive nor rich. Apart from small quantities of gold obtained as a by-product of tin-mining, almost the entire output up to the 1960s was from the Raub lode mine. But the Raub mine found it uneconomic to carry on production and closed down in 1962.

Peninsular Malaysia produces small quantities of the ferro-alloy metallic minerals. The only known deposits of manganese occur in Kelantan and Trengganu. Manganese mining began at Machang Stahun in 1925 and at Gual Priok in Kelantan in 1932. The total production from these two mines during the period 1925—45 was 440 500 tons. Another large deposit of high grade ore is believed to occur at the headwaters of the Sungei Aring in Kelantan. Manganese ore is mined on an insignificant scale today. The tungsten ores of commercial significance in Malaysia are wolframite and scheelite. Both are usually found associated with tin- and gold-ores. Scheelite occurs in many localities, but no large deposit has been discovered since the rich deposit at Kramat Pulai, near Ipoh, was worked out in 1939. Wolframite, too, occurs fairly widely. Production is on a small scale, and is mainly from the Bukit Kachi mine at Sintok, Kedah, and from the Chendrong Concession in Trengganu. Ore reserves, particularly those at Bukit Kachi, are believed to be considerable.

Ilmenite, columbite and monazite are minerals produced in commercial quantities as by-products of tin-mining. Ilmenite is an oxide of iron and titanium, and occurs as the main constituent of *amang*—the local term for the heavy minerals left over as a reject after the tin-ore has been separated as a marketable product in the treatment shed. The rise in demand for ilmenite as a source of titanium paint pigments has led to the production for export of this mineral from *amang*. Exports of ilmenite in 1973 were 182 400 tons. One of the constituents of *amang* is monazite, a valuable phosphate of rare earth metals with thorium. A new technique of separation enables high-grade monazite concentrates to be produced from *amang*. A few hundred tons are produced each year. Columbite is found in association with tin in the alluvium at Semiling and Karangan in Kedah, and at Bakri in Johore. At Semiling columbite is a by-product of tin mining, but at Bakri it is often the main mineral and tin-ore a by-product. Tin slags from the smelting companies contain appreciable quantities of columbium and tantalum, and nearly 20 000 tons of slags were exported in 1953 in response to high prices for columbite. Production of columbite reached a high of 236 tons in 1955 as a result of inducement premiums paid on the price by the United States, but has decreased since the withdrawal of the premium in 1955, and little is produced now.

Kaolin or china clay, from which porcelain may be made, was mined in small quantities until 1972, when production increased almost tenfold to 103 000 tons. The increased output was to meet the demand generated by the very large kaolin plant established in Tapah, Perak, producing kaolin for use in the paper, pharmaceutics, plastics, paint, ceramic, rubber and fertilizer industries. Output of kaolin in 1973 was 104 000 tons.

Petroleum

The very large increases in crude oil prices which were fixed by the OPEC countries at the end of 1973 and which may be compounded by further increases in the future have made oil an extremely important resource. A country fortunate enough to be a major oil producer will be in a position to earn substantial amounts of foreign exchange. Malaysia up to the last few years was a minor producer of oil, the quantity produced each year being insufficient to meet home demand. In 1974 production reached 100 000 US barrels a day which was 17 000 barrels more than needed for home use. However, since the low sulphur oil which Malaysia produces is in demand in pollution-conscious industrial countries, particularly Japan, and fetches a higher price than other crudes, Malaysia is able to earn as much as M$100 million annually by selling her oil and buying lower-priced Middle East oil for her own use.

All the oil produced so far has come from the four offshore oil fields of Bakau, Baram, west Lutong and Baronia in Sarawak. Until the discovery of the offshore fields production had been declining—from 435 000 barrels in 1960 to 328 000 barrels in 1967. When the first offshore fields were brought into production in 1968 the output of oil increased to 1 521 000 barrels. With the opening of the new fields of Baram and west Lutong in 1971 output leaped to 25 071 000 barrels, and reached a record of 35 400 000 barrels in 1973.

So far no oil is produced in Peninsular Malaysia, but an intensive

Fig. 12.3   Offshore oil concession areas and drilling sites.

search is being conducted by various oil companies in the offshore areas of both the east and west coasts (Fig. 12.3). The prospects appear quite favourable as up to 1974 five strikes had been made off the east coast: one about 160 miles (250 km) off the Trengganu coast with a test flow rate of about 2 500 barrels per day, and four about 100 miles (160 km) off Kuantan, Pahang, with test flow rates of 12 000 barrels per day. Commercial production will begin in a few years' time. So far no strikes have been reported off the west coast, but a number of oil and gas finds have been made on the Indonesian side of the Straits of Malacca, so that the chances of similar finds on the Malaysian side appear to be good.

Associated with the oil discoveries are the natural gas strikes. Once a nuisance to be burned away from the more precious crude oil, natural gas has become an important source of versatile, cheap and efficient energy. It can be used as a pollution-free fuel as well as feedstock for petro-chemical complexes. The offshore field off Kuantan is estimated to be capable of producing 11 million cubic feet per day; a second discovery in the same area in 1973 was rated at 56 million cubic feet per day, while the gas field off the Trengganu coast is believed to be even larger. Known reserves of natural gas in Malaysia as a whole were 10 000 billion cubic feet in 1972; reserves of oil were 1 500 million barrels. The post-1972 discoveries in Peninsular Malaysia as well as Sabah will have added substantially to these reserves.

The Government has established a national petroleum corporation, similar to Pertamina in Indonesia, known as Petroleum National Berhad (Petronas) which will have the exclusive rights to explore, exploit, win and obtain petroleum in Malaysia, whether lying offshore or onshore. The importance of this industry to the country is indicated by the expected production of 200 000 barrels of oil per day by 1977 and 400 000 to 500 000 barrels per day by 1980, apart from the output of liquified natural gas (LNG). Both oil and natural gas will be produced by international oil companies on a production-sharing basis with Petronas.

Future prospects

There is little likelihood of any of the minerals currently being mined in Peninsular Malaysia assuming an importance even remotely approaching that of tin in the mining economy. Tin will continue to be the dominant mineral as mining is extended to the Malay Reservations, to proved low-grade reserves, to offshore areas, and in time to come, to the lode deposits. The indications in the second half of the 1970s are that the output of iron-ore will continue to decline and that of bauxite maintained at current levels. The high price of gold may stimulate some small-scale mining of the alluvial deposits. The Government, as part of the Second Malaysia Plan, will undertake a comprehensive aerial and ground survey of the country to locate new mineral resources.

But the greatest change in the pattern of mining activities will come from the development of the petroleum and natural gas industry. The dimensions of this new industry are as yet unknown, but as seen earlier the oil and natural gas strikes off the east coast give promise of a major addition to the mineral wealth of Peninsular Malaysia.

13
Industry

In common with the other countries of Southeast Asia the mainspring of economic development in Peninsular Malaysia after the establishment of colonial rule in the nineteenth century was the production and export of primary raw materials, notably tin and rubber. The export sector of the economy expanded rapidly because of favourable world market demand conditions for these products. Peninsular Malaysia had an abundant supply of tin and of land resources (for rubber) so that she was able to produce tin and rubber in very large quantities, eventually becoming the world's largest producer of these commodities. The colonial government's policy of encouraging the development of the mining and plantation industries and the attractive profits that could be made there stimulated the flow of private foreign investment into these industries and into the lucrative import—export trade. The British colonies, including Peninsular Malaysia (then known as Malaya), were not only the suppliers of raw materials to the factories of Britain, but were also the markets for the manufactured goods from the metropolitan country.

This classic 'colonial pattern' of development created a lopsided economy, with a highly developed mining and plantation sector, a neglected indigenous rural sector and an industrial sector of minute dimensions. In fact, industrial development in the country was initially concerned with processing these raw materials to a form suitable for export. Thus plants and installations were set up to smelt tin, mill rubber, cure copra, can pineapples and extract oil from the fruit of the oil-palm. These processing factories could only function efficiently where there were establishments concerned with repairing and servicing and/or producing the equipment used in them. A second category of secondary industries therefore developed—light engineering works repairing, servicing, and making equipment and machinery, including small ships and boats, tanks, drums and pipes.

In addition to these ancillary industries, which sprang up with and were dependent upon the primary industries of agriculture and mining, were the cottage industries run by Malay families in their spare time. But cottage industries, concerned largely with the production of small

Plate 33   Dyeing cloth for *batik*, Kelantan. Much of the *batik* produced in Peninsular Malaysia is from the east coast states where *batik* cloth manufacture is an
important cottage industry.

quantities of hand-made consumption goods in everyday use, have never
been important in the industrial economy of the country. They were a
part of the Malay self-subsistence economy, the products of these industries going towards satisfying the meagre needs of the local *kampong*
population. Run on a small scale and without assistance from power-
driven machinery, the cottage industries declined in importance when
cheap factory-manufactured goods began to flood the market.

The scarcity of goods during the First World War stimulated the
development of light manufacturing industries to cater for some of the
needs of the local population. During the Great Depression of the 1930s
when the primary industries collapsed and international trade was at a
standstill the pace of industrialization quickened as resources were
diverted from the export industries to local manufacturing.

Industries established during the Japanese occupation were concerned
mainly with the production of items needed for the Japanese war effort
and of some miscellaneous items which could no longer be imported.
The manufacturing sector of the economy remained relatively small and
neglected during the immediate postwar period, and it was not until after
the attainment of political independence in 1957 that concerted efforts
were made to foster large-scale industrialization in the country as a

357

means of reducing its dependence on the export of a few primary products, bringing about a better balanced economic structure and providing employment opportunities for the rapidly growing population. The steadily rising national income, by raising the demand for manufactured goods, provided a stimulus to local entrepreneurs to produce some of the goods that had traditionally been imported, thereby not only expanding the industrial base but also saving on foreign exchange earnings.

As with other Southeast Asian countries, Peninsular Malaysia's initial manufacturing phase was one of import-substitution, that is, manufacturing those goods which were imported to meet home demand. Incentives were provided under the Pioneer Industry Ordinance whereby industries that qualified for pioneer status were given tax exemptions on profits for two to five years, allowed to import necessary raw materials free of duty, and provided with tariff protection as and when considered necessary.

The tariff protection for the domestic market in some manufactured goods and the favourable investment climate fostered by the Government brought about a progressive expansion of the manufacturing sector, the average annual rate of growth between 1967 and 1972 being 12 per cent. As Fig. 13.1 shows, the contribution of manufacturing to the Gross Domestic Production at constant prices increased from about 7 per cent in 1947 to 17 per cent in 1973, the rate of growth being most marked after 1958 when the pioneer industry policy came into effect. In contrast the contribution of the primary sector (agriculture, forestry, fisheries and mining) to the GDP has declined in recent years—from 38 per cent in 1967 to 33 in 1973. These changes are mirrored by similar changes in the workforce: in 1957, 7.4 per cent of the workforce was engaged in manufacturing while 59.7 per cent was in the primary sector; by 1970 the percentage in manufacturing had increased to 9.2 and that in the primary sector had dropped to 51.6. It is evident that the

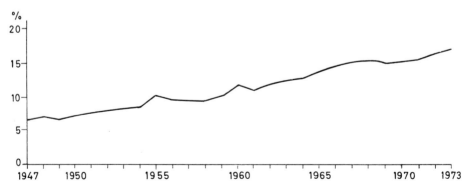

Fig. 13.1 Percentage contribution to Gross Domestic Product at constant prices by the manufacturing sector, 1947–73.

economy of Peninsular Malaysia has moved away considerably from the prewar pattern, typified by a high rate of dependence on the primary sector, towards a more balanced pattern, with the secondary (manufacturing) sector assuming a role of increasing prominence.

Manufacturing industries—structure and distribution

Manufacturing is defined as 'the mechanical or chemical transformation of inorganic or organic substances into new products, whether the work is done by power-driven machines or by hand, in a factory or in the worker's home, and whether sold at wholesale or retail. The assembly of component parts is included. Establishments primarily engaged in repair work are included, and classified according to the type of product repaired.' Comprehensive data on the industrial sector of the economy are available from the 1963 and 1968 censuses of Manufacturing Industries. The data for 1968 have been up-dated to 1970 and published in the Survey of Manufacturing Industries, Peninsular Malaysia. This survey covered 133 selected manufacturing industries and all pioneer industries not falling within the covered industries. The coverage for the survey accounted for 95 per cent of the value-added and 84 per cent of total employment in 1968. This examination of the structure and distribution of the manufacturing industries is based on data in the 1963 and 1968 censuses as well as the 1970 survey.

The 1968 census showed that 78 per cent of the 9 013 establishments were small-scale enterprises employing less than ten full-time paid employees. However, they accounted for only 8 per cent of the total manufacturing value added. In 1963 these small-scale enterprises made up 82 per cent of the total manufacturing establishments and accounted for 14 per cent of the total value added. It is therefore evident that such enterprises are on the decline, but are nevertheless still the most important group from the employment size point of view.

The greater part of the value added is derived from a relatively small number of the bigger establishments employing more than ten full-time paid employees. Large-scale industry, with access to both foreign and local capital and technological expertise, grew rapidly in the decade of the 1960s, as illustrated by the fact that the percentage of net value added in establishments employing 200 or more workers increased from 2.4 in 1963 to 39 in 1968. The highest rates of growth, on an industry-group basis, were recorded by those industries producing basic metal products, electrical machinery, textiles and transport equipment (Table 13.1). The most important developments in those industries during the period 1963—70 were the establishment of an iron and steel works at Butterworth (boosting the growth rate of the basic metal industries); the establishment of a battery factory and other factories producing electrical appliances (electrical machinery industries); the establishment

Table 13.1 Manufacturing industries by major industry groups, 1970, and growth index, 1963–70

Industry group	Establishments		Gross value of production		Value added		Paid full-time employment		Growth index, 1963–70*
	Number	Per cent	M$million	Per cent	M$million	Per cent	Number	Per cent	
Processing of agricultural produce off estates	174	5.4	720	18.4	129	10.9	13 103	8.8	2.63
Food processing	536	16.8	843	21.4	190	16.0	18 419	12.4	2.92
Beverage manufacture	60	1.9	80	2.0	43	3.6	2 622	1.8	3.30
Tobacco industries	67	2.1	275	6.9	85	7.2	3 931	2.7	3.04
Textiles	75	2.3	98	2.6	27	2.3	7 880	5.3	6.75
Footwear	102	3.2	48	1.2	13	1.1	5 765	3.9	3.25
Wood, rattan, atap and cork	498	15.6	331	8.5	118	10.0	25 942	17.5	2.41
Furniture and fixtures	131	4.1	30	0.8	9	0.7	2 499	1.7	1.12
Paper products	34	1.1	34	0.9	10	0.8	1 577	1.1	3.33
Printing and publishing	275	8.6	144	3.6	73	6.2	11 033	7.4	2.51
Leather goods	14	0.4	7	0.2	2	0.2	530	0.4	3.03
Rubber products	51	1.6	119	3.1	51	4.3	8 441	5.7	2.21
Chemical products	236	7.4	281	7.1	110	9.4	6 815	4.6	2.62
Petroleum and coal products	9	0.3	173	4.4	42	3.5	457	0.3	n.a.
Non-metallic mineral products	172	5.4	148	3.8	81	6.9	8 079	5.4	3.00
Basic metal products	51	1.6	105	2.6	33	2.8	3 279	2.2	9.17
Other metal products	201	6.3	141	3.6	45	3.8	7 814	5.3	1.96
Non-electric machinery	277	8.7	77	1.9	31	2.6	6 835	4.6	2.07
Electrical machinery	41	1.3	91	2.3	33	2.8	3 204	2.2	7.02
Transport equipment	76	2.4	127	3.2	36	3.1	4 776	3.2	6.00
Miscellaneous	112	3.5	58	1.5	21	1.8	5 304	3.5	n.a.
Total	3 192	100.0	3 930	100.0	1 182	100.0	148 305	100.0	2.81

* Ratio of value added in 1970 to value added in 1963.

Plate 34 Segamat Brick Factory, Johore, set in the midst of the oil-palm and rubber estates of central Johore. At the bottom left-hand corner of the photograph are market gardens producing fresh vegetables and pigs and poultry for the urban population of Segamat (see p. 364).

of large spinning and weaving factories as well as clothing factories (textiles industries); and the establishment of twelve vehicle assembly plants, six for cars, three for trucks and commercial vehicles, and three for motor cycles (transport equipment industries). Notable among the other large-scale enterprises set up were the petroleum refineries at Port Dickson, a chemical fertilizer plant at Port Klang, cement factories, a tyre factory, flourmills and animal feedmills.

The most important groups of industries in 1970, on the basis of value added, were those involved in food processing; the processing of agricultural produce off estates; wood, rattan, atap and cork manufacture; and chemical products manufacture. Together they accounted for 47 per cent of the total value added (Table 13.1). The first three of the industry-groups were also the most important employers of labour, together accounting for 39 per cent of all paid full-time employment.

The industries can be also classified on the basis of whether they are capital or labour intensive. Lim (1973) has demonstrated that the value added per employee is a reliable indicator of capital-intensity in Peninsular Malaysia. Using this criterion the clearly capital-intensive industry groups are those manufacturing petroleum and coal products, beverage,

361

tobacco, chemicals and chemical products, electrical machinery, and those involved in the processing of food and agricultural produce off estates. The clearly labour-intensive industry groups are those manufacturing footwear, leather products, furniture and fixtures, textiles, non-electric machinery and paper and paper products.

It would benefit the country on two counts to foster labour-intensive industries: first, it is in these industries that Peninsular Malaysia has a comparative advantage because wage levels are generally low. Second, such industries will provide employment to a greater proportion of the labour force, thereby helping to reduce the level of unemployment. However, during the period under survey the labour-intensive industries did not expand at a higher rate than the capital-intensive industries, mainly because there was no incentive for the entrepreneurs to do so: the Pioneer Industries Ordinance of 1958 only provided tax exemptions on the level of capital expenditure and not on the number of workers employed. The 1968 Investment Incentives Act which superseded the 1958 Ordinance did not change the situation in any significant way, and it was only in July 1971 that, through an amendment to the Act, provision was made for tax exemptions on the number of workers employed.

One of the most important measures to promote industrialization in Peninsular Malaysia was the granting of income tax exemptions and other reliefs for specified periods to industries which had pioneer status. Many industries have been established as pioneer industries since this policy came into force in 1958. In 1959 there were nineteen pioneer establishments employing 1 296 workers, with gross sales of M$10.7 million. By 1973 the number of pioneer establishments had increased to 349, the number of workers to 87 500 and the gross sales to M$2 446 million. Of the 100 000 new jobs generated in the manufacturing sector between 1971 and 1973, 41 per cent was from the pioneer industries; similarly the share of these industries in the total manufacturing net output rose from 33 per cent in 1970 to over 40 per cent in 1973.

Table 13.2 shows the relative contribution of the pioneer industries in 1970 in terms of number of establishments, average full-time employees per establishment, percentage of workers employed and percentage of value added. Several features stand out: within the manufacturing sector as a whole the pioneer industries contributed almost one-third of the value added. Within four specific industry groups the contribution of the pioneer industries to value added was very high (70–100%): petroleum and coal products, textiles, electrical machinery and basic metal products. The pioneer establishments were very much larger than the non-pioneer establishments in terms of average size, but they employed only 19 per cent of all full-time workers engaged in manufacturing, so that they did not contribute significantly to total employment.

Within the manufacturing sector the ten leading individual industries

Table 13.2   Pioneer and non-pioneer industries, 1968

Industry group	Number of establishments		Average full-time employees per establishment		Employment contribution (per cent)		Contribution to value added (per cent)	
	Pioneer	Non-pioneer	Pioneer	Non-pioneer	Pioneer	Non-pioneer	Pioneer	Non-pioneer
Food manufacturing	27	2 800	128	5	16	84	47	53
Beverages	2	72	202	26	18	82	51	49
Textiles	20	49	366	17	83	17	89	11
Wood products	19	800	254	22	9	91	10	90
Chemicals	37	282	85	10	48	52	55	45
Petroleum and coal	6	2	97	2	99	1	100	—
Non-metallic minerals	10	315	166	18	17	83	12	88
Basic metals	9	72	449	11	74	26	71	29
Metal products	16	1 189	117	5	21	79	24	76
Non-electrical machinery	7	448	66	12	3	97	5	95
Electrical machinery	17	302	108	2	63	37	73	27
Others	40	n.a.	145	n.a.	n.a.	n.a.	n.a.	n.a.
Total	210	8 867	155	11	19	81	32	68

Source: *Rao (1974), p. 163.*

in 1970 were rubber remilling factories off-estates, tobacco products, latex processing factories off-estates, sawmills, petroleum products, large ricemills, sugar refineries, crude coconut-oilmills off-estates, prepared animal feeds and other dairy products. Together they accounted for 48 per cent of the gross value of production, 37 per cent of value added, and 25 per cent of total paid full-time employment.

Table 13.3 shows the state-by-state distribution of industries based on data from the 1968 census and the 1970 survey. There is a very high concentration of industrial activity in four states—Selangor, Johore, Perak and Penang—in the Tin and Rubber Belt of the west coast. Together these four states account for more than four-fifths of both the total value added and the full-time paid employment. As seen earlier, the states within the Tin and Rubber Belt were historically the most intensively developed in the country, and the ones best served by infrastructural facilities. The postindependence growth of industry has favoured some of these areas locationally, notably those centres where industrial estates have been established (Fig. 13.2). Thus nearly 60 per cent of the manufacturing value added and 42 per cent of paid full-time employment were derived from industries located in these seven towns or in the industrial estates within or near them: Kuala Lumpur, Petaling Jaya, Port Dickson, Johore Bharu, Prai, Klang and Batu Tiga (Shah Alam). Kuala Lumpur and neighbouring Petaling Jaya were undoubtedly the main centres of industry, accounting for 40 per cent of the total manufacturing value added. There was a marked concentration of a few industries in some states. For example, the petroleum refineries dominated the industrial sector in Negri Sembilan, accounting for 53 per cent of the value added, although it employed only 8 per cent of the total paid full-time workers. Pahang was even more of a 'one-industry' state as sawmills contributed 80 per cent of the value added and 65 per cent of paid full-time workers. In Kedah, the padi-producing state, large ricemills contributed 28 per cent of value added and 22 per cent of paid full-time employment.

At present most of the manufacturing activities are concentrated along the western part of the Peninsula, where nearly all the industrial estates are located (Fig. 13.2). This has served to accentuate the imbalance in development between the west coast and the east coast states. One of the policies of the Government is to encourage the dispersal of industries so as to reduce this imbalance. Towards this end it has introduced a new incentive, known as the Locational Incentive, whereby companies located in designated growth centres, especially in the east coast states (and Sabah and Sarawak), will qualify for tax exemption up to a maximum of ten years. It will also develop the infrastructure of these areas as well as participate directly in the establishment of new enterprises. The creation of such 'growth poles' is a major step away from the historical *laissez-faire* attitude towards economic development. It reflects the

Table 13.3   Distribution of industries, by state, 1968 and 1970 (per cent)

State	Number of establishments		Gross value of production		Value added		Full-time paid employment	
	1968	1970	1968	1970	1968	1970	1968	1970
Selangor	23	35	43	47	51	52	39	40
Johore	12	13	14	14	12	12	18	18
Perak	19	17	12	10	11	11	14	14
Penang	15	14	11	11	9	10	12	12
Negri Sembilan	5	3	9	7	8	7	4	3
Pahang	4	4	2	2	2	2	3	4
Kedah	9	5	4	4	2	2	4	4
Malacca	5	3	3	2	2	2	2	2
Kelantan	4	4	2	2	2	1	3	2
Trengganu	3	1	—	1	1	1	1	1
Perlis	1	1	—	—	—	—	—	—
Total	100	100	100	100	100	100	100	100

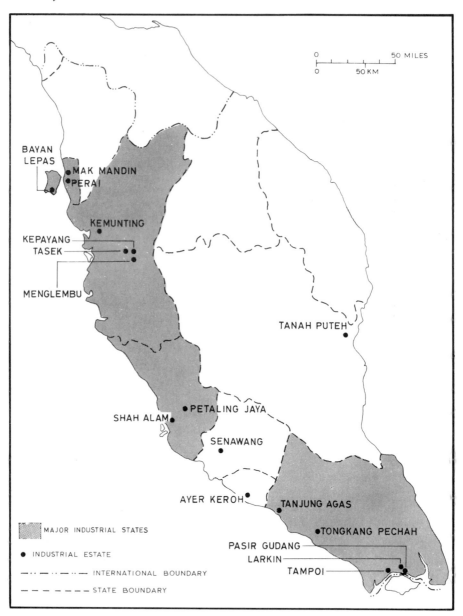

Fig. 13.2   Industrial estates.

desire of the Government to accelerate the modernization process in hitherto neglected areas, by widening job opportunities and adding an industrial sector to the traditional base of agriculture and fishing.

One indication of the extent of industrialization in a country is the proportion of the labour force engaged in the secondary sector, defined

Plate 35   Tasek industrial estate, on the outskirts of Ipoh. Recent industrial activity is being concentrated on such industrial estates, of which the first and most important was Petaling Jaya (see p. 364).

as manufacturing, building and construction. The Census of Population reports for 1947 and 1957 and various official statistical sources show that the proportion of the labour force engaged in this sector has increased steadily over the years, from 9.2 per cent in 1947, to 10.6 per cent in 1957, 11.9 per cent in 1965 and 12.7 per cent in 1970. In the decade of the 1960s the increase was due entirely to manufacturing as the percentage engaged in construction remained constant at 3.5. The actual number of people employed in manufacturing was 318 000 in 1970; by 1973 the number had increased to 418 000 (*Mid-term Review*). Most of the increase was due to the establishment of new industries.

Trends in industrialization

It is possible to discern three district trends in the industrialization process in Peninsular Malaysia. Traditionally industrial activity up to the early postwar period was limited to the processing of primary commodities, of which rubber was the most important, and to small-scale food industries, repair shops and handicrafts. The processing of estate produce in factories off estates was the dominant industrial activity up to the 1960s: in 1959, for example, 29 per cent of the total net manufacturing output was from the processing of agricultural produce, mainly rubber. However, as the industrial base broadened and new faster-growing industries such as those producing beverages, textiles, chemicals and chemical products, petroleum products, basic metals and metal products and transport equipment were established, the percentage share of processing activities declined, and by 1968 such activities were contributing only 10.5 per cent to the total net manufacturing output.

The second phase in industrialization was that of import substitution. The 1960s, spilling over into the early 1970s, was the period when this policy was most vigorously pursued, with new industries catering to the domestic market being added to the list each year. Many of these were pioneer industries, and were therefore granted tax concessions. Table 13.4 shows the progress in import substitution during the period 1960–67. It will be seen that in 1960 only three groups of industries—tobacco products, wood products and footwear—had a domestic production percentage of over 70. By 1967 this had increased to seven groups: beverages, textiles, wood products, furniture, printing and publishing, rubber products and non-metallic mineral products. Even at

Table 13.4   Import substitution, 1960 and 1967

Industry group	Percentage of domestic production in total supply	
	1960	1967
Food processing	43	63
Beverages	36	71
Tobacco products	74	96
Textiles	7	30
Footwear	10	13
Wood products	94	94
Furniture	87	93
Paper and paper products	9	23
Printing and publishing	68	73
Leather products	40	45
Rubber products	62	88
Chemicals	55	66
Non-metallic minerals	50	73
Metal products, machinery, etc.	17	25
Miscellaneous manufactures	44	46
Petroleum products	nil	47

Source: *Rao (1974), Table 5.9.*

that period the country had almost attained self-sufficiency in tobacco products, wood products and furniture, so that the import substitution phase based on the domestic market for these products could be said to have been completed.

Further progress in import substitution was recorded after 1967, so that by the early 1970s this phase in the industrialization programme of Peninsular Malaysia was regarded officially as being over. Thus the Finance Minister, in his budget speech of 1973, said '. . . we have gone as far as we are likely to go in the matter of import substitution'.

As Myint (1972) has pointed out, the import substitution process typically goes through an easy initial phase when domestic industries expand rapidly to take over the markets for imported consumer goods. As this phase is completed it is followed by a difficult phase when the small size of the domestic markets slows down further industrial growth. The official policy in Peninsular Malaysia today is to move industrialization from its predominantly domestic-market orientation towards export-market orientation. Hand-in-hand with this is the need to create more employment opportunities in industry because of the growing number of people moving into the labour market each year. Accordingly priority is being given to industries which are both export-oriented and labour intensive. One such type of industry is the electronics industry. To foster its growth the Government has declared it a priority industry and given it special tax relief for periods from four to ten years. By the end of 1972 twenty-one electronics factories had either started production, or were being established, or had been officially approved for establishment.

To promote other labour-intensive industries the Government introduced a labour utilization tax relief incentive in September 1971 whereby the larger a company's labour force the longer its period of tax relief. Thus a company employing 51 to 100 workers is eligible for two years' tax exemption, while one employing more than 350 workers is eligible for the maximum relief of five years.

An important means of promoting export-oriented industries is through the establishment of Free Trade Zones which allow manufacturing companies to import machinery, raw materials and component parts free of duty and export finished products with minimum customs formalities. By the end of 1973 five such zones had been established: Bayan Lepas, Prai, and Prai Wharf in Penang, Sungei Way in Selangor, and Batu Berendam in Malacca. Others to be developed include Pulau Jerejak (Penang), Ulu Klang (Selangor), Tanjong Kling (Malacca), and Pasir Gudang and Tanjong Agas (Johore).

During the import substitution phase of industrialization some industries in Peninsular Malaysia, under the shelter of protective tariffs and tax exemptions, might have been producing at prices higher than those prevailing in world markets. The ability of an industry to survive in world export markets depends on its competitiveness; that is, how cheaply it can produce its goods. In producing for the export market the industries of Peninsular Malaysia must therefore find ways and means of lowering costs, in some cases through economies of large-scale production or through lower labour costs. The Government, on its part and if it wishes, could encourage export production through devices such as export subsidies or through tax exemptions on profits.

The industry-groups that have shown the most promising export performance in recent years were textiles, clothing and footwear, food products and wood products. The country's natural advantage in timber has been used to good account to promote the export of wood products in the form of processed timber, especially veneer sheet, mouldings and plain plywood. Exports of machinery and transport equipment have also increased substantially.

Apart from plywood and veneer sheets, the other products which use locally produced raw materials and which have entered the export markets are canned pineapple and rubber products. Other individual industries which have successfully entered the export markets in spite of protection through import duties are those producing dairy products (using imported milk powder), sago and tapioca products, biscuits, soft drinks and carbonated beverages, and paints and varnishes (using imported resins and pigments). Electronic and related electrical equipment exports have also increased markedly in the post-1972 period.

On the whole the net exports of manufactured goods accounted for only 15 per cent of manufacturing gross sales in 1973. The export incentives provided for in the 1968 Investment Incentives Act were extended in 1973 whereby an export allowance is given for increases in the export sales of a taxpayer. The allowance is higher in the case of export products which have no less than 50 per cent of domestic materials or components. In all the scheme will have the effect of encouraging the establishment of export-oriented industries, especially those using locally produced raw materials. As these and the other incentives discussed earlier take effect it is likely that the percentage of net exports to total gross manufacturing sales will increase from the 15 per cent registered in 1973.

The New Economic Policy

Owing to its large growth potential the manufacturing sector is expected to play a leading part in assisting the Government to achieve the objectives of the New Economic Policy. One of these objectives is the creation of a Malay commercial and industrial community so as to correct the present economic imbalance between the Malays and the non-Malays in the country. In 1973 the Malays owned only 6 per cent of the total paid-up capital of pioneer companies. The Government now requires that at least 30 per cent of the equity of all approved companies, except the export-oriented companies, be reserved for Malays and other indigenous people. In addition efforts are being directed to increase Malay representation at all levels of manufacturing activities, especially at the executive and professional levels. Governmental-created institutions such as PERNAS, the national trading corporation, MARA, FIMA and the State Economic Development Corporations (SEDC) are participating in a number of industries either directly on a joint-venture basis with the private sector.

14
Trade

The economy of Peninsular Malaysia has been heavily dependent on trade since the earliest days of history. To a large extent this was due to the position of the Malay Peninsula in relation to the Straits of Malacca, a position which made it the natural doorway to the East Indies. Archaeological and historical evidence points towards the existence of Indian traders in the Malay world as early as Neolithic times. Medieval Malacca had a considerable *entrepôt* trade, attracting merchants with produce from Cairo, Arabia and other Arab countries, India and Burma, as well as merchants from countries east of the Malay Peninsular—China, Thailand, Cambodia and the Malay Archipelago.

The coming of the European powers greatly extended the trade connections of the Malay world. Penang, founded by the British in 1786, and Singapore, founded in 1819, together captured a large part of the trade of Malacca. All three ports came under British rule in 1824, and were constituted as the Straits Settlements in 1829. The British policy of free trade as well as its unique geographical position and the great natural advantages of its harbour rapidly turned Singapore into the major *entrepôt* of Southeast Asia, eclipsing Malacca, once the great trade centre of the Straits, and Penang. Penang's commerce was limited to trade with Burma, southern Thailand and northern Sumatra, while Malacca's trade connections rapidly dwindled until only those with Sumatra and the adjacent states of the Malay Peninsula remained. A contributing cause of Malacca's decline was the silting of its harbour. In 1825, only six years after its foundation, Singapore had captured over three-fifths of the total trade of the Straits Settlements, while Penang had slightly more than one-quarter of it.

The next twenty-five years saw the continued ascendancy of Singapore over the two other ports of the Straits Settlements. But sections of its great *entrepôt* trade were diverted with the establishment of Hong Kong in 1842 (which took away much of the China trade), the development of Saigon under the French and the extension of direct steamship channels of communication between Indonesia and Europe. Nevertheless, the development of major mining and agricultural enterprises in the adjacent territories, notably of tin and rubber in Peninsular

Malaysia, enabled it to add a large import and export trade to its *entrepôt* activities, and this has more than compensated for the contraction of the area served by the port.

The volume of trade almost doubled in the five years between 1895 (when the Federated Malay States were constituted) and 1900, and increased by two-thirds in the next five years. The rate of increase then slowed down until the 1920s, when it became more pronounced, reaching a climax in 1926 when the total trade of the country reached the record figure of nearly $619.5 million. The trade balance was always in Peninsular Malaysia's favour up to the beginning of the Second World War, due largely to the development of the tin, and later the rubber, industries. Tin was the dominant export until 1915, when rubber came to the fore, and by 1925 the exports of rubber were nearly four times as important (by value) as tin. Together these two primary products accounted for the larger part of the total export trade.

The postindependence period has seen two major changes in the pattern of trade of Peninsular Malaysia. First, the flow of goods through Singapore, traditionally one of the major ports of Peninsular Malaysia, has been gradually decreasing in importance since the two countries were politically separated in 1965. In that year 32 per cent by value of the external trade of Peninsular Malaysia passed through Singapore; by 1973 the percentage had decreased to 27. Second, the establishment of the Federation of Malaysia has resulted in the growth of intra-regional trade links between Peninsular Malaysia and Sarawak and Sabah. The main imports from Sarawak and Sabah to Peninsular Malaysia are petroleum, petroleum products and palm kernels, while Peninsular Malaysia's exports to the two partners are mainly food, beverages and tobacco, chemicals and fertilizers, and machinery and transport equipment. Trade between Peninsular Malaysia and Sarawak reached M$250 million in 1973.

The trade of Peninsular Malaysia is mainly of three kinds. First there is the internal trade largely concerned with the sale of locally grown foodstuffs and locally manufactured articles and handicrafts. Second there is the important external trade, consisting of imports and exports, and finally there is the *entrepôt* trade of Penang. The main trading centres are the *entrepôt* port of Penang in the northwest, and Kuala Lumpur linked with Port Klang near by. Ipoh and Malacca are the other important trade centres serving the tin and rubber belt of western Peninsular Malaysia. Eastern Peninsular Malaysia, separated from the west by mountainous country and still relatively undeveloped, trades through the small coastal ports of Kota Bharu, Kuala Trengganu and Kuantan.

Internal trade

The internal trade is mainly concerned with the sale of locally grown foodstuffs such as rice, vegetables, fruit, etc., and of locally manufactured goods and handicraft. Although no detailed statistical data are available on this aspect of the national economy, the dimensions of the internal trade are indicated by the fact that the value of locally grown rice alone came up to nearly M$774 million in 1973. If to this is added the value of other products grown or manufactured locally and sold in the internal markets, it becomes clear that the internal trade is of considerable importance.

Most of the foodstuffs produced figure prominently in the internal trade of the country. All of the surplus rice from the padi lands of the northwest and the other large rice-growing areas of Perak and Selangor are sold and consumed locally. The vegetables, food-crops, fruit and spices cultivated in market gardens, *kampongs*, New Villages and suburban areas are all sold and consumed within Peninsular Malaysia, except for small amounts which are regularly exported. A considerable number of the coconuts harvested enter into home trade, while part of the annual production of coconut-oil is sold in the domestic markets. Of the two other major export crops—rubber and palm-oil—only a very small proportion eventually finds its way into the local markets, rubber in the form of manufactured rubber articles and palm-oil in soaps and margarine.

There is also a fairly important internal trade in livestock—buffalo and oxen for meat and for draught purposes, sheep, goats, pigs and chickens for meat. A large number of livestock is also imported regularly since the country is not self-sufficient in meat. Most of the fish landed from the sea, as well as from freshwater sources, are also sold and consumed locally. Most of the annual output of sawn timber is exported; the remainder, including other forest products such as poles, charcoal and firewood, moves into local markets. A wide range of goods is manufactured and sold locally.

The directions of such trade depend mainly on the nature of the goods that are sold. Products which are in general demand by all sections of the population such as fish, rice and coconut-oil are sold in all parts of the country, although they are only produced in some regions. Generally speaking, there is a constant flow of the products of land, sea and forest into the urban markets, and a flow of locally manufactured articles into the rural markets, such flows consisting of the surpluses from the producing areas.

External trade

The import—export trade forms a very important part of the country's economy. Being a primary producing country, nearly all of the agricultural and mineral raw materials produced have to be exported to foreign markets. At the same time large quantities of goods, mainly food and manufactured articles, are imported for internal consumption.

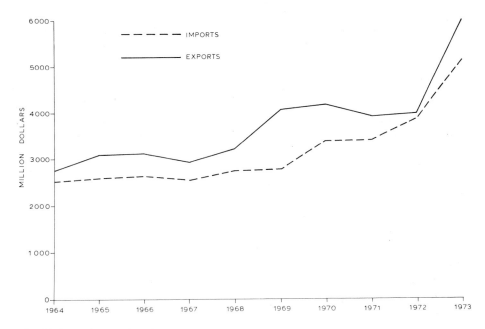

Fig. 14.1   Balance of trade, 1964—73.

Although Malaysia traditionally has a favourable balance of trade (Fig. 14.7), the balance fluctuates widely from year to year depending on the price and volume of the two principal exports—rubber and tin. The largest postwar export surpluses were reached in 1950 (M$1 297 million) and 1951 (M$1 510 million), during the Korean War boom.

Peninsular Malaysia has been able to attain a level of prosperity and affluence higher than most other countries in Southeast Asia through pursuing a policy of specialization in the production and export of those primary commodities, notably rubber, oil-palm and tin, in which she has a comparative advantage. She in turn imports a wide variety of essential foodstuffs and manufactured goods. This international trade was the mainspring of economic development in the country ever since it was opened up to such trade in the last quarter of the nineteenth century.

The basis for such development was the export of primary products. The share of Peninsular Malaysia's exports in her gross domestic product has always been high, as high as 60 per cent in 1950 and 1951, but declining to about 40 per cent in the 1960s. In 1973 it was 52 per cent. The export sector has consequently played a dominant role in the economy, influencing the other sectors, contributing to the development of infrastructure, to government revenue and, in the early years of its economic history, to the growth of its population through immigration.

There are however, two adverse consequences of this heavy dependence on the export sector. First, external capital into the country was

375

attracted towards the development of tin and rubber for export, with the consequent neglect of the domestic sector and particularly the indigenous rural sector. As pointed out earlier, one of the legacies of this over-concentration on these two primary commodities was an unbalanced economy. The development of roads, railways, sea and air transport and ports was primarily to meet the needs of these export industries. As these industries were concentrated along the western part of the Peninsula through a combination of circumstances, what eventually emerged was not only a lopsided economy but also a spatially unbalanced one, with the western Tin and Rubber Belt being the main region of economic growth and the eastern half of the Peninsula a relatively stagnant region. Second, the export-oriented economy of Peninsular Malaysia is correspondingly dependent on external markets and hence subject to the vagaries of external market forces over which it has no control. The prices of primary commodities such as tin and rubber are in the main determined by the advanced industrial countries (except in the special case of oil, where prices are set by OPEC), and any change in their economic policies can result in abrupt changes in the export trade of the primary producing countries. Similarly a major advance in technology which leads to a reduction in the use of certain raw materials can have serious long-term repercussions on the export trade of the countries producing these raw materials.

Exports

Table 14.1 shows the composition of Peninsular Malaysia's gross exports for the years 1947 to 1973 by value and by percentage. Up to 1960, three years after independence, rubber and tin accounted for 80 per cent of the value of total gross exports. Since then the growing emphasis on economic as well as export diversification has led to a gradual decline in the importance of these two commodities, their joint contribution falling to 70 per cent in 1965, 64 per cent in 1970 and 55 per cent in 1973.

Iron-ore has had a brief export history. Large-scale exploitation of iron-ore deposits started in the late 1950s, and up to 1965 iron-ore was the third most important export of Peninsular Malaysia. Gradual exhaustion of the deposits led in turn to a decline in the volume of iron-ore exports, and by the early 1970s iron-ore's short economic life-span had come to an end.

Palm-oil remained in the background until the 1960s, when official and private interest in the crop as an alternative to rubber led to large-scale planting on newly cleared land and on old rubber land. The volume of palm-oil exports began to increase significantly, and by 1971 the commodity had become the third most important export of the country. The contribution from palm-oil exports is expected to increase further as the newly planted areas come into bearing.

Table 14.1 Composition of exports, 1947–73

Year	Rubber M$m	Per cent	Tin M$m	Per cent	Iron-ore M$m	Per cent	Palm-oil M$m	Per cent	Timber M$m	Per cent	Others M$m	Per cent	Total M$m	Per cent
1947	587	70	114	14	0	0	19	2	19	2	96	12	835	100
1950	1 810	69	442	17	9	0	32	1	18	1	297	12	2 608	100
1955	1 584	67	434	18	33	1	36	2	26	1	259	11	2 372	100
1960	1 829	63	507	17	140	5	61	2	55	2	332	11	2 924	100
1964	1 303	47	728	26	163	6	81	3	87	3	412	15	2 774	100
1965	1 368	44	872	28	161	6	106	3	92	3	497	16	3 096	100
1966	1 396	45	792	25	136	4	118	4	99	3	578	19	3 119	100
1967	1 216	42	755	26	122	4	111	4	129	4	586	20	2 919	100
1968	1 301	40	830	26	111	3	117	4	182	6	676	21	3 217	100
1969	1 940	48	940	23	116	3	143	3	208	5	729	18	4 076	100
1970	1 663	40	1 013	24	107	2	246	6	250	6	913	22	4 192	100
1971	1 417	36	906	23	21	1	356	9	247	6	970	25	3 917	100
1972	1 260	31	924	23	9	0	325	8	325	8	1 200	30	4 043	100
1973	2 392	40	897	15	5	0	427	7	529	9	1 774	29	6 024	100

Timber exports, made up of sawn logs and sawn timber, have steadily increased in volume from the 1960s. The opening up of forested land on a country-wide scale for agriculture, especially by FELDA and other governmental agencies, has resulted in a large flow of timber from the land to the export markets. Unlike rubber and palm-oil, timber exports, though ranking third in importance in 1973, will gradually decrease in volume and importance as the contribution from such land development slows down, and also because the policy today is to increase foreign exchange earnings by processing the logs and timber into wood products and exporting these higher value products rather than exporting only sawn logs and sawn timber.

Table 14.1 shows not only the changing patterns of the traditional exports of primary commodities but also the increase in the percentage share of the 'Others' category: from 12 per cent in 1947 to 20 per cent in 1967 and to 29 per cent in 1973. Exports in this category are made up mainly of manufactured goods, transport equipment and machinery and chemical products. The percentage increase in the exports in this category is a reflection of the growing contribution from the industrial sector of the economy, as well as an indication of the extent to which the diversification policy has altered the export patterns of Peninsular Malaysia.

Table 14.2 shows the main destinations of Peninsular Malaysia's exports for the years 1958, 1965 and 1973. The dominant position of Singapore has not changed in the fifteen years between 1958 and 1973, and the island republic continues to be the single biggest customer of Peninsular Malaysia's products. Most of these exports are reexported by Singapore. Both the United States and Japan are the next main buyers of

Table 14.2   Destinations of exports, 1958, 1965 and 1973

Country	Percentage of exports		
	1958	1965	1973
Singapore	24	21	21
United States	11	18	12.5
Japan	9	13	10
United Kingdom	18	8	8
Netherlands	1.5	2	4
West Germany	5	3	4
France	3	3	3
USSR	4	7	4
Rest of the world	24.5	25	33.5
Total	100	100	100

the country's products, consisting largely of rubber, tin and in the case of Japan in the 1960s iron-ore. The United Kingdom's position declined considerably between 1958 and 1965, but since then has remained at fourth. The rest of the world imports Peninsular Malaysian products in smaller quantities. In general these importing countries are the developed countries rather than the developing countries.

Imports

The general pattern during the colonial period was one in which the bulk of the imports consisted of consumer goods such as food and manu-factured goods and only a very small percentage of the imports was made up of capital goods. After independence the pattern changed, mainly because of the policy of attaining self-sufficiency in rice and because of industrialization. Thus in 1965, eight years after independence, consumer goods constituted about half of the total imports, while the other half was made up of roughly equal proportions of capital goods and intermediate goods. The growing pace of industrialization since then had led to a significant increase in the importation of capital goods, so that by 1973 these goods made up over 30 per cent of the total imports.

Table 14.3 shows the composition of the imports of Peninsular Malaysia for the five-year period 1969—73. It will be seen that the three

Table 14.3 Composition of imports, 1969—73

SITC* Section	Percentage of imports by year				
	1969	1970	1971	1972	1973
0. Food	21	20	17	18	17
1. Beverages and tobacco	2	2	2	2	2
2. Crude materials, except fuel	11	9	7	7	7
3. Mineral fuels	7	6	7	7	6
4. Animal and vegetable oils	1	1	1	1	0
5. Chemicals	9	8	9	9	10
6. Manufactured goods	19	20	20	19	21
7. Machinery and transport equipment	23	28	31	32	30
8. Miscellaneous manufactured goods	5	5	5	4	6
9. Others	2	1	1	1	1
Total	100	100	100	100	100

* UN Standard International Trade Classification.

most important sections were food, manufactured goods and machinery and transport equipment, constituting 17, 21 and 30 per cent respectively of the total imports for 1973. There have been significant changes in two of these items between 1969 and 1973. Using 1969 as a base year the index for food in 1973 was 81, while the index for machinery and transport equipment was 130. The decrease in food imports was due to the increasing substitution of locally produced food, especially rice, for imported food. The increase in the importation of machinery and transport equipment was a reflection of the growing pace of industrialization in the country.

The other major group of imports in 1973 consisted of chemicals (SITC, Section 5). The main individual items, in descending order of importance, were chemical elements and compounds, plastic and related materials, medicinal products and fertilizers. The chemical and plastic materials were the imported inputs for the factories turning out various manufactured products based wholly or partly on these materials. The large import bill for medicinal and pharmaceutical products is an indication of the spread and use of modern medicine and health services. Although Peninsular Malaysia manufactures chemical fertilizers for its agricultural sector, domestic production is not sufficient to meet requirements, and substantial sums of foreign exchange are spent annually on imported fertilizers.

Table 14.4 shows the main sources of Peninsular Malaysian imports for the years 1958, 1965 and 1973. Three major changes are discernible: first, just as exports to the United Kingdom had declined considerably

Table 14.4   Sources of imports, 1958, 1965 and 1973

Country	Percentage of imports		
	1958	1965	1973
Japan	6	11	23
United Kingdom	25	20	11
Australia	5	6	8
United States	2	5	8
Singapore	8	11	7
West Germany	2	5	6
Mainland China	6	7	5
Thailand	11	10	4.5
Indonesia	14	0	2.5
Rest of the world	21	25	25
Total	100	100	100

between 1958 and 1973, so also had imports from the UK fallen, even though it remained the second most important supplier of goods to Peninsular Malaysia. Second, Japan, once a relatively minor supplier, had by 1973 become the single most important one. Imports from Japan consisted mainly of manufactured goods, machinery and transport equipment, miscellaneous manufactured articles and chemicals. Third, Indonesia, once an important supplier of primary raw materials such as tin, rubber, palm-oil and copra to Peninsular Malaysia for processing and reexport, had by 1973 ceased to be so, mainly because she had by then established her own processing facilities as well as because of her establishing direct trading links with her consumers.

Singapore's position as a port and *entrepôt* centre for Peninsular Malaysia has declined in the years since its political separation in 1965, and is expected to decline further when the new port at Pasir Gudang, on the tip of the Johore peninsula, is opened. Thailand has been one of the traditional sources of rice, rubber (for reexport), and tin ore (for smelting). Imports of rice have decreased since 1965 because of increased rice production within Peninsular Malaysia and that of tin-ore because of the establishment of a tin smelting plant in Thailand. Mainland China continues to supply Peninsular Malaysia with a variety of foodstuffs.

In recent years imports from Australia and the United States have grown rapidly, the two countries contributing 8 per cent each to the total imports of Peninsular Malaysia in 1973. Australia supplies large quantities of meat and dairy products. The most important imports from the United States in 1973 were beverages and tobacco.

The *entrepôt* trade of Penang

The *entrepôt* trade of Peninsular Malaysia is conducted through the port of Penang. An *entrepôt* port acts as an intermediary centre and temporary depot for goods passing from a foreign source to a foreign destination. In the process the goods entering the *entrepôt* port undergo some form of processing before being sent to their final destinations. In fact this value added is the best measure of the importance of the *entrepôt* trade. In official trade statistics the *entrepôt* trade of Penang consists of trade with Indonesia (Sumatra), Thailand and Burma on the one hand, and with mainland Peninsular Malaysia and the rest of the world on the other.

Up to the period of the formation of the Federation of Malaysia in 1963 the *entrepôt* trade of Penang made up from 15 to 20 per cent by value of its total foreign trade. Since then there has been a considerable decline of the *entrepôt* trade, in terms of absolute value as well as a percentage of total trade. By 1973 the *entrepôt* trade as a percentage of total foreign trade had declined to 6.2 per cent (Table 14.5).

The main reason for this decline is the policy of economic nationalism

Table 14.5   The *entrepôt* trade of Penang, 1961—73

Year	Value of total trade (M$million)	Value of entrepôt trade (M$million)			Entrepôt *trade as a percentage of total trade*
		Indonesia	Thailand	Burma	
1961	1 830	154	145	22	17.5
1965	1 931	1	202	7	10.8
1969	2 350	145	55	4	8.7
1973	3 213	103	85	12	6.2

followed by Penang's neighbouring trade partners, each of which aims to develop its own ports, establish its own direct trading links and foster its own import-substitution industries. Trade with Sumatra suffered from Indonesian regulations and came to a virtual standstill during the period of 'confrontation' between Indonesia and Malaysia in the mid-1960s. The post-confrontation period has seen a gradual though only still partial recovery of the Sumatra trade.

Thailand used to send its tin-ore and concentrates for smelting in Penang, as well as some of its rubber for processing. But the flow of tin-ore and concentrates came to a stop in 1965 when their smelter at Phuket was opened and the Thai Government prohibited the export of tin-ore. Trade with Burma has been on a minor scale in the postwar period, and became even less significant after 1965 because of economic problems within the country, but is now showing signs of recovery.

Associated with the *entrepôt* trade of Penang is its free port status. Penang was founded in 1786 as a free port, and in time became an *entrepôt* port, collecting and redistributing the produce from the surrounding region, and allowing the free entry of imported, mainly British, goods for eventual distribution to the mainland and elsewhere. This free port status has been maintained even after political independence was achieved. But it carried with it the drawback of acting as a disincentive to the establishment of industries, since local industries would have to compete against cheap duty-free imports from overseas.

The decline of the *entrepôt* trade, 'the traditional *raison d'être* of free port status' (Courtenay, 1972) has made it inevitable that Penang would eventually be drawn into the customs area of Peninsular Malaysia. As it is, there has already been a gradual loss of its free port status. The official view was put forward by the Minister of Finance in 1972, that it was '... absolutely vital in the national interests and the long-term interests of Penang that the process of industrialization must be accelerated ... To achieve this, it is necessary to introduce protective custom duties throughout Malaysia, including Penang. It is therefore inevitable that in the process of speeding up industrialization of the country, the free port status of Penang be eroded' (*Asia Research Bulletin*, September 1972). A likely compensation that could accrue to Penang should it be fully drawn into the main customs area of the Peninsular Malaysia would be the stimulation of industrial growth on the island, more so now that a causeway linking it to the mainland is to be built.

15
Transport

The evolution of the transport system

The history of transport development in Peninsular Malaysia can be divided into two phases—the earlier phase when movement was largely by water and the modern phase when rail, road and air transport superseded rivers as the main means of internal movement. Up to 1885, when the first railway line was constructed, movement in the Malay Peninsula was almost entirely by water with the seas and the rivers forming natural highways. The heavy and uniform rainfall gives rise to a multiplicity of rivers, and these in turn set the original pattern of Malay settlement and transport on the lowlands and coastal areas. The easiest lines of movement in that difficult landscape of lowland swamps and rain forest were along the rivers. Wet-padi cultivation, the basis of Malay agriculture, also tended to draw the Malay settlers towards flat land located near a convenient source of irrigation water. In addition the rivers provided potable water, and the rivers and sea were the natural sources of fish. In this amphibious environment the boat was the main means of communication and distances were usually calculated in terms of sailing or rowing hours or days.

Being a long narrow peninsula with an extensive coastline and good sheltered harbours along its western side, Peninsular Malaysia has since the earliest days been dependent on the sea as a means of communication. There is evidence that the first people to migrate and settle in the Peninsula were largely water-borne, as were also the later settlers who came from Sumatra and Java. The major cultural influences—Indian, Chinese, Arab and Western—that have helped shape the history of Malaysia also came by sea. The sea was not only a link between Peninsular Malaysia and other countries but acted, in the early days before the establishment of land transport, as a means of contact between neighbouring riverine Malay states within the Peninsula. The Malays of the Archipelago had a reputation for being fine and intrepid sailors, though not all of them used their navigational skill and knowledge of local waters for peaceful purposes. The Straits of Malacca and the neighbouring Indonesian seas were once the haunts of roving bands of pirates.

Interest in those early days centred around the peripheries of the Peninsula where a number of small petty kingdoms were set up near the mouths of rivers commanding lines of movement both coastwise and along the rivers. Most of the sultanates were backed by vast stretches of freshwater swamps lying between coast and interior. In a number of cases (e.g. Perak and Pahang) the territorial chief of a river-mouth settlement exerted control over subsidiary settlements at inland *kuala* sites. The rivers therefore served as the main means of internal transport, linking river-mouth settlements with upstream villages, and providing the only practicable means of penetrating the swamp belt into the interior. However, the Malays found little incentive to venture into the interior apart from an occasional excursion to collect jungle produce and mine tin and gold. On the contrary, settlements tended to be concentrated near the lower reaches of the rivers for agricultural as well as economic reasons, since the further upstream the settlement, the more toll-stations the villagers had to pass through and hence the more taxes they had to pay for their goods.

The rivers on either side of the main watershed of the Peninsula are not long and their catchment areas are small. The western side is broken up by an elaborate network of rivers and hence more accessible by water, whereas the eastern portion is less well served by rivers. Over the last few centuries many of the rivers have altered their courses and some their sizes as a result of river capture. The Pahang River used to flow further south than it does today. The Perak River once ran into the sea at Sungei Dinding. It has also increased its basin through capturing some of the major tributaries of the Sungei Bernam. Most of the larger rivers were sufficiently deep for the shallow-draught sailing craft and rowing boats employed by the Malays. River transport, however, had its share of hazards. All the rivers are perennial, though a local drought might reduce the depth of water below that needed for the larger craft. But floods rather than drought were the major hazards. The rivers exhibit a characteristic flattened profile, being swift and narrow at their headwaters in the mountains and slow, sinuous and broad in the lower reaches. A sudden intensive fall of rain in the upper reaches might send a torrent of water downstream at a rate which the rivers at the lower courses could not adequately cope with. Floods were therefore common. Such floods could occur suddenly with serious damage to river traffic. Because of its heavy rainfall from the northeast monsoon, the eastern part of the Peninsula was more liable to flooding. Sunken timber, rapids and shifting sand bars and sand banks added to the risks of river transport.

Land transport was little developed for a number of reasons. The constantly wet swampy environment inhibited movement on land. The dense jungle was difficult to penetrate. The rugged nature of the mountainous interior was another obstacle to movement. Jungle paths had to be kept clear of fallen tree trunks, and if not in regular use rapidly became overgrown. Further, the elephants and human porters used on these paths and tracks could not carry as large a load as even a small *sampan* could. Elephants were employed chiefly by the aristocracy, but they were an inefficient form of transportation, carrying only small loads, frequently falling ill and occasionally becoming dangerous to handle. As a result, movement on land was limited to movement along footpaths (usually sited on the higher ground of levees) leading from one *kampong* to another, minor excursions into the fringes of settlement to collect jungle produce and occasional ventures into the interior by river and thence by land to the tin and gold diggings. The footpaths and jungle tracks were subsidiary to the rivers, serving to extend the basic transport network formed by the rivers rather than existing as a separate network. Jungle paths also served as connecting links between two river systems. During the fifteenth and sixteenth centuries the *penarekan* or porterage route between the sultanates of Malacca and Pahang followed the Muar River to its headwaters where a short porterage across the watershed enabled travellers to continue their journey to Pahang by way of the Serting and Pahang rivers. Similarly it was possible to travel by river from Pahang to Kelantan by two alternative routes—one following the Pahang–Tembeling rivers across the watershed of the Lebir and into Kelantan via the Lebir and Kelantan rivers, and the other following the Pahang–Jelai rivers across the watershed into Kelantan via the Nenggiri–Galas–Kelantan rivers. Both of these passed through gold country.

The transformation of this early pattern of transport began with the establishment of British rule. Until 1874 the British controlled only the Straits Settlements of Singapore, Penang–Province Wellesley, and Malacca. The founding of the Straits Settlements ushered in an era of active road construction. These roads were, in fact, cart tracks, sinuous and badly surfaced, but a distinct improvement over the traditional foot-paths and jungle tracks. By the last quarter of the nineteenth century a network of cart tracks covering most of Malacca, the eastern half of Singapore island, the eastern side of Penang Island and most of Province Wellesley was established, supplementing the existing river network.

The other parts of the Peninsula were still very much dependent upon rivers for internal transport. With the discovery of the rich tin-fields of Larut, Kinta and the Klang Valleys in the latter half of the nineteenth century, the rivers leading to these regions were called upon to bear the strain of greatly increased traffic. The rivers were the only practicable means of access to the tin deposits, enabling the miners to move their mining equipment and stores inland as well as serving as a means of transporting the ore produced to the coast for eventual export. Mining operations were initially limited to the immediate vicinity of the main rivers and their tributaries, but as these operations gathered momentum the miners began to push further afield in their search for new tin lands. Gradually a new transport pattern evolved. This new pattern still hinged on the waterways, but rivers were supplemented by tracks and footpaths leading from the river banks to mines in the interior.

The extension of British control over the Malay States which began in 1874 paved the way for the large-scale development of the tin resources of the interior. The intensification of mining operations resulted in large quantities of tailings being discharged into the rivers of the main tin-producing states of Perak, Selangor and Negri Sembilan. The control of tin tailings was, in those early days, perfunctory and ineffective. Within a few years the rivers were silted up with tin tailings, and their channels became progressively shallower so that river travel became increasingly hazardous and difficult. The deterioration of the rivers set in just at that stage when the country was being opened up and improved transport and communications were necessary if the pace of development were not to be drastically slowed down.

It was evident that the rivers were no longer capable of coping with the increasing volume of traffic, and that a more reliable and efficient means of transport had to be found. The answer was found in rail transport, and the period of railway construction which began when the first line was completed in 1885 ushered in the modern phase of transport development in Peninsular Malaysia. Built originally to serve the mining industry, the railway system paved the way and set the pattern for the later development of the country. The existence of an excellent skeleton network of rail transport was one of the major factors responsible for the early and phenomenally successful establishment of the rubber industry. The rubber industry, in turn, provided the additional revenue needed to extend the rail system so as to cover most of the Peninsula.

The first phase of rail construction occupied the ten years from 1885 to 1895 when four short lines were laid along western Peninsular Malaysia, each line connecting a coastal port with an inland tin field, and taking over completely from the rivers as the carriers of supplies and tin-ore. The first line linking Port Weld with Taiping was built to serve the then principal mining region of Larut. Then came the Klang–Kuala Lumpur line serving the tin-rich Klang Valley. Similarly a line was built from Port Dickson to the Seremban fields. The fourth line to be completed joined Telok Anson to Ipoh and Batu Gajah, providing through communications to the Kinta Valley, which had displaced Larut as the leading mining region (Fig. 15.1).

The next phase of rail development occupied the period up to 1910, and involved the construction of a north–south trunk line joining the inland mining towns, following the grain of the country and running along the foothill zone where the main tin deposits were to be found. At the same time extensions northwards and southwards were made to the trunk line, and by 1903 through communications were established

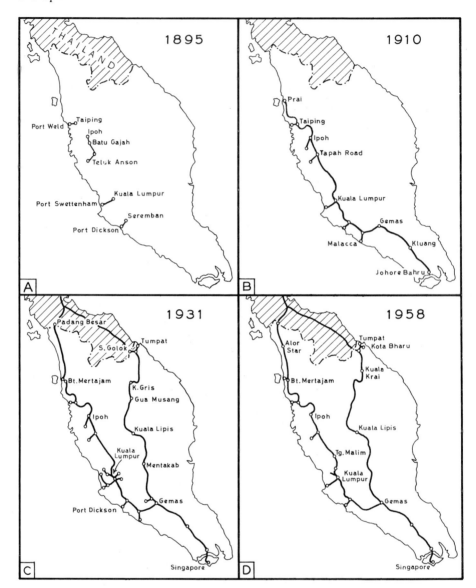

Fig. 15.1   The evolution of the rail network.

between Prai, immediately opposite Penang, and Seremban. The next few years saw further extensions being made southwards, first to Tampin where a branch line connected it to Malacca, then to Gemas, and finally to Johore Bahru. The pattern in 1910 is shown in Fig. 15.1. At this period the rubber-planting fever was reaching its height, and large areas of land were cleared on both sides of the railway line for the new crop.

The next twenty-one years saw the completion of the rail system, and apart from the temporary closure of the East Coast line and some branch lines as a result of the Japanese occupation, the pattern has remained basically the same up to the present day. The Kedah line, completed in 1918, extended the main trunk line further northwards to the Thai border. This line branched off from the main trunk line at Bukit Mertajam, and passed through Province Wellesley, Kedah and Perlis to Padang Besar at the border where it was connected with the Thai rail system. Thus by 1918 there was through communication from Johore Bahru in the south right up to Bangkok. The final southward extension to the railway was made when the causeway across the Johore Straits was built in 1923, connecting Singapore to the Malay Peninsula.

The other major achievement of this period was the construction of the East Coast line, connected with the main trunk line at Gemas. Although work began from Gemas as early as 1907 and from Tumpat in Kelantan in 1912, the line was not completed until 1931. A branch line from Pasir Mas to Sungei Golok was built in 1920. Sungei Golok was the connecting point between the Royal State Railways of Thailand and the Kelantan railway, and later, the East Coast line. Figure 15.1 shows the rail pattern in 1931.

During the Japanese occupation 276 miles (444 km) of line consisting of 200 miles (322 km) of the East Coast line from Mentakab to Krai, and the branch lines of Telok Anson, Tronoh and Malacca, were removed and used in the construction of the Burma—Siam railway. The Telok Anson line was relaid in 1946, but rehabilitation of the East Coast line was not completed until 1953 because of the outbreak of the Emergency in 1948. The Tronoh and the Malacca feeder lines were not replaced. Figure 15.1 shows the postwar pattern.

The development of rail transport in place of rivers was soon followed by complementary development of road transport. In the early days of mining, movement on land was by way of tracks and footpaths connecting mining centres with the nearest navigable river. Later these tracks gave place to bridle paths, and still further improvements came with the construction of cart-tracks designed for slow-moving bullock carts. None of these were metalled, and rivers and streams were crossed by very simple and cheap bridges. The fragmentary road network in the western Malay States were designed to serve the main highways—the rivers. Later, when river transport was replaced by rail, new feeder bridle paths and cart-tracks were constructed between mines, mining towns, administrative centres and the nearest railhead. As in the case of the railways, the additional revenue derived from rubber was used by the state governments to extend the road system. Each state was left to work out its own road system.

Roads did not attain any major significance until the beginning of the twentieth century because the main transport means—bullock-carts—were slow and of limited capacity, and could not in any way compete with the mechanical efficiency and carrying capacity of a locomotive and its rolling stock. But after the introduction of the motor-car in 1902, roads began to attain increasing importance as an alternative means of land transport, and not merely as subsidiary arms of the railway. Roads were systematically overhauled and improved for motor traffic. The standards aimed at were a metalled surface 16 ft (5 m) wide laid over a 22 ft (7 m) foundation between drains, with no gradients outside mountain areas to exceed one in forty. Many of the roads followed the old cart-tracks and were consequently sinuous and indirect. Road-making was considerably facilitated by the abundance of granite and limestone, the two rocks commonly used.

Road construction was so rapid that one decade after the introduction of motor vehicles there was through connection by trunk roads between Prai and Malacca, while another road crossed the mountainous backbone and linked Kuantan on the east coast with the western road system (Fig. 15.2). The very nature of road transport is such that it is more flexible than rail transport and more quickly responsive to changes in local conditions. High traffic density is less imperative to justify the construction of a road (which need not necessarily be of first-class standards until the volume of traffic has grown). They are therefore the most suitable media for linking up scattered points and creating a variety of routes in all directions. For these reasons, and as motorized vehicles came into general use roads began to compete with the railway and gradually a system of trunk roads was built which followed much the same directions in western Peninsular Malaysia as the railway. By 1928 the road network had extended northwards to cover the north-western states of Kedah and Perlis, and southwards to link Johore with the rest of western Peninsular Malaysia. Development in eastern Peninsular Malaysia was confined to a local network serving the Kelantan delta west of the river (Fig. 15.2).

The next decade saw the further expansion of the road network in all the states. The network in the west coast became denser, with subsidiary roads being built as the region was opened up for agricultural and mining development, but it was in the east coast states and Johore that the more important advances were made. In Johore a new road was constructed between Senggarang and Pontian Kechil, thereby completing the network covering the west coast of the state. A road between Kota Tinggi and Mersing similarly provided a direct link between Johore Bahru and the eastern portion of the state. Another road joining Yong Peng and Segamat opened up the rolling country of north-central Johore for rubber and oil-palm cultivation, and also provided an alternative through route north, by-passing Malacca. In Pahang a road from Kuantan was constructed southwards to Pekan, the old capital of the state, providing direct access to the undeveloped Pahang deltaic area. Perhaps the most significant advances were made in Trengganu, which up to 1928 was

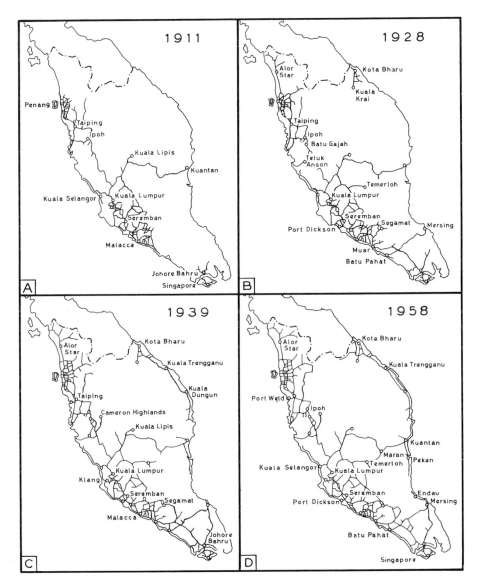

Fig. 15.2   The evolution of the road network.

isolated from the rest of Peninsular Malaysia and only accessible by sea. During the next decade a coast road was built running nearly the length of the state, and linking it with Kelantan though not with Pahang. Figure 15.2 shows the pattern at this stage.

Two major extensions were made in the road system in the early postwar period. The first was a main road linking Kuantan to Chukai, thus providing through communication with the north-eastern states of

391

Trengganu and Kelantan. The other was a 29 mile (47 km) stretch of new road between Temerloh on the Pahang River and Maran on the main east—west trunk road between Kuala Lumpur and Kuantan. The Temerloh—Maran road completed in 1955 by-passes the towns of Bentong, Raub and Kuala Lipis and cuts short, by 72 miles (116 km), the journey from Kuala Lumpur to Kuantan. This east—west road is still the only road link between western Peninsular Malaysia and the three eastern states of Pahang, Trengganu and Kelantan. There was as yet no through road between Johore Bahru and Kota Bharu, as the gap in the road system between Endau and Nenasi had not been bridged. Figure 15.2 shows the early postwar pattern.

A new phase in the history of Malaysian transport was inaugurated when an internal air service between Singapore and Penang began in 1937. The postwar period has seen a progressive expansion of air transport to cover most of the main towns of Peninsular Malaysia.

The present pattern

Two important and interconnected factors have exerted considerable influence in the development of the transport pattern. The first is the physical structure of Peninsular Malaysia—a long, narrow peninsula with extensive coastlines and flat, narrow coastal plains on the west and east separated by a mountainous backbone. The main transport routes by land, sea and air are aligned roughly north—south following the grain of the country, and the pattern is one of parallel coastal shipping, rail, road and air routes with few east—west land connections across the mountain barrier. The rivers of the Peninsula flowing east and west into the South China Sea and the Straits of Malacca are no longer of any consequence as highways, and the old *penarekan* route based on the Muar and Pahang rivers had long been abandoned. Secondly, a combination of circumstances has worked to establish the greatest concentrations of people and industries in western Peninsular Malaysia. This pattern of economic development is reflected in the transport network which shows its greatest and most elaborate development west of the Main Range. Although eastern Peninsular Malaysia (except Trengganu, which is not served by the railway) is connected to the rest of the country by the main arteries of the transport systems, these arteries carry little traffic and have very few branches in the way of feeder roads and feeder railway lines. Nearly all of Peninsular Malaysia's international traffic is carried by sea or by air. The major ports of Penang and Port Klang are the links between internal transport system and overseas transport, while Kuala Lumpur and, to a lesser extent, Penang are the connecting points for international air traffic. Peninsular Malaysia shares a common land frontier with Thailand. Although the frontier is crossed by two railway lines and two roads, most of the traffic between these two countries that goes by land is carried by rail since the road system in southern Thailand is relatively undeveloped.

River and sea transport

Rivers, once the main highways of Peninsular Malaysia, are no longer of significance as a means of communication, and inland water transport is of some importance only in the eastern states of Kelantan, Trengganu and Pahang where much of the interior is roadless and accessible only by river. Such traffic as moves along the river of the Peninsula is highly localized, and is usually made up of small launches and *sampans* moving between points up- or down-stream, or between one *kampong* and another. River transport is greatly hampered by silting of the channels due to mining and by the attendant problem of floods. The continual development of roads, especially in the interior and eastern Peninsular Malaysia, will result in a further decline in the importance of river transport.

Most of the traffic that moves by water is seaborne, being either coastal and local or oceanic and international. Peninsular Malaysia is well-served by a large number of major shipping lines connecting Penang and Port Klang with the United Kingdom, Western Europe, America, Africa, East Asia and Australia, and by local lines which trade with Indonesia, Borneo, the Indo-Chinese states, Burma, Thailand, the Philippines and Hong Kong. Nearly all of the *entrepôt* and import—export trade of Peninsular Malaysia is carried on by ships. In the ten-year period 1964—73 an annual average of 5 000 ships of over 75 net registered tons arrived at and departed from the ports of Peninsular Malaysia. Up to 1970 the cargo loaded exceeded that discharged, but since the closure of the two large iron mines in Dungun and Kuala Rompin in that year the pattern has reversed. In 1973, for example, 9 million tons of cargo were discharged as against 6 million tons loaded.

The ports of Peninsular Malaysia may be divided into three groups. The first consists of the two major ports of Port Klang and Penang, each run by an independent Port Authority. The second is made up of the ports owned and operated by the Malayan Railway Administration, namely Port Dickson, Port Weld and Telok Anson. The third comprises the remaining ports of Peninsular Malaysia—Malacca, Kuantan, Kuala Trengganu and Kota Bharu. In addition there are privately owned wharves and jetties to serve specific industries. An example is the wharf to serve the flourmill at Lumut.

Until the political separation of Singapore from the Federation of Malaysia in 1965 the major ports of Malaysia, in terms of the number of large vessels calling at the port and cargo handled, were Singapore, Penang and Port Klang (then known as Port Swettenham), in that order of importance. With the separation of Singapore, Penang was only able

Table 15.1   Cargo handled by Peninsular Malaysian ports, 1973

	Loaded	*Discharged* (freight tons)	*Total*	*Percentage*
Port Klang	3 464 000	2 960 000	6 424 000	42
Penang	1 405 000	2 356 000	3 761 000	24
Other ports	1 363 000	3 824 000	5 187 000	34
Total	6 232 000	9 140 000	15 372 000	100

to hold on to its new position as the premier port of Peninsular Malaysia up to 1967. By 1968 Port Klang had displaced Penang as the first port; in 1973 it handled 42 per cent of the total cargo of Peninsular Malaysia, as against Penang's 24 per cent (Table 15.1). These two ports together handled two-thirds of the international trade.

Port Klang is situated in a natural harbour protected from the occasional squalls of the Straits of Malacca by a group of islands (Fig. 15.3). The original intention of the Federated Malay States Government was to build a railway port serving west-central Peninsular Malaysia, thereby making the FMS Railway independent of Singapore and Penang, both of which were at that time under the Straits Settlements administration. The port was built on a site south of the point where the Klang River breaks up into an island-studded estuary, a site which however was a poor one from the navigational point of view since berthing and turning

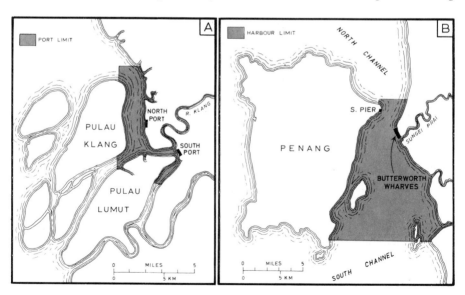

Fig. 15.3   The ports of Klang and Penang.

operations were difficult. The original planned capacity of the port was 400 000 tons a year, but even before the Second World War the volume of traffic had outgrown the port's capacity. Early in the postwar period the volume of traffic had increased to more than twice the planned capacity, so that the expansion of the port became an urgent matter. The main steps taken in the 1960s to increase the port's capacity were the construction of the North Port in the North Klang Straits, consisting of four ocean wharves with a draught of 30 ft (9 m), as well as wharf extensions to the South Port (the original site of Port Klang). The continued increase in the volume of traffic has made it necessary to expand the port even further, and by 1973 a new ocean wharf and a container wharf were added to the North Port.

Port Klang at present consists of the North Port, the South Port and a deepwater anchorage for loading timber and ore from privately owned lighters (Fig. 15.3). The facilities at the South Port include a main wharf of 1 490 ft (454 m) with three berths and 30 to 35 ft of water alongside, a coastal wharf of 950 ft (290 m) with two berths and 20 ft (6 m) of water alongside, and two lighterage wharves. Another wharf of 550 ft (168 m) was opened in 1974. The covered storage accommodation totals 394 000 sq ft (36 600 sq m) while the open storage areas total 120 000 sq ft (11 150 sq m). The North Port is 3½ miles from the South Port, and has five ocean wharves with a total length of 3 390 ft (1 030 m) and a container wharf of 2 100 ft (640 m) capable of accommodating two third-generation container ships or nine conventional vessels. Supporting facilities include transit sheds, a marshalling yard, a freight station and mechanized moving equipment. Plans have been drawn up to further extend the North Port wharves for conventional and container ships.

The port of Penang is the main point of entry and exit of goods to and from the entire north-western region of Peninsular Malaysia. It has a fine natural harbour in the channel between the island of Penang and the mainland. This channel, averaging 2 to 3 miles (3.2–4.8 km) wide, provides a deep and sheltered anchorage for vessels of all types. Approach to the harbour may be by the north channel, which is deeper and usually used by the larger vessels, or by the south channel, used by medium draught vessels. The port itself consists of three sections: Swettenham Pier on Penang Island, Butterworth Wharves on the mainland (Province Wellesley) and the Roads in the Straits of Penang (Fig. 15.3).

Swettenham Pier is 1 200 ft (367 m) long with two berths, each capable of accommodating an ocean-going vessel. The depth of water alongside is 32 ft. Facilities include transit sheds, storage godowns, bulk liquid facilities for palm-oil, coconut oil and latex, as well as mechanical moving equipment. Butterworth Wharves is 2 928 ft (890 m) long, and can berth five ocean-going vessels at any one time. The deepest depth of

Plate 36   The Butterworth wharves north of the Sungei Prai. These wharves are linked directly to the road and rail networks of the mainland (see p. 395).

water alongside is 32 ft. Two of the northern berths can handle container ships. The wharves are directly linked to the road and rail networks of Peninsular Malaysia. Altogether 379 000 sq ft (35 200 sq m) of covered storage space and 140 000 sq ft (13 000 sq m) of open storage space are available. Penang Roads provide a deep and safe anchorage for ships working their cargo to and from lighters. Such cargo is required to be offloaded into Swettenham Pier or Butterworth Wharves.

The other ports that are used to some extent by international shipping are Malacca and Dungun. Malacca, once the greatest port in the Malay Peninsula, has declined steadily in importance because of extensive silting of the harbour, the increased size of shipping and as a result of competition from Port Klang and Penang. It has now become, and in fact has been for the last century, only a lighterage port for occasional ships and small coastal steamers. The number of ships of over 75 net registered tons calling at Malacca has decreased from 217 in 1964 to 151 in 1973. The original *entrepôt* trade of Malacca has completely disappeared with the inclusion of the port in the customs area of Peninsular Malaysia. It now serves to export the rubber produced in its immediate hinterland, and to import some of the general cargo such as rice and sugar consumed in the region. However, the volume of traffic at Malacca is likely to increase in the future as a result of the planned construction of a deepwater jetty at Tanjung Kling, 7 miles (11 km) from Malacca. The depth of water alongside will be 36 ft, and vessels up to 15 000 tons can berth there.

The port of Kuala Dungun in Trengganu handles only a very small amount of commercial cargo, but used to be of considerable importance as a lighter port for the iron-ore shipped from Bukit Besi to Japan. Although iron was mined all the year round at Bukit Besi, shipment was possible only during the months of March to October because the lack of shelter at the port prevented it from being used during the northeast monsoon. The ore was loaded into lighters at Kampong Sura, south of the mouth of the Dungun River, and transported to the ore-ships at anchor a mile or so out to sea. The closure of the iron-mine has seen a sharp decrease in the volume of traffic. The number of ships calling at Dungun dropped from 140 in 1964 to only twenty-four in 1973.

The major ports of Peninsular Malaysia are connected to a large number of minor ports on both sides of the Peninsula by ships that ply the coastal trade (Fig. 15.4). Coastal shipping attained its greatest importance as a means of internal transport during the period after the First World War and before the mid-1920s when lorry transport established itself as a serious competitor for much of the traffic carried by rail and by coasters. In general, the development of road transport has had an adverse effect on coastal shipping in that it drove the railways out of short hauls, and into direct competition with shipping for the longer coastal trades. The position of coastal shipping has declined still further after the Second World War because of the great increase in the capital and running costs of small ships.

This competition between land and local sea transport has been most marked in western Peninsular Malaysia where the development of extensive networks of roads and railways has resulted in the relative decline of coastal shipping, but in eastern Peninsular Malaysia where land transport is still skeletal in pattern, movement by sea still retains much of its original significance. However, a number of physical handicaps stand in the way of sea transport development along the east coast. The northeast monsoon restricts movement by small coastal vessels during the months of November to March. The coast itself consists of a series of monotonous flat beaches shelving very gently seawards and interrupted at intervals by river mouths. All of the minor ports of the east coast are located at or near to a river mouth. The entrance to every port is obstructed by a shifting sand bar. The shallow approaches and the sand bar limit the use of such ports to small vessels with a shallow draught.

An average of about 3 000 vessels of over 75 net registered tons with a total tonnage of over 1 million tons as well as a very large number of small vessels are engaged in the coastal trade, calling at the major ports of Klang and Penang as well as the minor ports of Malacca, Port Dickson, Telok Anson, Muar, Batu Pahat, Port Weld, Lumut along the west coast,

Fig. 15.4   The pattern of sea and air transport, 1973.

and Dungun, Kuantan, Kuala Trengganu and Kota Bharu on the east coast. In general the coastal traffic that moves through the minor ports is small for a country that has over 1 000 miles of coast. This is partly a result of adverse physical conditions which make movement by sea difficult along the east coast during the northeast monsoon, and in part a consequence of the high level of development of other forms of transport.

The pattern of sea transport will undergo a significant change in the latter part of the 1970s with the development of two ports at Kuantan, Pahang and at Pasir Gudang, Johore (Fig. 15.4). The new Kuantan port

Plate 37   Tanjung Gelang, the site of the new port north of Kuantan. Two mile-long breakwaters will be constructed to provide a harbour capable of handling large vessels.

will be sited at Tanjung Gelang, about 16 miles (25 km) north of Kuantan town. The plan is to develop a modern port over a period of five years, capable of handling vessels of up to 35 000 tons deadweight. The harbour will be protected by two mile-long breakwaters. The port will draw its hinterland from the east coast states, and will be the first east coast port equipped for year-round shipping. It will also be the nearest major port to Sabah and Sarawak, and will facilitate the movement of goods between the Peninsula and these states.

The second port being developed is at Pasir Gudang about 20 miles (32 km) east of Johore Bharu. A major shipyard with two drydocks of 400 000 and 140 000 tons capacity will be established within the port area.

Rail transport

The basic pattern of the rail network covering the Peninsula was established as early as 1931 with the completion of the East Coast line. With the exceptions of the gaps caused by the removal of the Malacca and Tronoh branch lines during the Japanese occupation, the present rail network is essentially the same as in 1931, shaped in the form of the

399

letter Y, the left arm being the western and main line, the right arm the East Coast line, and the trunk of the Y running down the centre of Johore and joining both arms to Johore Bahru and Singapore. All three lines meet at Gemas. The main line runs from Singapore to Kuala Lumpur and Prai, a total distance of 488 miles (785 km). Prai is connected to Penang by ferry. The western line continues from Prai to Padang Besar where it joins the State Railway of Thailand. Despite its name, the East Coast line does not run parallel and adjacent to the coast, but through the interior of Pahang and Kelantan between the Main Range and the Trengganu Highlands, by-passing Trengganu altogether. The railway operates wharves at Port Dickson, Telok Anson and Port Weld, all connected to the main line by branch lines (Fig. 15.5).

Physical conditions in Peninsular Malaysia are not very favourable to railway construction and maintenance. The orographic barrier of the Main Range has prevented the construction of an east–west line, and Kelantan can be reached by rail from west-central Peninsular Malaysia only by going north to Haadyai Junction in Thailand and then south by the East Coast line. The ruling gradient is 1 : 100 except in the Taiping Pass section where it is 1 : 80. While it has been relatively easy to lay lines without exceeding the ruling gradient along the low-lying and gently undulating country in western Peninsular Malaysia and central Johore, the construction of the East Coast line across the rugged terrain of northern Pahang and southern Kelantan was difficult and expensive, and in places involved tunnelling through granite masses.

Heavy rainfall and occasional floods add to the difficulties and cost of railway maintenance. Persistent and excessive falls, especially during the northeast monsoon, may cause landslips and landslides in cuttings and embankments in unstable soil. Floods may inundate portions of the track in both eastern and western Peninsular Malaysia, and railway bridges are sometimes washed away in serious floods.

The establishment of a north–south rail network following the grain of the country entailed the spanning of numerous east–west-flowing rivers by bridges, thereby adding considerably to the cost. Other conditions are, however, otherwise more favourable to railway construction than in many other parts of the tropics. Material suitable for ballast is obtained from the railway-owned granite and limestone quarries at Kodiang, Ipoh, Kuala Lipis and Segamat. Local coal, though poor in quality, was available in sufficient quantity from the Batu Arang coalfields to supply the needs of the entire system until the changeover to oil as a source of fuel. Local hardwood sleepers, pressure-creosoted in the railway plant at Gemas, are sufficiently durable to resist the ravages of climate and white ants for periods up to twelve years. Timber from local hardwood forests is also used for coach building.

The railway provides passenger and freight services within Peninsular Malaysia as well as between Peninsular Malaysia and Singapore on the

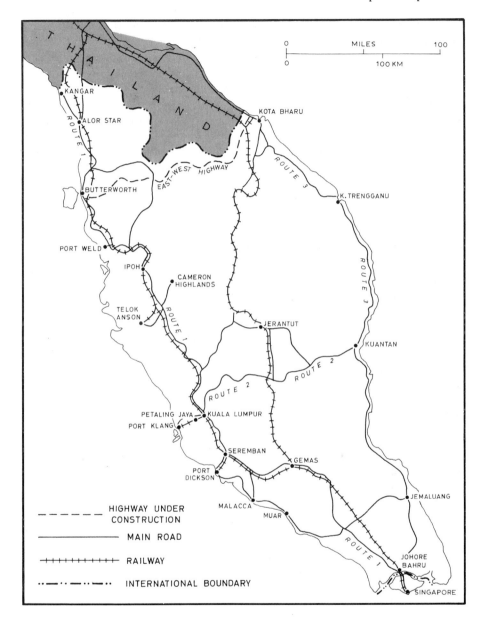

Fig. 15.5   The land transport pattern, 1973.

south, and Thailand on the north. The traffic pattern reflects closely the pattern of economic activities, with the western (and main) line carrying the greatest traffic and the East Coast line insufficient traffic to cover running costs. The greatest passenger loads are carried on the main line linking Singapore, Kuala Lumpur, Ipoh and Prai. The railway handles

401

about 18 per cent of the total tonnage of goods traffic in the country, as compared with 40 per cent handled in 1961. However, the railway has a competitive edge in the movement of long distance bulk traffic such as petroleum, cement, timber and logs, rubber and latex, palm-oil, rice and fertilizers. It carries about half of all such bulk traffic in Peninsular Malaysia each year.

The serious and increasing competition from road and air transport has made major inroads into the passenger service section of the railway. The total number of passengers carried by the railway in the ten-year period 1964--73 has decreased from 6 million in 1964 to 5.6 million in 1973, while the average revenue per net ton mile for goods traffic has also dropped. The result has been a net operating loss of a few million dollars for the railway each year.

In order to make the railway more competitive and economically viable a programme of rehabilitation and modernization was initiated during the Second Malaysia Plan period (1970–75). The steps to be taken include the dieselization of the railway and the replacement of out-of-date rolling stock. The dieselization programme was completed in 1972 with the purchase of forty new and powerful diesel–electric locomotives which can haul higher loads, thereby reducing the unit cost of operations. Repair and maintenance costs will also be reduced considerably as all the wagons over forty-five years old are replaced by new wagons with greater loading capacities and greater speed capability.

Road transport

Peninsular Malaysia has the best road system in Southeast Asia. Roads provide access to all the developed parts of the country. The main roads in western Peninsular Malaysia follow closely the line taken by the main railway as evidenced by the fact that the roads and the railway lines meet or come within half a mile of each other at over a hundred places, and are never more than 15 miles (24 km) apart throughout the length of the Peninsula. The main roads along the much less developed eastern sector, however, do not run side by side with the East Coast railway (which passes through the interior) but hug the coastline (in the case of the Kota Bharu to Johore Bahru trunk road). Another road runs in an east–west direction joining Kuantan to Kuala Lumpur, while in Johore a similar east–west road joins Batu Pahat, Kluang and Mersing. A road from Mersing to Johore Bahru through Kota Tinggi serves eastern Johore (Fig. 15.5). The areas served by the road and the rail systems do not overlap in eastern Peninsular Malaysia so that the keen competition between the two forms of transport in western Peninsular Malaysia does not exist in this part of the country. The coastal alignment of the road network in the eastern states emphasizes the interest in coastal sites, recalling conditions in the Peninsula during the nineteenth century and earlier when most of the people were concentrated in riverine and deltaic locations.

The main roads are connected to and augmented by an elaborate network of other feeder roads, more especially along western Peninsular Malaysia. The result is a pattern composed of a dense network of roads running the length of the Peninsula along its western side from Perlis to south Johore, and on the eastern side, a skeleton system of roads running from Kota Bharu and the Kelantan delta southwards through the Trengganu coast to Kuantan, Pekan on the Pahang River, and to Johore Bahru. The road pattern reflects the peripheral development of Peninsular Malaysia, the continuing interest in coastal sites for development and settlement, and the large central mountainous and swampy areas between the two coastal networks of roads that still remain unopened and inaccessible except by river and tracks.

There are 10 950 miles (17 600 km) of developed roads in Peninsular Malaysia, of which over 80 per cent are paved. About 30 per cent of the roads are Federal roads, 65 per cent state roads and the remainder municipal roads. The three Federal Highways (Routes 1, 2 and 3) are the main trunk roads. Route 1 is the main trunk road from Johore Bahru to the Thai border, serving the western economic heartland of the country. Route 2 runs from Port Klang to Kuantan, a distance of nearly 200 miles (320 km), while Route 3 is the stretch of 237 miles (380 km) from Kuantan to Kota Bharu (Fig. 15.5).

The Federal road network will be extended under the Second Malaysia Plan. The most important project is the East–West Highway which will link Kelantan on the east coast to Penang on the west (Fig. 15.5). The plan calls for the construction of a 75 mile (120 km) road joining Jeli in Kelantan to Kampong Kuala Rui in Perak. The highway will rise to a maximum elevation of about 3 000 ft (900 m) above sea-level and will be a two-way highway with provision for widening in the future. The completion of this highway will pave the way for the further development of the isolated east coast states of Kelantan and Trengganu. The second Federal road project is the Kuantan–Segamat highway, which will be 112 miles (180 km) long and will provide access to the Pahang–Tenggara region. The third project is the realignment and relocation of the part of Route 2 between Kuala Lumpur and Karek.

Most of the roads of Peninsular Malaysia have a bituminous surface which provides a good riding surface. Vehicles last much longer on these roads than on, say, the unpaved, corrugated roads of many parts of Africa, where it has been estimated that a car using such roads has a life of only about 20 000 miles (32 187 km). Many of the tortuous bends which were a characteristic feature of the early roads have been straightened out and banked. Road gradients are fairly gentle except in mountainous country. Owing to the wet conditions which prevail all the year round, a waterproof surface is necessary if a road is to carry even light traffic. Waterproofing is usually through the use of bitumen. A related problem of road construction in an equatorial setting is the need to drain away the water that runs off the road surface. In urban areas the road-side drains also function as antimalarial drains, while in rural areas they may be combined with land drainage and padi irrigation canals. A further problem is that of bridging the numerous rivers, especially in the coastal plains where the rivers are wide and shallow. The construction of culverts and bridges add considerably to the costs of road making. Many of the rivers, particularly in eastern Peninsular Malaysia, were not bridged but were crossed by ferries. Up to 1974 all but the ferries at the Endau and Rompin rivers had been replaced by permanent bridges.

Road construction is facilitated by the abundance of good road-stone, generally within a short haul of the job. Most of the stone quarries are owned by the Public Works Department. Road maintenance costs are nevertheless high due to the need for keeping down vegetation on the side margins, and the need to keep the drains as well as the road surface in good order. Construction and maintenance costs vary over the different classes of roads, and here lies one of the main advantages of road over rail in an underdeveloped tropical country, namely, the possibility of beginning modestly and improving the standards as traffic grows, whereas in the case of railways the full cost of a prohibitively high standard must be borne at the outset.

Road traffic in Peninsular Malaysia comprises all types of wheeled vehicles from the bullock-cart, bicycle and trishaws to large motor lorries. Table 15.2 shows the number and types of motor vehicles registered in 1973.

Table 15.2   Motor vehicles registered in Peninsular Malaysia, 1973

	Number
Motor-cycles	507 000
Motor-cars	317 000
Buses	7 300
Taxis and hire-cars	7 500
Lorries and vans	72 000
Road rollers, trailers, etc.	29 000
Total	939 800

There is in addition a very large number of bicycles both in urban and rural areas. In the rural areas the bicycle is the universal carrier, carrying heavy and bulky loads along roads as well as cart-tracks and footpaths not normally accessible to motor vehicles. Bullock-carts are still in use in some localities. In the urban centres motor-cycles, cars, buses, taxis and bicycles are the common means of transport. The number of motor

Plate 38   A ferry at Endau, Johore. Such ferries once common along the main east coast road are rapidly becoming relics of the past. At the time of writing only two of the rivers on the east coast have not been bridged—the Endau and Rompin rivers. Plans are already on hand to replace these two ferries with permanent bridges.

Plate 39   The Batu Pahat bridge spanning the Batu Pahat River. The construction of this bridge and a similar one at Muar has eliminated the two main bottlenecks to road traffic between Johore and Malacca.

405

vehicles has increased greatly in the larger towns such as Kuala Lumpur, Ipoh and Penang, creating problems of traffic congestion which are difficult to solve because of the narrow streets of these unplanned towns. Trishaws are also employed for passenger transport in urban areas. Buses operate on all the major and most of the minor roads of Peninsular Malaysia. Lorries are usually employed for freight hauling, and in the transportation of less bulky goods have a distinct advantage over the railway in that goods are carried from door to door without the need for any transference. An increasingly large number of private cars are being used for personal transportation in town and country.

Air transport

Air transport has become an accepted and important means of movement in the postwar world. The declaration of a State of Emergency in 1948 had the effect of greatly increasing the number of people travelling by air between the main towns as neither road nor rail travel was very safe. Many small landing grounds were constructed throughout the Peninsula for use by military light aircraft and, with the ending of the Emergency, they have become useful to civil aviation.

Up to 1971 Peninsular Malaysia and Singapore ran a joint national carrier known as Malaysia—Singapore Airlines (MSA) which had a monopoly of the domestic and international air services in the two countries. However, in 1972 this airline was split and reorganized into two separate national airlines, the Malaysian carrier being named the Malaysian Airline System (MAS). Coinciding with the birth of MAS was the completion of a National Airport Master Plan which will provide guidelines on the development of new and existing airports in Peninsular Malaysia as well as Sarawak and Sabah.

Table 15.3   Air traffic at Peninsular Malaysian airports, 1973

Airport	Aircraft landings and take-offs		Number of passengers		Cargo		Mail	
	Number	Per cent	Number	Per cent	Tonnes	Per cent	Tonnes	Per cent
Kuala Lumpur	31 438	56	1 172 939	65	6 672	76	1 374	74
Penang	12 232	22	441 231	25	1 831	21	239	13
Ipoh	4 313	8	72 788	4	101	1	86	5
Malacca	2 886	5	24 395	1	75	1	13	—
Kota Bharu	1 670	3	55 322	3	87	1	89	5
Kuantan	1 340	2	12 060	1	29	—	19	1
Alor Star	638	1	6 138	—	12	—	12	—
Others	2 016	3	9 680	1	19	—	32	2
Total	56 533	100	1 794 553	100	8 826	100	1 864	100

There are two international airports in Peninsular Malaysia, Kuala Lumpur and Penang. Kuala Lumpur airport at Subang is fully equipped to handle its growing international traffic. The importance of Kuala Lumpur airport is attested by the large number of passengers and the amount of general cargo and mail handled (Table 15.3). Penang airport is the second busiest in the country. The number of aircraft landings and take-offs at these two airports has increased steadily in the past decade. In contrast the volume of traffic at the other airports has shown little or no increase.

Recent developments include the opening of a new airport at Senai, near Johore Bahru, which will form the southernmost link in the internal air transport system (Fig. 15.4) and will also facilitate direct air links between the southern part of the Peninsula and Sabah and Sarawak. The new national airline will be acquiring wide-bodied aircraft as it extends its international services. Feeder services within Sabah and Sarawak will probably be taken over by the newly formed airline in East Malaysia.

16
Problems and prospects

In less than two centuries Peninsular Malaysia has emerged from obscurity to occupy an outstanding place among the new nations of Southeast Asia. For most of this period it was a colony, a small part of the British Empire. The revolutionary changes that have occurred in this country were by-products of colonialism: the development of an economy based on agriculture, mining and trade, and the transformation of a homogeneous society into a multi-racial one were the fruits of a policy which delegated to Peninsular Malaysia, as indeed to the other British colonies, a role as a source of raw materials and a market for British manufactured goods. In fulfilling this role, Peninsular Malaysia started with two natural advantages. Its western coastline adjoins the narrow Straits of Malacca, one of the great trade routes of the world along which pass the ships plying between Western Europe and the Far East. From the earliest times Peninsular Malaysia has been in a position to take advantage of the opportunities for trade afforded by this sea-way crowded with traffic. Malacca, of historic fame, and, more recently, Penang, Singapore and Port Swettenham served as convenient refuelling stations and as points of entry and exit for goods and people.

The other natural advantage was in possessing some of the richest tin resources of the world in an easily accessible and easily mined form. The revenue derived from the development of these resources paved the way for the early establishment of modern land transport which in turn was one of the main factors contributing to the remarkable rise of the rubber industry. Tin was the magnet which drew in thousands of Chinese miners, just as much as rubber was later to draw in further thousands of Indian labourers. The material results of the development of the tin and rubber industries are striking. Physically, it led to the opening up of large expanses of once unproductive forests. A country which less than a century ago had only about 500 000 acres (202 000 ha) under crops now has almost 7 million acres (2.8 million ha) cultivated, and a further 600 000 acres (243 000 ha) alienated for mining. In addition one-third of the total land area of the Peninsula is under productive and protective forest reserves. The attendant benefits of prosperity have permeated into

408

all phases of life, in the forms of modern health and medical facilities, roads, railways, schools and universities, and social services. Equally striking was the parallel expansion of population following upon the influx of great numbers of immigrants from China, India and Indonesia.

In the early days of the colonial era the major problem was the comparatively straightforward one of locating the natural resources of the country, assessing their potentialities and developing them. Development was along *laissez-faire* lines. The colonial government regulated many, and established some, of the economic and social institutions necessary for such development to take place. Likewise it brought stability to a land once racked by internal strife, and ensured that the returns of production were not seized upon by the exercise of arbitrary right. In an atmosphere which saw everyone preoccupied with making a living, and some with accumulating a fortune, it was not surprising that politics were relegated to the background. There was little friction among the different peoples not only because there was plenty of land and room for expansion, but also because they did not compete for the same jobs. This divergence of economic interests among the races also meant that their settlements were physically separate. The Malays and the immigrant Indonesians continued growing padi along river and coast. The other immigrants, on the other hand, were drawn to the towns, villages, tin-mines and estates along what later came to be known as the Tin and Rubber Belt of western Peninsular Malaysia, between the coast and the Main Range.

The present level of economic development was not attained without many mistakes and failures caused through lack of understanding of and adaptation to the environmental conditions of the Peninsula. Many thousands of acres of land were destroyed by the 'land-mining' techniques adopted by the early planters in their search for quick profits. The top-soil from further thousands of acres of rubber land was stripped off by erosion because the planters kept the estates clean-weeded in the manner of orchards in Europe. During the earlier and extremely destructive phase of tin-mining, whole countrysides were exposed to severe erosion because of the removal of the protective forest cover, while the natural regime of many of the rivers of west-central Peninsular Malaysia was permanently disrupted through the uncontrolled discharge of mining effluent into the riverbeds.

The European as well as Asian pioneers were also confronted from the onset with the problem of health maintenance in a country rife with many deadly endemic and epidemic diseases. The hot, wet climate is highly favourable to the development of a large number of diseases as well as of the vectors which transmit them. Vector-borne diseases are especially dangerous because the physical conditions are ideal for the year-round propagation of many of the vectors, notably insects. Perhaps the most deadly and certainly the most notorious of the disease-carrying insects is the anopheline mosquito which transmits malaria. Climatic conditions are continuously favourable to mosquito life, and malaria took a heavy toll of life before effective measures were discovered to control the disease. The extensive clearing of forested land for tin-mining, rubber cultivation, fuel, for the construction of roads and rail-ways and other forms of land-use inevitably disturbed the ecological balance of nature, and where such clearing took place on hilly and undulating land drained by swift-flowing streams, led to the rapid multiplication of *Anopheles maculatus*. Since the most suitable locations for rubber are the free-draining foothills of western Peninsular Malaysia, the rubber estates suffered heavily from malaria transmitted by *A. maculatus*, with mortality rates reaching 63 per 1 000 in 1911. But over the years malaria and the other major tropical diseases such as cholera were brought under control, and today the developed parts are among the healthiest areas in the tropical world. But constant vigilance by the health authorities is needed to keep this record, for the breakdown of health and medical services during the latter days of the Japanese occupation has shown how easily and quickly malaria, cholera, smallpox, yaws and other endemic and epidemic diseases can sweep across the country once health measures are relaxed.

When the new Government achieved independence for the country in 1957, it inherited a land rich by the standards normally applied to tropical areas. The *per capita* income was, and still is, one of the highest in Asia. But in common with many other countries there is a marked imbalance in the distribution of income, with the rural smallholders, engaged in small-scale agriculture and fishing, occupying the lowest rungs in the income ladder.

Many factors are responsible for the poverty of these smallholders. One of the most important is the difficult physical environment of the Peninsula. The climate, with its constantly high temperature and humidity, and especially its monotony, is a handicap to the efficient working of farmers and fishermen engaged mainly in outdoor manual work. They are also regularly exposed to disease-carrying mosquitoes, mites, flies and other insects, and the nature of the occupations is such that they are often in contact with infected soil. Living as they do, on an inadequate and badly balanced diet, in insanitary surroundings and without proper medical facilities, it is not surprising that they find it difficult if not impossible to maintain a high level of health and efficiency. Their output consequently is low. The great number and variety of insects and other pests which flourish in the hot and humid climate also contribute directly to the low output by attacking the farmers' crops. Moreover, as noted earlier, the soils of the Peninsula are, with few exceptions, infertile and easily eroded, and require regular fertilization to support good crops. Few of the farmers use fertilizers, mainly because they are too poor to be able to afford them, but also because some of them are not convinced of their value. This vicious circle of low output and low incomes is difficult to break.

But the low living standards of the smallholders are also caused by other non-physical factors. Rural indebtedness, poor marketing and transport facilities in the rural districts, excessive price fluctuations, agricultural holdings which are too small for their labour capacity and made smaller year by year through increasing pressure of population on the land, through land laws and customs which lead to the repeated subdivision and fragmentation of land, and insecurity of land tenure, among others, are also directly or indirectly responsible.

Coupled with these are the less tangible, but no less important, questions of the prevailing social and religious attitudes towards economic matters. Smallholders who place custom and religion above economic status, would understandingly find it difficult to change their outlook overnight, even assuming that they do want to change it. Most economists writing on the problems of developing the underdeveloped countries conceive of the internal impetus to economic development as coming through an increase in the consumptive wants of the people, which will in turn generate the incentive to earn more money in order to be able to satisfy these wants. Such a move implies the acceptance of the Western principle of insatiability, with economic and material considerations instead of social and cultural factors occupying the foremost place in the scale of values. To bring about an adoption of such values, assuming again that it is desirable to do so, is more an educational and sociological problem than an economic one, although it has undoubted economic implications.

The economic elevation of the rural (as well as the urban) poor is one of the objectives of the New Economic Policy. The strategy is to modernize the rural sector through the development of infrastructural facilities such as roads, water supplies, electricity, educational and training centres emphasizing science and technology; through the establishment of governmental institutions such as rural banks, the Farmers' Organization Authority (FOA), the National Padi and Rice Authority (LPN), the Malayan Rubber Development Corporation (MRDC), the Rubber Industry Smallholders' Development Authority (RISDA) and the Credit Guarantee Corporation (CGC) which will extend financial, capital, marketing and technical assistance to the rural sector; and through the opening up of new farmland by the major land development agencies—the Federal Land Development Authority (FELDA), the Federal Land Consolidation and Rehabilitation Authority (FELCRA), RISDA, and the State Economic Development Corporations (SEDC). Included in the land development programmes are the masterplans drawn up for the comprehensive and integrated development of the Pahang Tenggara and Johore Tenggara areas (Fig. 16.1). The Pahang Tenggara region covers about 2.4 million acres (971 000 ha) in southeast Pahang, of which nearly half is

Plate 40   Clearing land for cultivation in the Hutan Percha FELDA Scheme, Malacca. Such bare land is an unusual sight in Peninsular Malaysia. It marks the first phase in the conversion of forested land into crop land (see p. 411).

suitable for agriculture. It is the largest contiguous area of potential agricultural land in Peninsular Malaysia. The Johore Tenggara region covers about 700 000 acres (283 000 ha), of which about 300 000 acres (121 000 ha) are potential agricultural land.

All these measures represent a concrete effort on the part of the Government to move away from the *laissez-faire* attitude of its colonial past towards the direction whereby the future growth of the hitherto neglected rural sector is shaped and guided by conscious planning. To this end, and in order to combat the twin problems of inflation and stagnation, the Government launched a programme at the end of 1974 which seeks to double food production to the level of self-sufficiency and to increase the earnings of the rural people. Named the Green Book Plan, the programme called for the creation of development policies and strategies at central, state and district levels; the full concentration of government machinery in production and marketing activities of rural produce; and organizing the rural people and channelling their efforts through institutional and agricultural agencies to increase their productivity.

There is a real danger, however, that the rate of growth in the rural as well as the other sectors of the national economy may be too slow in

412

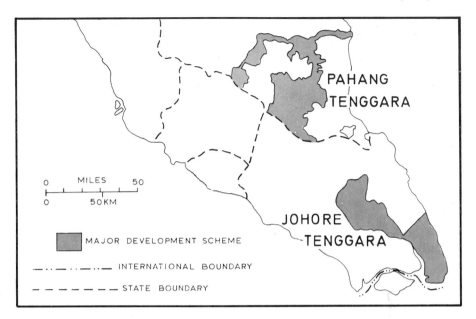

Fig. 16.1   The Pahang Tenggara and the Johore Tenggara areas.

relation to the rate of population increase to make for a net increase in the overall standards of living. The rate of natural increase of the population in Peninsular Malaysia is 2.7 per cent per annum. It is safe to assume that large-scale immigration will no longer be a factor of importance in the future growth of the population, and that such growth will depend on the excess of births over deaths. Death rates have fallen with the spread of modern medical science to cover all sections of the population, but birth rates continue to be high among each of the main racial groups. The question of birth control, a complex one in any society, is even more complex in Peninsular Malaysia where the peoples differ so widely in their history, culture, language, religion and education. In general most of the population are by nature conservative in outlook, and traditional family practices tend towards large families. Under such circumstances resistance to any form of family planning is likely to be high.

It is necessary to find ways and means of encouraging the expansion of the economy to keep pace with the rate of population increase. At the same time it is vital to ensure that economic expansion be channelled along lines that will reduce the country's extreme vulnerability to world market fluctuations. Although Peninsular Malaysia was the most successful colony in Southeast Asia from the economic point of view, its success has been achieved at the expense of a lack of balance in the economy. Like most other colonial countries, Peninsular Malaysia had a set function—to produce only those goods which gave the best returns,

413

namely, rubber and tin. Most of its needs have had to be imported. The result was an inflexible economic structure, ill-equipped to withstand the strains caused by changes of up to 30 per cent in the national income in a single year.

As seen earlier, this lopsided economy was the result of a colonial policy which allowed the free entry of private foreign investment into the primary export sector; free international trade with low tariff rates; a free internal market system to stimulate export expansion; and which, in following the principle of comparative advantage in resource allocation, led Peninsular Malaysia to specialize in the production of tin and rubber for the export market. Accordingly, when the country gained its independence in 1957, she had a well-developed export sector; an under-developed and largely neglected domestic sector; and a manufacturing sector confined mainly to the processing of agricultural products. The relative importance of the primary sector is seen in the high percentage (61%) of the labour force engaged in agriculture, forestry, fishing, mining and quarrying in 1957.

The declared policy of the independent Government was to diversify the country's economy through industrialization while retaining the established methods of economic development through export expansion. The extent to which it has progressed can be gauged by the fact that the percentage of the labour force engaged in the primary sector decreased to 52 in 1970, while that engaged in the secondary sector (manufacturing and construction) increased from 9 in 1957 to 14 in 1970. The economy of Peninsular Malaysia today can be regarded as being in a transitional stage towards self-sustained growth, with an increasing share of the gross domestic product contributed by manufacturing.

Diversification of the economy has also been pursued in the traditional primary sector. In mining, the dominance of tin has been further emphasized by the sharp decline in iron-ore production. The output of bauxite has remained at around the same level since 1966, and is not likely to show any marked increase because of the limited extent of the deposits. However, the pattern of mining is likely to change dramatically in the future with the development of the petroleum and natural gas fields which have been located off the east coast.

Diversification has progressed furthest in agriculture. The introduction of new crops into the agricultural scene presents many problems. In the first instance the crops must be suitable for cultivation in an equatorial environment, that is, they must be capable of giving sustained yields over a period of time without straining the fertility of the soil. In the Malay Peninsula, where the climax vegetation is composed of trees, perennials such as trees and shrubs will be ecologically more suitable for cultivation than annuals. Unlike the shallow-rooted annuals which require continuous cropping and rapidly deplete the soil fertility, perennials remain

414

on the land for several years so that the soil is little disturbed. Their foliage, augmented by cover crops, shade and protect the soil from the direct effects of solar radiation and from being eroded by the heavy rains. Moreover, most perennials yield regular and frequent crops, an important feature if they are to be taken up on a wide scale for small-holder cultivation as this means that the farmers will have income at regular intervals and are less liable to be forced into debt to meet their daily needs. But, as pointed out earlier, the ecological advantage of perennials is marred by two serious economic handicaps. Perennials suffer from both short-run and long-run price inelasticity of supply. Because they have long economic life-spans they tend to immobilize land and other fixed capital for lengthy periods of time.

Moreover, planters taking up the cultivation of any new crops will have to face competition from other tropical areas growing the same crops. Such areas might have advantages derived from an early start and established markets, from some peculiarly favourable physical factor of soil or climate, or from proximity to markets. Most of the known tropical crops are already grown on an extensive scale in one tropical country or another, and any attempt to compete with an established rival territory implies a capacity to produce the same crop cheaper or better, provided that the market for the crop is not already saturated.

Nevertheless the range of crops cultivated in Peninsular Malaysia has been significantly enlarged in the last decade—through the expansion of the oil-palm industry, and the cultivation of sugar-cane, cocoa, tapioca and maize on a commercial scale.

The economic base has therefore been significantly broadened in the last fifteen years through industrialization and through diversification of the traditional primary sector. However such diversification will not, *ipso facto*, reduce price fluctuations unless the new products are stable in price and profits or unless such prices and profits move in a direction counter to that of the products currently being produced and exported.

Viewed in general terms, Malaysia (including Peninsular Malaysia) shares two major problems with many other developing countries—the promotion of national unity and identity and the uplifting of the material welfare of the people. The first problem is being tackled through a series of measures designed to promote common values and loyalties among all communities. In education, language, literature, art and music the main objective is to foster the sense of belonging to one society and one nation.

The May 1969 riots are an indication of the tragedy that can happen to a country that remains divided. They have added a new sense of urgency to the attainment of national unity. But, as has been pointed out, national unity cannot be achieved if economic conditions create deep cleavages within the country. As stated in the Second Malaysia Plan (pp. 3–4):

National unity is unattainable without greater equity and balance among Malaysia's social and ethnic groups in their participation in the development of the country, and in the sharing of the benefits of modernization and economic growth. National unity cannot be fostered if vast sections of the population remain poor and if sufficient productive employment opportunities are not created for the expanding labour force.

To correct these economic anomalies the Government formulated the New Economic Policy (NEP). The NEP seeks to promote national unity through (a) the reduction and eventual eradication of poverty by raising income levels and increasing employment opportunities for Malaysians, irrespective of race; and (b) the restructuring of Malaysian society to correct the existing economic imbalance so as to reduce and ultimately eliminate the identification of race with economic function.

Differences in the distribution of income among Malaysians are marked. The post-enumeration survey of the 1970 Census of Population on the distribution of household income indicates that the mean household income in Peninsular Malaysia was only M$264 per month. While the mean household income of the Chinese was 48 per cent higher and that of the Indians 15 per cent higher than the national average, that of the Malays was 35 per cent lower. The poverty line has been taken as M$130 or below by the Economic Planning Unit. On this basis, 40 per cent of the households enumerated were living in poverty, the Malays making up three-quarters of this group.

There is a close correlation between income levels and sectoral employment. Thus most (70%) of the poor were employed in agriculture and primary production, mainly as coconut and rubber smallholders, single-crop padi farmers, tenants and sharecroppers in padi cultivation and inshore fishermen. Their low productivity and low incomes were due to uneconomic sized and often fragmented holdings, traditional farming methods and lack of access to modern agricultural imports and techniques. In contrast the productivity of the Chinese engaged in mining, manufacturing and construction was two to three times higher; their incomes were consequently higher.

The poor in the urban areas were mainly those engaged in low productivity urban activities such as petty trading, hawking, domestic services and a variety of unskilled occupations. Most of them live in congested dwellings, often in squalid conditions.

The two objectives of the NEP, of eradicating poverty and correcting economic imbalance, are complementary to each other. For example, programmes aimed at raising productivity and incomes in the largely Malay rural sector will not only increase the living standards of this section of the population but will also help to correct racial economic imbalance. In the same manner measures to correct such racial economic

416

imbalance in the urban areas by increasing the participation of Malays and other *bumiputras* (sons of the soil) in new urban activities will also serve to raise living standards through the generation of new employment opportunities.

The objectives of the NEP are to be realized within a period of twenty years from 1970. They are ambitious objectives, aimed at influencing growth along lines which will create a new society at the end of this century, a society in which absolute poverty and racial economic imbalance will no longer be obstacles to national unity and harmony. Their attainment will undoubtedly demand the full utilization of all the physical and human resources of the country.

Appendix: Time chart showing major political changes in the Malay Peninsula and Borneo

Year	Event
Year	*Event*
1786	Occupation of *Penang* (Prince of Wales Island) by the British East India Company.
1800	Occupation of *Province Wellesley* by the British East India Company.
1819	Founding of *Singapore* by Sir Stamford Raffles.
1824	*Malacca* ceded to the British under the terms of the Anglo–Dutch treaty.
1826	Penang (and Province Wellesley), Malacca and Singapore grouped together to form the *Straits Settlements*.
1841	Sir James Brooke became the ruler of *Sarawak*.
1874	*Perak, Selangor* and *Negri Sembilan* came under British control.
1881	Occupation of *North Borneo* (*Sabah*) by the British North Borneo Chartered Company.
1888	*Pahang* came under British control.
1895	Perak, Selangor, Negri Sembilan and Pahang grouped together to form the *Federated Malay States*.
1909–10	*Kelantan, Trengganu, Kedah* and *Perlis* came under British control.
1914	*Johore* came under British control.
1942–45	Japanese occupation.
1946	All the states in the Malay Peninsula, including Penang and Malacca but excluding Singapore were amalgamated to form the *Malayan Union*. Singapore, Sarawak and North Borneo became Crown colonies.
1948	Dissolution of the Malayan Union and formation of the *Federation of Malaya* consisting of the nine Malay states and Penang and Malacca. Singapore remained a separate colony.
1957	The Federation of Malaya became a fully independent country.
1959	Singapore became a self-governing state within the Commonwealth.

1963 The Federation of Malaya, Singapore, Sarawak and Sabah (North Borneo) were merged to form a new independent political unit—the *Federation of Malaysia.*

1965 Singapore separated from the Federation of Malaysia and became the *Republic of Singapore.* The Federation of Malaysia today consists of the eleven states of *Peninsular Malaysia* (formerly *West Malaysia*) and the two Borneo states of *Sabah* and *Sarawak.*

List of references

This list of references supplements that published in the first edition. The works listed here are those consulted by the author for the present revised edition. The statistical data used in this edition are drawn mainly from offical sources.

Abdul Latif b. Nordin and Harun b. Ismail (1970) 'Utilization of rubber, wood and waste from primary wood-based industries for chips', *Malayan Forester*, 334—41.

Abdullah b. Abdul Kadir (1971) 'The pineapple industry in Malaysia', *Malaysian Pineapple*, 1—3.

Andriesse, J. P. (ed.) (1968) *Proceedings of the 3rd Malayan Soil Conference* (Kuching).

Arnott, G. W. and Lim, H. K. (1966) 'Animal feeding stuffs in Malaya', *Malaysian Agricultural Journal*, 370—403.

Bank Negara Malaysia (1970) *Annual Report, 1970* (Kuala Lumpur).

Bank Negara Malaysia (1971) *Annual Report, 1971* (Kuala Lumpur).

Bank Negara Malaysia (1972) *Annual Report, 1972* (Kuala Lumpur).

Bank Negara Malaysia (1973) *Annual Report, 1973* (Kuala Lumpur).

Bank Negara Malaysia (1974) *Annual Report and Statement of Accounts, 1973.*

Barlow, C. and Chan, L. K. (1969) 'Towards an optimum size of rubber holding', *Proc. Natural Rubber Conference 1968* (Kuala Lumpur), 613—53.

Bateman, L. (1974) 'The place of natural rubber in future rubber markets', *Singapore Stock Exchange Journal*, February, 16—21.

Bekema, N. P. (1969) 'Consumer appraisals of natural rubber', *Proc. Natural Rubber Conference*, Pt. II (Kuala Lumpur), 1—13.

Bevan, J. W. L. *et al.* (1966) *Planting Techniques for Oil Palms in Malaya* (Kuala Lumpur).

Bevan, J. W. L. and Goering, T. J. (1968) 'The oil palm in Malaysia: an estimate of product prices and returns to investment', *Incorporated Society of Planters* (Kuala Lumpur).

Blencowe, E. K. and Blencowe, J. W. (eds) (1970) *Crop Diversification in Malaysia* (Kuala Lumpur).

Blencowe, J. W. and Turner, P. D. (eds) (1968) *Cocoa and Coconuts in Malaya* (Kuala Lumpur).

Burgess, P. F. (1969) 'Ecological factors in hill and mountain forests of the states of Malaya', *Malayan Nature Journal*, 22, 119—28.

Burley, T. M. (1974) 'Malaysia's tin industry', *Asia Research Bulletin*, 2, 524—6.

Burnham, C. P. (1966—68) 'Landscape and soils in Malaya', *Malayan Agriculturist*, 7, 64—9.

Burton, C. K. (1964) 'The older alluvium of Johore and Singapore', *Journal of Tropical Geography*, 18, 30—42.

Caldwell, J. C. (1963a) 'The demographic background', in Silcock, T. H. and Fisk, E. K. (eds), *The Political Economy of Independent Malaya* (Singapore).

420

Caldwell, J. C. (1963*b*) 'Urban growth in Malaysia: trends and implications', *Population Review*, 59—66.

Caldwell, J. C. (1964) 'New and old Malaya: aspects of demographic change in a high growth rate, multi-racial society', *Population Review*, 29—36.

Camoens, J. K. (1972) *An Investigation into the Possibility of Utilizing Sandy Loam for Cattle Rearing* (Kuala Lumpur).

Chan, Heun Yin, *et al.* (1973) 'Management of soils under Hevea in West Malaysia', *RRIM Planter's Conference 1973* (Kuala Lumpur), Preprint No. 14, 14 pp.

Chand, F. and Singh, D. Santokh (1970) 'Mineral resources maps in West Malaysia', *Second Technical Conference on Tin, Bangkok, 1969,* 3 (The Hague), 1,145—53.

Chander, R. (1971) *1970 Population and Housing Census of Malaysia: Field Count Summary* (Kuala Lumpur).

Chow, Weng Tai and Ng, Siew Kee (1969) 'A preliminary study on acid sulphate soils in West Malaysia', *Malayan Agriculturist Journal*, July, 253—67.

Chung, S. K. (1970) *Annual Report of the Geological Survey Malaysia, 1968* (Kuching, Sarawak).

Chye, Kooi Onn and Loh, Wee Yet (1971) 'The tapioca processing industry in Perak', *FAMA Agriculture Economic Bulletin*, 1—59.

Corley, R. H. V. *et al.* (1973) 'Optimal spacing for oil palms', in Wastie, R. L. and Earp, D. A. (eds), *Advances in Oil Palm Cultivation* (Kuala Lumpur).

Courtenay, P. P. (1972) *A Geography of Trade and Development in Malaya* (London).

Crotty, R. (1967) *An Economic Survey of the Livestock Industry in West Malaysia* (Kuala Lumpur).

Dale, W. L. (1959) 'The rainfall of Malaya, Pt. I', *Journal of Tropical Geography*, 13, 23—37.

Dale, W. L. (1960) 'The rainfall of Malaya, Pt. II', *Journal of Tropical Geography*, 14, 11—28.

Dale, W. L. (1964) 'Sunshine in Malaya', *Journal of Tropical Geography*, 19, 20—6.

Department of Statistics (n.d.), *Rubber Statistic Handbook, 1970* (Kuala Lumpur).

Department of Statistics (1970) *Employment and Unemployment, West Malaysia* (Kuala Lumpur).

Department of Statistics (1971*a*) *Employment and Unemployment, West Malaysia,* 2, 'Zones and Strata' (Kuala Lumpur).

Department of Statistics (1971*b*) *Oil Palm, Coconut and Tea Statistics 1971* (Kuala Lumpur).

Devendra, C. (1966) 'Goat breeds of Malaysia', *Malaysian Agricultural Journal*, 268—74.

Devendra, C. *et al.* (1972) *Proceedings of the Symposium on the Pig Industry* (Kuala Lumpur).

Dorall, R. F. (1970) 'Some aspects of settlement hierarchy in West Malaysia', *Geographica*, 36—46.

Eyles, R. J. (1967) 'Laterite at Kerdau, Pahang, Malaya', *Journal of Tropical Geography*, 25, 18—23.

Eyles, R. J. (1968) 'Physiographic implications of laterite in Malaya', *Singapore Nat. Aca. of Science* (mimeo. 1st long.).

FAMA (1967) *Annual Report and Statement of Accounts 1965 and 1966* (Kuala Lumpur).

FAMA (1968) *The Coconut Industry in West Malaysia* (Kuala Lumpur).

FAMA (1968) *Poultry and Egg Industry in West Malaysia* (Kuala Lumpur).

FAMA (1969) *The Cultivation of Maize, Banana and Tapioca in West Malaysia* (Kuala Lumpur).

FAO (1965) *Report to the Government of Malaysia on Development of Inland Fisheries* (Rome).

421

References

Federal Industrial Development Authority (1969) *Malaysia: A New Industrial Development Strategy* (Kuala Lumpur).

Federation of Malaya (1963) *Report of the Subdivision of Estates Committee* (Kuala Lumpur).

FELDA, Malaysia (various years) *Annual Report* (Kuala Lumpur).

Fernando, H. M. A. B. and Grimwood, B. E. (1973) *Study of the Coconut Industry in the ADB Region* (Asian Development Bank, Philippines).

Flemmish, C. O. (ed.) (1959) 'Timber utilization in Malaya', *Malayan Forest Records*, No. 13 (Singapore).

Fryer, D. W. (1970) *Emerging Southeast Asia* (London).

Gobbett, D. J. (1964) 'The Lower Palaeozoic rocks of Kuala Lumpur, Malaysia', *Federation Museums Journal*, No. 9 (New Series), 67–79.

Gobbett, D. J. (1965) 'The formation of limestone caves in Malaya', *Malayan Nature Journal*, 4–12.

Gobbett, D. J. (1968) 'The Permian system in Malaya', *Studies in Malaysian Geology*, Geol. Soc. of Malaysia, Bull., No. 1, 17–22.

Gobbett, D. J. and Hutchison, C. S. (eds) (1973) *Geology of the Malay Peninsula* (New York).

Goering, T. J. (1968) 'A note on investment decisions in oil-palm and rubber', *Review of Agricultural Economics*, Malaysia, June.

Graham, D. J. (1969) 'New presentation processes and SMR scheme', *Proc. Natural Rubber Conference 1968* (Kuala Lumpur), 14–25.

Grant, J. S. (1957) 'Forests and streamflow', *Malayan Forester*, 20, 122–6.

Gray, B. S. (1969) 'Ground covers and performance', *Proc. Natural Rubber Conference, 1968* (Kuala Lumpur), 107–12.

Grubb, P. L. C. (1968) *Geology and Bauxite Deposits of the Pengerang Area*, Southeast Johore, Geol. Survey, West Malaysia, District Memoir 14 (Ipoh).

Guha, M. M. (1969) 'Recent advances in fertilizer usage in Malaya', *Proc. Natural Rubber Conference 1968* (Kuala Lumpur), 207–16.

Hacharan Singh Khera (1974) *The State and Peasant Innovation in Rural Development: The Case of FELDA Oil Palm Schemes* (mimeo., unpub. Kuala Lumpur).

Hamzah, Sendut (1960–61) 'Problems of rural–urban migration in Malaya', *Community Development Bulletin*, 86–91.

Hamzah, Sendut (1962) 'Patterns of urbanization in Malaya', *Journal of Tropical Geography*, 16, 114–30.

Hamzah, Sendut (1964) 'Urbanization', in Wang, Gungwu (ed.), *Malaysia*, 82–96.

Hamzah, Sendut (1965) 'Statistical distribution of cities in Malaysia', *Kajian Ekonomi Malaysia*, 49–66.

Hamzah, Sendut (1969) 'The structure of Kuala Lumpur, Malaysia's capital city', in Breese, G. (ed.), *The City in Developing Countries* (Englewood Cliffs, N.J.), 461–73.

Hartley, C. W. S. (1967) *The Oil Palm* (London).

Henderson, M. R. (1939) 'The flora of the limestone hills of the Malay Peninsula', *Journal of the Royal Asiatic Society*, Malayan Branch, 17, 13–87.

Hill, R. D. (1969) 'Pepper growing in Johore', *Journal of Tropical Geography*, 28, 32–9.

Hill, J. H. (1964) *The Mineral Belts of Malaya* (Ipoh, mimeo.).

Hoffmann, Latz and Tan, Tew Nee (1971) 'Pattern of growth and structural change in West Malaysia's manufacturing industry', *Kajian Economi Malaysia*, December, 44–69.

Hosking, K. F. G. (1970) 'Aspects of the geology of the tin fields of S.E. Asia', *Second Technical Conference on Tin*, Bangkok, 1969, 1 (The Hague), 41–80.

Hosking, K. F. G. (1973a) 'The primary tin mineralisation patterns of West Malaysia', *Geological Society Malaysia, Bulletin*, No. 6, 297–308.

422

Hosking, K. F. G. (1973*b*) 'Primary mineral deposits', in Gobbett, D. J. and Hutchison, C. S. (eds), *Geology of the Malay Peninsula* (New York), 335–90.

Hosking, K. F. G. (1969) *Offshore Tin Deposits* (Johannesburg).

Hutchison, C. S. (1968) 'Physical and chemical differentiation of West Malaysian limestone formations', *Studies in Malaysian Geology*, Geol. Soc. of Malaysia, Bull., No. 1, 45–56.

Incorporated Society of Planters (1968) *Oil Palm Developments in Malaysia* (Kuala Lumpur).

Incorporated Society of Planters (1969*a*) *Progress in Oil Palm* (Kuala Lumpur).

Incorporated Society of Planters (1969*b*) *The Quality and Marketing of Oil Palm Products* (Kuala Lumpur).

International Rubber Study Group (1972) *Rubber Statistical Bulletin*.

Jack, H. W. (1923) *Rice in Malaya* (Kuala Lumpur).

Jones, Alun (1968) 'The Orang Asli: an outline of their progress in modern Malaya', *Journal of South East Asian History*, 9, 286–305.

Jones, C. R. (1961) 'A revision of the stratigraphic sequence of the Langkawi Islands, Federation of Malaya', *Proc. 9th Pac. Sc. Cong.*, 1957, 12, 287–300.

Jones, C. R. (1965) 'The limestone caves and cave deposits of Perlis and North Kedah', *Malayan Nature Journal*, 21–30.

Jonge, P. de (1969) 'Exploitation of Hevea', *Proc. Natural Rubber Conference, 1968* (Kuala Lumpur), 283–91.

Joseph, K. T. (1960–61) 'Malaya's soil potential', *Malayan Agriculturist*, 1, 41–4.

Joseph, K. T. (1964) 'Sedentary rocks of Kedah and their suggested utilization', *Journal of Tropical Geography*, 18, 101–10.

Kanapathy, K. (1966) 'Acid swamp soils and problems in their utilization', *Proc. 2nd Malaysian Soil Conference* (Kuala Lumpur), 208–13.

Kanapathy, K. and Thamboo, S. (1970) 'West Malaysian soils in relation to cocoa', in Blencowe, E. K. and Blencowe, J. W. (eds), *Crop Diversification in Malaysia* (Kuala Lumpur).

Kanapathy, V. (1970) *The Malaysian Economy* (Singapore).

Khoo Swee Joo (1964) 'The Malayan oil palm industry', *Kajian Ekonomi Malaysia*, 1, 1–13.

Koopmans, B. N. (1972) 'Sedimentation in the Kelantan Delta', *Sedimentary Geology*, 65–84.

Lam, Thim Fook (1970) 'Urbanization and the Chinese community in the Malay Peninsula', *ANZAAS 42nd Congress*, Port Moresby (mimeo.).

Law, Wei Min and Selvadurai, K. (1968) 'The 1968 Reconnaissance Soil Map of Malaya', in Andriess, J. P. (ed.), *Proceedings of the 3rd Malayan Soil Conference* (Kuching), 229–39.

Leamy, M. L. and Panton, W. P. (1966) *Soil Survey Manual for Malayan Conditions* (Kuala Lumpur).

Lee, S. A. (1972) *Economics of Pineapple Smallholdings in Johore* (Pekan Nenas, Johore).

Lee, Peng Choong (1973) 'Multi-use management of West Malaysia's forest resources', *Proc. Symposium on Biological Resources and National Development* (Kuala Lumpur), 93–101.

Leigh, C. H. and Low, K. S. (1973) 'An appraisal of the flood situation in West Malaysia', *Proc. Symposium on Biological Resources and National Development* (Kuala Lumpur), 57–72.

Lian, Kwen Koo (1966) 'The future of the sawmilling and plywood industries in West Malaysia', *Malayan Forester*, 245–50.

Liew, Khooi Cheng and Lopez, D. T. (1968) 'Development of the sawmilling industry in West Malaysia', *Malayan Forester*, 33–42.

References

Lim, Chong Yah (1966) 'West Malaysian external trade, 1947–65', in Morgan, T. and Spoelstra, N. (eds), *Economic Interdependence in Southeast Asia* (University of Wisconsin Press).

Lim, David (1970) 'Export-oriented industrialisation: a case study of Malaysia', *Kajian Ekonomi Malaysia*, 17–25.

Lim, David (1973) *Economic Growth and Development in West Malaysia, 1947–70* (OUP, Kuala Lumpur).

Lim, Han Kuo (1968) 'Animal feeding stuffs', *Malaysian Agricultural Journal*, 405–20.

Lim, Sow Ching (1969) 'Analysis of smallholders' rubber marketing in West Malaysia', *Proc. Natural Rubber Conference, 1968* (Kuala Lumpur), 604–12.

Lim, Sow Ching and Chong, Kow Ming (1973) 'Merits of estate participation and incentive wage system in public sector land development', *RRIM Planters' Conference, 1973* (Kuala Lumpur), Preprint No. 2, 16 pp.

Lim, Sow Ching *et al.* (1973) 'Economics of Maximising early yields and shorter immaturity', *RRIM Planters' Conference, 1973* (Kuala Lumpur), Preprint No. 1, 15 pp.

Lo, Sum Yee (1972) *The Development Performance of West Malaysia* (Kuala Lumpur).

Lockwood, J. G. (1971) 'Does Malaysia really have a hot, wet climate?', in Fenley, J. R. (ed.), *The Water Relations of Malaysian Forests* (University of Hull).

Low, Kim Wah (1967) 'Fish marketing in Malaysia', *Rev. of Agric. Economics, Malaysia*, 28–33.

MacDonald, S. (1967) *Geology and mineral resources of North Kelantan and North Trengganu*, Geol. Survey, West Malaysia, District Memoir 10 (Ipoh).

Malaysian Business (1973) *Our Pineapple Industry faces Big Challenges* (Kuala Lumpur).

Malaysian Centre for Development Studies (1972), Kuala Lumpur.

McCulloch, G. C. (1968) 'The economics of coconut monoculture planting in Malaya', in Blencowe, J. W. and Turner, P. D. (eds), *Cocoa and Coconuts in Malaya* (Kuala Lumpur), 96–102.

McGee, T. G. (1964) 'Population: a preliminary analysis', in Wang, Gungwu (ed.), *Malaysia: A Survey* (London), 67–81.

McTaggart, W. D. (1972) *Industrialization in West Malaysia 1968* (Arizona State University).

Mehmet, O. (1969) *An Outline of the Manpower Situation in West Malaysia* (mimeo., Kuala Lumpur).

Mid-Term Review of the Second Malaysia Plan 1971–1975 (1973) (Kuala Lumpur).

Ministry of Agriculture and Co-operatives (1966) *The Oil Palm in Malaya* (Kuala Lumpur).

Ministry of Agriculture and Co-operatives (1967) *West Malaysia: Census of Commercial Poultry, Farms and Hatcheries, 1966* (Kuala Lumpur).

Mohd. Noor b. Wahab and Arun, K. C. (1969) 'Smallholdings in West Malaysia', *Proc. Natural Rubber Conference 1968* (Kuala Lumpur), 581–91.

Mohd. Salleh Nor and Tang, H. T. (1973) 'Some aspects of the utilization and conservation of the forest resources of West Malaysia', *Proc. Symposium on Biological Resources and National Development* (Kuala Lumpur), 103–11.

Mohd. Shaari b. Sam Abdul Latiff (1971) *A Guide to Trawl Species in Penang Waters* (Kuala Lumpur).

Morris, J. E. (1969) 'Hevea crumb process', *Proc. Natural Rubber Conference, 1968* (Kuala Lumpur), 39–55.

Muttukumaru, E. (1968) *Economic Survey of the Coconut Growing Industry* (FAO, Rome).

Myint, H. (1972) *Southeast Asia's Economy* (London).

Nair, S. and Abdul Kadir Mohammed (1973) 'Expansion of the SMR scheme', *RRIM Planters' Conference, 1973* (Kuala Lumpur), Preprint No. 27, 21 pp.

Narkswasdi, Udhis and Selvadurai, S. (1967) 'Economic survey of padi production in West Malaysia', Reports Nos 1 (Selangor), 2 (Collective padi cultivation in Bachang, Malaya), and 3 (Malacca) (Kuala Lumpur).

Ng, Choong Sooi *et al.* (1969) 'Factors affecting the profitability of rubber on West Malaysian estates', *Proc. Natural Rubber Conference, 1968* (Kuala Lumpur), 654—82.

Ng, Eng Kok (1969) 'Economic analysis of tapping experiment', *Proc. Natural Rubber Conference, 1968* (Kuala Lumpur), 360—87.

Ng, Siew Kee (1968*a*) 'Soil suitability for oil palm in West Malaysia', in *Incorporated Society of Planters* (1968), 11—17.

Ng, Siew Kee (1968*b*) 'Padi soil of West Malaysia', in Andriess, J. P. (ed.), *Proceedings of the 3rd Malayan Soil Conference* (Kuching), 67—72.

Ng, Siew Kee (1969*a*) 'Soil resources in Malaya', in Stone, B. C. (ed.), *Natural Resources in Malaysia and Singapore* (Kuala Lumpur), 141—51.

Ng, Siew Kee (1969*b*) 'Soils of South Johore and manuring oil palms', *The Planter*, June, 348—58.

Ng, Siew Kee and Law, Wei Min (1971) 'Pedogenesis and soil fertility in West Malaysia', in UNESCO, *Soil and Tropical Weathering* (Paris), 129—39.

Ng, Siew Kee *et al.* (eds) (1966) *Proceedings of the 2nd Malaysian Soil Conference* (mimeo., Kuala Lumpur).

Nieuwolt, S. (1968) 'Diurnal rainfall variation in Malaya', *Annals, Association of American Geographers*, June, 313—26.

Nossin, J. J. (1962) 'Coastal sedimentation in eastern Johore (Malaya)', *Zeitschrift für Geomorphologie*, 6, 296—316.

Nossin, J. J. (1965) 'Analysis of younger beach deposits in eastern Malaya', *Zeitschrift für Geomorphologie*, 9, 186—208.

Oh, Kong Yew (1965) 'Hydrology in Malaya: rainfall and river discharge', *Malayan Agricultural Journal*, 182—90.

Ooi, Jin-Bee and Chia, Lin Sien (eds) (1974) *The Climate of West Malaysia and Singapore* (OUP, Kuala Lumpur).

Ooi, Jin-Bee (1975) 'Urbanization and the urban population in Peninsular Malaysia', *Journal of Tropical Geography*, 40, 40—7.

O'Reilly, J. M. H. (1963) 'An assessment of the Malayan tin mining industry in the twentieth century', *Journal of Tropical Geography*, 17, 72—8.

Osman b. Mohd. Noor (1972) *Cashewnut in Trengganu*.

Panton, W. P. (1964) 'The 1962 soil map of Malaya', *Journal of Tropical Geography*, 18, 118—24.

Paramananthan, S. (1969) 'Characteristics of some soils derived from igneous rocks of West Malaysia', *Malayan Agricultural Journal*, July, 239—52.

Paton, J. R. (1964) 'The origin of the limestone hills of Malaya', *Journal of Tropical Geography*, 18, 134—47.

Pelinck, E. (1970) 'An analysis of commercial timber outturn from forest reserves in West Malaysia', *Malayan Forester*, 374—86.

Pimm, A. C. (1967) 'Triassic volcanic rocks in East and West Malaysia', *Geological Papers, 1966*, Collenette, P. (ed.), Geol. Survey, Borneo Region, Malaysia (Kuching), 36—40.

Poore, M. E. D. (1961) 'River control and conservation in Malaya', in *Nature Conservation in Western Malaysia 1961*, Wyatt-Smith, J. and Wycherley, P. R. (Kuala Lumpur), 48—51.

Procter, W. D. (1966) 'Some recent advances in Malayan geology', *Geol. Survey Paper 66/P/015* (Ipoh), unpublished.

425

References

Pryor, R. J. (1973) 'The changing settlement system of West Malaysia', *Journal of Tropical Geography*, 37, 53—67.

Pushparajah, E. *et al.* (1973) 'Towards modernization of smallholders', *RRIM Planters Conference, 1973* (Kuala Lumpur), Preprint No. 3, 14 pp.

Rao, V. V. Bhanoji (1974) *The Postwar Development Pattern and Policy of the Malaysian Economy* (unpublished PhD thesis, University of Singapore).

Robbins, R. G. and Wyatt-Smith, J. (1964) 'Dry land forest formations and forest types in the Malayan Peninsula', *Malayan Forester*, 188—216.

Rosenquit, E. A. (1964) 'Soils and the fertilization of rubber and oil palm', *Journal of Tropical Geography*, 18, 148—56.

Sainsbury, C. L. (1969) *Tin Resources of the World* (Washington).

Sandhu, K. S. (1964) 'Emergency resettlement in Malaya', *Journal of Tropical Geography*, 18, 157—83.

Saw, Swee Hock (1966) 'Regional differences in the structure of the labour force in Malaysia', *Kajian Ekonomi Malaysia*, 50—8.

Saw, Swee Hock and Cheng, Siok Hua (1971) 'Migration policies in Malaya and Singapore', *Nanyang Quarterly*, September, 45—61.

Selvadurai, S. (1968) *A Preliminary Report on the survey of Coconut Smallholdings in West Malaysia* (Kuala Lumpur).

Selvadurai, S. (1972a) *Socio-economic Survey of Rubber Smallholdings in West Johore* (Kuala Lumpur), 40 pp.

Selvadurai, S. (1972b) *Padi Survey: Sungei Manik and Changkat Jong Irrigation Areas, Perak* (Kuala Lumpur).

Selvadurai, S. (1972c) *Padi Farming in West Malaysia* (University of Agriculture and Land, Kuala Lumpur), 139 pp.

Selvadurai, S. (1972d) *Krian Padi Survey* (Kuala Lumpur).

Selvadurai, S. and Ani b. Arope (1969) *Socio-economic Survey of Padi Farms in Province Wellesley, 1968* (Kuala Lumpur).

Selvadurai, S. and Jegatheesan, S. (1968) *An Economic Survey of Pineapple Smallholdings in Pontian, Johore* (Kuala Lumpur).

Selvadurai, S. and Othman b. Mohd. Lela (1967) *An Evaluation of the Minyak Beku (Johore) Coconut Replanting and Rehabilitation Scheme* (Kuala Lumpur).

Selvadurai, S. *et al.* (1969) *Socio-economic Study of Padi Farms in the Kemubu Area of Kelantan, 1968* (Kuala Lumpur).

Second Malaysian Plan 1971—1975 (Kuala Lumpur).

Shailes, H. J. (1970) 'Some problems facing Malaysian ports', *Institute of Transport (Malaya section) Journal*, 55—61.

Shallow, P. G. (1956) *River Flow in the Cameron Highlands* (Central Electricity Board, Kuala Lumpur).

Shamsul Bahrin (1965) 'Indonesian labour in Malaya', *Kajian Ekonomi Malaysia*, June, 53—70.

Shamsul, Bahrin (1967a) 'The growth and distribution of the Indonesian population in Malaya', *Bijdragen tot de Taal-land en Volkenkunde*, 267—85.

Shamsul, Bahrin (1967b) 'The pattern of Indonesian migration and settlement in Malaya', *Asian Studies*, 5, 233—57.

Shamsul, Bahrin (1970) 'The Indonesian immigrants and the Malays of West Malaysia: a study in assimilation and integration', *Geographica*, 1—12.

Shelling, N. J. *et al.* (1968) 'Ages of Malayan granites', *Geol. en. Mijnbouw*, 358—9.

Shirle, Gordon (ed.) (1973) 'Chinese New Villages in Malaya: a community study' (Singapore).

Short, D. E. and Jackson, J. C. (1971) 'The origins of an irrigation policy in Malaya: a review of development prior to the establishment of the drainage and irrigation department', *Journal of the Malayan Branch, Royal Asiatic Society*, 44, Pt. 1, 78—103.

Silcock, T. H. and Fisk, E. K. (eds) (1963) *The Political Economy of Independent Malaya* (Singapore), 59—92.

Smiley, C. J. (1970) 'Later Mesozoic flora from Maran, Pahang, West Malaysia, Pt. 1', Papers in Geology and Stratigraphy', *Geol. Soc. of Malaysia Bull. No. 3* (Kuala Lumpur), 77—88.

Soong, Min Kong (1965) 'The role of science and technology in fisheries development in Malaysia', *Malaysian Agricultural Journal*, 21—7.

Stone, B. C. (ed.) (1969) *Natural Resources in Malaysia and Singapore* (Kuala Lumpur).

Suntharalingam, T. (1968) 'Upper Palaeozoic stratigraphy of the area west of Kampar, Perak', *Studies in Malaysian Geology*, Geol. Soc. of Malaysia, Bull. No. 1, 45—56.

Swettenham, Sir F. (1948) *British Malaya, An Account of the Origin and Progress of British Influence in Malaya* (London).

Tan, Kee Meng (1969) 'A case study of pineapple smallholdings', *Kajian Ekonomi Malaysia*, June, 11—36.

Tan, Soon Peng (1973) 'The significance of sump ponds in harvesting paddy-field fishes in North Krian, Perak', *Malayan Nature Journal*, April, 26—31.

Tay, T. H. (1969) 'The distribution, characteristics, uses and potential of peat in W. Malaysia', *Journal of Tropical Geography*, 29, 58—63.

Thomas, P. (ed.) (1964) *Report of the 1st Conference of Malaysian Soil Survey Specialists, Sabah, Malaysia* (mimeo., Sabah).

Thomas, P. O. and Allen, P. W. (1973) 'Some aspects of competition between natural and synthetic rubber', *RRIM Planters' Conference, 1973* (Kuala Lumpur), Preprint No. 4, 9 pp.

Thuraisingham, S. (1969) *Proposals for Large-scale Dairy Development in West Malaysia* (Kuala Lumpur).

Tin Industry Board (n.d.) *Tin Mining in Malaysia* (Ipoh).

Turner, P. D. (ed.) (1968) *Oil Palm Developments in Malaysia* (Kuala Lumpur).

Van Bemmelen, R. W. (1949) *The Geology of Indonesia, Vol. 1a* (The Hague).

Veterinary Division (1967) *Proposals for the Development of the Livestock Industry* (Kuala Lumpur).

Vickers, M. E. H. (1969) *Growing and Grazing Good Grass in West Malaysia*, May and June, 1—26.

Wastie, R. L. and Earp, D. A. (eds) (1972) *Cocoa and Coconut in Malaysia* (Kuala Lumpur).

Wastie, R. L. and Earp, D. A. (eds) (1973) *Advances in Oil Palm Cultivation* (Kuala Lumpur).

Watson, J. G. (1928) *Mangrove Forests of the Malay Pensinula* (Singapore).

Watts, I. E. M. (1954) 'Line-squalls of Malaya', *Journal of Tropical Geography*, 3, 1—14.

Wee, Y. C. (1970) 'The development of pineapple cultivation in West Malaya', *Journal of Tropical Geography*, 30, 68—75.

Wee, Y. C. and Tay, T. H. (1965) *Pineapple Cultivation in West Malaysia* (Pekan Nenas, Johore).

Wharton, C. R., Jr. (1963) *Monocultural Perennial Export Dominance: The Inelasticity of Southeast Asian Agricultural Trade* (mimeo., 25 pp.).

Wheelwright, E. L. (1965) *Industrialization in Malaysia* (Melbourne University Press).

Wikkramatileke, R. (1972) 'Federal land development in West Malaysia 1957—1971', *Pacific Viewpoint*, 62—86.

Williams, C. N. and Hsu, Y. C. (1970) *Oil Palm Cultivation in Malaya* (Kuala Lumpur).

Williams, C. N. and Thomas, R. L. (1969) 'Some considerations on sugar cane growing in Malaya', *The Planter*, November, 593—7.

References

Wong, I. F. T. (1970a) *A Soil Suitability Classification for Malaysia* (mimeo., Kuala Lumpur).

Wong, I. F. T. (1970b) *Reconnaissance Soil Survey of Selangor* (Kuala Lumpur).

Wong, I. F. T. (1971) *The Present Land Use of West Malaysia, 1966* (Kuala Lumpur).

Wong, I. F. T. (1972) 'Suitable cocoa soils in West Malaysia', in Wastie, R. L. and Earp, D. A. (eds), *Cocoa and Coconut in Malaysia* (Kuala Lumpur).

Wyatt-Smith, J. (1965a) 'An introduction to forest types', in *Malayan Forest Records, No. 23*, 7/1—7/44.

Wyatt-Smith, J. (1965b) 'Heath forest', *Malayan Forest Records, No. 23*, 13/1—13/17.

Wyatt-Smith, J. (1965c) 'Hill forest', *Malayan Forest Records, No. 23*, 14/1—14/133.

Wyatt-Smith, J. (1965d) 'Swamp forest', *Malayan Forest Records, No. 23*, 15/1—15/54.

Wycherley, P. R. (1967) 'Rainfall probability tables for Malaysia', *Rubber Research Institute of Malaya* (Kuala Lumpur).

Wycherley, P. R. (1969a) *Conservation in Malaysia* (Morges, Switzerland).

Wycherley, P. R. (1969b) 'Breeding in Hevea', *Proc. Natural Rubber Conference, 1968* (Kuala Lumpur), 38—55.

Yip, Yat Hoong (1966) 'Development prospects of the Malayan tin industry', *Kajian Ekonomi Malaysia*, June, 25—50.

Yip, Yat Hoong (1969) *The Development of the Tin Mining Industry of Malaya* (Kuala Lumpur).

You, Poh Seng (1965) 'Population structure and growth in Malaya and Singapore, in You, Poh Seng (ed.), *Economic Problems of Malaysia* (Singapore), 7—17.

Index

The most important references are in **bold** type.

429